RAILROAD ECONOMICS

RESEARCH IN TRANSPORTATION ECONOMICS

Series Editor: Martin Dresner

Volume 1–6:	Research in Transportation Economics – Edited by B. Starr McMullen
Volume 7:	Railroad Bankruptcies and Mergers from Chicago West 1975–2001: Financial Analysis and Regulatory Critique – Michael Conant
Volume 8:	Economic Impacts of Intelligent Transportation Systems: Innovations and Case Studies – Evangelos Bekiaris and Yuko Nakanishi
Volume 9:	Road Pricing: Theory and Evidence – Georgina Santos
Volume 10:	Transportation Labor Issues and Regulatory Reform – James Peoples and Wayne K. Talley
Volume 11:	Interurban Road Charging for Trucks in Europe – José Manuel Viegas
Volume 12:	Shipping Economics – Kevin Cullinane
Volume 13:	Global Competition in Transportation Markets: Analysis and Policy Making – Katsuhiko Kuroda and Adib Kanafani
Volume 14:	Measuring the Marginal Social Cost of Transport – Christopher Nash and Bryan Matthews
Volume 15:	Procurement and Financing of Motorways in Europe – Giorgio Ragazzi and Werner Rothengatter
Volume 16:	Port Economics – Kevin Cullinane and Wayne K. Talley
Volume 17:	Devolution, Port Governance and Port Performance – Mary R. Brooks and Kevin Cullinane
Volume 18:	Bus Transport: Economics, Policy and Planning – David A. Hensher
Volume 19:	Investment and the Use of Tax and Toll Revenues in the Transport Sector – Andre de Palma, Charles Robin Lindsey, and Stef Proost

RESEARCH IN TRANSPORTATION ECONOMICS VOLUME 20

RAILROAD ECONOMICS

EDITED BY

SCOTT M. DENNIS
US Department of Transportation, Washington, DC, USA

WAYNE K. TALLEY
Old Dominion University, Norfolk, VA, USA

ELSEVIER
JAI

Amsterdam – Boston – Heidelberg – London – New York – Oxford
Paris – San Diego – San Francisco – Singapore – Sydney – Tokyo
JAI Press is an imprint of Elsevier

JAI Press is an imprint of Elsevier
Linacre House, Jordan Hill, Oxford OX2 8DP, UK
Radarweg 29, PO Box 211, 1000 AE Amsterdam, The Netherlands
525 B Street, Suite 1900, San Diego, CA 92101-4495, USA

First edition 2007

British Library Cataloguing in Publication Data
A catalogue record for this book is available from the British Library

ISBN: 978-0-7623-1255-9
ISSN: 0739-8859 (Series)

For information on all JAI Press publications
visit our website at books.elsevier.com

Printed and bound in the United Kingdom

07 08 09 10 11 10 9 8 7 6 5 4 3 2 1

The views, opinions, and statements contained in this volume are solely those of the authors, and do not represent the official policy of the U.S. Department of Transportation or any of its units, Old Dominion University, or any other institution with which any of the authors in this volume may be affiliated.

CONTENTS

LIST OF CONTRIBUTORS

Michael W. Babcock	Department of Economics, Kansas State University, Manhattan, KS, USA.
John D. Bitzan	College of Business Administration, North Dakota State University, Fargo, ND, USA.
James L. Bunch	Kansas Army National Guard, Topeka, KS, USA.
Scott M. Dennis	US Department of Transportation, Washington, DC, USA.
Marc Ivaldi	Toulouse School of Economics, Universite des Sciences Sociales, 21 Allee de Brienne, Toulouse, France.
William Lythgoe	Institute for Transport Studies, University of Leeds, Leeds, UK.
Gerard McCullough	Department of Applied Economics, University of Minnesota, St. Paul, MN, USA.
James Peoples	Department of Economics, University of Wisconsin-Milwaukee, Milwaukee, WI, USA.
Russell Pittman	Economic Analysis Group, Antitrust Division, US Department of Justice, Washington, DC, USA.
Ian Savage	Department of Economics, Northwestern University, Evanston, IL, USA.
Wayne K. Talley	Old Dominion University, Norfolk, VA, USA.

Kenneth Train	Department of Economics, University of California, Berkeley, CA, USA.
Mark Wardman	Institute for Transport Studies, University of Leeds, Leeds, UK.
William G. Waters II	Centre for Transportation Studies, Sauder School of Business, The University of British Columbia, Vancouver, Canada.
Gerard Whelan	MVA Consultancy Ltd., Piccadilly Plaza, Manchester, UK.
Wesley W. Wilson	Department of Economics, University of Oregon, Eugene, OR, USA.

INTRODUCTION

Scott M. Dennis and Wayne K. Talley

While railroads may appear to be an old technology, they are, in fact, the original network industry. Railroad rates were once regarded as one of the most fundamental puzzles in Economics, and were studied by the most eminent economists of the time, including J. B. Clark, J. M. Clark, F. Y. Edgeworth, A. C. Pigou, and F. W. Taussig. The study of railway pricing has played an important role in the development of the economic theory of pricing, and modern theories of multi-product costing and pricing have their origin in railroad rate theory.

Railroad economics is the study of economic issues arising in the provision of freight and passenger railroad transportation services. Railroads provide utility of place and time for the people and goods transported. The demand for railroad transportation is, therefore, derived from the demands of consumers and producers. Railroads incur large sunk costs before any service can be provided. Once built, the railroad may provide transportation service to a variety of users, each with differing demands. The complexity of the underlying technology of multiple capital-intensive operations serving diverse markets at different locations gives rise to difficult economic issues. The inability to uniquely establish the costs of specific rail services resulted in decades of debate about rail pricing in relation to costs.

This volume provides original contributions to the study of railroad economics. The contributions address: the evolution of railroad economics; economic theories underlying the restructuring of state-owned railroads; railroad costs; freight transportation spatial demand; railroad passenger

Railroad Economics
Research in Transportation Economics, Volume 20, 1–10

ISSN: 0739-8859/doi:10.1016/S0739-8859(07)20001-0

demand; railroad pricing; trespassing on railroads; impacts of railroad abandonment on energy use and pollutant emissions; and the earnings differentials of railroad managers and labor.

Chapter 2 by W. G. Waters II reviews major themes in the evolution of railroad economics over the past century and a half: (1) railroads and economic development; (2) railroad pricing; (3) economic regulation in North America; (4) railroad cost analysis; (5) disappointment with railroad regulation; (6) competitive forces in railroad markets; (7) economic deregulation and its effects; (8) government ownership; and (9) the ongoing interest in and approaches to public intervention to address pockets of railroad market power.

Initially, railroad economics was concerned with the role of railroads in the overall economic development of regions and nations. But economists soon moved on to examining economic characteristics of railroads and their market structure. Reconciling railroad rate making with economic principles of prices related to costs proved to be an enduring challenge in railroad economics. The need for differential pricing of railroad services is now accepted by economists. In the nineteenth and for much of the twentieth century, rail market power existed in many markets in North America. The public response was to economically regulate North American railroads as opposed to direct government ownership.

Railroads and their data provided a 'test bed' for empirical estimation of cost functions, techniques that would be equally valuable for other industries. Railroad cost analysis has developed along two approaches – utilizing aggregate cost functions to investigate whether scale and density economies exist among railroads (the aggregate approach) and developing cost estimates for specific railroad operations (the disaggregate approach).

Railroad regulation was cumbersome; other modes had to be regulated in order to maintain the regulatory order. Many characterize the Interstate Commerce Commission as regarding the U.S. railroad industry as a client to be protected and served, and traffic to be shared among railroads and other modes. Over time, population and market growth, and technological change gave rise to competition in many transportation markets. The historical regulatory regime became obsolete. By the 1960s, the rail industry was in financial difficulty and was becoming worse.

The deregulation of the U.S. railroads resulted in significant productivity improvements, innovations, and financial improvements for these railroads. Unlike North America, many countries have chosen direct government ownership and operation of railroads rather than regulation and private enterprise. In Europe, railroads are often seen as an instrument of public policy to combat roadway congestion and pollution as well as to provide an alternative to truck transport of freight. In North America, even with deregulation, concerns persist about rail market power in some markets. One suggestion for promoting rail intra-modal competition in these markets is to foster access to shared track. A railroad's track may be shared by another railroad, for an access fee, or the ownership of the track would be separated from rail operations (i.e., a railroad that owns track would not be allowed to be an operating railroad and vice versa). The feasibility of and issues arising in alternate access regimes are a major topic of interest in current railroad economics throughout the world. This theme is addressed in Chapter 7 below.

Chapter 3 by John Bitzan and Wesley Wilson estimates a hedonic cost function for multi-product railroad firms. Many previous authors have estimated multi-product railroad cost functions, and hedonic output specifications are now commonly used. However, the unique contribution of this research is to estimate costs for specific types of railroad services, where shipment attributes are allowed to vary by the type of service and not just for the firm as a whole.

Railroad costs are specified as a translog function of input prices, technological characteristics (such as miles of road), and ton-miles of unit train service and way and through train service. Each type of service is specified as having different hedonic characteristics. Unit train service, which typically involves large volumes of traffic moving in a dedicated fashion from point to point, has larger shipment size and different length of haul than way and through train service, which tends to involve smaller shipment size and hub-and-spoke movement.

Bitzan and Wilson find an elasticity of cost with respect to all outputs is approximately 0.6, which suggests significant economies of density. More importantly, they find large differences in the elasticities of different outputs and substantial impacts of the hedonic variables on marginal costs. In their preferred model, with fixed effects, the elasticity of cost with respect to way and through train service is approximately 0.48, while it is 0.16 with respect to unit train service. The hedonic coefficients indicate that way and through train service becomes less expensive for longer hauls, and that unit train service becomes less expensive for larger shipments. The wide variation in cost elasticities for unit train and way and through train output, and the large changes in these marginal costs as shipment characteristics vary, illustrate the importance of accounting both for the different outputs produced by railroads and the service characteristics of these outputs.

In the last section of the paper, Bitzan and Wilson use their hedonic cost results to estimate costs for individual movements of farm products, chemicals, and coal from the Surface Transportation Board's Carload Waybill Sample. These examples illustrate how cost estimates can be made to vary with the characteristics of individual shipments, and may suggest how to estimate individual movement costs in a way that is consistent with economic theory.

Chapter 4 by Kenneth Train and Wesley Wilson presents a freight transportation demand model that considers spatial effects and the access that shippers have to transport markets. Specifically, the model recognizes that shippers who are not located at a rail or barge access point have the option of shipping to an access point some distance away. A survey of agricultural shippers in the U.S. Upper Midwest found that about one-half of the shippers only have access to truck carriers. Thus, these shippers must first ship by truck in order to then ship by rail or barge.

First, Train and Wilson estimate a discrete choice model in which each shipper has two alternative modes available for shipping their cargo to a final destination, barge and rail. The connection to barge and/or rail is treated as an access cost (i.e., truck cost per ton of cargo). The explanatory variables considered in the logit estimation model include barge and rail rates, barge and rail access costs, shipper distances to barge and rail access, barge and rail leg-distances of shipments, and rail car loading capacity (the number of rail cars that can be placed on the shipper's siding). The estimation results suggest that as access costs increase for a particular alternative relative to the other (e.g., barge versus rail), the likelihood of that alternative being chosen decreases.

The estimated choice model is then augmented by rate functions defined over space and used to derive spatially generated modal demand functions. A river and a rail terminal are assumed to exist, located 100 miles apart on a line. There are 50 shippers and each transports 100 tons of cargo. Each shipper faces different access costs and thus has different probabilities of using barge and rail. The demand functions reveal that spatially distributed demanders have options in moving goods to markets and that these choices are directly connected to spatial considerations.

Chapter 5 by Mark Wardman, William Lythgoe, and Gerard Whelan advances the cross-section modeling methodology of inter-urban rail passenger travel demand as well as provides new empirical insights into this demand. One methodological advance is the incorporation of catchment areas around stations in cross-section rail passenger demand models. These models are then estimated using ticket-sales data for Great Britain for rail passenger journeys between stations.

The cross-section catchment demand models are further refined by separating population and accessibility to rail stations from rail service quality, in order to allow for the estimation of station access and egress passenger time elasticities. The egress time elasticities were found to exceed access time elasticities. The rationales for this finding include: (1) fewer egress transport modes tend to be available at destination stations and (2) greater uncertainties exist as to how to get from destination stations to ultimate destinations.

The catchment area approach is further extended to deal with the issue of competition between stations. The authors illustrate how to estimate the number of new trips generated as the result of improved service at a particular station by comparing the total number of trips generated at the station with the number of trips attracted to the station from other nearby stations.

Overall, estimates of cross-section catchment inter-urban rail passenger travel demand models suggest that passenger generalized cost elasticities do not depend on the specification of station catchments, but population elasticities do. The estimates also suggest that the cross-section catchment demand models are appropriate alternative models to time series demand models in estimating inter-urban rail passenger travel demand when time-series data problems exist – e.g., when there is little variation in the values of one or more time-series variables such as the quality of service over time on particular routes. The methods developed by Wardman, Lythgoe, and Whelan have applicability to any mode of passenger transit, not just intercity rail.

Chapter 6 by Marc Ivaldi and Gerard McCullough examines the level and structure of railroad rates since deregulation, and assess their impact on the U.S. railroad industry. While the U.S. freight railroads have always price-discriminated among shippers of different commodities, analysis of the relationship between commodity-specific rates and their corresponding marginal costs is necessary in order to understand the varying economic conditions that railroads and shippers face in different commodity markets, and to help determine whether the revenues that railroads receive will be adequate to cover their costs.

Ton-mile data (such as that used by Bitzan and Wilson in Chapter 3) and rate data are not available on a commodity-by-commodity basis. Ivaldi and McCullough therefore draw on the results of their previous work with Generalized McFadden cost functions to estimate marginal costs per car-mile for bulk and general traffic. They then use revenue per car-mile data to estimate rates for five different classes of cars (bulk, inter-modal, chemical, automotive, and general), which reflect rates for the corresponding commodities. Lerner indices are then constructed by combining rates for the five general car types with the corresponding marginal cost estimate (bulk or general traffic). The Lerner indices relate the markup of price over marginal cost to the elasticity of demand in a market. Individually, the Lerner indices reflect the competitiveness of a specific market through the elasticity term. In aggregate, the Lerner indices can be used to determine whether railroad revenues are adequate to cover railroad costs.

The Lerner index analysis shows a significant reduction over time in the level of markups over marginal cost (except for in bulk markets), and some change in the structure of rates. Markups in the bulk markets for coal and grain have increased dramatically since deregulation. This may be due either to an increase in railroad market power or a reduction in costs due to productivity. There has been a significant increase in recent years in the Lerner indices in the inter-modal market. Again, this may be due to either an increase in railroad market power or a reduction in costs due to productivity. The relatively high indices for chemical and automotive traffic are mainly indicative of the high value of these cargoes. Lastly, the indices for general freight movements appear to reflect a cost advantage that railroads have over trucks.

Chapter 7 by Russell Pittman presents various options for restructuring a state-owned railroad system to create intra-modal rail competition within the state. These options include: (1) parallel competition, (2) source competition, and (3) third-party access. Parallel railroad competition exists when two or more railroads provide service between the same city-pairs. However, the creation of parallel competition among vertically integrated freight railways may prevent the competing lines from achieving available economies of density in all but the highest volume corridors.

Source (geographic) competition exists when a shipper at a given origin can use different railroads to reach different markets for the same product, or a customer at a given destination can use different railroads to receive the same product from different origins. In these cases, the presence of two or more railroads serving a given location provides shippers with access to alternative markets, thus promoting rail competition for transportation of their shipments. Source competition has become more prevalent as geographic markets expand, but is an imperfect substitute for parallel competition.

Third party access requires an integrated railroad (having rolling stock and tracks) to provide access for independent, non-integrated railroad operating companies to its track. A problem with third party access is that the integrated railroad is likely to discriminate among non-integrated railroad operating companies. The often proposed solution is to have a complete vertical separation – i.e., a railroad system that includes one company owning track but having no railroad operations, and non-integrated railroad operating companies without their own track. A problem with vertical separation is the difficulty of creating appropriate investment incentives, both maintenance and new capacity, for the vertically separated infrastructure company. Also, economies of vertical integration are lost with the adoption of vertical separation. Only in rare circumstances are the benefits of complete vertical separation likely to outweigh the losses from the process of vertical separation itself.

Chapter 8 by Ian Savage provides an analysis of trespassing casualties, which have become an increasingly important safety issue on the U.S. railroads. Installing gates and/or warning lights at rail-highway crossings, improved lighting on locomotives, closing little-used crossings, and increased public education through Operation Lifesaver have been remarkably successful in reducing casualties at rail-highway crossings. However, reductions in trespassing casualties (injuries plus fatalities) have been far more elusive, pointing to an increased need by the professional community to understand the causes of trespassing and what can be done to reduce the annual casualty count.

Federal Railroad Administration (FRA) data and a number of published studies are used to sketch the demographics of trespasser casualties. The data indicate that about half of the trespasser casualties can be characterized as single adult males in their 20s and 30s who are loitering on the right of way. Many of them are under the influence of alcohol or drugs. While suicides are not supposed to be included in FRA trespasser data, perhaps a quarter of all trespasser deaths are suspected suicides, or are documented suicides that were mistakenly reported to the FRA. (In addition, documented suicides that are not reported to the FRA would inflate the annual death toll by 20%.) The remaining casualties represent people on railroad property for purposes of theft, vandalism, thrill seeking, catching a ride on a freight train, or taking short cuts over or along the right of way.

While the trespasser casualty rate per capita and per line-haul train mile varied substantially over the last 100 years, these rates remained largely unchanged over the last 30 years. More detailed time-series analysis of trespasser casualty data reveals that the lack of change over the past few decades is the result of two nearly equal but opposite trends. Increases in factors that tend to increase trespassing, such as population size and train miles, were almost exactly balanced by factors that tend to reduce trespassing, such as line abandonment, increasing wealth, installation of ditch lights on locomotives, and an aging population.

The demographic sketch and the time-series analysis suggest countermeasures that may be adopted to help reduce railroad trespassing casualties. Many casualties have resulted from individuals loitering on the railroad to consume, or recover from, alcohol or drugs and engaging in other risky activities. The most appropriate response falls into the field of public health. Fencing the right of way may prove to be counterproductive in these cases because this type of trespasser values privacy. Clearing vegetation and installing lighting where appropriate may be helpful. Suicides, too, would appear to be a public health issue, though it is important that we have a better understanding of the magnitude of this problem. Trespassing for purposes of illicit transportation is related to the prevalence of illegal immigration, which is a topic of national debate. Casualties from more generic forms of trespass by thieves, vandals, thrill seekers, or those taking a short cut across the tracks might be reduced by increased signage or the use of fencing. However, money spent on such measures would likely result in a much greater reduction in casualties if it were applied to installing warning devices at rail-highway crossings that do not currently have them.

Chapter 9 by Michael Babcock and James Bunch develops a methodology for measuring the energy use and pollutant emissions from potential abandonment of shortline railroads. The methodology is adapted to the Kansas wheat transport market. Specifically, the transport of Kansas wheat is modeled as a transshipment network with individual wheat farms as supply nodes, grain elevators and unit train loading facilities as transshipment nodes, and export terminals at Houston, Texas as the final demand node. The movement of wheat is modeled assuming the availability of the Kansas shortline railroads, and then assuming abandonment and thus deletion of these railroads from the transportation network.

The methodology and data (e.g., wheat production and various transport costs by truck and rail) for the State of Kansas were used to obtain estimates of energy use and pollutant emissions in the transport of Kansas wheat. Truck ton-miles in the transport of wheat increased 105.4% with the abandonment of the Kansas shortline railroads. A shift occurred from relatively long-haul shortlines to relatively short-haul trucks in the transportation of wheat. Class I railroads were still the dominant mode in the transportation of Kansas wheat; their ton-miles were unaffected by shortline abandonment.

The net effect of the shortline abandonment was 2% fewer ton-miles of Kansas wheat transported due to the shift from relatively long-haul shortlines to relatively short-haul trucks coupled with the dominance of Class I railroads in the wheat logistics system. With railroads being more energy efficient than trucks and with the increase in truck ton-miles with shortline abandonment, energy consumption under shortline abandonment increased by 2.1% in the transport of Kansas wheat. The conventional wisdom that railroads produce fewer emissions than trucks was not confirmed in this case, because large trucks have lower emissions factors than shortline railroad locomotives. Total emissions in the transport of Kansas wheat were 1.4% lower under shortline abandonment.

The methodology developed by Babcock and Bunch has broad applicability in the calculation of energy and pollution effects whenever traffic is shifted between modes.

Chapter 10 by James Peoples and Wayne Talley investigates the earnings patterns of managers, union, and non-union employees in the U.S. railroad industry under regulation and deregulation. Economic theory provides no clear a priori predictions on the effect of deregulation on railroad non-managerial labor earnings. On one hand, the elimination of unprofitable routes and competitive cost-cutting steps may reduce the demand for labor and depress earnings. This prediction may be reinforced by the reduction of economic rents under deregulation. On the other hand, improvements in productivity and profitability may improve the earnings for workers left in the industry. Predictions about the expected earnings of railroad managers are just as unclear. On one hand, cost cutting and a decline in economic rents under deregulation would cause the earnings of railroad managers, like those of railroad labor, to decline. On the other hand, the incentive to improve firm performance following deregulation may make owners more likely to compensate managers for enhancing productivity.

Peoples and Talley use data from the U.S. Current Population Survey to estimate a wage equation for railroad managers and four categories of union and non-union labor (engineers, conductors, brakemen/switchmen, and mechanics) for the years 1973–2001. The wage equations specify weekly earnings as a function of hours worked plus a vector of control variables such as age, sex, education, region, and unemployment rate, as well as a dummy variable equal to 0 for the regulated era (1973–1980) and 1 for the deregulated era (1981–2001).

The results of the wage equation indicate that railroad managers, union, and non-union labor all experienced declines in real weekly earnings under deregulation. These results are consistent with the view that deregulation promoted a more cost-conscious business environment that placed downward pressure on earnings for union and non-union labor as well as managers. With the exception of non-union conductors, who experienced virtually no decline in wages, managers suffered less of a wage reduction than union labor, who in turn suffered less of a wage reduction than non-union labor. These results support the view that managers and union workers were better able than non-union workers to negotiate relatively small wage losses during the deregulation period. Union workers may have benefited from their negotiation strength associated with a highly unionized work force, while managers may have benefited from a post-deregulation business environment that encourages performance pay.

EVOLUTION OF RAILROAD ECONOMICS

William G. Waters II

ABSTRACT

This paper reviews major themes in the evolution of railroad economics over the past century and a half. The earliest writings emphasized links between railroads and economic development generally. Increasing returns and their implications for market structure and efficiency became a rationale for public intervention (regulation or government ownership). Railway rate theory was the precursor to modern multiproduct pricing theory, and railroads were the data source and focus for the development of cost function estimation. The economic analysis of regulatory performance and subsequent deregulation in North America were models of modern applied economics. The persistent problem of rail market power in some markets still stimulates debate about policy interventions to either regulate or stimulate competition to promote efficiency.

1. INTRODUCTION

Economics as a discipline only slightly predates the railroad.[1] The economic characteristics of railroads and the issues associated with this industry have had significant influence on the evolution and development of Economics

Railroad Economics
Research in Transportation Economics, Volume 20, 11–67

ISSN: 0739-8859/doi:10.1016/S0739-8859(07)20002-2

itself. Many of the themes and issues in modern industrial organization (IO) economics had their origin in the issues and controversies regarding the rail industry. IO focuses on the links between industry structure, its institutional and market organization, and the implications for the behavior of firms and their performance. Issues regarding the extent of competition, regulation, or other government controls and performance are intertwined. The underlying technology of multiple capital-intensive operations serving diverse markets at different locations gives rise to complex management decisions, carrier-shipper disputes, and debates over appropriate public policy intervention.

The parallels between rail economics and modern IO can be seen in several themes to be reviewed in the evolution of rail economics. This chapter begins with the earliest and broadest links between railroads and economic development generally. A subsequent section provides a brief overview of economic, operational, and public policy issues regarding railways over the past century and a half. The chapter then turns to reviews of major themes in the evolution of rail economics:[2] (1) the economics of railway pricing and rationales for public intervention; (2) the rise of regulation in North America; (3) the development of rail cost analysis; (4) the disappointment with and critiques of rail regulation; (5) the working of competitive forces in rail markets; (6) deregulation and its effects; (7) government ownership as an alternative to regulation, its rationales and performance; and (8) the ongoing issues and approaches to government intervention to deal with pockets of rail market power including proposals to separate ownership of track from rail operations. A brief conclusion follows.

2. RAILROADS, ECONOMIC DEVELOPMENT, AND THE DEVELOPMENT OF ECONOMICS

Partly because of the importance and prominence of railroads in the evolution of industrial economies, the initial interest of economics in railroads focused on their role in the overall economic development of regions and nations.

> Every improvement in the art of transport having a tendency to diminish cost, and augment speed and safety, operates in a variety of ways to stimulate consumption and production, and thereby advance national wealth and prosperity. (Lardner, 1850, p. 29)

Because the railroad was such an advance over previous land transport, the reductions in travel time and cost were dramatic. Lardner cites several examples of travel times in England reduced from days to a matter of hours with the advent of rail services. The importance of railroads on the development of Western North America is widely cited, although hyperbole occasionally exceeded reality. Douglas North summarizes the popular view:

> In addition to its revolutionary role in lowering transport costs, the railroad has also been credited with still further substantial effects upon economic development. The size of investment – that is, the amount of capital invested – in railroads in the United States in the nineteenth century make it the first billion-dollar industry by the time of the Civil War. Not only was it a large-scale industry; the railroad in the course of its building needed iron, steel, machinery, and timber; therefore, it was given credit for inducing expansion in still other industries. (North, 1966, p. 108)

This view is most notably associated with Rostow's (1952, 1960) "Stages of Economic Growth." This view of railroads as being the underpinning of western economic development came under question by economic historians, notably Fogel (1964), who even questioned the need for the technology at all (see also Fishlow, 1965).

Nonetheless, the railroad is the defining technology of its time and is intimately identified with the economic development process of that era. But we have learned that economic development is not reducible to one or two over-riding causes. The key issues in rail economics are not its broader links with economic growth, but rather characteristics of rail production and costs, and associated implications for market structure, competition, and industrial organization questions.

An incidental characteristic of railroads with potentially significant economic implications concerns its influence on the development of corporate management generally (e.g., see Chandler, 1965). "... as a large-scale enterprise, the railroad required the development of sophisticated methods of large-scale business organization and has been looked upon as a pioneer in the development of corporate organization in the United States." (North, 1966, p. 108). North notes that there were other large-scale industries developing in the nineteenth century, and he particularly notes the various financial schemes and manipulation by promoters that may have hampered market development. Certainly there were previous large-scale long-distance organizations (e.g., the Hudson's Bay Company). But arguably the railroad was the first large-scale example of real-time management of spatial operations. The need for standardized time grew out of rail management. The modern JIT spatial organization of production, logistics, and supply chains are the evolved result of the operations management problems that grew out of rail operations.

Another characteristic in North America was the important role that land grants played in financing railroad development, so they could cash in on the economic activity that was stimulated by their presence. Indeed, some railroads made more from land-value enhancement than they could make directly from transportation services. Modern ideas of capturing location rents at or near urban transit stations to help finance them is a recent example of recognizing and trying to take advantage of the interrelationship between transport, economic activity, and land values.

Around the end of the nineteenth century, especially in North America, railroads became leading examples of public regulation of private business. This led to decades of debates over the theory and practice of regulation generally. Alternatively, in many countries railways became a prime example of public enterprise, i.e., enterprises owned by government yet requiring substantial managerial discretion to operate at least a quasi-commercial operation. The economics of railways is intimately linked to regulatory constraints and related public intervention in rail markets. These issues are taken up in several sections of the chapter.

The collection of data on railway companies and operations would provide the basis for the development of empirical analysis of production and cost functions, techniques that would become of widespread importance in economics generally. Rail cost analysis is taken up in Section 6.

But the closest link between railway economics and economic theory, in general, is pricing for multiproduct enterprises. Railways were – and remain – a major example of multiproduct enterprises. This required modification to standard economic theory, which normally is focused on single product firms. Indeed, in the decades around 1900, railway rate theory was regarded as one of the fundamental branches of economic theory. This literature is summarized in Section 4.

3. ECONOMICS OF RAILROADS, THEN AND NOW

Some of the basic operational and cost characteristics have not changed much in over a century. There is the heavy capital investment in way and structure before service can commence, investments that become largely sunk once they are incurred. There is also substantial investment required in terminals. There are substantial investments required in rolling stock although over time it has become possible to lease much of this equipment thereby reducing this element of ownership risk. Railways are network industries, requiring real time coordination often over very long distances. For large-scale urban passenger operations, often there is a traffic control problem of great complexity.

While these characteristics have persisted, there have been major advances in rail technology and performance such as the size and speed of trains, scale of operations, specialized rail cars, pooled rail car fleets, and especially the information technology to manage all of this. Cost analysis has improved notwithstanding the inherent difficulty of assigning costs. In North America, the most significant change in the economics of railroads has been the shift from being heavily regulated, where the economic and managerial issues were focused on a regulatory process, to the deregulated environment, whereby rail companies are now commercial enterprises pursuing profitability with only limited regulatory restrictions. But the world is not static. Recent economics literature concerned with railways are once again focusing on rail market power in selected markets and exploring alternate institutional arrangements to either regulate such markets or foster greater competition for them.

Inevitably, the earliest writings on rail economics were primarily descriptive, but there was also analysis and discussion of the economic implications of rail operations. Among the earliest treatises on rail economics is Lardner (1850). He initially emphasizes the significance of transportation improvements on economic activity from ancient times, and the profound influence the railway had brought. Later chapters discuss the various components of rail operations and their characteristics (way and works, locomotives, "carrying stock" and its maintenance, stations, clearing house, passenger and goods traffic, characteristics of expenses, revenue and tariffs, accidents), and chapters on railways in different countries.

Hadley (1885) made insightful comparisons of rail development in America, England, and continental countries, including discussions of economic characteristics and their implications.

> The feature of the English railroad system which most forcibly strikes an American observer, is its stability... . It shows itself in their construction, their management, and their legal relations. The mere traveler sees it in the massive stone bridges, the tunnels and viaducts, the station accommodations, and a thousand details of less importance which combine to produce an impression of solidity and finish, entirely wanting in the majority of American railroads. The statistician sees it in the figures showing the cost per mile of road, which in America is little over $60,000, and in England is more than $2,00,000 ...
>
> Many writers on both sides of the Atlantic assume that the differences in railroad management between England and the United States are in large measure the result of

> differences in legislation. This is a mistake … . The fact probably is that the different systems, of management and legislation both, are an almost inevitable outgrowth of the different industrial conditions of the two countries … . The English railroads were mainly built to accommodate and extend existing business … . The American railroads have been mainly built with a view to the development of new lines of traffic, new establishments, or even new cities. The Englishman built for the present and future both; the American chiefly, and sometimes entirely, for the future.
>
> This hope of future gains, out of all proportion to present traffic, of necessity gave railroad business in America a more speculative character than in England … (Hadley, 1885, pp. 146–147)[3]

Hadley includes a chapter on "ownership and speculation" since that was an important characteristic of the industry especially in the U.S. He also discussed competition versus combination in the industry, which is an important theme that continues to the present.

There were several major books on rail economics, including Acworth (1905), Ripley (1923), Wellington (1915), and Williams (1909). They reviewed the various activities involved in producing rail transportation, both construction and operations, and the economic implications, and chapters on rail freight classification and rate-making. The history of railroads was also a topic in most rail books.

Implicit in some authors (such as in Lardner) but explicit in others (Knoop, (1913, 1923), also Clark, 1923) was an emphasis on sources of increasing and decreasing returns, both in the economy generally and in railways. Increasing returns could be gained in manufacturing by the expansion of market territories made possible by railroads. Similarly, diminishing returns as in agriculture could be avoided by expanding territory for new agricultural production. In rail operations themselves there were many possibilities of increasing returns associated with the growth of operations. The characteristics of competition versus monopoly were major topics for review, including the problem that railways tended to be somewhere between the two economic models, a mix of competitive and monopoly powers depending on markets and the presence of differential rate structures. And competitive forces could arise in subtle forms, Knoop (1923, pp. 151–152) recognized competition among markets served as an indirect competitive restrain affecting railways.

Railway issues dominated the major textbooks on the economics of transportation up to 1970. Locklin's text on *The Economics of Transportation* was first published in 1935 and went through numerous editions. Although Locklin's and other texts (notably Pegrum, 1963) addressed transportation generally, the texts were dominated by rail issues, usually with one or two chapters devoted to each of the other modes. There was an emphasis on understanding rules, regulations, and government institutions, and analysis of significant regulatory cases and the arguments associated with them.

It was accepted that railroads (along with public utilities) were businesses affected with the public interest, and were subject to economies of scale thus making competition unworkable. And these public interest concerns were presumed to carry over to other modes. Regulation was deemed necessary and economic analysis focused on conflicts between efficiency and fairness issues.

But starting about the 1960s, a "sea-change" in the economic thought about railways came about. The performance of regulation was increasingly questioned, the belief in scale economies in railroading was not supported in empirical studies, and the rise of competitive modes of transportation came to be recognized. A deregulation movement was underway (and is discussed in Sections 7 and 9).

But first we return to one of the most fundamental themes in railway economics, the theory of railway pricing.

4. RAILWAY PRICING

Railway rates once occupied a very important place in the development of economic theory. For a time, it was considered to be one of the mainstream branches of economics. Some of the leading academics devoted considerable attention to it, e.g., Hadley (1885, then president of the American Economics Association), F. Y. Edgeworth, J. B. Clark, and what became known as the Pigou–Taussig debates stimulated many papers in the leading journals of economics. Locklin (1933) provides an insightful review of the literature. A central issue in the debates concerned whether the observed variability of railway rates among customers was discriminatory pricing associated with monopoly power, or whether a complex differential rate structure was an inevitable outcome of ambiguity in trying to identify what portions of the enterprise's total costs could be associated with a specific output. In fact, both positions are correct, there will be some markets where railways will have some discretionary market power, yet it is also true that costs shared among multiple outputs cannot necessarily be assigned uniquely among the outputs.

4.1. Railway Rates and Economic Theory

An inability to measure costs with precision posed a serious dilemma for economists. Economics is a cost of production theory of value. In the long run, perfectly competitive markets would result in products being produced as efficiently as possible and priced at minimum long-run average costs. This is an attractive prospect, and provides a theory about the social validity of market prices (although with the caveat that this is for a given distribution of income).

Railway rate structures emerging in practice did not produce uniform prices, but rather a mixture of rates. And differences in rates did not seem related to measurable differences in costs, but reflected the "value of service" or influences of demand. Unlike the cost concepts of economic theory, it appeared that substantial portions of the railway's costs did not vary with levels and mixes of outputs. These came to be known as "overhead" costs (and by many other labels, see Locklin, 1933, p. 174).[4] There were indivisibilities and at least some elements of excess capacity present that resulted in some costs not varying with output, or varying in an irregular way. In these circumstances, there is a clear logic for a firm to attract additional traffic even at very low markups to utilize any spare capacity. Differential prices make economic sense. How does one reconcile railway prices with the standard economic theory of a direct and unique link whereby prices reflect costs exactly?[5]

Most economists assumed that it was monopoly power that would enable price discrimination among customers, and this explained why rail prices were not conforming to the expectations of pricing by competitive firms. If competition were present, then some normal set of prices would emerge. But this did not happen. Where competition took place, price differentials persisted, and/or prices were bid down covering only the direct variable costs. In that case, bankruptcy would eventually result, leaving the surviving railway in a position of market power. Add to this the prospect that there would be inherent economies of scale, and railways (and some utilities) became special cases in economics, and the standard theory about competition, costs, and prices could not apply.

Taussig's (1891) contribution was to emphasize joint costs as explaining a substantial part of differential pricing. Analogous to beef and hides or wool and mutton, railways were characterized by joint production: one fronthaul unavoidably generated one backhaul (it was not emphasized at the time, but peakload characteristics are another example of joint production). In this case, there is a clear theoretical explanation for the prices of joint products reflecting the relative demands (willingness to pay) for the joint products, i.e., an established theory to explain price differentials even in competitive markets (the differential prices of different cuts of meat is a good modern example of joint product prices).

The Pigou–Taussig debate (Pigou, 1913; Taussig, 1913; see Locklin, 1933 for a full account) involved many more authors than the two central figures, but it had to do with how prevalent are true joint costs in railways, as opposed to monopoly power, and also the problem of overhead costs which are not joint but nor are they assignable in any unique way between multiple products.

The need for some differential pricing of railway outputs has now been accepted by economists for some decades (e.g., Baumol et al., 1962), although periodic debates still arise by those who hope that better cost accounting might somehow enable all costs to be assigned so that prices would be tied to costs as in perfectly competitive markets. But this misses the point about the unallocability of costs and that accepting price-sensitive business at low markups lowers the amount of revenue that must be collected from other customers to cover all costs. The real public policy issue is that – granted that differential prices are necessary and inevitable – how does one identify and prevent exploitation of monopoly power in this environment? This is taken up below but for the moment the economic principles about differential pricing are summarized.

4.2. Pricing and Public Policy

The economic theory of optimal resource allocation emphasizes marginal cost pricing. In the absence of economies of scale, competition will result in minimum long-run average costs, which also equal marginal costs. If economies of scale are present, competition in the market is not feasible. If marginal cost pricing were followed, the firm would incur a financial deficit and not survive. Either a subsidy would be necessary to enable a private firm to survive, or such a firm could be operated as a public enterprise, and the financial deficit absorbed in the government budget. The presence of overhead costs do not necessarily mean there are economies of scale, but there will be economies of utilization and the same problem that pricing at direct variable (marginal) costs would result in a deficit.

At this juncture, public policy about railways can follow two paths. A commitment to strict marginal cost pricing means the government must accept the need for on-going subsidy, either of private railroads or a public enterprise. If the prospect for subsidy is large, countries are likely to have government-owned railways. One might also note that once rail financial losses are accepted as normal, this may invite other social rationales for subsidy, and the political process will respond. The alternative policy path is to require that the rail industry try to be self-financing. This is the path followed in North America. This path was privately owned railroads, although would come under government regulation to oversee rail pricing. (The next few sections review themes in rail economics related to North American rail regulatory experience before addressing the government-ownership approach.)

Pricing aimed at full cost recovery can follow two broad approaches. First is an average or full cost approach that requires allocation of joint and overhead costs and set prices to reflect these "fully distributed" or "fully allocated" costs. But arbitrary allocations of unallocable costs means inevitably that some price-sensitive customers will be lost, and the "contributions" they could have made toward the overhead costs (even if below the average contribution of other traffic) are lost, leaving a larger "burden" of overhead costs to be covered by other customers. The alternative is to allow differential pricing, whereby markups over direct marginal costs are lower on price-sensitive traffic and higher on traffic which is able to bear higher prices. The latter is the practice that evolved in self-financing railways, and it has an economic efficiency rationale behind it even if it proved controversial regarding equity or fairness of differential markups.

What is labeled a "second-best" approach is to allow a multiproduct firm to raise prices above marginal costs on different outputs just sufficient to cover the overheads and a normal return for the business overall. It turns out that there is an optimal set of markups that will raise the needed revenue with a minimum loss of business due to prices exceeding the identifiable marginal costs of each business. These markups vary with the elasticity of demand. These are known as Ramsey prices following Ramsey (1927) but also identified with the French economist Boiteux (1956), see Baumol and Bradford (1970) for the evolution of this concept. For railroads, Ramsey pricing is consistent with profit-maximizing "value of service" pricing, also called "charging what the traffic will bear."[6] This practice is especially appropriate for railways or other high overhead cost industries. It is not necessarily economies of scale per se that results in a financial deficit from marginal cost pricing, but rather the "burden" of overheads (or "constant costs"[7]) that need to be covered by traffic in total but are not assignable to individual outputs. Often there are indivisibilities resulting in unused capacity, and differential pricing can stimulate utilization of such assets, raising total output and spreading the overhead burden among more customers.

The second best efficient pricing system is to allow differential pricing up to the point where the total overhead costs are covered including a normal return on investment. If revenues were any greater, this would be entering the realm of economic or monopoly profits. The test for monopoly profits (assuming the firm is efficient) is whether or not total revenues collected exceed total economic costs. The height of a markup on any specific output is not a test for monopoly.[8] This Ramsey or modern value of service pricing is an economically efficient way to cover all costs of the firm with minimum loss of traffic due to prices exceeding marginal costs. This is an efficiency concept, it does not necessarily mean the differential pricing will meet tests of fairness. For example, Ramsey pricing could be consistent with having high markups on food and low markups on luxury goods, if the former were relatively inelastic and the latter elastic; but public policy might object on fairness grounds. Efficiency versus fairness concerns have haunted regulatory debates for decades. This provides a segway to review the rise and dominance of regulation over railroads that would last over much of the twentieth century.

5. RAIL REGULATION IN NORTH AMERICA

The capital intensity and associated financial risks for railways result in a market structure where the number of firms generally is limited, often only one serving a particular market. That is, there are prospects for monopoly elements in railways, although it is more complicated than just counting the number of firms. Eventually, there were possible competitive pressures from other modes and/or competition among alternate markets and sources of supply. But in the nineteenth century, there was rail market power in many markets. The traditional economic concern about monopoly power is the deadweight loss associated with a firm reducing output to increase price (or restricting qualities of service for the same price). This also can raise equity concerns about the fairness of income redistribution in favor of rail shareholders at the expense of their customers. Given the plethora of markets served, there was the likelihood of discrimination among markets, which in fact became recognized and even accepted as an important component in determining rail rate levels and structures.

Note, however, that the prospect of discrimination reduces the traditional economic efficiency concern that monopolists tend to restrict output. A discriminating monopolist has an incentive to carry additional traffic as long as it makes some contribution to overheads and profit (although a concern about income distribution would be aggravated since, ceteris paribus, a discriminating monopolist should be able to raise more money than a non-discriminating one).

There is also an irony in rail market structures: where competition does exist, there have long been concerns that competition in such circumstances could be "destructive," that competition would drive prices toward the minimum identifiable variable costs of the movement and not generate sufficient revenues to sustain the full costs of the enterprise. This outcome must make a number of assumptions about the behavior and possible myopia of competitors, ruling out prospects for collusion even if only tacit. Nonetheless, fears of "cutthroat pricing" or "destructive competition" were also part of the rationale of government intervention in the rail industry.

Faced with these market structures, public policy reacted in two broad ways historically. Some countries relied on direct government ownership of railways, and some accepted privately owned rail companies and used regulation to combat the concerns for monopoly and/or destructive competition. North American experience followed the regulatory approach (until about the 1970s). Several European countries and Australia adopted state-ownership of railways. Both approaches emerged in different countries in South America. Most Asian countries favored government ownership. The U.K. had a more complex history of private companies, nationalization, and more recently a radical restructured privatization of operations.

The major railway decisions regarding operations, pricing, and investment arise both under nationalization or regulated private companies. But there are differences in the vision or expectations about the role of railways in the economy, differences in the perceived role of the state in relation to railways, and differences in rail management strategy and tactics. This section focuses on North American rail regulation.

The Interstate Commerce Commission (ICC) existed from 1887 through 1995, although its regulatory influence was starting to wane by the late 1970s. (The Board of Railway Commissioners, later Canadian Transport Commission played a similar role in Canada.) The ICC was formed partially in response to populist pressures from Prairie regions, i.e., farmers dependent on individual railroads to carry their produce to distant markets and also for all the goods they purchased. There was also widespread concern about the behavior of large corporations generally around the turn to the twentieth century, i.e., the era of "Robber Barons." The rail concerns were not only about levels of rates and service, but also discrimination including fears in both Canada and the U.S. that railroad pricing might restrict economic development prospects in western regions and leave them dependent on "eastern" manufacturing. Rail cartel arrangements were common although unstable. The ICC did not eliminate discrimination but attempted to adjudicate matters, to avoid "undue discrimination." And it sought stability for the industry.

Regulation is usually characterized as being imposed on the rail industry, although some have noted that railroads benefited from the stability that regulation brought and thus the railroads may have actually welcomed and even sought regulation (Kolko, 1965; MacAvoy, 1965; Spann & Erickson, 1970).

The basic concept of price regulation was straightforward: shippers objecting to rate increases (or alleged inadequacies of service) have the right to appeal to the regulatory agency to hear their case and potentially intervene. In time, other parties could become involved such as competitors objecting one company's proposed rate changes. But the process was time-consuming, criteria for decisions were not necessarily clear and might involve a mix of efficiency and fairness considerations, often emphasizing precedent from previous cases. And there was the prospect of judicial appeal of decisions. It was a ponderous process with disincentives for efficient and innovative rail operations (more in Section 7).

During the early decades of regulation, the railroads were the dominant transport technology. Competitive alternatives would arise later. Because of fairness concerns and the desirability that the transportation system serve as many as possible, even in relatively remote regions, a complex rate structure evolved which included cross-subsidy of services (although cost analysis was not well developed hence explicit measures of cross-subsidy usually were not available). As competition began to emerge, primarily from motor carriers but also inland barge or coastal ship movements, the solution was to regulate these other modes, to bring them into the regulatory orbit (Hilton, 1972). Railway rate structures continued to set the pattern. Early motor carriers often set rates using rail tariffs. Over time, high-valued, high-markup traffic began to divert to motor carriers with their greater flexibility and convenience for many shippers. This would undermine railroad profitability. Motor carriers would seek the high-markup traffic and not what was less attractive. The ICC response tried to preserve the rail rate structure and tended to pursue a policy of trying to share traffic between the modes, i.e., enable both to compete, share business, and survive financially.

Another ICC regulatory characteristic to note was an ambivalence and often reluctance to allow mergers among railroads, although several were permitted in the post World War II years (Keeler, 1983, p. 36). Skepticism of mergers is not too surprising. Part of the rationale for regulation was to control or avoid monopoly. The ICC was more suspicious of parallel merger proposals than end-to-end, but even the latter were often opposed. A merger between a strong and weak (financially) railroad might be looked on with some favor because it might be regarded as a way to preserve operations that might otherwise go bankrupt (but strong railroads had little incentive to takeover bankrupt operations). While a number of rail mergers were permitted over the decades, nonetheless the end result of ICC merger policy was a legacy of a large number of the U.S. railroads, none of whom could offer transcontinental service.

The "big story" in the economics of North American railroads is the substantial (although not complete) deregulation of the industry. But before addressing the circumstances that gave rise to it and the economic analyses associated with it, it is useful to review a major theme of analysis of the rail industry which was important for assessing the costs of rail regulation: The estimation of rail costs.

6. EVOLUTION OF RAIL COST ANALYSIS

The first point to note is the influence of railways (or more accurately, their data) on the development of empirical analyses of costs for the economics profession generally. The large number of private rail companies in the U.S. all had to file statistics about their operations and expenditures. This treasure chest of data facilitated analysis of rail cost characteristics, including the earliest empirical investigations of cost and production functions. More particularly, the data enabled empirical investigation of rail cost characteristics, both questions of broad interest such as the extent of economies of scale or density, as well as development of more micro cost estimates for individual components of rail operations, for rail management and regulators. Both of these cost investigation themes proved to be valuable for the advance of costing procedures in other industries.

Rail cost analysis has developed in two streams. First are aggregate cost functions (total costs of each firm for one year is one observation) to identify broad cost characteristics such as scale and density economies. The second approach to rail cost analysis is to develop cost estimates for specific components and individual outputs of rail operations. These are labeled disaggregate or practitioner cost analyses. Both have a long history and make use of statistical methods, but there has been surprisingly little cross fertilization between them.

6.1. Development of Aggregate Cost Functions[9]

The pioneering work of applying statistical methods to rail cost characteristics is generally credited to Clark (1923), although the methods were primarily data compilation, scatter plots and charts. In contrast to the popular notion that the majority of rail costs were fixed, he pointed out that over time there was correlation between the level of costs and levels of operations. He drew from even earlier analysis by Lorenz (1916) of the ICC, who plotted cost per gross ton mile (GTM) as well as cost/mile of track against GTM/mile of track for the U.S. railroads. Both Lorenz and Clark were able to show that there was greater variability of costs with output levels than was popularly believed. Also note that both recognized the relevance of traffic density in explaining cost characteristics, a feature that remains very important in understanding and interpreting rail cost functions.

The first studies of rail costs that would be labeled "econometric" were those of Borts (1952, 1954, 1960) and Klein (1953). Borts (1952) estimated rail production functions separately for switching and line-haul operations for a 1948 cross-section of the U.S. railroads. His calculated cost-elasticities were ambiguous about the presence of scale economies. Borts' subsequent papers were conceptual discussions of the problems in trying to measure scale economies when there is unused capacity.

Klein (1953) estimated a rail production function using the 1936 U.S. rail data, specifying two outputs (passenger miles and net ton miles of freight) and found evidence of economies of scale. Klein's data were later reexamined using flexible functional forms by Hasenkamp (1979) and Brown, Caves, and Christensen (1979).

The next notable work was Friedlaender (1971) who estimated a long-run cost function from a cross-section of the U.S. railroads stratified by region and time period, as well as a short-run cost function estimated from quarterly data. Combining the cost elasticities showed evidence of substantial excess capacity in the industry, a critique of the impacts of the regulatory environment on the industry.

Keeler (1974) was critical of Friedlaender (and Bort's) analyses because of inherently contradictory assumptions they had to make: The long-run cost function assumes that firms are operating at designed output of their long-run cost function, whereas the short-run cost functions estimated for the same firms assume that operations are not at their long-term planned level of operations. Keeler postulated a Cobb–Douglas production function for freight and passenger operations, with track as a fixed input. He used pooled cross-section and time series data for 51 railroads for 1968–1970 to estimate his cost function. Similar to Borts and Friedlaender, his estimated cost elasticities implied substantial excess capacity in the industry. His results indicated constant returns to scale but increasing returns from higher utilization of existing capacity.

Another important analysis of aggregate cost functions during this period was Griliches (1972). He reviewed rail cost estimation methods and was critical of the ICC practice of dividing costs and output by miles of track before running their regressions (note that this practice dated back to Lorenz, 1916; Meyer, Peck, Stenason, & Zwick, 1959 were also critical of this ICC practice). Instead, Griliches used weighted regression to deal with heteroskedasticity. His cost model used a cross-section of the U.S. railroads 1957–1961 separated into two size classes, above or below 500 miles of track. He found no evidence of economies of scale but drew attention to the importance between scale (the change in costs with equiproportionate increases in all outputs) as opposed to economies from greater utilization of indivisible plant by increases in some outputs.

Harris (1977) took up the issue of economies of scale versus density. He used revenue ton-miles RTM rather than gross ton-miles as his output measure, and first postulated a total cost TC function that was consistent with the linear functions used by the ICC:

$$\mathrm{TC} = \mathrm{b1RTM} + \mathrm{b2RFT} + \mathrm{b3MR} \tag{1}$$

where RFT are revenue freight tons (i.e., ignoring distance which is captured by RTM) and MR is miles of road, a proxy for network size. Dividing by RTM yields:

$$\frac{\mathrm{TC}}{\mathrm{RTM}} = \mathrm{b1} + \mathrm{b2}\frac{\mathrm{RFT}}{\mathrm{RTM}} + \mathrm{b3}\frac{\mathrm{MR}}{\mathrm{RTM}} \tag{2}$$

or

$$\frac{\mathrm{TC}}{\mathrm{RTM}} = \mathrm{b1} + \mathrm{b2}\frac{1}{\mathrm{ALH}} + \mathrm{b3}\frac{1}{\mathrm{DENSITY}} \tag{3}$$

where ALH is average length of haul. He included a dummy variable for urban operations, and his results showed the strong influence of traffic density on rail costs.

The next significant development in rail cost analysis (and cost functions generally) was the use of flexible functional forms, especially the translog function. These were introduced by two research teams, Friedlaender and Spady of the Massachusetts Institute of Technology and Caves, Christensen et al., of the University of Wisconsin, publishing their work at about the same time.[10] The translog function has been widely used since because it enables researchers to explore possible nonlinearities in the coefficients as well as cross-relationships among the variables in a cost function.

Spady (1979) and Friedlaender and Spady (1981) estimated translog cost functions for both rail and trucking. They used the translog with firm-specific technology variables, specifically low-density route miles and freight tons per train, which they interpreted as exogenous route characteristics for different firms. The initial study used data for 1968–1972, but subsequently reduced the sample to 1970 (prior to the formation of AMTRAK, the government-owned carrier that took over most rail passenger operations). They employed four traffic output categories, and found some evidence of diseconomies of scale for freight traffic, and economies of route density, train, and load consolidation.

Caves, Christensen et al., conducted a number of rail costs studies over a longer span of time. They were particularly interested in measuring productivity changes as well as the traditional rail production characteristics. Productivity is indicated by the downward shift of cost functions over time. Caves, Christensen, and Swanson (1980, 1981c) estimated a cost function using 1955, 1963, and 1974 data and interpolating and extrapolating the productivity (technology shift) variable over the full period. Their initial studies showed some evidence of economies of scale, but this was before their later formulations to explicitly separate economies of scale and density. Their studies showed the rail productivity growth in the U.S. was lower than what many believed. Even more interesting were their subsequent studies (Caves, Christensen, & Swanson, 1981b and with Tretheway (Caves, Christensen, Swanson, & Tretheway, 1982)), which included the two Canadian Class I railways (Canadian National (CN) and Canadian Pacific (CP)). Their productivity growth was much higher than that of the U.S. railroads. This was attributed to the deregulation and greater managerial freedom in Canada.

A significant development in all of this research was refining the distinction between economics of scale and density. The latter is the behavior of costs as output expands over a given network, whereas economies of scale focuses on the behavior of costs if the network size increases as output expands. Route miles is usually used as a proxy for network size (e.g., Caves, Christensen, Tretheway, & Windle, 1985).

Four developments affected the U.S. rail data around the time of deregulation. The formation of AMTRAK in 1970, the government-owned rail passenger service, removed passenger service from the railways.[11] Second was a major revision in the data collection itself in about 1978, as well as a shift in treatment of capital and maintenance expenditures about 1983. Third was the deregulation of the U.S. rail industry primarily identified with the Staggers Act 1980. A fourth complication taking place after deregulation is the increase in mergers after 1980 which results in a discontinuity of data before and after the merger. Estimation of cost functions using rail data overlapping the regulated and deregulated periods pose econometric challenges in separating the impact of deregulation or mergers from changes in the data itself.

Berndt, Friedlaender, Chiang, and Vellturo (1993) and Friedlaender, Berndt, Chiang, Showalter, and Vellturo (1993) employed 1974–1986 data. Their formulation separated route miles from way and structures capital and included percentages of different output types to reduce the aggregation in RTM output measures, using a hedonic specification of output, that is the output measures adjusted for cost-influencing characteristics such as length of haul rather that list length of haul as a separate argument in the cost function. They found increasing returns to density and slightly increasing returns to firm size. A contribution of Friedlaender et al. (1993) was to recognize the intensity of capital utilization and capital stock adjustments as a factor complicating the estimation of cost functions.

Another contribution as well as challenge in rail cost functions was separating firm-specific effects from estimates of industry-wide characteristics such as economies of scale or density (especially the latter, Caves et al., 1985). Braeutigam, Daugherty, and Turnquist (1984) used a time series for a single firm to avoid an influence of several firm-specific effects. Caves et al., pointed out a problem in that the dummy variables for individual firms can distort the estimates of scale or density economies (or other coefficients) because there can be correlation between the firm-specific measures and that of scale or density economies (Caves, Christensen, Tretheway, & Windle, 1987).

A recent analysis is Bitzan (2000, 2003) who uses data for 30 U.S. railroads (some of whom merge during the data period) for 1983–1997 (a total of 215 observations) in an investigation of possible sub-additivity properties of rail cost functions, following Shin and Ying (1992). He employs a translog function with three output categories (types of train service) and other firm characteristics including average speed. Tests show the superiority of separating rather than leaving output categories combined. He employs both a capital stock measure and miles of road as firm inputs and characteristics, respectively. Previous researchers often use miles of road as a proxy for network size or scale. Bitzan argues that miles of road might be interpreted as a measure of scope economies because it could represent adding new territories and markets and not necessarily greater scale of existing outputs. Hence, there is some ambiguity between scale and scope economies by his definition, and the results do show some increasing returns. The particularly interesting analysis is to reformulate a "quasi cost function" that separates costs associated with track as opposed to train operations. This enables a test of possible interaction between track-related costs and those of train operations. He finds there are cost complementarities, which would imply some increase in costs if one were to separate track from rail operations. Ivaldi and McCullough (2001) found some ambiguity in cost interdependencies, but a later study (2004) found significant increases in costs, if operations were separated from infrastructure supply.

Bitzan (2000, 2003) goes further in evaluating components of rail costs to test if there are economies in train operations considered separately from way and structure (track) costs. He finds increasing returns indicating possible increased costs, if rail services were provided by multiple firms rather than one. Ivaldi and McCullough (2004, 2007) found substantial cost increases if track and operations were separated and if there were multiple operators.

6.2. Development of Disaggregate or Practitioner Cost Functions

In contrast to studies of broad cost characteristics of scale or density, railway companies and rail regulators desire cost functions applicable to specific traffic movements, to assist in assessing profitability. Railways supply thousands of customers, but need some means of estimating costs of serving various customers. The basic approach to this type of rail costing is a two stage analysis (e.g., see Waters, 1985 or Talley, 1988). Railways involve a number of operations or intermediate outputs: yard operations, dispatching, line-haul, track maintenance, car (wagon) ownership and repairs, etc. Railways try to estimate the unit costs of each of these activities. This might be done by simply assigning specific cost categories to the various activities and dividing by the annual amount of activity (direct assignment), or sometimes by engineering analysis (e.g., link fuel consumption to train weight, gradients, speed, etc.). Railways (and regulators) also estimate statistical cost functions using various company and yearly data for certain cost accounts and measures of these intermediate activities (e.g., annual track maintenance expenditures related to gross ton miles). Linear regression analysis is used, which usually has a positive constant term indicating that the costs are not 100-percent variable. The regression coefficients (or the percent variable implied by the regression) are used to estimate a per unit expense for this cost category, linked to the appropriate intermediate activity measure.

Given these unit cost coefficients for various activities, the cost of a specific traffic movement consists of describing the amounts of intermediate activities for the movement (e.g., so many car-days and/or car-miles, a share of train operating expenses, yard switching time, etc.). Then multiplying each of these activity requirements times the appropriate unit cost coefficient, results in an estimate of the variable costs of that specific traffic movement. All railways will have a costing manual for this purpose. Regulatory agencies such as the Canadian Transportation Agency and the U.S. Surface Transportation Board (formerly ICC) have costing procedures for regulatory purposes that will include estimates from statistical cost functions.

This approach to costing is applicable to other multiproduct industries and is generally known as "activity-based costing." This costing approach was pioneered by the railroads, partly linked to the development of the ICC's Rail Form A (primarily direct accounting estimates in its origin but with some regression analysis) and modifications made by various railroad research departments trying to develop better cost estimates.

The statistical advances came about in the late 1950s and early 1960s, in both Canadian (MacPherson Royal Commission, 1962, vol. 3; Stenason & Bandeen, 1965) and the U.S. railroads (Association of American Railroads, 1964). The appendices in Meyer et al. (1959) made extensive use of these analyses of rail cost components in developing measures of rail costs for their "classic" book on the feasibility of competition in the then-regulated transportation industry.

These unit cost procedures are very valuable for decision making in railways and, where necessary, in evaluating individual rates in regulatory disputes. But as valuable as they are for railways and regulators, it is a bit surprising that the statistical methods in use have had very little updating. Generally, simple linear regressions are still used. There is an econometric concern about this procedure. Each cost function is estimated independently, i.e., implicitly assuming that each cost function is separable from all others. But this is unlikely in many instances. It is an example of Zellner's (1962) "seemingly unrelated regressions." Waters and Woodland (1984) did an exploratory analysis showing the change in regression estimates when a set of these activity–cost functions were estimated jointly. But it would be a substantial task to estimate all the disaggregate cost functions simultaneously.

The Uniform Rail Costing System (URCS) is the regulatory-sanctioned costing system in the U.S. It still relies on a series of linear regressions (with direct assignment for some accounts). URCS did undergo some research and analysis to amend the procedures in the 1980s (ICC Ex Parte 431 proceedings), but this review ceased when the ICC's functions were transferred to the STB.

6.3. Conclusions Regarding Cost Analysis

The improvements in and evidence from empirical analysis of rail costs were not only valuable for the rail industry, these tools of analysis were also applicable for investigating cost characteristics and performance of other transportation modes. In the rail industry itself the distinction between scale and density economies, and the lack of empirical support for the former, were part of the foundation for rethinking the need for regulation.

7. CRITIQUES OF RAIL REGULATION

There were major changes underway in the economy generally over the course of the twentieth century. There was the rise of alternate transport technologies, especially the growth of motor carriers making use of public roads. There were advances in technology, generally, and productivity, the real costs of distance fell bringing greater trade and competition among market centers. There was population growth as well as growth in income levels. These made for larger and more markets, hence more demand for transportation to be served by all modes. The general growth of the economy and technology would undermine much of monopoly powers of railways and undermine the effectiveness of regulation because it would become difficult or impossible to sustain historical regulated rate structures in this new era.

There were early criticisms of ICC regulation, including suggestions that market competition could play an important role (e.g., Nelson, 1942). The criticisms of the ICC escalated over time. The regulatory was cumbersome, even oppressive. New modes (such as trucking) had to be regulated in order to maintain the regulatory order (Hilton, 1972). The ICC (and other utility regulatory commissions) became the inspiration for new economic theories of regulation. Commissions are seen as "captured" by the regulated (or perhaps even founded in the first place for the protection of the industry). The regulatory agency comes to regard the industry as a client to be protected and served, and the well-being of the industry becomes the focus of the regulatory agency. Regulation can be seen as supplied in response to a demand for protection from the rigors of the market place (e.g., Stigler, 1971; Posner, 1974; Peltzman, 1976).

By the 1960s, the U.S. rail industry was sinking financially. The story was similar in Canada although a long distance trucking industry did not evolve as rapidly as in the U.S., in part because of the more sparse population and markets, but also because Canadian transport policy granted some freedoms for their large railways to compete with new modes as they arose.

The break-through book arguing that the U.S. rail regulation (and that of other modes) was obsolete and reliance on markets could work was Meyer et al. (1959).[12] They reviewed the shortcomings of transport regulation as it had evolved, both the static effects leading to higher costs and also the adverse long-run impacts on managerial performance and innovation. They conducted substantial cost analyses for all modes, and the prospects for greater reliance on market forces to guide the allocation of resources rather than regulatory direction. This would include freedom to abandon services that were not economic. They foresaw a need for some residual regulation on the most capital-intensive modes (railroads) serving bulk shippers with limited alternatives, but overall they called for a dramatically different approach to transportation than had prevailed in the past.

Meyer et al. (1959) made extensive use of statistical and quantitative methods demonstrating their practical value in assessing existing performance and prospects for alternate arrangements in transportation. Empirical studies of transportation costs were important because, contrary to popular belief, the cost studies turned up little evidence of economies of scale, even for railroads. Economies of scale traditionally had been a major rationale of the need for regulation. As discussed earlier, empirical measures of increasing returns tended to reflect greater utilization of indivisible assets, not size per se.

The book by Meyer et al. (1959) set the tone for much of the academic research (and teaching) on transportation for the next decade or two, viz., analysis of the working of transportation markets and the feasibility of greater reliance on market competition. Initially, the idea of relying on market systems for transportation was almost exclusively an academic idea. There was little or no support among carriers or political parties. But this gradually changed as argument and evidence accumulated.

A number of economists were stimulated by Meyer et al.'s work. Friedlaender (1969) reviewed the economic issues and consensus from a conference organized by the Brookings institution. By analyzing supply and demand conditions in the industries (rail and other modes), some predictions could be made about the outcomes of greater reliance on markets for resource allocation. Much of the focus continued to be on the shortcomings of the policies and actions of ICC regulation.

Keeler (1983) provides an excellent review of the economic thinking and research results at that time. Several economists produced estimates of the economic costs of regulation (e.g., Harbeson, 1969; Moore, 1975; Levin, 1981). Early estimates (including Meyer et al., 1959) thought that reallocation of road-to-rail traffic would result (e.g., shifts of long distance truck to rail). Others were skeptical of the size of intermodal shifts (e.g., Boyer, 1977; Levin, 1978). But there were several costs associated with regulation, summarized by Gallamore (1999, p. 500n):

> Regulatory costs stemmed from forced cross-subsidy of unprofitable services, unwillingness to permit abandonment of certain facilities, delayed approval of inflation-driven cost increases, protection of existing traffic patterns and gateways, protection of competing modes, protection of employees adversely affected by railroad restructuring, excessive use of quasi-judicial procedure, and excessive paperwork. It is impossible to say which of these factors were the most costly to railroads; all were enormously aggravating to management.

At about the same time as the publication of the book by Meyer et al. (1959), a Royal Commission on Transportation (MacPherson Commission, (1962) in Canada recommended that regulations of Canadian railways be reduced to give them greater freedom to respond intermodal competition and greater flexibility in negotiating rates with shippers. The National Transportation Act of 1967 adopted these principles. It retained some regulations on rates that had high markups over variable costs, but the wording ended up providing the railways with more rate freedom than was intended. But the events in Canada provided a case study of the adjustments and performance of the railways as they adapted to a more commercial environment (Heaver & Nelson, 1977).

Caves et al. (1980, 1981c) provided evidence on the poor productivity of American railroads over the recent decades, and their papers (Caves, Christensen, & Swanson, 1981a, 1981b, also with Tretheway, 1982) were able to integrate Canadian rail data with their U.S. rail data, and empirically show the much higher productivity that emerged in Canada with rail pricing freedom. This added to the mounting evidence on the shortcomings of rail regulation and the cure.

The prospects for rail intramodal competition in this oligopoly industry were problematic, but some prospects were there (e.g., Levin, 1981). There were fears that rail rates could increase substantially in some markets without regulatory restrictions, although the deadweight loss in these markets might be offset by the gains in efficiency in rail operations and the prospect that the industry could be self-financing.

The combination of mounting evidence of the failures of regulation, compelling arguments that markets could work in transportation markets, and the sinking financial condition of the U.S. railroads, led to major legislative changes in the late 1970s and culminating with the Staggers Rail Act of 1980 to largely deregulate the industry. Gallamore (1999) provides an excellent overview the major factors leading to deregulation of the U.S. railroads, as well as the experience after deregulation.

8. UNDERSTANDING COMPETITION IN RAIL MARKETS

The disenchantment with regulation and rise of competitive forces in the transportation industry generally did not necessarily imply that rail markets could function in a highly competitive manner in all markets. Because of the capital intensity of rail lines, and that service is supplied along narrow corridors relative to the total landscape, direct competition among multiple railroads is rare. Even very large centers may be served by only a couple of railroads. Many communities or regions will have only one railway nearby. The perfectly competitive image of many homogeneous firms competing for business does not fit rail markets. Grimm and Winston (2000) illustrate ways that some competition can arise between railroads.

Where intramodal competition is feasible, there have long been concerns about the stability and sustainability of competition between firms with long-lived sunk assets and substantial overhead costs, in modern terminology, the possibility of an empty core.[13] Vigorous competition could drive prices down near directly identifiable variable costs and threaten long-term viability. Oligopoly competition can have various outcomes depending on the behavior of firms. Prices could be any where between destructively competitive levels (pricing even below variable costs in hopes of driving out competitor) to pure monopoly outcomes as a result of collusion. So assessing the behavior of firms is important to understand likely outcomes of oligopoly competition.

Even without intramodal competition, there are some competitive forces at work. Intermodal competition has been important in many markets. Trucks compete for high-valued shipments, where timely and frequent service is important. In some markets, shipping or barge movements might compete for bulk movements. Over the middle of the twentieth century, the rise of motor carriers was a major competitive force for many markets previously served by railways.

A third form of competitive pressures is known as market competition.[14] The ability of a railroad to charge high rates can be limited by competition in the marketplace for the commodity to be carried. Too high of a price and a supplier could not compete. There are alternate sources of supply and alternate logistics chains that can limit the market power a railway has over an apparently "captive" shipper. Over time, the advance of technology and growth of markets and alternative sources of supply have made market competition more feasible and important. Nonetheless, such competitive forces may be not nearly as forceful as intramodal competition could be.

Railways are neither perfectly competitive nor pure monopoly. Competition among railways is some form of oligopolistic competition, and varies among specific markets. Some economists have emphasized the importance of studying the specific and dynamic characteristics of the workings of markets, to assess if there is "workable competition" (Clark, 1961). Railroads sometimes compete directly on prices, but often compete more readily in other dimensions of service. But as noted above, often whatever competitive forces exist arise indirectly such as through market competition. Although some of the institutional and regulatory constraints are now different, Heaver and Nelson (1977, Chapters 4 and 9) provide an insightful discussion of the workings of competitive forces in rail markets.

There is another model of competition that could arise in some circumstances. It is a concept that has grown out of the concept of contestability as an alternative to traditional emphasis on competition (Baumol, Panzer, & Willig, 1982). This is a distinction between competition *in* a market as opposed to competition *for* a market. Even if there are scale economies or similar barriers to entry, it may be possible to obtain the results of competitive markets. Suppose firms had to bid for a franchise to supply specified services at specified prices. Even though investments might become sunk, prior to this commitment there could be competition *for* the market. Great Britain has tried this approach for franchises for passenger rail services (see Welsby & Nichols, 1999, for a review). Contestability can work in some circumstances, however, the usefulness of this concept for the working of existing rail markets is less clear. There remains the problem that investors can avoid costs prior to investment, but once invested the costs are sunk and competitive options still become greatly constrained. Contestability is the concept behind discussions about possibly restructuring the rail industry to separate the sunk costs of track and way facilities from potentially contestable train operating companies sharing the track (more below).

9. THE DEREGULATION EXPERIENCE IN NORTH AMERICA

The overall experience of rail deregulation has largely borne out economists' predictions at the time, with some surprises. The evidence of only limited economies of scale – as opposed to density – meant that most economists did not anticipate the extent of mergers and consolidations that would take place. Nor did major reallocations of traffic take place among modes. Nonetheless, competitive forces worked. The gains from deregulation reflected efficiency improvements and stimulated markets; significant innovations and productivity improvements came about.

There are three themes to review performance under deregulation: (i) the impact on firms' financial condition; (ii) productivity and cost efficiency; and (iii) impacts on customers (a fourth category, not pursued here, would be to look at the impacts on railroad employees).[15] A fourth development with debated implications for performance is the substantial consolidation that took place in the industry. This is addressed first, followed by the other rail performance topics.

9.1. Mergers and Consolidation of the Rail Industry

After deregulation, rail mergers and acquisitions were still subject to regulatory approval, although the oversight was first by the ICC and then by the Surface Transportation Board (STB), not the Department of Justice antitrust division. Concern has been expressed by economists that the STB was too lenient in merger approvals. Most (but not all) merger proposals were approved, and many situations of poorer service and reduced competition are alleged to have resulted (Tye & Horn, 2000, p. 2n). Merger approvals (in any industry) often involve tradeoffs between efficiency gains versus increased market power. These require case-by-case evaluation, and are not reviewed here. Suffice to say that the earlier empirical evidence on lack of (or limited) scale economies made economists skeptical of claimed efficiency gains from mergers.[16]

On the other hand, Harris and Winston (1983) developed a model to estimate the impact on rail costs and service quality of prospective merger activity in the early years of deregulation. They concluded that there were promising gains in cost reduction especially for vertical mergers, and also prospects for improved service. They also saw the danger of increased prices for some shippers, but these would not be so great as to offset the projected benefits of merger activity. The recent empirical analysis of rail freight rates by Grimm and Winston (2000) showed that while captive shippers do pay higher freight rates than others, the overall reductions in rail rates and service quality would offset the deadweight losses of higher rates associated with deregulation, although this does not necessarily defend the amount of merger activity.

The consolidation of the U.S. railroads after 1980 is shown in Fig. 1. (The Canadian Class Is were already transcontinental carriers and they increased their presence in the U.S. during this period as well.)[17]

There has been a theme receiving special attention in railroad economics regarding mergers. This is concern about "foreclosure" or control over bottlenecks in a rail network. The fear is that a railroad controlling a bottleneck could use its position to extract monopoly profits and/or restrict competing railroads from making use of the bottleneck. These issues are taken up in Section 11 below on ongoing issues in rail economics and public policy.

9.2. Market Growth and Financial Performance since Deregulation

Rail traffic has grown substantially since 1980 although there is no prospect of railroads regaining the high market shares it once had. Those times are gone. There has been substantial growth in some markets, notably long distance bulk cargo such as coal, and high-valued intermodal traffic. (The Association of American Railroads publishes several reports and statistical summaries, see www.aar.org).

> As railroads learned how to benefit from reduced regulation and as the economy improved, traffic volumes broke loose from decades of decline and stagnation. Class I railroad ton-miles increased 27 percent in the four years 1992–1996 alone. Revenues began a mild upswing, and ordinary income, which was only $144 million for all the Class I railroads in 1975 (in nominal dollars) reached $3.9 billion in 1996. (Gallamore, 1999, p. 495)

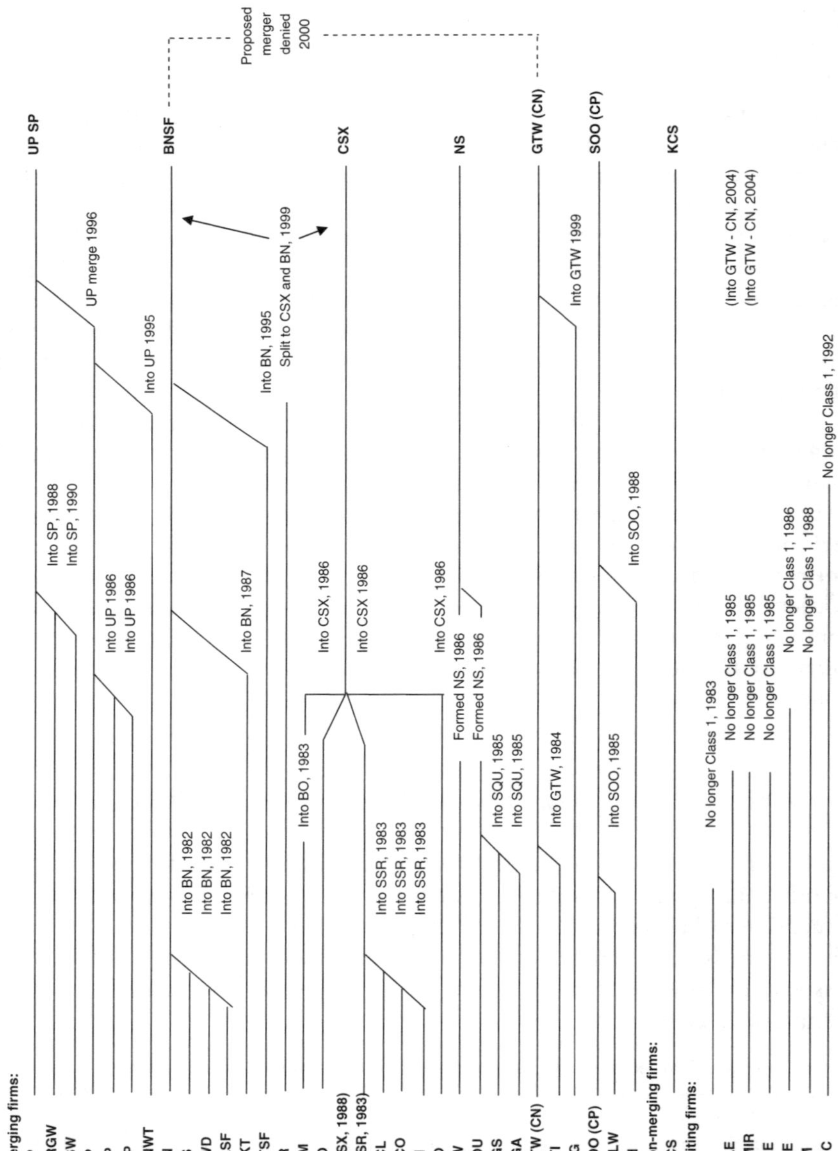

Fig. 1. Consolidation of the U.S. Class I Railroads, 1980–2004.

Equally or more important as increased revenues was cost control, so that net revenues have improved. There is no doubt that railroads are financially better off now than during the regulated era. One indicator is the operating ratio, operating expenses relative to revenues. This shows the proportion of the sales dollar absorbed by operating expenses, and thus indicates how much is left to cover capital costs and profit. Before 1980, the operating ratio of the U.S. Class I rail industry was a very unhealthy middle 90s percent. It was down to the low to mid-80s percent by the late 1990s. This is a significant improvement although the highly capital-intensive rail industry needs an even lower operating ratio to sustain competitive level rates of return. All is not rosy for the industry but the financial position has improved and some railroads are approaching acceptable rates of return.

The story in Canada is similar to the U.S. CTAR (2001a, pp. 45–47) showed trends in the CN and CP operating ratio generally improving since 1992, and rates of return reaching 14–15 percent in the year 2000. But they note that one must look over a full business cycle to assess the financial condition of the industry. CTAR (2001a, p. 47) showed rail capital expenditures had not kept pace in mid-1980s–1995.

9.3. Productivity and Efficiency Performance

Rail productivity gains and cost reductions were a major benefit of deregulation. There were significant efficiency gains under deregulation in the early years by eliminating the inefficiencies that were fostered under regulation. Berndt et al. (1993) estimated a cost function for a panel of railroads and years overlapping deregulation. They found major gains from deregulation including some benefit from the mergers that took place in those early years (but about 90 percent of the benefits were from deregulation rather than efficiencies from mergers).

Deregulation enabled sustained improvements in efficiency, marketing, and cost control.

> The railroads' new emphasis on asset utilization energized dramatic plans for restructuring physical plant and for learning how to manage smarter with computerized applications for data collection and analysis. Railroads caught the quality bug, earnestly pursuing customer satisfaction and business process reengineering initiatives. Struggling with century-old customers and regulatory legacies, the industry nonetheless negotiated significant changes in contractual agreements with labor unions and aggressively reduced employment levels.

> Realizing notable success in all these areas, total factor productivity soared. Ton-miles per constant dollar of operating expense increased almost 2.5 times between 1980 and 1995. (Gallamore, 1999, p. 495).

Bereskin (1996) and Wilson (1997) both examined rail productivity post-Staggers and found significant productivity increases. They estimated rail cost functions looking for downward shifts in the function over time, indicating productivity gains. Wilson's (1997) data covered 1978–1989; he found substantial productivity gains, especially in the early years after deregulation. Bereskin's (1996) data set extended through 1993. He found the annual downward shift of the estimated cost function varied substantially over the years, but there were sizeable productivity gains extending into the early 1990s. The two authors used different formulations of rail cost relationships but their findings were similar. Both found the major gains just after deregulation, but productivity continued to grow after that. Bitzan and Keeler (2003) also examined the downward shift of a rail cost function separating out two important specific productivity improvements, reductions in crew size, and elimination of the caboose. These were important but they found productivity growth besides this with no sign it was slowing down.

Productivity gains have continued into recent years. Industry statistics continue to show a striking improvement in ton-miles per employee or by various other performance ratios. Partial productivity measures are not definitive because there is the possibility that other inputs are not being used efficiently. A more comprehensive productivity measure is total factor productivity TFP. This is an index of the total quantities of output produced compared to an index of total input quantities.[18] The STB calculates an index of TFP (it is used to adjust an automatic rail cost escalator, the rail cost adjustment factor or RCAF, for productivity gains). The author took the STB series for 1990–2004 and Exhibit 1 shows the output and input quantity indices for the Class I rail industry in total (TFP is plotted in Exhibit 4).[19] (Irregularities in the input quantity index reflects "special charges" such as write-downs that disturb individual years but not the overall trend.) Total input use has not changed much despite the substantial growth in output over the years, which indicates productivity gains (although the rise in input use after 2000 indicates slower productivity growth after that point).

The productivity record of the Canadian railways continued to be strong (Tretheway, Waters, & Fok, 1997), although calculations have not been carried out since 2000.

The efficiency of North American railroads relative to the rest of the world railways is well known. Rail productivity performance has done well

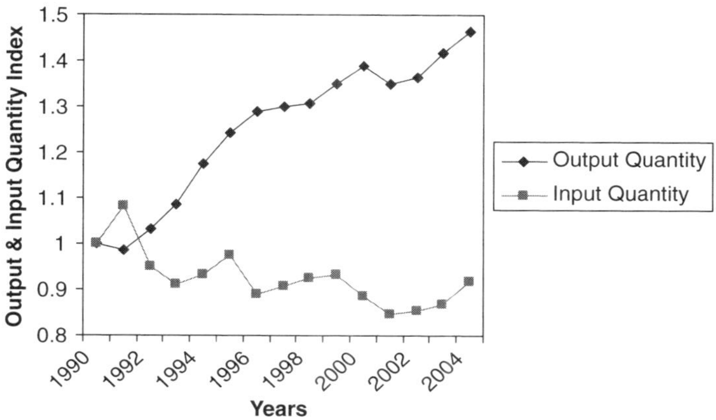

Exhibit 1. 1990–2004 U.S. Class I Rail Quantity Indices. *Note:* Output quantity is total Revenues deflated by Output price index constructed by STB. Input quantity index is total expenditures (including special charges) deflated by the RCR (Rail cost recovery) factor. *Source:* Surface Transportation Board, supplied by Association of American Railroads.

under deregulation. This still leaves the question about the distribution of the gains in efficiency, i.e., how did shippers benefit from the productivity improvements?

9.4. Benefits to Shippers/Customers since Deregulation

Measuring the benefits of economic deregulation can be approached by the converse of the arguments about the costs of regulation, i.e., that deregulation enables firms to be more innovative, that traffic can move by the most efficient mode rather than in accordance with outmoded regulatory-constrained freight rates and market restrictions.

At least for a time, a financially healthier industry is able to provide better and more reliable service to customers. The improved financial condition of the rail industry following deregulation enabled the railroads to carry out substantial investments in track and rolling stock, at the same time that regulatory freedom enabled them to abandon or sell off low-density lines. But this leaves unanswered whether or not shippers were better off as a result of deregulation.

Winston, Corsi, Grimm, and Evans (1990) attempted to estimate the value to shippers of the improvements in rail and trucking deregulation. They estimated aggregate cost functions for rail and road, and a choice model for traffic facing the two modes. They concluded that some shippers were adversely affected by increases in rail freight rates, but overall benefiting by more than offsetting improvements in quality of service (Winston et al., 1990, pp. 24–29). They expressed concern about possible adverse effects of the considerable consolidation in the U.S. rail industry (*ibid.*, pp. 52–59).

The trend in freight rates over time is important for assessing the impacts on rail customers. Deregulation saw substantial real declines in rail prices *on average*, and even declines in nominal terms. A simple measure is to plot average revenue per ton-mile, see Exhibit 2. Average freight rates had been rising sharply through the 1970s, but when into steady decline after 1980, until about the year 2000. But overall revenue per ton-mile could reflect the growth of higher volume relatively low-priced traffic, and could be misleading. A better freight rate index is a weighted average of many freight movements over time weighted by their respective freight charges. The STB calculates an output price index for the U.S. Class I railroads. This uses data from a one percent waybill sample. A plot of the output price index is in Exhibit 3 along with the rail cost recovery indicator which is what the industry and the STB uses as an input price index for the rail industry. These data are available from 1990. Exhibit 3 shows that the index of rail output

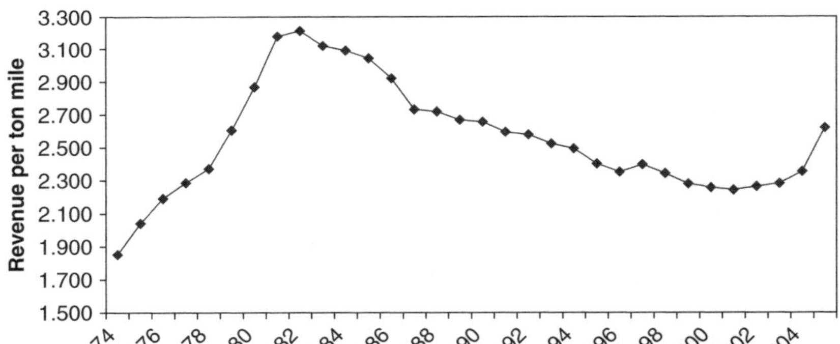

Exhibit 2. Revenue Per Ton Mile U.S. Class I Rail, 1974–2005. *Source:* Data supplied by the Association of American Railroads.

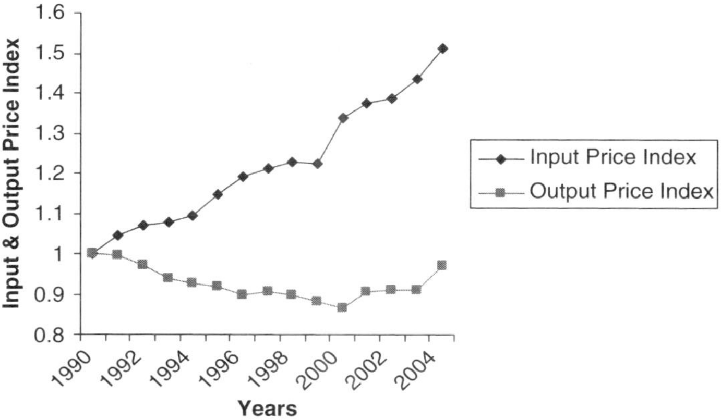

Exhibit 3. 1990–2004 U.S. Class I Rail Price Indices. *Note:* Input price index is the AAR Rail Cost Recovery (RCR) factor. Output price index is constructed by STB based on waybill sample. STB price index provided by Association of American Railroads.

prices (nominal, not constant dollars) declining until 2000 and then rising. This is despite substantial rises in the input prices faced by railroads. Expressed another way, *on average*, the railroads have not had to increase prices to keep pace with the rising input costs. Productivity gains have made this possible.

Waters and Tretheway (1999) show that one can compare the growth of TFP with the growth of an index of input prices relative to an index of prices received for the rail's outputs. Productivity enables (average) output price increases to rise less than the increase in input prices that they face. They label this total price performance TPP. Tracking the input and output price indexes (TPP) relative to TFP reveals the sharing of productivity gains, *on average*. In Exhibit 4, for the period 1990–2004, the STB indices show that the vast majority of productivity gains were absorbed in keeping rate increase below the rise in input costs. That is, on average the productivity gains have been passed through to shippers.[20]

Martland (1997, 1999, 2006) has also calculated a productivity index and tracked the U.S. railroad pricing, productivity, and financial results over an extended period. Despite the substantial increases in productivity, railroad finances did not improve much over the period. In the more recent years:

> Productivity did improve, but at a slower rate. Rail rates continued to decline and did offset the financial benefits of productivity improvements. Various strategic problems,

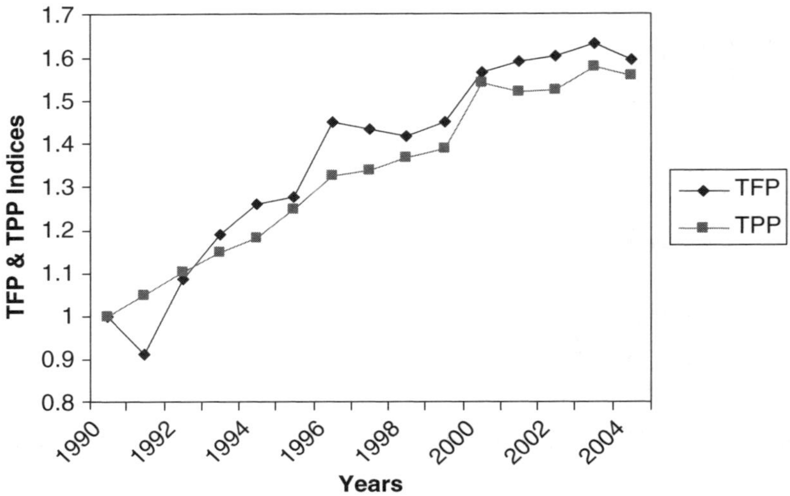

Exhibit 4. 1990–2004 TFP & TTP. *Note:* TFP is output quantity index/input quantity index (Exhibit 1). TPP is input price index/output price index (Exhibit 3).

> including capacity and service quality did become more pressing. As a result the financial performance for the industry peaked around 1996, then declined until the very end of the period. (Martland, 2006, p. 779)

Bitzan and Keeler (2003) find similar results.

The Canadian data are not available after 2000, but CTAR showed TFP compared to the TPP for 1985–1999 for the two Canadian Class I railways. "before the mid-1990s, rail productivity was not sufficient to offset declines in average rail prices relative to prices paid for inputs, and railways were weakening financially. Between 1988 and 1999, about 75 percent of the productivity gains were passed on to shippers. In more recent years, railways have retained a greater proportion – about 60 percent since 1995. Whether this trend will continue remains to be seen.(CTAR, 2001a, pp. 42–43).

On average, the evidence is that North American rail shippers have benefited from rail productivity improvements in terms of lower freight rates or increases below the rate of increased prices of rail inputs.[21] However, aggregate statistics can conceal a great deal of variability in the data. Even if rail freight rates decline *on average*, there can be price increases in some markets. Some shippers with limited competitive options, so-called "captive" shippers, have experienced price increases while other shippers were experiencing price declines.[22] This raises questions about what residual regulatory protection can be available to shippers in markets where there competitive restraints on railways are very limited. This is taken up shortly as an ongoing issue in railroad economics.

10. GOVERNMENT-OWNED RAILWAYS

The foregoing five sections trace the evolution of regulation and deregulation in North America. But as noted earlier, many countries chose direct government ownership and operation of railways rather than rely on private enterprise and regulation. Several countries have experimented with both; indeed, there are many variations in rail organization and operating practices around the world.

The belief in public ownership of railways can be motivated by many factors, well-captured by Knoop (1925) in his discussion of pressures for nationalization of British railways in the early twentieth century:

> Many people seem favorably disposed towards the idea of the nationalization of the railways, though for very various reasons. Some who hold socialist views would welcome it as bringing about an important extension of the functions of the State. Many traders appear to believe that it would be the means of securing a considerable reduction in charges ..., and that section of the community that travels by rail has visions of lower fares ... Some people see in it the possibility of realizing a large surplus ... to relieve the burden of taxation ... ; other people look forward to the railways being used by the State to assist in carrying out social reforms, by certain services being performed at a cost price or even at a loss. Those districts ... which have not enjoyed the same ample services and facilities which are provided where railway competition is keen, trust that they would secure a more generous treatment from the State, quite apart from the question whether the desired services and facilities were remunerative or not. Many working class people ... anticipate that nationalization would be accompanied by better working conditions, shorter hours, and higher wages. (Knoop, 1925, pp. 249–250)

With these incompatible expectations, publicly owned railways face a significant challenge in achieving high performance, and what constitutes best performance is not usually commercial success.

Recall that a fundamental economic characteristic of railways is declining average costs, whether from scale or density economies. Economic theory calls for marginal cost pricing, but this will lead to a financial deficit. Private companies had to be allowed to charge above marginal costs in order to be financially viable. Government-owned railways could have deficits directly absorbed in overall public expenditures. In sum, there are economic rationales for government ownership of natural monopolies – the ability to pursue marginal cost pricing albeit with a deficit to be underwritten by the public purse. The emphasis on marginal cost pricing is explicitly recognized in several European countries (including the U.K.). But there is no unanimity. Doubts can be raised about the real feasibility of implementing rigorous marginal cost pricing (e.g., Rothengatter, 2003). Nonetheless, it is a recurrent theme in European transport policy and a major influence on research directions (Nash & Sansom, 2001, Nash & Matthews, 2005b; Quinet, 2005).

Although the connection could be incidental, there seems to be a correlation between government ownership of railroads and the importance of rail passenger service in contrast to freight service.[23] Especially in high-density corridors or networks, passenger operations are highly complex with tight time tables and rigorous traffic control. These are major and costly operating requirements compared to that of long distance freight operations such as in North America. Passenger markets, particularly urban and short-haul intercity travel, raise some economic arguments for subsidy. There is the traditional characteristic of highly divisible demands facing indivisible or lumpy supply, hence situations of very low marginal costs and the possibility of incentive pricing to increase utilization. Another argument for a subsidy to support social marginal cost pricing is the "Mohring effect" (introduced by Mohring, 1972). This is a source of increasing returns in collective waiting time of passengers on scheduled transport service.[24] Low prices to stimulate consumption also stimulate supply which leads to increased capacity and shorter headway and waiting time. It is a type of externality: increased consumption by individuals can benefit others via reduced wait times as supply of service is stimulated. This is particularly important on lower density routes where headway intervals are longer. This is an important rationale for subsidy of public transport, in bus systems as well as rail. (see Doll & Jansson, 2005; also Nash, Sansom, & Still, 2001).

The converse of this is congestion, a situation of rising marginal costs and, especially, the externality costs of delays imposed on other users. Both on roads and public transit, additional users during peak periods impose delays on others that are not recognized by the individual. Social marginal cost pricing would call for higher prices during congestion to signal marginal users of their full impact on costs of the transport system including user-borne time costs. In these circumstances, the financial outcome of marginal cost pricing is not necessarily financial deficits, or at least they are reduced depending on the degree and duration of congestion (and responsiveness of users to price increases). Financial surpluses would accrue during congested periods as an offset to subsidies required to finance uncongested service.

Passenger transport pricing and subsidies are not just a function of economic arguments; social/political forces are at work too. The presence of passenger service tends to result in political pressures to keep rates low and extend service (Pittman, 2007). Rail management must look beyond commercial or economic efficiency motivations in their decisions. Service frequency is usually more important than minimizing unit costs via larger train sizes. And usually there are pressures to keep prices low for social (income-level) reasons as well as service to some low-density markets.

Particularly in Europe, the potential environmental advantages of rail technology are also an important public policy consideration. Railways are often seen as an instrument of public policy, to combat auto congestion and pollution, as well as the prospect of substituting rail for truck transport of freight. Measuring environmental costs and incorporating them into pricing and investment decisions are a major research interest and policy direction in Europe (see Nash et al., 2001, also Nash & Matthews, 2005a, especially Bickel, Schmid, & Fredrich, 2005; van den Bossche, Certan, Veldman, Nash, & Mathews, 2005). But it should be noted that railways in different countries are not united regarding current practices and prospective directions, e.g., Monami (2000) and Nash (2005c).[25]

There are other implications of public ownership of railways. With the accompanying social or political obligations and acceptance of deficit operations, is a greater emphasis on broad evaluation of pricing and investment proposals. Investment plans must be vetted on political as well as economic grounds and defended against funding requests from other government departments. Similarly, pricing regimes and traffic forecasts project the size of deficits which have to be approved by central government. In contrast, pricing and investment decisions in private companies are internal management decisions (although possibly subject to regulatory review in some cases). Being internal to the companies, there is less public literature on estimates of projected demands, price elasticities, and/or public evaluation of investment plans as in North America. In countries with intimate government involvement in rail decisions, there are debates over whether to emphasize financial criteria for investments or broader social cost-benefit analysis (Nash & Preston, 1991). (A classic example of social cost-benefit of rail investment is Foster & Beesley, 1963.) Other themes important for passenger rail systems are forecasts of traffic volumes and their price sensitivity (e.g., Fowkes & Nash, 1991; British Railways Board, 1994; Wardman, 2006, and references cited therein).

It should be acknowledged that public ownership can take on various forms with varying degrees of public control versus managerial autonomy. In the absence of a strong commercial mandate, rail management tends to be very operations-oriented, running the trains on time being more important than the financial return. But it is possible to cultivate a strong commitment to management efficiency as opposed to some stereotyped vision of a bureaucratic rail company. Canada had the publicly owned but substantially autonomous CN competing with the private CP. Railway prior to 1995, and the CN productivity performance rivaled and even exceeded that of CP (Caves & Christensen, 1980; Caves et al., 1981b, 1982). Oum and Yu (1994) reviewed the efficiency of passenger rail systems in many countries and were able to show superior performance in different institutional environments including the degree of managerial autonomy (see also discussion in the review by Oum, Waters, & Yu, 1999).

It should also be noted that some countries with government-ownership are the most innovative at exploring new approaches to the industrial organization of railways, viz., the separation of rail track from rail operations and hence the possibility of fostering greater competition in rail than is possible in vertically integrated operations (discussed further below), notably the U.K., Sweden, and Australia (BTRE, 2003; Thompson, 2003). We return to this theme in the final section.

11. RAILROAD MONOPOLY CONCERNS REVISITED

The last few decades saw the North American rail industry undergo a dramatic transformation and renewal. Decades of regulation had become stultifying and inefficient; freeing the railroads brought financial renewal, significant gains in productivity and – for the most part – customers benefited from the economic makeover. But while the consensus has been that society is better off than the days of detailed rate and service regulation, concerns persist about rail market power in some markets. There are some ongoing themes in rail economics literature about pockets of rail market power and possible public policy directions to alleviate them.

Looking back, the deregulation era came in when there was substantial excess capacity in many rail assets, with incentives to stimulate even low-valued traffic through pricing freedom. Uneconomic services could be abandoned and many of these were markets where alternate modes or rail shortlines could fill the gap. Railways did undertake substantial investments in upgrading and capacity where needed. It is evident that some manners of competitive forces were at work because average freight rates fell in real and often even in nominal terms. Railways improved financially, approaching normal rates of return for the first time in decades. To characterize it: railways were granted pricing freedom to pursue differential pricing and maximize profits. They became more efficient in the process and the overall levels of return rose but did not reach monopoly levels. That is, despite superficial appearances of market power due to a limited number of firms, a combination of some other competitive forces and the limited ability to pay by many of the markets that rely on rail transportation, the railroads were unable to achieve monopoly rates of return. These fortuitous circumstances meant that there was not much of an economic case for regulatory intervention. Potential rail monopoly was seen to be relatively benign. But not completely; there have been persistent complaints by some shipper groups with limited (or no) transportation alternatives.

But by about the late 1990s and in 2000s, concerns about possible rail monopoly powers were on the rise. Dissatisfaction was reported about rail service following major mergers. Aside from mergers, there were structural changes in rail plant and equipment. Railways in both Canada and the U.S. were downsizing unnecessary track and uneconomic lines, i.e., reducing spare capacity. Railways were "right-sizing." Then rail traffic began to grow more rapidly than previously, associated with an expansion of international trade and an economic boom. The excess capacity of railways that characterized most of the years after deregulation was no longer the case. As capacity approaches full utilization, marginal costs begin to rise, traffic rationing by price becomes commercially attractive, and railroads have little interest in attracting low contribution or marginal traffic to a congested system. This is in contrast to the motivations in the early years of deregulation. In these circumstances, the possibility of monopoly prices may reappear.

One can identify at least three major themes in the recent economic literature regarding regulation of railroads and potential monopoly power:[26]

1) The traditional concern for maximum price regulation of a monopolist and guidelines for maximum rate regulation;
2) Restrictions on rail operations and pricing that arise in connection with mergers, specifically, the concern about "foreclosure" whereby a merged railroad may be able to restrict competition from other railroads;
3) Promoting competition by enabling access to other railroads over a shared track, whether by mandatory interchange, forced access for a fee, or separation of track from rail operations and encouraging competition among rail operating companies.

These respective literatures are largely separate from one another. The latter two share an interest in determining the appropriate fee to allow a railway access to a specific portion of a network. This is an issue relevant for both private and public railways. All three themes have an underlying common thread which is the economic efficiency principles about optimal pricing from the point of view of a firm with market power versus a socially optimal price.

11.1. Traditional Maximum Price Regulation

The classic concern about monopoly is restricting quantity supplied to obtain a higher price. Regulation imposes a maximum allowed price below that desired by the firm, which also results in increased output due to the lower price. Judicious setting of the maximum price can emulate the cost-based price competitive markets would produce.

But as discussed in Section 4, railroads are multi-product firms with shared costs including indivisible inputs hence economies of utilization (declining average costs). Marginal costs of individual outputs may be ambiguous, and marginal cost pricing (the competitive ideal) would not recoup the full costs of the enterprise. The "second-best" policy principle that underlay modern North American rail regulation was to allow railroads to practice differential pricing, freedom to charge prices reflecting demand (value of service) until the total costs of the firm are covered, including a competitive return on investment. Note that a monopolist able to engage in price discrimination would not have an incentive to restrict output because they can reduce the price-to-price sensitive traffic without foregoing revenue from other higher priced traffic.

This idealized regulatory framework must assume that railroads are operating with maximum efficiency, that they can accurately assess customers' willingness to pay, and follow optimal investment policies.[27] Imperfections in the functioning of markets could negate the "hands-off" policy prescription.

This refers only to economic efficiency concerns (and accepting the second-best constraint that the industry is to be self-financing). There can be other grounds for regulatory intervention, including all manner of equity or fairness concerns. These go beyond economic efficiency criteria, but the latter is the primary concern in this review.

North American railroads are not exempt from restrictions on maximum rates. In the U.S. there is a jurisdictional threshold of 180 percent above estimated variable costs that must be exceeded before maximum rate review can take place (this does not apply to confidential negotiated contract rates). This does not mean there will be a regulated rate, only that the case will not be heard unless that threshold is reached. Because the working of value of service (differential) pricing is accepted until railroads reach revenue adequacy, higher markups are often accepted. In 1967, Canada originally specified a 250 percent markup as an upper limit on pricing freedom, but it proved open-ended and not really any limit at all because of a narrow definition of costing procedures. The maximum rate limit was later removed. Canada sought other methods to either stimulate some competition between railways and/or facilitate procedures to settle rate disputes. Regulated interswitching rates ensure that shippers have access to alternate nearby rail carriers at a regulated connection rate. Frameworks have been put in place to assist in resolving carrier/shipper disputes, such as final offer arbitration. Nonetheless, shipper groups in both countries maintain that regulatory measures are inadequate.

Even in the present differential pricing framework, a significant regulatory challenge may be approaching. Some of the major railroads are approaching or reaching "revenue adequacy" or normal rates of return. The unrestrained exercise of differential pricing has an economic justification up to this point of normal profits. But once railways exceed this amount, the optimal Ramsey markups become very difficult to review. Society was fortunate during the deregulated era, unrestrained differential pricing did not lead to overall monopoly rates of return despite significant improvements in efficiency. A relatively modest regulatory intervention could be justified economically. The theoretical regulatory solution is known for when and if rail profits become above normal: it would call for differential reductions in rail rates that would lead to an equiproportionate expansion of all outputs (Baumol & Bradford, 1970, pp. 263–264). That is, high-markup traffic would have a greater proportionate reduction in rates than that for more price-sensitive traffic. But the prospect of moving toward widespread regulatory intervention on rail rates is not appealing given the past experience with detailed rate regulation regimes.

One other point is that one must look at the full business cycle when assessing rail performance and rates of return. At the peak of a boom, one expects capacity to be under strain, and rising prices. Over a longer period, investment takes place to expand capacity adequate for permanently increased traffic. It is difficult to know whether rising prices and capacity shortages is a symptom of the peak in a business cycle, or if it heralds a time of increased rail market power. Both could be true.

11.2. Rail Competition and Regulation: Foreclosure

Regulation is a substitute for inadequate competition. Public policy might be able to promote competition rather than rely on regulatory controls. This theme is emphasized in two streams of literature in rail economics, both emphasize possible competition among railroads over shared track. One body of literature focused on foreclosure in rail mergers, and there is a related literature exploring alternate methods to increase competition among railroads over a common track.

The fears of foreclosure are that a merger between connecting railways could then exclude competition from a third carrier that had been interlining with one of the merging carriers. This is illustrated in Exhibit 5. At issue is the market between X and Z, where there are parallel railroads A and B serving to intermediate point Y, and another railroad serving Y to Z. Initially, railroads A and B can compete for X–Z traffic by interlining with railroad C. But if A and C merge, they could prevent railroad B from competing. There are many analyses of this problem and what might be done about it. One of the key issues concerns incentives. The so-called Chicago school approach points out that if rail route B is the lowest cost, profit-maximizing railroads A and C would want to make an agreement to use route B. If B were not a less costly route, then it would not survive in competition. The issues then are whether or not the pure economics of the situation would determine the outcome. Could there be strategic reasons why railroad A–C would want to exclude B, perhaps to try to reserve future markets for A–C?

An alternative way of looking at this is to focus on the initial situation of three railroads, and C is the "bottleneck" carrier. Because C is the only connection, is there need for regulatory restrictions on the price C would charge for connecting to market Z, and what would the guideline be? Again, the "Chicago school" answer would be that even a profit-maximizing monopolist would want to use the more efficient connector of

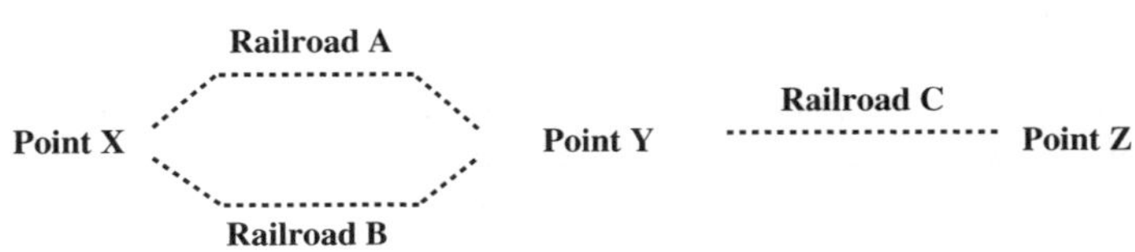

Exhibit 5. Illustration of Bottleneck.

A or B. But should there be limits on the price that C would charge, i.e., limits on its share of the revenue that traffic are willing to pay between X and Z? And if A and C were to have merged, what would be the limit that C would be allowed to charge B in order for it to compete with A–C?

According to Baumol (2000), the limit should be what would attract a hypothetical efficient railroad to invade the market, i.e., making the assumption that the market is contestable.[28] In what is called the efficient component pricing rule (ECPR) or parity principle, the access fee should be one that treats the incumbent and hypothetical entrant equally, i.e., an incumbent firm should be indifferent between providing service itself or using an equally efficient "foreign" carrier that yielded the same contribution to the incumbent's overhead. This way, only a more efficient carrier would be able to penetrate the market. Expressed still another way, if one were to impose a regulated maximum price in the X–Y market, the appropriate limit would be the price that would be charged by a hypothetical efficient carrier entering this market. This is the standalone cost. Note that standalone cost does not refer to building a railway solely for one piece of traffic; the hypothetical carrier could invade other markets and capture the contributions to overhead and profit from other markets. If the hypothetical entrant is just earning a competitive return over all, the allowed revenue for the traffic in question is its standalone cost less the contributions to overheads from other traffic. Comparing this to an estimate of the identifiable marginal costs will yield the markup that this hypothetical entrant would require. Note that if the incumbent railroad is efficient, and not earning above a normal rate of return overall, then the incumbent firm's markup will at least approximate what will emerge from a standalone cost analysis. That is, the incumbent firm's markup will be deemed optimal. One can appreciate that shippers seeking regulatory relief are not enamored with this argument.

There are critiques of ECPR (or parity pricing principle), particularly that real markets offer subtle opportunities for the exercise of market power by large incumbent firms with asymmetric knowledge.[29] (One could also raise equity or fairness concerns separate from the efficiency arguments that underlie ECPR.) Note that the ECPR is primarily a static argument. If one believed that competition stimulated by a favorable access price could lead to innovation and productivity improvement, such dynamic gains might offset the static efficiency concern. But there are several issues here. These are taken up in the next section.

11.3. Rail Competition and Regulation: Fostering Access to Shared Track

There are two approaches for promoting rail competition by fostering shared use of rail track. A regulatory approach would require granting access to one railroad's track by some other carrier, for an access fee. The other approach would be to separate the ownership of rail track (and way) from rail operations. This would remove the major sunk cost component of rail operations and make it possible for multiple operators to compete over a common facility, analogous to multiple trucking companies competing over public highways. Crucial to either approach is the basis for establishing an access fee, and the discussion about efficiency and ECPR still arises.

Introducing either approach to an existing industry and regulatory regime raises various transition issues especially property rights and compensation. This discussion bypasses these and focuses on the basic economics pro's and con's.

Regulations to grant rights of access to another railroad's track could stimulate competition with downward pressures on prices and incentives for innovation and increased service. That is the goal, but several issues arise particularly linked to the price and conditions of access. An access charge that is prohibitively high would bring no change. But an access fee too low raises serious incentive problems for the incumbent (track-owning) railroad. In the present North American regulatory structure, if railroads are not yet revenue-adequate, the second-best efficiency principles allow higher differential rates on traffic willing and able to pay it. The previous subsection noted that an access fee below the implicit fee being collected by the incumbent carrier would enable less efficient carriers to enter the market. This is the rationale behind the ECPR arguments. If one were to follow the ECPR approach, note that this would require an access fee that varies with the particular traffic following value of service (demand-based pricing) principles. If the incumbent railroad is revenue-adequate, and/or if competition would stimulate cost-cutting innovations, then a lower access fee could be efficient, although still it would likely be a charge varying according to value of service principles. But if the incumbent is not covering its full costs, a high access fee to approximate existing price markups would enable more efficient carriers to enter the market, but it would not result in much change in the overall rail rate structure.

An alternative access fee regime might be a flat or uniform fee, perhaps analogous to highway user charges such as a fuel tax. This is an average cost framework (cf., Holder, 1999, p. 113). If full cost recovery is still a goal, this regime would price out the most price-sensitive traffic and raise the average fee that needs to be paid by other traffic.[30] Traffic facing the highest differential markups would probably benefit, but subject to the potentially important caveat that if the incumbent railway is not revenue-adequate under differential pricing, adoption of an at least partial average cost markup would leave the firm even farther from revenue adequacy. Overall rail financial viability is weakened unless the competition stimulated would produce more than offsetting innovative cost reductions.

A separation of track from operations could herald a shift toward a simpler marginal cost pricing structure in that cost-recovery of rail track might not be required, there would be public subsidy to underwrite financial shortfalls associated with marginal cost pricing when increasing returns are present (the existence of joint costs and unallocable costs in train operations would probably still result in differential prices but less extreme than when track costs are included in rail pricing) (e.g., Nash, 2005). This would result in reductions in average freight rates. The net effect on overall economic efficiency (welfare) depends on the deadweight losses associated with differential pricing in the rail industry versus the welfare costs of raising the public funds to underwrite the subsidized rail infrastructure.

There are a couple additional efficiency concerns involved. One is that cost function studies confirm that there are cost complementarities between above-the-rail and below-the-rail costs (Bitzan, 2000).[31] Separation of track and operations will face these inherent inefficiencies, and/or will require regulatory supervision to avoid one group imposing uncompensated costs on the other (e.g., operators running excessively heavy trains that damage the track). The magnitude of these cost interrelationships is uncertain but need to be considered. A second empirical result from cost function studies (Bitzan, 2000, 2003; Ivaldi & McCullough, 2004) is that there are some increasing returns in quasi cost functions that focus on the above-the-rail operations separate from provision of way and track. That is, there may be cost advantages to fewer, larger railways even in operations alone. This might limit the amount of entry and competition that could be expected from an open-entry system.

Nonetheless, if the rise of increased rail competition from an open access regime could stimulate significant productivity and service gains, the industry restructuring might result in positive net benefits.[32] In North America there are at least two reservations. First is that the existing productivity record of the rail industry since deregulation has been impressive. It would have to become all the more productive under the altered industrial structure. Related to this is that, unlike telecommunications – where access regimes are associated with significant productivity and service gains – there are no pending technological developments in the rail industry that could unleash dramatic reductions in costs.

Most of the foregoing discussion referred to North American conditions, where the rail industry is acknowledged to be relatively efficient and close to cost recovery. This is not true for railways in many other countries. Many have a legacy of costly operations under government ownership and control. Most of these have extensive passenger operations and already are heavily subsidized. Passenger service tends to operate with set timetables compared to more random movements of freight. Demand forecasts for passenger service might be more predictable than for freight. If so, allocation and pricing of specific track time slots (e.g., by auction) might be more feasible for passenger operations. If so, the case for separation of track from operations may be more compelling for railroads with these latter characteristics. It is no accident that there is much more interest and actual experimentation with this restructuring of the rail industry in Europe, Australia, and the U.K. Economists as well as the rail industries the world over are watching these experiments very closely (e.g., Thompson, 2003).

12. CONCLUSION

Once the defining technology of its age, railroads continue to play an important although more narrow and specialized role in the economy. Several characteristics of rail technology and operation – and their economic implications – persist to the present. The indivisibilities in capital investment and scale of operations result in situations of decreasing average costs. The inevitable ambiguity in measuring costs makes it difficult to compare prices and costs. There are diverse competitive forces at work; rail competition is not just a matter of counting the number of firms serving a market. But the large scale of operations spread over long distances and multiple markets makes it inevitable that there will be specific markets where rail has substantial market power. There is an ongoing challenge to try to balance the benefits of commercial freedom for railroads with desires for some public oversight.

Much has been learned about rail economics and market performance. The North American experience first with regulation and then deregulation, spanning a century, has been intimately linked with economic concepts and empirical analyses. Railroad economics reflected industry characteristics and public policy issues, and in time the economic analyses reshaped perspectives on the industry and public policies toward it.

Outside North America, rail passenger travel generally is a high priority. Passenger service often involves complex operations with high costs. Both economic and social considerations influence policies and operations, and result in sizeable subsidies. There can be several public policy concerns to be reconciled with a desire for efficient management of rail operations. Cost control is harder to achieve in these environments, but evidence shows that organizational arrangements can make a difference.

Issues in rail economics extend over 150 years. Some issues seem almost timeless, such as the dilemma posed by untraceable overhead costs and the role of differential pricing. Other themes change over time, such as the rise of regulation and subsequent deregulation. In North America, railroads now are primarily self-financing freight carriers. In Europe and some other countries, rail is still an important passenger mode and an instrument of environmental policy. New economic concepts arise and modify our interpretation of rail economics, such as contestability and understanding the implications of contracting and institutional design, even raising the old prospect of separating rail operations from the provision of track. Like the rail industry itself, railroad economics evolves, building on the past and incorporating new ideas and new techniques to advance our understanding of the industry and its relationship to the economy and economic performance.

NOTES

1. The terms "railroads" and "railways" are used interchangeably here. The former tends to be the American phrase, and "railways" dominant in the rest of the English-speaking world, but both words are used everywhere.
2. There is more coverage of North American experience and rail economics. Partly this reflects the author's background but also there is extensive academic literature on the economics associated with the evolution of North American railroads. These themes are covered before addressing the most prominent differences between North America and most other countries, which are government ownership and control, as well as the emphasis on passenger operations.
3. The author reviewed a number of early texts and articles in preparing this chapter. For the record, Hadley's (1885) book proved to be the most interesting, it is still a 'good read' over a century since it was written.
4. Locklin cites several early writers commenting on differential prices to increase utilization of capacity, including Lardner (1850) and the French engineer J. Dupuit (1844, 1849).
5. "This subject, of costs which are not traced to units of output, or do not vary with output, has challenged the author's scientific interest for years. From being a mere exception to the general laws of value and efficiency it has grown to be a large and important section of economic principles. And now the question seems to be

whether it can best function as an autonomous department of economics, or whether the whole body of economic thought must become an 'economics of overhead costs'..." (Clark, 1923, p. 9)

6. More accurately stated as "not charging what the traffic will not bear." (Baumol & Bradford, 1970) cite Hadley (ca. 1880s) as the origin of this phrase.

7. There is a risk of confusion with the phrase "constant costs." In railway parlance, constant costs are synonymous with overhead costs, i.e., the bundle of costs that cannot be assigned to individual outputs although they might vary with all outputs considered together. In standard economic theory, constant costs refer to the absence of economies of scale, i.e., industries where long-run average costs will be constant for various output levels. To avoid confusion, this paper uses the phrase "overhead" costs to refer to this cost characteristic of railways.

8. If portions of a rail operation were wholey separable, then one could apply the monopoly test to that separable operation, think of two geographically-distinct and separate railroads that just happen to be owned by a single company.

9. This review of rail cost functions draws on Waters and Woodland (1984) and Bitzan (2000). For more thorough reviews of transportation cost functions generally, see Braeutigam (1999), Jara-Diaz (1982), or Oum and Waters (1996).

10. Harmatuck (1979) also was an early use of the translog for rail costs and provides a good introduction to this functional form. He used the imputed price of rail intermediate activities rather than factor prices in his formulation.

11. The presence or absence of rail passenger service limited the sample size of railroads for cost function estimation because one had to use one category or the other. Caves, Christensen, and Tretheway (1980) solved this with a generalized translog function using a Box-Cox metric for output, which enabled including railroads with zero values for passenger service along with railroads with passenger service.

12. Nelson (1959) published his important critique of the U.S. rail policy about the same time.

13. The concept of the "core" is concerned with the conditions necessary for an equilibrium outcome under competition (Telser, 1978, 1987, 1994; see also Bittlingmayer, 1982). A stable equilibrium is not a guaranteed outcome. For example, a limited number of competitors, highly divisible demands and indivisibilities in supply are conditions that may result in an empty core, i.e., an unsustainable outcome. (Explorations of the concept of an empty core have been explored for ocean shipping (Sjostrom, 1989; Pirrong, 1992) and airlines (Button, 1996; Raghavan & Raghavan, 2005).

14. Sometimes further distinguishing between product and geographic competition, the former referring to the possibility that some other product could be substituted for the traffic in question, and the latter referring to competition from suppliers from other locations.

15. Insofar as deregulation facilitated greater competition and cost savings, organized labor tended suffer from deregulation. Efficiency gains are reductions in input use, which means fewer jobs. Rail employment declined as railways became more efficient, although there were also some jobs created in expansion of short lines, but these often were nonunion positions.

16. There can be demand-side advantages of firm size in terms of market coverage, i.e., customers value dealing with a single carrier who is responsible for the movement from origin to destination. This has been important in understanding consolidation in parcel service, trucking, and air transport.

17. The North American rail industry has restructured in two directions. There is the consolidation of the large Class I carriers into long distance, high volume carriers serving large networks. At the same time, many shortlines have been spun off from the major carriers. These typically are feeder lines to the Class I carriers. They are characterized by local entrepreneurial skills and more flexible labor arrangements.

18. Index number measurement of TFP is not identical to the downward shift of a cost function, but they can be linked (Waters, 2000).

19. The output quantity index is total revenues divided by the STB's detailed output price index, not a simple revenue per ton-mile or similar aggregate index. Similarly, the input quantity index is total rail expenditures divided by the RCR or rail cost recovery index, the agreed guide to rail input prices.

20. The apparent reduction in TFP for 1991 is a data anomaly. The STB input quantity index is obtained by dividing total expenditures by an input price index. There were some accounting write-downs that year which distorts the input measure for that one year. This does not alter the trend which is what is important.

21. See also the discussion in Morrison and Winston (1999).

22. Grimm and Winston's (2000) econometric analysis of rail freight charges and levels of service conclude that captive shippers pay about 20 percent higher rates, although they also conclude the deadweight losses of these higher rates do not offset the substantial benefits from the gains to other shippers and efficiency gains overall.

23. Privately-owned Japanese passenger railways are an exception to this pattern.

24. The concept applies to freight transport too but the topic has been discussed primarily for passengers.

25. A useful and more general reference is Thompson (2003).

26. The focus here is on the maximum price a firm with market power would be allowed to charge. There are other regulatory issues including safety, quality of service, minimum rates that can be charged, permission to abandon markets, etc. These issues are not addressed.

27. See CTAR (2001b) for discussion of some qualifications about the validity of the Ramsey pricing framework.

28. There are many potential references to Baumol and colleagues articles and testimony. Baumol (2000) is straight-forward statement and is readily accessible on the Internet. See also Baumol and Willig (1999).

29. Again, there are many references that could be cited. For example see Tye 1998, Tye and Horn (2000), and the exchange between Tye (1993a, 1993b) and Kleit (1993); also Grimm and Harris (1983, 1988) on the foreclosure issues.

30. Simulations by Preston et al., of possible competition for British rail passenger transport noted that it would lead to increased consumer surplus but greater losses in producer surplus. "In cases where there is no competition, the incumbent is able to price-discriminate in such a way that the profit-maximizing and welfare-maximizing results are similar. When competition is introduced such price discrimination is no longer possible. The regulatory authorities must, therefore, take a view on the

appropriate weight to attach to producer and consumer surplus..." (Preston, Whelan, & Wardman, 1999, p. 92)

31. Ivaldi and McCullough, 2001 found some ambiguity in cost interdependencies, but a later study (2004) found significant increases in costs if operations were separated from infrastructure supply.

32. Gallamore and Panzar (2004) and Pittman (2007) are quite pessimistic about the prospects that access regimes could result in improved performance compared to vertically integrated railroads.

ACKNOWLEDGMENT

The author wishes to thank the editors and anonymous referees, as well as John Bitzan, Curt Grimm, and Trevor Heaver, for helpful comments. The usual caveat applies that the author remains responsible for the contents of the paper. This is a heavy burden in this case. The long time span for this subject, and the large number of authors and contributions, means it is inevitable that some important works will be overlooked. Space and publication deadlines limited the author's ability to correct these injustices.

REFERENCES

Acworth, W. H. (1905). *The elements of railway economics*. Oxford: Clarendon Press.

Association of American Railroads. (1964). *A guide to railroad cost analysis.* Washington, DC.

Baumol, W. J. (2000). Public interest standards for Canadian rail rate regulation: Differential prices, access and price ceilings. Submitted to the Canada Transportation Act Review (CTAR) Panel. Available at http://reviewcta-examenltc.gc.ca/submissions-soumissions/June30/Baumol%20William%20J%20(CN).pdf

Baumol, W. J., Bonbright, J. C., Bronzen, Y., Dean, J., Edwards, F. K., Hoover, C. B., Pegrum, D. F., Roberts, M. J., & Williams, E. W., Jr. (1962). Role of cost in the minimum pricing of railroad services. *Journal of Business,* 357–366; Reprinted in: T. H. Oum et al. (Eds), *Transport economics: Selected readings* (1997, pp. 237–251). Harwood Academic Publisher and Korea Research Foundation.

Baumol, W. J., & Bradford, D. F. (1970). Optimal departures from marginal cost pricing. *American Economics Review, 60*, 265—283; Reprinted in: T. H. Oum et al. (Eds), *Transport economics: Selected readings* (1997, pp. 253–284). Harwood Academic Publisher and Korea Research Foundation.

Baumol, W., Panzar, J., & Willig, R. (1982). *Contestable markets and the theory of industry structure.* New York: Harcourt Brace Jovanovich Inc.

Baumol, W. J., & Willig, R. (1999). Competitive rail regulation rules – should price ceilings constrain final products or inputs? *Journal of Transport Economics and Policy, 33*(January), 43–53.

Bereskin, C. G. (1996). Econometric estimation of post-deregulation railway productivity growth. *Transportation Journal, 35(4)*, 34–43.

Berndt, E. R., Friedlaender, A. F., Wang Chiang, J. S., & Vellturo, C. A. (1993). Cost effects of mergers and deregulation in the U.S. rail industry. *Journal of Productivity Analysis*, *4*, 127–144.

Bickel, P., Schmid, S., & Fredrich, R. (2005). Environmental costs. In: C. Nash & B. Matthews (Eds), *Measuring the marginal social costs of transport* (pp. 185–209). Amsterdam: Elsevier.

Bittlingmayer, G. (1982). Decreasing average costs and competition. *Journal of Law and Economics*, *25*, 201–229.

Bitzan, J. (2000). Railroad cost conditions – implications for policy. Report for the Federal Railroad Administration, Washington, DC.

Bitzan, J. (2003). Railroad costs and competition: The implications of introducing competition to railroad networks. *Journal of Transport Economics and Policy*, *37*(2 (May)), 201–275.

Bitzan, J., & Keeler, T. (2003). Productivity growth and some of its determinants in the deregulated U.S. railroad industry. *Southern Economics Journal*, *70*(2), 232–253.

Boiteux, M. (1956). Sur la gestion des monopoles publics astreints a l'equilibre budgetaire. *Econometrica,* 24. Translated and republished as On the management of public monopolies subject to budgetary constraints. *Journal of Economic Theory,* 3, 1971.

Borts, G. H. (1952). Production relations in the railway industry. *Econometrica,* January, 71–79.

Borts, G. H. (1954). Increasing returns in the railway industry. *Econometrica,* January, 316–333.

Borts, G. H. (1960). The estimation of rail cost functions. *Econometrica,* January, 108–131.

Boyer, K. D. (1977). Minimum rate regulation, modal split sensitivities and the railroad problem. *Journal of Political Economy*, *85*, 493–512.

Braeutigam, R. R. (1999). Learning about transport costs. In: J. A. Gomez-Ibanez, W. B. Tye & C. Winston (Eds), *Essays in transportation economics and policy* (pp. 57–97). Washington, DC: Brookings.

Braeutigam, R. R., Daugherty, A. F., & Turnquist, M. A. (1984). A firm specific analysis of economies of density in the railroad industry. *Journal of Industrial Economics*, *33*(1), 3–20.

British Railways Board. (1994). Passenger demand forecasting handbook (2nd ed.). London: HMSO.

Brown, R. S., Caves, D. W., & Christensen, L. R. (1979). Modeling the structure of cost and production for multiproduct firms. *Southern Economics Journal,* July, 256–273.

Bureau of Transport and Regional Economics (BTRE). (2003). Rail infrastructure pricing: Principles and practice. Report 109, BTRE, Canberra, Australia.

Button, K. G. (1996). Liberalizing European aviation: Is there an empty core problem? *Journal of Transport Economics and Policy,* 30(3), 275–291.

Caves, D. W., & Christensen, L. R. (1980). The relative efficiency of public and private firms in a competitive environment: The case of Canadian railroads. *Journal of Political Economy*, *88*, 959–976.

Caves, D. W., Christensen, L. R., & Swanson, J. A. (1980). Productivity in U.S. railroads, 1951–1974. *Bell Journal of Economics*, *11*, 166–181.

Caves, D. W., Christensen, L. R., & Swanson, J. A. (1981a). The high cost of regulating U.S. railroads. *Regulation,* Jan/Feb, 41–46.

Caves, D. W., Christensen, L. R., & Swanson, J. A. (1981b). Economic performance in regulated and unregulated environments: A comparison of U.S. and Canadian railroads. *Quarterly Journal of Economics*, *96*(November), 559–581.

Caves, D. W., Christensen, L. R., & Swanson, J. A. (1981c). Productivity growth, scale economics, and capacity utilization in U.S. railroads, 1955–1974. *American Economic Review*, *71*(December), 994–1002.

Caves, D. W., Christensen, L. R., Swanson, J. A., & Tretheway, M. W. (1982). Economic performance of U.S. and Canadian railroads: The significance of ownership and the regulatory environment. In: W. T. Stanbury & F. Thompson (Eds), *Managing public enterprises* (pp. 123–151). New York: Praeger.

Caves, D. W., Christensen, L. R., & Tretheway, M. W. (1980). Flexible cost functions for multiproduct firms. *Review of Economics and Statistics*, *62*, 477–481.

Caves, D. W., Christensen, L. R., Tretheway, M. W., & Windle, R. J. (1985). Network effects and the measurement of returns to scale and density for U.S. railroads. In: A. F. Daughety (Ed.), *Analytical studies in transport economics* (pp. 97–120). Cambridge: Cambridge University Press.

Caves, D. W., Christensen, L. R., Tretheway, M. W., & Windle, R. J. (1987). An assessment of the efficiency effects of U.S. airline deregulation via an international comparison. In: E. E. Bailey (Ed.), *Public regulation: New perspectives on institutions and policies* (pp. 285–320). Cambridge: MIT Press.

Chandler, A. D., Jr. (1965). *The railroads: The nation's first big business*. Harcourt, Brace and World, Inc.

Clark, J. M. (1923). *Studies in the economies of overhead costs*. Chicago, IL: Unviersity of Chicago Press.

Clark, J. M. (1961). *Competition as a dynamic process*. Washington DC: Brookings.

CTAR Canada Transportation Act Review Panel. (2001a) *Vision and balance*. Ottawa: Minister of Public Works and Government Services.

CTAR Canada Transportation Act Review Panel. (2001b). The role of differential pricing: Implications and remedies (in CD Rom supplement, Additional rail info). In: Vision and balance. Ottawa: Minister of Public Works and Government Services.

Doll, C., & Jansson, J. O. (2005). User costs and benefits. In: C. Nash & B. Matthews (Eds), *Measuring the marginal social costs of transport* (pp. 125–154). Amsterdam: Elsevier.

Dupuit, J. (1844). De la mesure de l'utilite des travaux publique, *8 Annales des Ponts et Chaussees* 2d series, 332.

Dupuit, J. (1849). De l'influence des peages sur l'utilite des voies de communication, *17 Annales des Ponts et Chaussees* 2d series, 170.

Fishlow, A. (1965). *American railroads and the transformation of the antebellum economy*. Cambridge: Harvard University Press.

Fogel, R. W. (1964). *Railroads in American economic growth*. Baltimore: Johns Hopkins.

Foster, C., & Beesley, M., (1963). Estimating the social benefit of constructing an underground railway in London. *Journal of the Royal Statistical Society*, 126, 46–58 plus appendices.

Fowkes, T., & Nash, C. (Eds). (1991). *Analysing demand for rail travel*. Aldershot, Hants: Avebury Academic Publishers.

Friedlaender, A. F. (1969). *The dilemma of freight transport regulation*. Washington, DC: Brookings Institution.

Friedlaender, A. F. (1971). The social costs of regulating the railroads. *American Economic Review*, *71*(May), 226–234.

Friedlaender, A. F., Berndt, E. R., Wang Chiang, J. S., Showalter, M., & Vellturo, C. A. (1993). Rail costs and capital adjustments in a quasi-regulated environment. *Journal of Transport Economics and Policy*, *27*(2), 131–152.

Friedlaender, A. F., & Spady, R. H. (1981). *Freight transportation regulation: Equity, efficiency, and competition in the rail and trucking industry*. MIT Press: Cambridge, Mass.

Gallamore, R. E. (1999). Regulation and innovation: Lessons from the American railroad industry. In: J. A. Gomez-Ibanez, W. B. Tye & C. Winson (Eds), *Essays in transportation economics: A handbook in honor of John R. Meyer* (pp. 493–529). Washington, DC: Brookings Institution.

Gallamore, R. E., & Panzar, J. (2004). When is competition not good? The case of compulsory access and maximum rate regulation for railroad "captive shippers." Manuscript final draft, Northwestern University, October 6, 2004.

Griliches, Z. (1972). Cost allocation in railroad regulation. *Bell Journal of Economics and Management Science*, Spring, 26–41.

Grimm, C. M., & Harris, R. G. (1983). Vertical foreclosure in the rail freight industry: Economic analysis and policy prescriptions, *ICC Practitioners Journal*, July–August, 508–531.

Grimm, C. M., & Harris, R. G. (1988). A qualitative choice analysis of rail routings: Implications for vertical foreclosure and competition policy. *Logistics and Transportation Review*, March, 24(1), 49–67.

Grimm, C., & Winston, C. (2000). Competition in the deregulated rail industry: Sources, effects and policy issues. In: S. Peltzman & C. Winston (Eds), *Deregulation of network industries: What's next?* (pp. 41–71). Washington, DC: Brookings Institution.

Hadley, A. T. (1885). *Railroad transportation*. New York: Putnam's and Sons (19th impression, 1908).

Harbeson. (1969). Toward better resource allocation in transport. *Journal of Law and Economics*, *12*, 321–338.

Harmatuck, D. J. (1979). A policy sensitive railway cost function. *Logistics and Transportation Review*, *5*(2), 277–315.

Harris, Robert, G. (1977). Economies of traffic density in the rail freight industry. *Bell Journal of Economics*, 556–564.

Harris, R. G., & Winston, C. (1983). Potential benefits of rail mergers: An econometric analysis of network effects on service quality. *Review of Economics and Statistics*, *65*, 32–40.

Hasenkamp, G. (1979). A study of multiple-output production functions: Klein's railroad study revisited, *Journal of Econometrics*, 23–62.

Heaver, T. D., & Nelson, J. C. (1977). *Railway pricing under commercial freedom: The Canadian experience*. Vancouver: UBC Centre for Transportation Studies.

Hilton, G. W. (1972). The basic behaviour of regulatory commissions, *American Economics Review*, May, 47–54.

Holder, S. (1999). Recent developments in rail infrastructure charging in the European Union. *Journal of Transport Economics and Policy*, *33*(1), 111–118.

Ivaldi, M., & McCullough, G. J. (2001). Density and integration effects on Class I US freight railroads. *Journal of Regulatory Economics*, *19*(2), March.

Ivaldi, M., & McCullough, G. J. (2004). Subadditivity tests for network separation with an application to U.S. railroads. London, CEPR Discussion Paper 4392.

Ivaldi, M., & McCullough, G. J. (2007). Railroad pricing and revenue-to-cost margins in the post-Staggers era. In: S. Dennis & W. Talley (Eds), *Railroad economics*. Elsevier Science.

Jara-Diaz, S. (1982). The estimation of transport cost functions: A methodological review. *Transport Reviews*, *2*, 257–278.

Keeler, T. E. (1974). Railroad costs, returns to scale and excess capacity. *Review of Economics and Statistics*, *56*, 201–208.

Keeler, T. E. (1983). *Railroads, freight and public policy*. Washington DC: The Brookings Institute 1983.

Klein, L. R. (1953). *A textbook on econometrics*. Evanston, IL: Row, Peterson and Company.

Kleit, A. N. (1993). Problems come before solutions: Comment on pricing market access for regulated firms. *Logistics and Transportation Review*, *29*(1), 69–73.

Knoop, D. (1923). *Outlines of railway economics*. London: Macmillan and Co.

Kolko, G. (1965). *Railroads and regulation 1877–1916*. Princeton, NJ: Princeton University Press.

Lardner, D. (1850). *Railway economy: A treatise on the New Art of Transport, Its management, prospects and relations*, New York: A.M. Kelley, (1968 reprint).

Levin, R. C. (1978). Allocation in surface freight transportation: Does rate regulation matter? *Bell Journal of Economics*, 9, 18–45.

Levin, R. C. (1981). Railroad rates, profitability and welfare under deregulation. *Bell Journal of Economics*, *12*(Spring), 1–26.

Locklin, D. P. (1933). The literature on railway rate theory. *Quarterly Journal of Economics*, *47*, 167–230.

Lorenz, M. O. (1916). Cost and value of service in railroad ratemaking. *Quarterly Journal of Economics*, *21*, 205–218.

MacAvoy, P. W. (1965). *The economic effects of regulation – The trunkline railroad cartels and the ICC before 1900*. Cambridge: MIT Press.

Martland, C. D. (1997). Sources of financial improvement in the U.S. rail industry 1966 to 1995. In: *Proceedings of the 39th annual transportation research forum* (pp. 58–86).

Martland, C. D. (1999). Productivity and prices in the U.S. rail industry: Experience from 1965 to 1995 and prospects for the future. *Journal of the Transportation Research Forum*, *381*, 12–25.

Martland, C.D. (2006). Productivity, pricing and profitability in the rail industry: 1995–2004. In: *Proceedings of the Canadian Transportation Research Forum*, University of Saskatchewan Printing Services, Saskatoon (pp. 778–792).

Meyer, J. R., Peck, M. J., Stenason, J., & Zwick, C. (1959). *The economics of competition in the transportation industries*. Cambridge, MA: Harvard University Press.

Mohring, H. (1972). Optimization and scale economies in urban bus transportation. *American Economic Review,* September, 591–604.

Monami, E. (2000). European passenger rail reforms: A comparative assessment of the emerging models. *Transport Reviews*, *20*(1), 91–112.

Moore, T. G. (1975). Deregulating surface freight transportation. In: A. Phillips (Ed.), *Promoting competition in regulated markets*. Washington, DC: Brookings Institution.

Morrison, S., & Winston, C. (1999). Regulatory reform of U.S. intercity transportation. In: J. A. Gomez-Ibanez, W. B. Tye & C. Winson (Eds), *Essays in transportation economics: A handbook in honor of John R. Meyer* (pp. 469–492). Washington, DC: Brookings Institution.

Nash, C. (2005). Rail infrastructure charges in Europe: Review of current practice, rationales. *Journal of Transport Economics and Policy*, *39*(3), 259–278.

Nash, C., and Matthews, B. (Eds). (2005a). *Measuring the marginal social costs of transport*. Amsterdam: Elsevier.

Nash, C., & Matthews, B. (2005b). Transport pricing policy and the research agenda. In: C. Nash & B. Matthews (Eds). *Measuring the marginal social costs of transport* (pp. 1–18). Amsterdam: Elsevier.

Nash, C., & Preston, J. (1991). Appraisal of rail investment projects: recent British experience. *Transport Reviews*, 295–309.

Nash, C., & Sansom, T. (2001). Pricing European transport systems: Recent developments and evidence forom case studies. *Journal of Transport Economics and Policy*, *35*(3), 363–380.

Nash, C., Sansom, T., & Still, B. (2001). Modifying transport prices to internalize externalities: Evidence from European case studies. *Regional Science and Urban Economics*, *31*, 413–431.

Nelson, J. C. (1942). *New concepts in transportation regulation. In: Transportation and National Policy*. Washington, DC: U.S. Government Printing Office.

Nelson, J. C. (1959). *Railroad transportation and public policy*. Washington, DC: Brookings Institution.

North, D. (1966). *Growth and welfare in the American past*. Englewood Cliffs, NJ: Prentice-Hall.

Oum, T. H., & Waters, W. G., II (1996). A survey of recent developments in transportation cost function research. *Logistics and Transportation Review*, *32*(4), 423–460.

Oum, T. H., Waters, W. G., II, & Yu, C. (1999). A survey of productivity and efficiency measurement in rail transport. *Journal of Transport Economics and Policy*, *33*(January), 9–42.

Oum, T. H., & Yu, C. (1994). Economic efficiency of railways and implications for public policy: A comparative study of the OECD countries' railways. *Journal of Transport Economics and Policy*, *28*(2), 121–138.

Pegrum, D. F. (1963). *Transportation economics and public policy*. Richard D. Irwin, and various revised editions.

Peltzman, S. (1976). Toward a more general theory of regulation. *Journal of Law and Economics*, *19*, 211–240.

Pigou, A. C. (1913). Railway rates and joint costs. *Quarterly Journal of Economics*, 27, 535–536, 687–692.

Pirrong, S. C. (1992). An application of core theory to the analysis of ocean shipping markets. *Journal of Law and Economics*, *35*, 89–131.

Pittman, R. (2007). Options for restructuring the state-owned monopoly railway. In: S. Dennis & W. Talley (Eds), *Railroad economics*. Elsevier Science.

Posner, R. A. (1974). Theories of economic regulation. *Bell Journal of Economics*, *5*(Autumn), 335–358.

Preston, J., Whelan, G., & Wardman, M. (1999). An analysis of the potential for on-track competition in the British passenger rail industry. *Journal of Transport Economics and Policy*, *33*(January), 77–94.

Quinet, E. (2005). Alternative pricing doctrines. In: C. Nash & B. Matthews (Eds), *Measuring the marginal social costs of transport* (pp. 19–47). Amsterdam: Elsevier.

Raghavan, V. S., & Raghavan, J. (2005). Application of core theory to the U.S. airline industry. *Journal of the Academy of Business and Economics,* March, 1–22.

Ramsey, F. P. (1927). A contribution to the theory of taxation. *Economics Journal*, *27*, 47–61.

Ripley, W. Z. (1923). *Railroads: Finance and organization*. New York: Longmans, Green and Co.

Rostow, W. W. (1952). *The process of economic growth*. New York: W.W. Norton and Co.

Rostow, W. W. (1960). *The stages of economic growth*. Cambridge, UK: Cambridge University Press.

Rothengatter, W. (2003). How good is first best? Marginal costs and other pricing princles for user charges in transport. *Transport Policy*, *10*, 121–130.

Royal Commission on Transportation (MacPherson Commission). (1962). Royal commission on Transportation (3 Vol.) Ottawa: Queen's Printer.

Shin, R. T., & Ying, J. S. (1992). Unnatural monopolies in local telephone. *Rand Journal of Economics*, *23*(2), 171–183.

Sjostrom, W. (1989). Collusion in ocean shipping: A test of monopoly and empty core models. *Journal of Political Economy*, *97*(5), 1160–1179.

Spady, R. (1979). *Econometric estimation for the regulated transportation industries*. New York: Garland Press.

Spann, R. W., & Erickson, E. (1970). The economics of railroading: The beginnings of cartelization and regulation. *Bell Journal of Economics and Management Science*, *1*(2), 227–244.

Stenason, J., & Bandeen, R. A. (1965). Transportation costs and their implications: An empirical study of railway costs in Canada, In: *Transportation Economics* (pp. 121–138). New York: National Bureau of Economic Research.

Stigler, G. (1971). The theory of economic regulation. *Bell Journal of Economics*, *2*(Spring), 3–21.

Talley, W. (1988). *Transport carrier costing*. New York: Gordon and Breach Science Pub.

Taussig, F. W. (1891). A contribution to the theory of railway rates. *Quarterly Journal of Economics*, *5*, 438–465.

Taussig, F.W. (1913). Railway rates and joint costs once more. *Quarterly Journal of Economics*, 27, 378–384, 537–538, 692–694.

Telser, L. G. (1978). *Economic theory and the core*. Chicago: University of Chicago Press.

Telser, L. G. (1987). *A theory of competition and cooperation*. Cambridge: Cambridge University Press.

Telser, L. G. (1994). The usefulness of core theory in economics. *Journal of Economic Perspectives*, *82*, 151–164.

Thompson, L. (2003). Changing railway structure and ownership: Is anything working? *Transport Reviews, 23*(3), 311–355.

Tretheway, M. W., Waters, W. G., II, & Fok, A. K. (1997). The total factor productivity of Canadian railways, 1956–1991. *Journal of Transport Economics and Policy*, *31*(1), 93–113.

Tye, W. B. (1993a). Pricing market access for regulated firms. *Logistics and Transportation Review*, *29*(1), 39–67.

Tye, W. B. (1993b). Pricing market access for regulated firms: Reply. *Logistics and Transportation Review*, *29*(1), 75–80.

Tye, W. B. (1998). Achieving competitive neutrality in rail competitive access disputes. *Journal of Transportation Law, Logistics and Policy*, *65*(4), 348–355.

Tye, W. B., & Horn, R. (2000). Rail merger and access issues before the U.S. Surface Transportation Board, Paper for symposium on competition and access in the rail industry, for the Canada Transportation Act Review Panel, Saskatoon, SK.

van den, B., Certan, C., Veldman, S., Nash, C., & Mathews, B. (2005). In: C. Nash & B. Matthews (Eds), *Measuring the marginal social costs of transport* (pp. 287–314). Amsterdam: Elsevier.

Wardman, M. (2006). Demand for rail travel and effects of external factors. *Transport research, eLogistics and transportation review*, *42*, 129–148.
Waters, W. G., II (1985). Rail cost analysis. In: K. G. Button & D. Pitfield (Eds), *International railway economics* (pp. 101–135). Aldershot, UK: Gower Publishing.
Waters, W. G., II (2000). Productivity measurement. In: K. Button & D. Hensher (Eds), *Handbook of transport modeling* (pp. 335–351). Oxford: Elsevier.
Waters, W. G., II, & Tretheway, M. W. (1999). Comparing total factor productivity and price performance: Concepts and application to Canadian Railways. *Journal of Transport Economics and Policy*, *33*(2), 209–220.
Waters, W. G., II, & Woodland, A. D. (1984). *Econometric analysis and railway costing*. UK: Centre for Transportation Studies, University of British Columbia, and North Oxford Academic Press.
Wellington, A. M. (1915). *The economic theory of the location of railways*. New York: Wiley London: Chapman & Hall.
Welsby, J., & Nichols, A. (1999). The privatisation of Britain's railways: An inside view. *Journal of Transport Economics and Policy*, *33*(1), 55–76.
Williams, S. C. (1909). *The economics of railway transport*. London: MacMillan.
Wilson, W. W. (1997). Cost savings and productivity in the railroad industry. *Journal of Regulatory Economics*, *11*, 21–40.
Winston, C., Corsi, T. M., Grimm, C. M., & Evans, C. (1990). *The economic effects of surface freight deregulation*. Washington, DC: Brookings.

A HEDONIC COST FUNCTION APPROACH TO ESTIMATING RAILROAD COSTS☆

John D. Bitzan and Wesley W. Wilson

ABSTRACT

This study estimates a hedonic railroad cost function. It allows for differences in marginal costs across different outputs with different shipment characteristics. Cost and shipment data are included to examine the elasticity of costs with respect to two outputs – unit train output and way & through train output. We find differences across these two measures, which suggest the use of aggregate output measures may lead to significant bias in cost elasticities. Moreover, our approach also allows the effects of different shipment characteristics (e.g., shipment size, average length of haul) on marginal cost of each output to be considered.

1. INTRODUCTION

There is a long history of examining the structure of railroad costs by academic economists. Investigations of railroad costs have examined a

☆This study was completed under partial funding from the Federal Railroad Administration.

Railroad Economics
Research in Transportation Economics, Volume 20, 69–95

ISSN: 0739-8859/doi:10.1016/S0739-8859(07)20003-4

variety of important issues, including the extent of economies of scale, productivity gains resulting from changes in technology and regulatory change, the extent to which railroads need to pursue differential pricing, and the desirability of competition for railroad services.

During this time period, there have been several advancements in estimating railroad costs in a way that is consistent with economic theory. Some important advancements have included distinguishing between two different types of scale economies – economies of density and economies of size (Keeler, 1974), the introduction of flexible functional forms (Brown, Caves, & Christensen, 1979), distinguishing between way and structures capital (a factor of production) and route mileage (an obligation to serve markets) (Friedlaender & Spady, 1981), the importance of including firm effects in estimating railroad cost functions (Brauetigam, Daughety, & Turnquist, 1984; Caves, Christensen, Trethaway, & Windle, 1985), the introduction of many new technological variables aimed at capturing differences in railroad networks and operations, and the consideration of multiple outputs provided by railroads (Ivaldi & McCullough, 2001; Bitzan, 1999; Bitzan & Keeler, 2007).

However, while these important innovations have occurred, there has been only scant attention paid to the effects of different outputs emanating from different network structures with associated differences in commodity traffic. Railroads move products over a network according to two types of traffic. Way & through train traffic reflect a hub-and-spoke type of flow. Way train traffic tends to be of small shipment volumes to a consolidation point, while through train traffic is between freight terminals. Unit train traffic is typically of larger volumes, occurring in a dedicated fashion from point to point. The incremental costs of unit train traffic are generally thought to be much lower than way & through train traffic. Of course, in addition, shipments often tend to be of different sizes and lengths of haul. Each of these also has differences in costs.

The previous literature that attempts to recognize differences in output is varied. Friedlaender and Spady (1981) estimated a hedonic railroad cost function wherein the generic outputs were delineated by freight and passenger services. But, since their study, passenger service by Class I railroads has been transferred to AMTRAK, and there have been serious innovations in the marketing of railroad services that have resulted in increases in multiple car and unit train traffic. Other studies have incorporated summary statistics of differences across railroads with respect to output. For example, Wilson (1997) included the percent of ton-miles in unit trains as an explanatory variable. Some studies have explicitly considered the different outputs provided by railroads. Bitzan (1999), Bitzan and Keeler (2007), and Ivaldi and McCullough (2001) each estimated multiple output cost functions, but differed in the specification of output. Ivaldi and McCullough included car-miles in bulk, high-valued, and general traffic as outputs, while Bitzan (1999) and Bitzan and Keeler (2007) estimated cost functions that included unit train ton-miles, way train ton-miles, and through train ton-miles as outputs. None of these studies, however, considered differences in the characteristics of different outputs (e.g., shipment size and length of haul) and their impacts on costs.

Our approach closely follows Chiang and Friedlaender's (1984) study of cost functions for the motor carrier industry. In their study, they used financial and operating statistics of trucking firms and combined those data with shipment data to estimate a hedonic cost function. Chiang and Friedlaender (1984) showed that using aggregate output measures in the estimation of truck costs can lead to substantial bias. When using multiple outputs that were hedonically adjusted using shipment characteristics they found constant returns to scale, while estimation with a single aggregate output showed decreasing returns to scale.

The current study estimates a hedonic cost function that considers the different types of services provided by railroads and differences in the nature of such services among railroads. Specifically, this study estimates a hedonic cost function, where railroad costs are a function of input prices, technological characteristics, and outputs for specific types of services, where shipment attributes are allowed to vary by types of services. The cost function data are from the R-1 Reports filed by the Class I railroads. These data are supplemented by shipment specific data from the confidential waybill sample. The estimated model shows how the marginal cost of different outputs can vary with different output characteristics. In addition, an illustration of how this cost function might be used to estimate individual railroad shipment costs is presented.

The following section of the paper presents the theoretical hedonic cost model. After a brief discussion of the data, results and an illustration of how marginal costs of different outputs may vary based on output characteristics is presented. Next, the model is used to simulate costs for a series of actual U.S. railroad shipments. Finally, conclusions and implications are presented.

2. HEDONIC MODEL OF RAILROAD COSTS

Railroads are multiproduct enterprises, carrying a variety of commodities between a variety of geographic locations, and with varying service characteristics. Ideally, a railroad cost function should include measures of each unique output provided. That is, each movement of a specific commodity between a particular origin and destination, and with unique service characteristics, would be included as one of many outputs. However, given the fact that existing econometric techniques cannot handle this many outputs and comprehensive movement specific data are not generally available, most previous studies have focused on a single aggregate output – ton-miles.[1] Unlike the bulk of previous research in railroad economic cost functions, our specification is multiproduct and allows for heterogeneity in outputs. Specifically, we model costs using a hedonic translog cost function.[2] As noted by Spady and Friedlaender (1978), the hedonic approach rests on the definition of an "effective output." The effective output depends on a physical measure of output (e.g., a ton-mile) and also on a set of attributes (e.g., shipment size and length of haul). That is, the hedonic output, $\psi^i = \psi^i(y^i, q^i)$, is a function that measures effective outputs in terms of a generic output (ton-miles, y^i) and a set of attributes or qualities associated with the generic output (shipment size and average length of haul, q^i). The underlying assumption of such a specification is that a continuum of different [attributes] measures of physical outputs exists, which can be consistently aggregated by the function $\psi^i = \psi^i(y^i, q^i)$.

In this study, we define two distinct outputs, using a hedonic aggregator for each. The two generic outputs used in the hedonic functions are (1) unit train services and (2) way & through train services. Unit train services are those provided to high-volume shippers in a routine fashion. Trains are dedicated to the movement of a single commodity between a particular origin–destination pair. Way services encompass the gathering of cars at individual shippers for delivery to major freight terminals, while through services are shipments between major freight terminals. As discussed in Bitzan (1999) and Bitzan and Keeler (2007), each of these three types of services are unique and we should expect each to have a different cost.[3] However, because we are unable to distinguish between way & through services in compiling hedonic attributes, the two outputs are combined in this study.[4] We note that the delineation of outputs into multiple hedonic outputs allows factor utilization to vary across the hedonic outputs.[5] The hedonic cost model we employ, in general form, is given by:

$$C = C(\psi^{WT}(z^{WT}), \psi^{U}(z^{U}), w, N)$$

where ψ^i represents the ith generic output ($i = U, WT$) with characteristics z^i, w is a vector of factor prices including labor (l), equipment (e), fuel (f), materials and supplies (m), and way and structures (r), and N is a vector of variables indexing the network and technology.

The hedonic function, we used is:

$$\ln \psi^i = \ln y^i + h^i_{ss} \ln SS^i + h^i_{ALH} \ln ALH^i$$

where y^i is the generic measure of output (e.g., way train ton-miles and unit train ton-miles), SS^i is shipment size (average cars per train) for generic output i, and ALH^i is average length of haul for generic output i.

The empirical specification used to estimate our cost function is the usual translog form:

$$\begin{aligned}\ln C = \alpha_0 &+ \sum_i \alpha_i \ln w_i + \sum_j \beta_j \ln \psi_j + \sum_n \delta_n \ln N_n \\ &+ \tfrac{1}{2} \sum_i \sum_m A_{im} \ln w_i \ln w_m \\ &+ \tfrac{1}{2} \sum_j \sum_k B_{jk} \ln \psi_j \ln \psi_k \\ &+ \tfrac{1}{2} \sum_n \sum_l C_{nl} \ln N_n \ln N_l \\ &+ \sum_i \sum_j D_{ij} \ln w_i \ln \psi_j + \sum_i \sum_n E_{in} \ln w_i \ln N_n \\ &+ \sum_j \sum_n F_{jn} \ln \psi_j \ln N_n + \varepsilon\end{aligned}$$

where all variables (including the time trend) are divided by their sample means, serving as a point of approximation. As in previous cost function estimations, we make use of Shephard's Lemma in order to obtain factor share equations:

$$s_i = \alpha_i + \sum_m A_{im} \ln w_m + \sum_j D_{ij} \ln \psi_j + \sum_n E_{in} \ln N_n + \varepsilon$$

We also impose symmetry and homogeneity of degree one in factor prices. That is:

$$A_{im} = A_{mi},\ B_{jk} = B_{kj},\ C_{nl} = C_{\ln},\ D_{ij} = D_{ji},\ E_{in} = E_{ni},\ F_{jn} = F_{nj}$$

and

$$\sum_i \alpha_i = 1,\ \sum_i A_{im} = \sum_m A_{im} = \sum_i D_{ij} = \sum_i E_{in} = 0$$

We substitute hedonic output equations into the above cost function and share equations, and estimate them jointly through seemingly unrelated regressions.

2.1. Data Sources and Variables

Most of our data are from the R-1 Reports of Class I railroads reporting to the Interstate Commerce Commission (ICC) and the Surface Transportation Board (STB).[6] These data cover all Class I railroads over the 1983 through 1997 period.[7] In addition, we use the confidential waybill sample and the Association of American Railroads' materials and supply index to supplement some of the data provided in the R-1 Reports. All nominal variables are deflated to 1992 levels using the Gross Domestic Product Price Deflator available in the *Economic Report to the President*.

During the time when data are available, there are 240 possible firm years. In 1983, there were 28 railroads. By 1997, that number fell to nine.[8] Most of the reduction in firms has been due to firm consolidation. In Table 1, we provide a summary of the firms used in the analysis and acronyms used to identify them.

In developing our model, we use total annual costs as the dependent variable. This variable and all other variables are defined in Table 2. Total annual costs include the sum of expenditures on all factor inputs.

Two hedonic outputs are used in our analysis. These are way & through gross ton-miles and unit train gross ton-miles.[9] The hedonic attributes used for each output are shipment size (cars per shipment) and average length of haul. Shipment sizes and lengths of haul are calculated from the waybill statistics for each movement type, railroad, and year. Since the type of movement (i.e., way & through versus unit train) is not available in the waybill data, we proxy movement type by using shipment size.[10] We define a unit train as a multiple-car movement with a shipment size of 50 cars or more.[11] In the R-1 data, there are occasions in which this approach is inappropriate. Specifically, in a few cases, the waybill yields non-zero unit train movements (i.e., 50 cars or more), but the R-1 data have zero unit train operations. In these cases, observations are deleted.[12]

Five factors of production are employed in our cost specification, consisting of labor, equipment, fuel, materials and supplies, and way and structures. Included in the definition of costs is a return on investment (ROI) for way and structures, and equipment. For the ROI, we use the cost of capital from the American Association of Railroad's publication *Railroad*

Table 1. Observations in Data Set—with Merger Definitions.

Railroad	Years in Data Set (RRs with 0 unit train gross ton-miles are excluded from the data set)
Atchison Topeka & Sante Fe (ATSF)	1983–1995 – merged into BN
Baltimore & Ohio (BO)	1983–1985 – merged with CO SCL to form CSX
Boston & Maine (BM)	1983–1986 – lost Class I status
Burlington Northern (BN)	1983–1997 – from 1996 to1997 includes merged ATSF BN system
Chesapeake & Ohio (CO)	1983–1985 – merged with BO SCL to form CSX
Chicago & Northwestern (CNW)	1983–1994 – merged into UP
Consolidated Rail Corporation (CR)	1983–1997
CSX Transportation (CSX)	1986–1997 – formed with the merger of BO CO SCL
Delaware & Hudson (DH)	1983–1987 – lost Class I status
Denver Rio Grande & Western (DRGW)	1983–1993 – merged into the SP
Detroit Toledo & Ironton (DTI)	1983 – merged into GTW
Duluth Missabe & Iron Range (DMIR)	1984 – lost Class I status
Florida East Coast (FEC)	1985–1991 – lost Class I status
Grand Trunk & Western (GTW)	1983–1997 – from 1984 to 1997 includes merged GTW DTI
Illinois Central Gulf (ICG)	1983–1997
Kansas City Southern (KCS)	1983–1991 and 1995–1997 – data for hours of work not reported for 1992–1994
Milwaukee Road (MILW)	1983–1984 – acquired by SOO
Missouri-Kansas-Texas (MKT)	1983–1987 – merged into UP
Missouri Pacific (MP)	1983–1985 – merged into UP
Norfolk Southern (NS)	1985–1997 – formed with the merger of SRS NW
Norfolk & Western (NW)	1984 – merged with SRS to form NS
Pittsburgh Lake Erie (PLE)	1983–1984 – lost Class I status
SOO Line (SOO)	1984–1997 – from 1985 to 1997 includes merged SOO MILW
Southern Railway System (SRS)	1983–1984 – merged with NW to form NS
Southern Pacific (SP)	1983–1996 – from 1990 to 1993 includes merged SP SSW – from 1994 to 1996 includes merged SP SSW DRGW – merged into UP
Saint Louis Southwestern (SSW)	1988–1989 – merged into SP
Union Pacific (UP)	1983–1997 – from 1986 to 1987 includes merged UP WP MP system – from 1988 to 1994 includes merged UP WP MKT system – from 1995 to 1996 includes merged UP CNW system – for 1997 includes merged UP SP system
Western Pacific (WP)	1984–1985 – merged into UP

Source: Dooley, Wilson, Benson, and Tolliver (1991) and consultation with the Surface Transportation Board.

Table 2. Variable Definitions and Sources.

Variable	Source
Costs	
Real total cost	(OPERCOST−CAPEXP + ROIRD + ROILCM + ROICRS)/GDPPD
OPERCOST	Railroad operating cost (R1, Sched. 410, line 620, Col F)
CAPEXP	Capital expenditures classified as operating in R1 (R1, Sched. 410, lines 12–30, 101–109, Col F)
ROIRD	Return on investment in road (ROADINV− ACCDEPR) × COSTKAP
ROADINV	Road investment (R1, Sched. 352B, line 31) + CAPEXP from all previous years
ACCDEPR	Accumulated depreciation in road (R1, Sched. 335, line 30, Col G)
COSTKAP	Cost of capital (AAR, *Railroad Facts*)
ROILCM	Return on investment in locomotives [(IBOLOCO + LOCINVL)−(ACDOLOCO + LOCACDL)] × COSTKAP
IBOLOCO	Investment base in owned locomotives (R1, Sched. 415, line 5, Col. G)
LOCINVL	Investment base in leased locomotives (R1, Sched. 415, line 5, Col. H)
ACDOLOCO	Accumulated depreciationowned locomotives (R1, Sched. 415, line 5, Col. I)
LOCACDL	Accumulated depreciation leased locomotives (R1, Sched. 415, line 5, Col. J)
ROICRS	Return on investment in cars [(IBOCARS + CARINVL)−(ACDOCARS + CARACDL)] × COSTKAP
IBOCARS	Investment base in owned cars (R1, Sched. 415, line 24, Col. G)
CARINVL	Investment base in leased cars (R1, Sched. 415, line 24, Col. H)
ACDOCARS	Accumulated depreciation owned cars (R1, Sched. 415, line 24, Col. I)
CARACDL	Accumulated depreciation leased locomotives (R1, Sched. 415, line 24, Col. J)
Generic and hedonic outputs	
WTGTM	Way & through gross ton-miles (R1, Sched. 755, line 100 + line 101, Col. B).
UTGTM	Unit train gross ton-miles (R1, Sched. 755, line 99, Col. B)
Adjustment factor multiplied by each generic output	RTM/(WTGTM + UTGTM)
SSW&T	Way & through train shipment size. From waybill sample
SSunit	Unit train shipment size. From waybill sample
ALHW&T	Way & through average length of haul. From waybill sample
ALHunit	Unit train average length of haul. From waybill sample
Factor Prices (all divided by GDPPD)	
Labor price	Labor price per hour (SWGE + FRINGE−CAPLAB)/LBHRS
SWGE	Total salary and wages (R1, Sched. 410, line 620, Col. B)
FRINGE	Fringe benefits (R1, Sched. 410, liness 112—114, 205, 224, 309, 414, 430, 505, 512, 522, 611, Col. E)
CAPLAB	Labor portion of capital expenditure classified as operating in R1 (R1, Sched. 410, lines 12—30, 101—109, Col. B)
LBHRS	Labor hours (wage form A, line 700, Cols. 4 + 6)
Equipment price	Weighted average equipment price (ROI and Annual Depriciation per car and locomotive – weighted by that type of equipment's share in total equipment cost)
Fuel price	Price per gallon (R1, Sched. 750)
Materials and supply price	AAR materials and supply index

Table 2. (*Continued*)

Variable	Source
Way and structures price	(ROIRD + ANNDEPRD)/MOT
ANNDEPRD	Annual depreciation of road (R1, Sched. 335, line 30, Col. C)
MOT	Miles of track (R1, Sched. 720, line 6, Col. B)
Technological and network conditions	
Miles of road	(R1, Sched. 700, line 57, Col. C)
Average length of haul	RTM/REVTONS
Loss and damage per ton-mile	(R1, Sched. 410, lines 412 + 428 + 504 + 511)/GDPPD/RTM
Percent of tons originated	Constructed from QCS form. Report of Freight Commodity Statistics. (Total tons originated and delivered + total tons originated and terminated)/total tons carried

Facts. Labor prices are defined in terms of total labor costs (including fringe benefits) and are expressed on an hourly basis. Equipment prices are defined as a weighted average of locomotive and car depreciation, and ROI (weighted by expenditures). Fuel price is expenditures on fuel divided by the number of gallons purchased. Materials and supplies price is reflected by the American Association of Railroad's Materials and Supplies Price Index for railroads operating in the eastern and western portions of the United States. Finally, we include a price for way and structures expressed on a miles-of-track basis. A net investment base is first calculated from the R-1 Report. Then a ROI is applied to derive ROI cost of way and structures. We then add this to an annual depreciation of way and structures and divide the annual cost by miles of track to define the price.

Four variables index the technology that can be classified as operating and/or network variables. These include miles of road, the percentage of tons that are originated on the railroad's network (versus other railroads), the loss and damage expense per revenue ton-mile, and a time trend to allow for technological change. Miles of road measures the size of the network and is expected to have an increasing effect on costs.[13] The percentage of tons that are originated is included in this specification (also in Bitzan & Keeler, 2003) to reflect the extra costs associated with originating a shipment. As this percentage increases, it should have a positive influence on costs due to the costs associated with placing empty cars at shipper sidings, the time equipment sits idly at shipper sidings, picking up cars at shipper sidings, and classification and blocking of cars for originated shipments. We also include loss and damage expense per ton-mile to reflect the extra costs associated with hauling more valuable and fragile products. Finally, we include a time trend to reflect technological change. Over time, there have been many innovations in the industry, some of which are not reflected in the specification (e.g., see Keeler, 1983; MacDonald, 1989; Gallamore, 1999; Bitzan, & Keeler, 2007, who provide extensive discussions). Improvements in technology should have a reducing effect on costs.

2.2. Econometric Results

We estimate two versions of this model. The first set of results excludes fixed effects, while the second specification allows for fixed effects.[14] The model is estimated with non-linear, seemingly unrelated regressions.[15] Table 3 presents the results without fixed effects, while fixed effects results are in Table 4.

The models fit the data well, and are consistent with comparable previous work. Because all variables (including time) are divided by their sample means, the first-order terms can be interpreted as individual elasticities when all other variables are at their sample means. For the most part, the coefficients are in the range of a priori expectations.

At sample means, elasticity of cost with respect to all outputs is approximately 0.6 in both models. This is consistent with recent studies by Bitzan and Keeler (2003, 2007), and suggests significant economies of density. Moreover, there are large differences in the elasticities of different outputs. In the fixed effects model, the elasticity of cost with respect to way & through train service is approximately 0.48, while it is 0.16 with respect to unit train service.[16] These widely varying elasticities further illustrate the importance of accounting for the different outputs produced by railroads. The elasticity of costs with respect to factor prices is very similar in both models. Labor, way and structures, and materials account for the largest shares of total costs for the average railroad, at 31%, 27%, and 24% of total costs, respectively.[17] Equipment and fuel account for 11% and 7% of total costs, respectively.

The coefficient for miles of road is positive and significant in both models, but with large differences in magnitude. In the fixed effects model, a one percent increase in miles of road increases costs by 0.58%. This is very similar to previous long-run cost function estimates (Bitzan & Keeler, 2003, 2007). In the non-fixed effects model, a one percent increase in miles of road

Table 3. Estimation Results without Fixed Effects.

Variable	Parameter Estimate	Variable	Parameter Estimate	Variable	Parameter Estimate
Intercept	−0.0595* (0.0257)	1/2 Ψ_2^2	0.0689* (0.0247)	wL × LD	0.0068 (0.0043)
wL (labor price)	0.3083* (0.0042)	$\Psi_1 \times \Psi_2$	−0.2113* (0.0513)	wE × LD	−0.0012 (0.0042)
wE (equipment price)	0.1137* (0.0040)	wL × Ψ_1	0.0186*** (0.0103)	wF × LD	−0.0007 (0.0021)
wF (fuel price)	0.0682* (0.0022)	wE × Ψ_1	0.0287* (0.0097)	wM × LD	0.0096*** (0.0056)
wM (materials price)	0.2387* (0.0053)	wF × Ψ_1	−0.0045 (0.0053)	wL × TIME	−0.0196* (0.0048)
Ψ_1 (way & through service)	0.5408* (0.0646)	wM × Ψ_1	0.0168 (0.0137)	wE × TIME	−0.0208* (0.0043)
Ψ_2 (unit train service)	0.0602* (0.0276)	wL × Ψ_2	−0.0151* (0.0034)	wF × TIME	0.0001 (0.0030)
MOR (miles of road)	0.3833* (0.0803)	wE × Ψ_2	0.0077* (0.0033)	wM × TIME	0.0156** (0.0062)
ORG% (percent tons originated)	0.0318 (0.0789)	wF × Ψ_2	0.0066* (0.0016)	MOR × ORG%	−0.2345 (0.1561)
LD (loss & damage per rtm)	0.1089* (0.0359)	wM × Ψ_2	0.0007 (0.0044)	MOR × LD	−0.0465 (0.0865)
TIME	−0.2424* (0.0342)	1/2 MOR^2	−0.1788 (0.1843)	MOR × TIME	−0.0511 (0.0817)
1/2 wL^2	0.1106* (0.0141)	1/2 ORG%^{2}	−1.0987* (0.2150)	ORG% × LD	−0.2230* (0.0790)
1/2 wE^2	0.0142* (0.0053)	1/2 LD^2	0.1122* (0.0310)	ORG% × TIME	0.0537 (0.0723)
1/2 wF^2	0.0357* (0.0072)	1/2 TIME^2	−0.0923** (0.0418)	LD × TIME	0.0150 (0.0237)
1/2 wM^2	0.0502* (0.0209)	wL × MOR	0.0012 (0.0112)	Ψ_1 × MOR	0.2033 (0.1717)
wL × wE	−0.0259* (0.0050)	wE × MOR	−0.0421* (0.0105)	Ψ_1 × ORG%	0.3071** (0.1497)
wL × wF	−0.0140* (0.0061)	wF × MOR	−0.0038 (0.0055)	Ψ_1 × LD	0.0116 (0.0777)
wL × wM	−0.0069 (0.0140)	wM × MOR	−0.0203 (0.0147)	Ψ_1 × TIME	0.0159 (0.0728)
wE × wF	0.0088* (0.0026)	wL × ORG%	0.0058 (0.0096)	Ψ_2 × MOR	0.1086*** (0.0642)
wE × wM	0.0193* (0.0066)	wE × ORG%	0.0164*** (0.0094)	Ψ_2 × ORG%	0.1019 (0.0645)

Table 3. (*Continued*)

Variable	Parameter Estimate	Variable	Parameter Estimate	Variable	Parameter Estimate
wF × wM	−0.0131	wF × ORG%	−0.0031	$\Psi_2 \times$ LD	0.0176
	(0.0089)		(0.0047)		(0.0215)
1/2 Ψ_1^2	0.0219	wM × ORG%	−0.0404*	$\Psi_2 \times$ TIME	−0.0374
	(0.1809)		(0.0124)		(0.0250)

$$\Psi_1 = q1 - \underset{(0.1128)}{0.1998^{***}} \times SS\text{W\&T} - \underset{(0.0219)}{0.1772^{*}}\, ALH\text{W\&T},$$

$$\Psi_2 = q2 - \underset{(0.4813)}{3.3528^{*}} \times SS\text{Unit} - \underset{(0.0853)}{0.3454^{*}}\, ALH\text{Unit},$$

Adjusted $R^2 = 0.9879$, RMSE = 0.1316.

*Significant at the 1% level
**Significant at the 5% level
***Significant at the 10% level

only increases costs by 0.39%. The smaller parameter estimate for the non-fixed effects model may reflect unmeasured network specific efficiencies associated with some of the larger railroad networks.

The parameter estimates of other network variables are somewhat mixed. Loss and damage expense per ton-mile is positive and significant in both models, suggesting that carrying more valuable and fragile products increases costs. The percent of tons originated is not significant in either model, and has a different sign in each. It was expected to have a positive sign due to the extra costs associated with originating a shipment. Finally, the time trend is significant and negative in both models suggesting productivity gains over time.

The estimated hedonic functions are shown at the bottom of Tables 3 and 4. In the model without fixed effects (Table 3), shipment size and average length of haul are negative and significant for way & through train output (ψ_1) and for unit train output (ψ_2). These suggest that way & through train output and unit train output are less expensive to provide when their shipment sizes and lengths of haul are larger. In the fixed effects model (Table 4), shipment size is negative for both outputs, but only significant for unit train output. Average length of haul is negative and significant for way & through train output, while it is positive but not significant for unit train output. While not entirely consistent with expectations, the significant

Table 4. Estimation Results with Fixed Effects.

Variable	Parameter Estimate	Variable	Parameter Estimate	Variable	Parameter Estimate
Intercept	0.3363* (0.0771)	1/2 Ψ_2^2	0.0896* (0.0205)	wL × LD	0.0072*** (0.0040)
wL (labor price)	0.3054* (0.0042)	$\Psi_1 \times \Psi_2$	0.0498 (0.0374)	wE × LD	−0.0018 (0.0034)
wE (equipment price)	0.1131* (0.0036)	wL × Ψ_1	0.0158 (0.0098)	wF × LD	−0.0011 (0.0017)
wF (fuel price)	0.0699* (0.0019)	wE × Ψ_1	0.0214* (0.0083)	wM × LD	0.0108** (0.0055)
wM (materials price)	0.2405* (0.0057)	wF × Ψ_1	0.0013 (0.0044)	wL × TIME	−0.0187* (0.0045)
Ψ_1 (way & through service)	0.4796* (0.0719)	wM × Ψ_1	0.0135 (0.0138)	wE × TIME	−0.0193* (0.0035)
Ψ_2 (unit train service)	0.1559* (0.0312)	wL × Ψ_2	−0.0141* (0.0028)	wF × TIME	−0.0015 (0.0026)
MOR (miles of road)	0.5869* (0.0987)	wE × Ψ_2	0.0050** (0.0024)	wM × TIME	0.0153** (0.0060)
ORG% (percent tons originated)	−0.0839 (0.0826)	wF × Ψ_2	0.0067* (0.0012)	MOR × ORG%	0.3464** (0.1599)
LD (loss & damage per rtm)	0.0608** (0.0290)	wM × Ψ_2	0.0012 (0.0038)	MOR × LD	0.0276 (0.0521)
TIME	−0.2102* (0.0262)	1/2 MOR^2	0.3515* (0.1070)	MOR × TIME	0.1448* (0.0464)
1/2 wL^2	0.1008** (0.0132)	1/2 ORG%^{2}	−0.3740** (0.1543)	ORG% × LD	0.0132 (0.0512)
1/2 wE^2	0.0157* (0.0044)	1/2 LD^2	0.0655* (0.0196)	ORG% × TIME	0.1638* (0.0440)
1/2 wF^2	0.0336* (0.0064)	1/2 TIME^2	−0.0689* (0.0229)	LD × TIME	0.0086 (0.0149)
1/2 wM^2	0.0222* (0.0200)	wL × MOR	0.0049 (0.0106)	Ψ_1 × MOR	−0.1593 (0.0972)
wL × wE	−0.0267* (0.0048)	wE × MOR	−0.0340* (0.0088)	Ψ_1 × ORG%	−0.0013 (0.1165)
wL × wF	−0.0136* (0.0054)	wF × MOR	−0.0102** (0.0047)	Ψ_1 × LD	−0.0345 (0.0456)
wL × wM	0.0074 (0.0132)	wM × MOR	−0.0172 (0.0146)	Ψ_1 × TIME	−0.1220* (0.0406)
wE × wF	0.0086* (0.0022)	wL × ORG%	0.0081 (0.0092)	Ψ_2 × MOR	−0.1127** (0.0455)
wE × wM	0.0182* (0.0065)	wE × ORG%	0.0169** (0.0078)	Ψ_2 × ORG%	−0.1264* (0.0397)

Table 4. (*Continued*)

Variable	Parameter Estimate	Variable	Parameter Estimate	Variable	Parameter Estimate
wF × wM	−0.0109	wF × ORG%	−0.0052	$\Psi_2 \times$ LD	0.0080
	(0.0080)		(0.0040)		(0.0183)
$1/2\ \Psi_1^2$	0.1583	wM × ORG%	−0.0414*	$\Psi_2 \times$ TIME	−0.0473*
	(0.1015)		(0.0124)		(0.0141)

$$\Psi_1 = q1 - \underset{(0.1816)}{0.0639^{***}} \times SS\text{W\&T} - \underset{(0.0367)}{0.1067^{*}}\ ALH\text{W\&T},$$

$$\Psi_2 = q2 - \underset{(0.5270)}{3.9052^{*}} \times SS\text{Unit} + \underset{(0.0677)}{0.0472^{*}}\ ALH\text{Unit},$$

Adjusted $R^2 = 0.9981$, RMSE = 0.0523.

*Significant at the 1% level
**Significant at the 5% level
***Significant at the 10% level

parameter estimates suggest that way & through train service is less expensive for longer hauls and that unit train service is less expensive in larger shipments.

There are many second-order terms (interactions in the model). However, while there are a number of important second-order effects, we do not provide an in-depth discussion of these interactions.

At this point, one might wonder how important it is to include the hedonic attributes of each output in the cost function. In other words, while the inclusion of output specific shipment size and length of haul is interesting, do changes in average shipment size and length of haul have a very big impact on costs?

In order to gain insight into the answer to this question, we use the fixed effects results to estimate the marginal cost of a ton-mile for way & through and for unit train traffic for a given railroad and time period (BNSF in 1997), when the average characteristics of each output (shipment size and length of haul) vary.[18] Fig. 1 shows the estimated marginal cost of a way & through and a unit train ton-mile, when average length of haul varies between 200 and 1,000 miles.[19] As the figure shows, the estimated marginal cost of a way & through train ton-mile on the BNSF in 1997 is nearly 2.3 cents when way & through train average length of haul (W&T ALH) is 200 miles, while it is less than 2 cents when W&T ALH is 1,000 miles. The

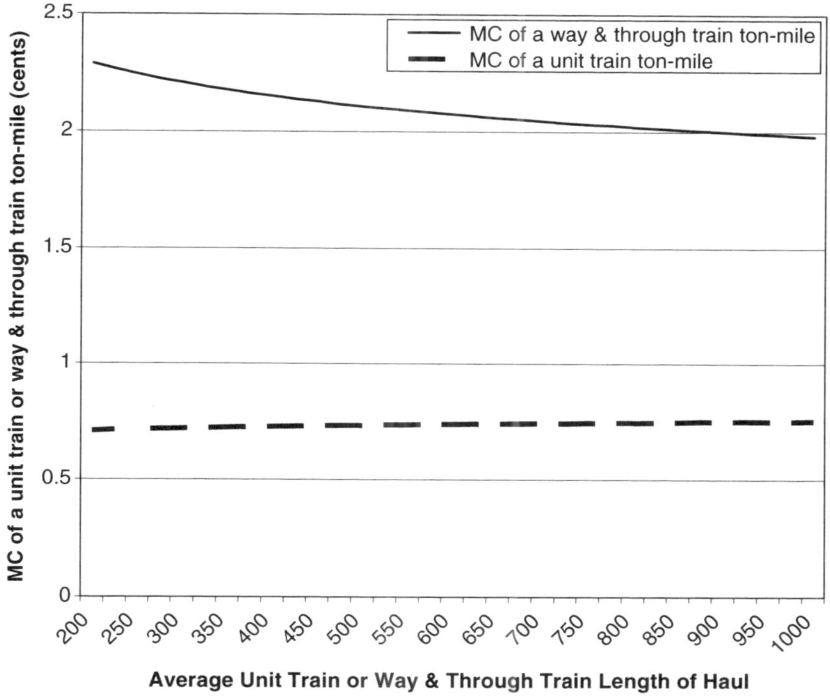

Fig. 1. Estimated Marginal Cost of a Unit Train Ton-Mile and a Way & Through Train Ton-Mile at Various Unit Train and Way & Through Train Average Lengths of Haul (BNSF in 1997).

marginal costs of a unit train ton-mile are relatively flat (it increases slightly but the linear coefficient is not statistically significant).[20]

Fig. 2 shows the estimated marginal cost of a way & through train ton-mile when the average way & through shipment size varies between 1 and 5 cars.[21] As the figure shows, marginal cost ranges from over 2.05 cents when average W&T shipment size is 1 car, to less than 1.9 cents when average W&T shipment size is 5 cars. Fig. 3 shows the large changes in the estimated marginal cost of a unit train ton-mile that occur as average unit train shipment size varies between 50 and 110 cars.[22] At 50 cars per unit train shipment, estimated marginal cost on the BNSF in 1997 is estimated to be nearly 4.5 cents, while it is just over 0.5 cents for an average shipment size of 110 cars.

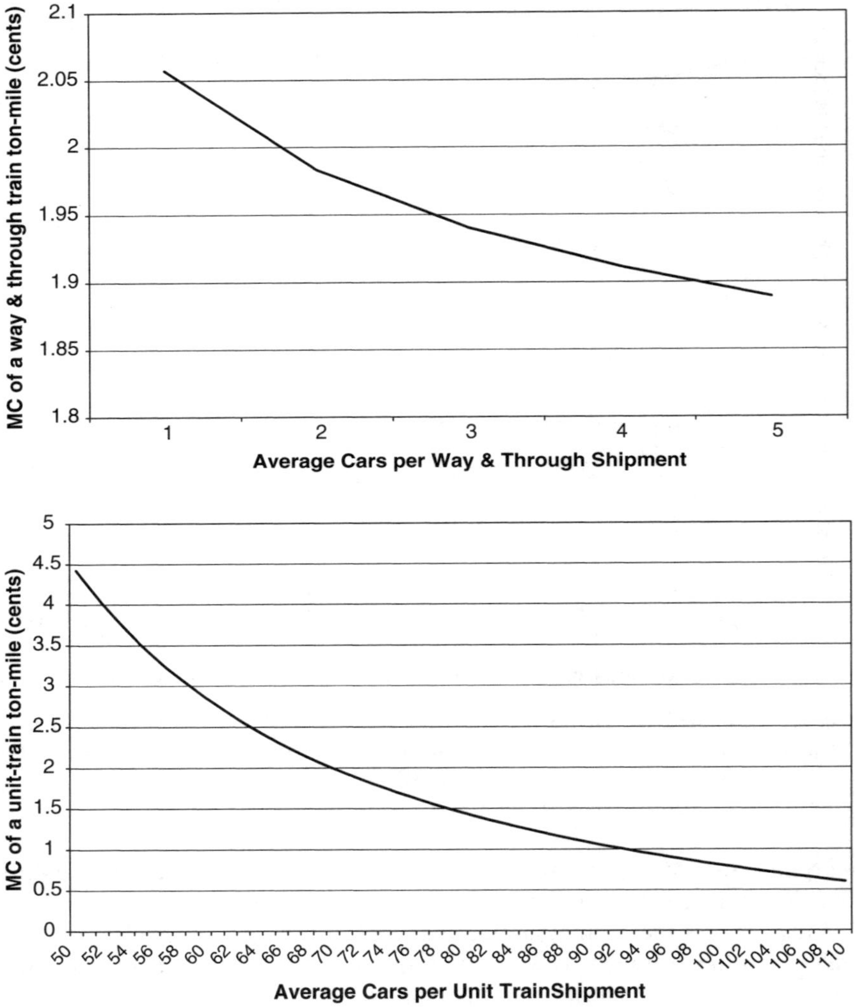

Fig. 2. Estimated Marginal Cost per Way & Through Ton-Mile for Various Average Way & Through Shipment Sizes (BNSF in 1997).

These figures, while only for one railroad, highlight the differences in marginal costs of different types of railroad output (unit trains and way & through trains), and the large changes that can occur in these marginal costs as the service characteristics of these outputs change. The following section

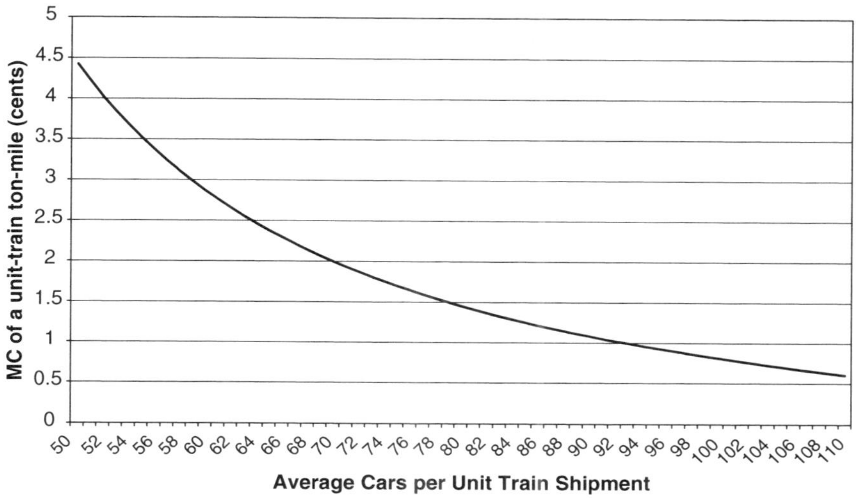

Fig. 3. Estimated Marginal Cost of a Unit Train Ton-Mile for Various Average Unit Train Shipment Sizes (BNSF in 1997).

of the report examines the potential for using our hedonic cost function to estimate individual rail shipment costs.

3. USING THE HEDONIC COST FUNCTION TO INFER INDIVIDUAL MOVEMENT COSTS

Previously, we discussed the many innovations that have occurred in estimating railroad cost functions. At the same time as the innovations have occurred in measuring railroad costs that are consistent with economic theory, rail costing (i.e., the costing of a specific movement) has evolved for regulatory and bargaining purposes. In contrast to the academic studies of railroad costs, rail costing has not estimated cost functions. Instead, rail costing has applied linear regression techniques to a series of subcategories of railroad costs in an attempt to estimate the portions of these cost components that are fixed and variable. While railroad costing has been much better suited to estimating individual movement costs due to the highly aggregate nature of the academic studies, the inconsistency with economic theory and the ad hoc use of statistical techniques suggest that the accuracy of individual costs obtained from railroad costing might be questioned.

There have been two attempts to bridge these two lines of railroad cost analysis. Waters and Woodland (1984) applied a variety of econometric techniques to estimating the various subcategories of railroad costs. Some of the improvements made by Waters and Woodland included estimating cost categories in a system of equations, pooling cross-sectional and time series data in a random coefficients model, specifying cost subcategory models as distributed lag models, and using a non-linear model to estimate cost subcategory–output relationships. Bereskin (1989) also estimated expense subcategories using non-linear models. While both of these studies made important improvements to railroad costing, they still retained the assumption that expense categories were separable. This suggested that each category of expenses (e.g., running track maintenance) was optimized on a stand-alone basis. Moreover, they assumed that inputs were not substitutable for one another.

In this section of the report, we estimate individual railroad movement costs in an attempt to explore the potential for future utilization of a hedonic cost function approach to estimate individual movement costs in a way that is consistent with economic theory.

We use the hedonic model to simulate movement costs.[23] In doing so, we use the waybill sample to identify movements for farm products, coal, and chemicals. We use the 1996 Waybill sample movement data to identify the added way & through train and the unit train ton-miles from specific shipments. In this regard, we calculate the added net ton-miles from the waybill. We then add the shipment ton-miles to the railroad's traffic base, calculate incremental costs of the movement, and express it on a ton-mile basis. In mapping the waybill shipment characteristics to the railroad costs, we make an arbitrary distinction between way & through train movements and unit train movements analogously to that used in calculating average shipment size. That is, any movement involving more than 50 cars is classified as unit train movement, and all others are classified as way & through train movements.

In estimating incremental movement costs, we use two alternative simulations. The first simulation includes only the added ton-miles without making any adjustments to the composition of the hedonic outputs. The second simulation includes added ton-miles and makes an adjustment in the hedonic output shipment size and average length of haul based on a weighted average of existing characteristics and the characteristics of the new shipment. An explanation of each of these simulations follows.

3.1. Simulation 1: Hedonic Output Unchanged

Our first simulation only includes the added ton-miles. Theoretically, the added cost of a movement of type i can be written as:

$$\Delta C = C\left(\psi_1^i(z_1^i), \psi_0^j\left(z_0^j\right), X_1\right) - C\left(\psi_0^i(z_0^i), \psi_0^j\left(z_0^j\right), X_0\right)$$

where $\psi_1^i(z_1^i) - \psi_0^i(z_0^i)$ is the change in output i due to incremental ton-miles and changes in shipment characteristics, and $X_1 - X_0$ is the change in remaining explanatory variables.

In the first simulation, we assume that the characteristics of the hedonic outputs and the remaining explanatory variables remain the same. This simulation seems reasonable, given the fact that hedonic characteristics and remaining explanatory variables are system averages, and therefore, change by small amounts with incremental output. Thus, in the first simulation:

$$\psi_1^i(z_1^i) - \psi_0^i(z_0^i) = \Delta Q^i$$

In applying our approach, we use the 1996 Waybill sample for farm products, chemicals, and coal. From this sample, we calculate net ton-miles for each movement. We then use the net ton-mile figure along with shipment type (i.e., way & through versus unit), and add that to the traffic base of the railroads. We then simulate the added costs per ton-mile as described above.

The simulations are presented in Table 5, showing incremental costs per ton-mile, by railroad, commodity, and shipment type, and showing the associated movement characteristics. The translog cost simulations show large differences in incremental costs among railroads and among shipment types for a given railroad. However, there is very little variation in costs for different shipments of a particular type on a particular railroad. This is not surprising, since all variables other than the generic output are assumed to remain constant. In an attempt to capture more of the shipment-to-shipment cost variation, we perform a second simulation.

3.2. Simulation 2: Hedonic Output Changes

Our second simulation estimates incremental costs by estimating the change in costs due to the incremental ton-miles and due to the change in hedonic characteristics introduced by the new shipment. Hedonic characteristics (shipment size and average length of haul) are changed by taking weighted averages of the overall railroad characteristic and the incremental shipment

Table 5. Fixed Hedonic Outputs and Incremental Costs by RR, Commodity and Shipment Type.

RR	Commodity	Shipment Type	Obs	Cars	Tons per Car	Distance	Ton-miles	Translog
BN	CHEM	W&T	2,677	2.88	80.75	1,063.8	1,82,555	2.12
BN	CHEM	Unit	11	72.55	100.33	836.36	58,21,910	0.6
BN	COAL	W&T	390	32.22	98.69	319.74	5,83,364	2.12
BN	COAL	Unit	3,259	107.69	108.87	653.36	80,85,301	0.6
BN	FARM	W&T	4,151	10.14	73.35	1,197.19	8,96,946	2.12
BN	FARM	Unit	549	58.33	99.35	1,255.62	70,90,214	0.6
CR	CHEM	W&T	932	1.07	74.18	511.91	32,585	1.67
CR	COAL	W&T	159	25.42	94.86	327.79	7,58,546	1.67
CR	COAL	Unit	1,898	97.79	99.99	329.16	32,59,668	1.14
CR	FARM	W&T	495	5.69	57	659.25	2,46,027	1.67
CR	FARM	Unit	7	76.43	100.9	619.86	50,65,894	1.14
CSX	CHEM	W&T	4,062	3.17	80.17	515.52	64,246	2.84
CSX	CHEM	Unit	180	79.8	61.91	41.68	2,05,114	1.34
CSX	COAL	W&T	1,289	16.02	93.56	394.2	6,10,114	2.84
CSX	COAL	Unit	5,390	93.93	102.94	381.62	37,06,787	1.34
CSX	FARM	W&T	961	8.34	84.06	664.16	5,07,430	2.84
CSX	FARM	Unit	274	63.64	94.72	737.74	44,21,160	1.34
GTW	CHEM	W&T	28	1.46	90.55	288.32	37,922	1.54
GTW	COAL	W&T	3	31.33	108.34	355	12,08,893	1.54
GTW	COAL	Unit	77	109.96	108.07	259.34	32,12,772	2.54
GTW	FARM	W&T	39	6.72	98.77	182.46	70,283	1.54
GTW	FARM	Unit	21	66.05	98.95	44.19	3,14,900	2.54
ICG	CHEM	W&T	597	1.29	94.12	391.16	47,559	1.54
ICG	COAL	W&T	9	47.22	97.68	177.11	7,86,810	1.54
ICG	COAL	Unit	424	91.09	102.02	276.91	28,40,250	0.63
ICG	FARM	W&T	494	21.67	95.57	378.26	9,29,114	1.54
ICG	FARM	Unit	40	74.68	93.55	732.83	50,71,661	0.63
KCS	CHEM	W&T	369	1.28	82.87	445.31	34,760	1.28
KCS	FARM	W&T	404	13.61	71.94	593.76	7,94,649	1.28
NS	CHEM	W&T	2,179	1.74	77.48	562.54	71,887	1.82
NS	CHEM	Unit	1	52	104.67	151	8,21,893	2.2
NS	COAL	W&T	1,1003	4.87	100.34	386.92	1,25,186	1.82
NS	COAL	Unit	2,403	90.55	104.54	341	34,16,456	2.2
NS	FARM	W&T	1,762	14.52	92.09	555.82	7,51,767	1.82
NS	FARM	Unit	126	62.77	102.13	491.52	32,92,112	2.2
SOO	CHEM	W&T	241	1.11	85.05	343.83	29,853	0.98
SOO	COAL	W&T	2,299	2.56	104.68	248.56	47,381	0.98
SOO	COAL	Unit	341	105.34	104.38	207.09	23,46,071	0.77
SOO	FARM	W&T	2,217	6.51	98.19	464.3	3,03,540	0.98
SOO	FARM	Unit	19	60.32	99.27	531.47	32,15,282	0.77
SP	CHEM	W&T	1,645	1.08	65.47	1,168.54	65,610	1.48
SP	FARM	W&T	395	9.89	58.39	980.83	4,83,055	1.48

Table 5. *(Continued)*

RR	Commodity	Shipment Type	Obs	Cars	Tons per Car	Distance	Ton-miles	Translog
SP	FARM	Unit	18	62.22	61.75	634.44	31,29,969	1.85
UP	CHEM	W&T	2,134	2.49	85.64	963.61	1,95,159	2.1
UP	CHEM	Unit	23	65.83	98.54	924.3	59,48,611	0.83
UP	COAL	W&T	154	27.42	98.22	440.89	11,60,753	2.1
UP	COAL	Unit	459	96.16	101.54	482.99	49,58,643	0.83
UP	FARM	W&T	1,219	16.29	91.39	670.47	8,64,459	2.1
UP	FARM	Unit	528	80.15	98.49	885.97	76,15,232	0.83

characteristic, where ton-miles is the weighting factor. An example of calculating shipment size to estimate the incremental costs of a new way & through train movement is:

$$SS_1^{WT} = \left(\frac{incr.W\ \&\ TTM}{existing\ W\ \&\ TTM + incr.W\ \&\ TTM}\right) SS_{shipment}^{WT} + \left(\frac{existing\ W\ \&\ TTM}{existing\ W\ \&\ TTM + incr.W\ \&\ TTM}\right) SS_{existing}^{WT}$$

The incremental cost of the new way & through train movement is then estimated by:

$$\Delta C = C(\psi_1^{WT}(Q_1^{WT}, SS_1^{WT}, ALH_1^{WT}), \psi_0^{UNIT}(Q_0^{UNIT}, SS_0^{UNIT}, ALH_0^{UNIT}), X_0) - C(\psi_0^{WT}(Q_0^{WT}, SS_0^{WT}, ALH_0^{WT}), \psi_0^{UNIT}(Q_0^{UNIT}, SS_0^{UNIT}, ALH_0^{UNIT}), X_0)$$

where Q_1^{WT}, SS_1^{WT}, ALH_1^{WT} are new way & through output, shipment size, and average length of haul, respectively and Q_0^{WT}, SS_0^{WT}, ALH_0^{WT} are existing way & through output, shipment size, and average length of haul, respectively.

The simulations are presented in Table 6, showing incremental costs per ton-mile estimated with the translog by railroad, commodity, and shipment type.[24] As the table shows, there is a lot more variation in costs among shipments of the same type by an individual railroad than in the previous simulation. Unfortunately, however, there is no basis for assessing the accuracy of the individual movement costs simulated from our hedonic cost function, as no generally accepted measure of individual movement costs exists.

Table 6. Variable Hedonic Outputs and Incremental Costs by RR, Commodity, and Shipment Type.

RR	Commodity	Shipment Type	Obs	Cars	Tons per Car	Distance	Ton-miles	Translog
BN	CHEM	W&T	2,556	1.68	79.67	1,087.6	1,14,661	1.87
BN	CHEM	Unit	11	72.55	100.33	836.36	58,21,910	1.29
BN	COAL	W&T	119	10.39	97.32	683.13	6,99,150	0.99
BN	COAL	Unit	3,259	107.69	108.87	653.36	80,85,301	0.49
BN	FARM	W&T	2,827	2.18	61.16	1,331	1,51,373	1.72
BN	FARM	Unit	549	58.33	99.35	1,255.62	70,90,214	1.61
CR	CHEM	W&T	932	1.07	74.18	511.91	32,585	1.61
CR	COAL	W&T	46	8.89	94.18	309.15	2,69,297	0.95
CR	COAL	Unit	1,607	93.22	99.33	320.15	29,78,368	0.97
CR	FARM	W&T	451	2.92	53.03	676.27	1,03,886	1.35
CR	FARM	Unit	7	76.43	100.9	619.86	50,65,894	1.82
CSX	CHEM	W&T	3,900	2.03	80.23	530.24	52,725	2.21
CSX	CHEM	Unit	145	68.6	62.28	41.37	1,75,527	2.27
CSX	COAL	W&T	801	7.82	92.47	380.73	3,06,052	1.61
CSX	COAL	Unit	4,543	85.01	102.76	394.13	35,48,028	1.28
CSX	FARM	W&T	807	5.13	81.83	643.59	2,61,897	1.59
CSX	FARM	Unit	272	63.23	94.98	740.8	44,36,726	2.66
GTW	CHEM	W&T	28	1.46	90.55	288.32	37,922	1.51
GTW	COAL	Unit	75	108.83	108.04	256.79	31,40,556	0.94
GTW	FARM	W&T	33	2.03	99.83	202.61	43,023	1.5
GTW	FARM	Unit	21	66.05	98.95	44.19	3,14,900	5.36
ICG	CHEM	W&T	597	1.29	94.12	391.16	47,559	1.58
ICG	COAL	Unit	281	81.4	100.68	223.03	21,08,934	0.75
ICG	FARM	W&T	199	6.77	91.08	260.87	1,86,246	1.18
ICG	FARM	Unit	40	74.68	93.55	732.83	50,71,661	0.97
KCS	CHEM	W&T	369	1.28	82.87	445.31	34,760	1.18
KCS	FARM	W&T	244	3.56	54.56	571.18	1,10,745	0.96
NS	CHEM	W&T	2,159	1.5	77.26	563.67	61,273	1.6
NS	CHEM	Unit	1	52	104.67	151	8,21,893	5.21
NS	COAL	W&T	9,894	1.67	100.58	402.96	54,572	1.69
NS	COAL	Unit	1,950	86.08	103.4	315.96	29,43,716	1.62
NS	FARM	W&T	1,234	3.3	88.77	571.27	1,53,273	1.42
NS	FARM	Unit	124	62.1	102.08	486.31	32,00,194	4.21
SOO	CHEM	W&T	241	1.11	85.05	343.83	29,853	0.95
SOO	COAL	W&T	2,218	1.03	105.32	251.94	27,220	0.99
SOO	COAL	Unit	68	76.94	94.18	221.13	18,31,977	1.04
SOO	FARM	W&T	1,794	1.75	98.08	461.73	74,891	0.87
SOO	FARM	Unit	19	60.32	99.27	531.47	32,15,282	1.68
SP	CHEM	W&T	1,645	1.08	65.47	1,168.54	65,610	1.28
SP	FARM	W&T	290	3.43	49.88	1,120.49	1,63,639	1.1
SP	FARM	Unit	18	62.22	61.75	634.44	31,29,969	4.12
UP	CHEM	W&T	2,070	1.45	85.23	964.8	98,568	1.93

Table 6. (*Continued*)

RR	Commodity	Shipment Type	Obs	Cars	Tons per Car	Distance	Ton-miles	Translog
UP	CHEM	Unit	23	65.83	98.54	924.3	59,48,611	1.98
UP	COAL	W&T	53	11.13	96.91	506.49	5,89,345	0.99
UP	COAL	Unit	448	93.72	102.29	483.48	49,34,359	1.09
UP	FARM	W&T	667	4.87	86.99	782.78	2,95,394	1.61
UP	FARM	Unit	528	80.15	98.49	885.97	76,15,232	1.53

4. SUMMARY AND IMPLICATIONS

This study estimates a railroad cost function that accounts for the varying impacts of different outputs on costs. Moreover, unlike previous railroad cost studies, this study considers differences in the ways that such outputs are provided by different railroads and by the same railroad over time.

In examining the elasticity of costs with respect to two unique outputs – unit train output and way & through train output – we find large differences. Unit train services, which are provided in a dedicated fashion between a particular origin and destination, have an elasticity of 0.48. Way & through services, which are gathering services and terminal-to-terminal services, respectively, have an elasticity of 0.16. These differences suggest that using an aggregate output to estimate cost functions may lead to bias.

Estimates of the marginal cost of each output show large changes when the characteristics of each output change. The estimated marginal cost of a way & through train ton-mile on the BNSF varies between 2.29 and 1.98 cents, as the average way & through train length of haul changes from 200 to 1,000 miles. The estimated marginal cost of a unit train ton-mile on the BNSF varies between 0.71 and 0.76 cents for changes in unit train average length of haul from 200 to 1,300 miles. Similarly, changes in shipment size (cars per shipment) affect marginal cost estimates. A change in average way & through train shipment size from 1 to 5 cars causes estimated marginal cost of a way & through train ton-mile on the BNSF to vary between 2.06 and 1.89 cents. Changing unit train average shipment size from 50 to 110 cars causes estimated marginal cost of a unit train ton-mile on the BNSF to fall from 4.5 to 0.5 cents. These changes in marginal cost with changes in output characteristics suggest that controlling for such differences is important.

Finally, because the hedonic cost function approach has the ability to capture differences in output characteristics, it seems to hold promise for overcoming the problems inherent in measuring individual movement costs with economic cost functions. That is, the large number of unique outputs provided by railroads is difficult to account for with existing econometric methodology. Nonetheless, the hedonic approach with further disaggregation of outputs and with more output characteristics is likely to improve the estimation of more disaggregated costs in a way consistent with economic theory.

NOTES

1. Exceptions to this approach include Bitzan (1999), Bitzan and Keeler (2007), and Ivaldi and McCullough (2001).

2. The hedonic translog cost function was first introduced by Spady and Friedlaender (1978) for a single generic output. It was extended by to multiple generic outputs by Friedlaender and Spady in 1981 and Chiang and Friedlaender in 1984. Spady and Friedlaender (1978) and Chiang and Friedlaender (1984) dealt with the trucking industry, while Friedlaender and Spady (1981) estimated a hedonic rail cost function.

3. Bitzan and Keeler (2007) found that the elasticity of costs with respect to unit train, through train, and way train services were 0.17, 0.38, and 0.09, respectively at the point of means.

4. We use shipment size and average length of haul for hedonic attributes. These are compiled from the master waybill sample, where no shipment type identifiers exist. As a proxy to distinguish between unit trains and way/through trains, we used a cutoff of 50 cars per shipment.

5. Friedlaender and Spady (1981) use hedonic functions for passenger and freight services for railroads, and Chiang and Friedlaender (1984) use hedonic functions for less-than-truckload (LTL) and truckload (TL) services. The factor mixes used to produce these different outputs quite likely are different, but they are likely the same within each class of output.

6. The R-1 database was first established in 1978. In 1983, there was a change from betterment to depreciation-based accounting. Using betterment accounting methods, long-term investments often were included as expenses. Under depreciation-based accounting standards, such items are depreciated rather than expensed.

7. Unfortunately, we are unable to obtain data beyond the 1997 period. R-1 annual reports are publicly available beyond 1997. However, the waybill sample data used to measure hedonic attributes is confidential and not generally available unless it is used as part of a project for a government agency. We performed this study under a contract with the Federal Railroad Administration, who provided access to the waybill sample through 1997.

8. These data correspond quite closely with the American Association of Roads *Railroad Facts* (1984–1998). However, there are some differences. Throughout the data, EJE and Long Island are Class I carriers in *Railroad Facts*. However, as the EJE is a switching line and Long Island is a commuter rail line, they were omitted

from our data. Other differences between our data reflect differences in the timing of mergers and in the availability of data. We used merger definitions of Dooley, Wilson, Benson, and Tolliver (1991) for pre-1989 mergers and consulted with STB officials for the timing of other mergers.

9. Each is multiplied by the ratio of revenue ton-miles to gross ton-miles for an estimate of revenue ton-miles by shipment type. This is done in an attempt to match shipment types with the true output provided by railroads – ton-miles. This same adjustment was applied in Bitzan (1999), Bitzan (2003), and Bitzan and Keeler (2007).

10. In reality, unit trains are not defined by shipment size. According to the Annual Reports to the Surface Transportation Board (formerly Interstate Commerce Commission), "Unit Trains, for the purpose of this report, are defined as a solid train with a fixed, coupled consist operated continuously, in shuttle service under load from origin and delivered intact at destination, and returning empty for reloading at the same origin." R-1 Annual Reports to the Interstate Commerce Commission, 1983.

11. Technically, a unit train is a dedicated point-to-point movement. Generally, it is of a large shipment size. Way & through traffic is not dedicated, and, is typically of smaller shipment sizes. The use of 50 cars to delineate the two was based on discussions with the FRA and others.

12. Previous discussions with officials at the Surface Transportation Board have raised doubt about the validity of such observations. See Bitzan (1999).

13. It is important to note that these are route miles, and not track miles. Thus, they represent the scope of service provided by the railroad, not the amount of capital stock the railroad employs. We estimate a long-run cost function, where the railroad makes optimal adjustments to way and structures (which may include changes in track miles) in order to serve a given amount of route miles.

14. There is some disagreement in the literature over whether fixed effects should be included. Some authors are concerned that collinearity between output or network variables and firm dummies may reduce statistical significance or change the size of the output and network variable parameter estimates (see Oum and Waters, 1996). However, collinearity still does not lead to biased parameter estimates. Moreover, if some unobserved network variables influence costs and they are correlated with included variables, a bias will result from not including firm effect variables. Thus, it seems that firm effects should be included. Nonetheless, we provide both estimates here.

15. We did not estimate a three-stage least squares system. A Hausman test suggests that SUR and 3SLS estimates are not statistically different. The omitted variables interpretation of the Hausman Test yields an F-statistic of 1.75 in the model without fixed effects and an F-statistic of 0.75 in the model with fixed effects.

16. These are very similar to output elasticities found by Bitzan (1999) and Bitzan and Keeler (2007). In the model without fixed effects, there are also large differences in output elasticities, but they are different than those in the fixed effects model.

17. The elasticity of total costs with respect to factor price is the share of total costs accounted for by that factor, according to Shephard's Lemma.

18. Similar changes in marginal costs occur for other railroads when average characteristics of each output are varied. The BNSF is used only as an illustration.

19. In 1997, way & through average length of haul ranged from 180 for CSX to 705 for BNSF.
20. In 1997, unit train average length of haul ranged from 207 for GTW to 1,248 for UP.
21. In 1997, way & through train shipment size ranged from 1.03 for GTW to 1.24 for CSX.
22. In 1997, unit train shipment size ranged between 81 cars for SOO and 102 cars for BNSF and KCS.
23. Because of the potential bias from not including fixed effects and the broader consistency of the fixed effects results with previous findings, we only use the fixed effects model to simulate incremental costs.
24. In some cases, allowing hedonic characteristics to change resulted in negative incremental costs. These observations are deleted.

ACKNOWLEDGMENTS

Comments from Bill Gelston and the staff of the FRA are gratefully acknowledged as are numerous conversations with Denver Tolliver.

REFERENCES

Association of American Railroads. (1984–1998). *Railroad facts.* Washington, DC: American Association of Railroads.

Bereskin, G. C. (1989). An econometric alternative to URCS (Uniform Railroad Costing System). *The Logistics and Transportation Review*, *25*(2), 99–128.

Bitzan, J. D. (1999). The structure of railroad costs and the benefits/costs of mergers. *Research in Transportation Economics*, *5*, 1–52.

Bitzan, J. D. (2003). Railroad costs and competition: The implications of introducing competition to railroad networks. *Journal of Transport Economics and Policy*, *37*(May), 201–225.

Bitzan, J. D., & Keeler, T. E. (2003). Productivity growth and some of its determinants in the deregulated U.S. railroad industry. *Southern Economic Journal*, *70*(2), 15–36.

Bitzan, J. D., & Keeler, T. E. (forthcoming 2007). Economics of density and regulatory change in the U.S. Railroad Freight Industry. *Journal of Law and Economics.*

Brauetigam, R. R., Daughety, A. F., & Turnquist, M. A. (1984). A firm specific analysis of economies of density in the railroad industry. *The Journal of Industrial Economics*, *33*(1), 3–20.

Brown, R. S., Caves, D. W., & Christensen, L. R. (1979). Modelling the structure of cost and production for multiproduct firms. *Southern Economic Journal*, *46*(1), 256–273.

Caves, D. W., Christensen, L. R., Trethaway, M. W., & Windle, R. J. (1985). Network effects and the measurement of returns to scale and density for U.S. railroads. In: A. F. Daugherty (Ed.), *Analytical studies in transport economics* (pp. 97–120). New York: Cambridge University Press.

Chiang, S. J. W., & Friedlaender, A. F. (1984). Output aggregation, network effects and the measurement of trucking technology. *The Review of Economics and Statistics*, *66*(2), 267–276.

Dooley, F., Wilson, W., Benson, D., & Tolliver, D. (1991). Post staggers productivity for Class I railroads. MPC-91-6. Mountain Plains Consortium Report.

Friedlaender, A. F., & Spady, R. H. (1981). *Freight transportation regulation: Equity, efficiency, and competition in the rail and truck industries*. Cambridge, MA: MIT Press.

Gallamore, R. E. (1999). Regulation and innovation: Lessons from the American railroad industry. In: J. Gomez-Ibanez, W. B. Tye & C. Winston (Eds), *Essays in transportation economics and policy: A handbook in honor of John R. Meyer* (pp. 493–530). Washington: The Brookings Institution.

Ivaldi, M., & McCullough, G. J. (2001). Density and integration on Class I U.S. freight railroads. *Journal of Regulatory Economics*, *19*(2), 161–182.

Keeler, T. E. (1974). Railroad costs, returns to scale and excess capacity. *Review of Economics and Statistics*, *56*(2), 201–208.

Keeler, T. E. (1983). *Railroads, freight, and public policy*. Washington: The Brookings Institution.

MacDonald, J. M. (1989). Railroad deregulation, innovation, and competition: Effects of the Staggers Act on grain transportation. *Journal of Law and Economics*, *32*, 63–96.

Oum, T. H., & Waters, W. G. (1996). A survey of recent developments in transportation cost function research. *Logistics and Transportation Review*, *32*(4), 423–460.

Spady, R. H., & Friedlaender, A. F. (1978). Hedonic cost functions for the regulated trucking industry. *The Bell Journal of Economics*, *9*(1), 159–179.

Waters, W. G. II, & Woodland, A. D. (1984). *Econometric analysis and railway costing* (pp. 1–101). The Centre for Transportation Studies, University of British Columbia: North Oxford Academic Publishing Co.

Wilson, W. W. (1997). Cost savings and productivity gains in the railroad industry. *Journal of Regulatory Economics*, *11*, 21–40.

SPATIALLY GENERATED TRANSPORTATION DEMANDS☆

Kenneth Train and Wesley W. Wilson

ABSTRACT

Transportation demanders are located at different points in geographical space and have differential access to modes. Central to the planning of transportation infrastructure is the aggregation of different shippers by mode over space. We estimate a modal choice model for rail and barge. However, shippers may not have direct access to one or both modes and incur access (truck) costs. The results indicate that access costs, barge and rail rates, and shippers' attributes matter significantly in mode choice. The choice model is then augmented by rate functions defined over space and used to derive spatially generated modal demand functions.

1. INTRODUCTION

The demand for freight transportation is a derived demand. Shippers make shipment decisions that usually involve the choice of mode or modal

☆This research was funded under the Navigation and Economic Technologies Program (NETS) of the Army Corps of Engineers directed by Keith Hofseth. Comments from Keith and the staff of the Army Corps of Engineers are gratefully acknowledged.

Railroad Economics
Research in Transportation Economics, Volume 20, 97–118

ISSN: 0739-8859/doi:10.1016/S0739-8859(07)20004-6

combinations and size of the shipment. Shippers, however, are often located at different points in geographic space and have different costs to access modal options. These "access costs" are directly related to distance from rail/barge access points as well as shipper characteristics such as rail car loading capacity. For example, shippers located on a waterway with the ability to load barges are more likely to ship by barge than shippers located some distance away from the waterway that must truck or rail to the river access point. The latter shippers may have access to both rail or truck or just one of the two surface modes and may have plant characteristics, e.g., significant rail loading capacity, which substantially reduces the cost of using rail. Finally, there are some shippers that have neither rail nor barge access. Their only option is to either truck to a rail or barge access point.

In this paper, we focus on the access that shippers have to transportation markets. To illustrate, we estimate a discrete choice model which is framed around the access shippers have to transport markets and then use the model to aggregate shipment decisions to provide "spatially generated transportation demands." That is, in analysis there are usually well-identified locations over which market clearing conditions are identified (e.g., ports). Typically, demands at these points are spatially generated transportation demands. These spatially generated demand functions then can be combined with supply conditions to establish equilibrium over a network (e.g., Anderson & Wilson, 2004).

The demand for freight transportation has historically taken two different approaches.[1] Early studies used aggregate data across locations, shipments, and/or commodities, and modeled aggregate demands. In locations, demand functions are aggregated across shippers in a region, e.g., Wilson, Wilson, and Koo (1988) or Yu and Fuller (2005). At the shipment level, there is a component of the literature in which individual shipment decisions are aggregated for each shipper. In such cases, demands are commonly modeled using a transportation cost function and associated factor demands by mode, e.g., Oum (1979), Friedlaender and Spady (1980), Westbrook and Buckley (1990). In the last 30 years, however, it has become more common to model transportation demands at a disaggregate level. In this framework, transportation demands are typically modeled at a shipment level using choice methods.[2] Generally, differences in options available to shippers are taken as differences in the choice set from which demand decisions are made. For example, in a model with three options that include truck, rail, or barge, a shipper that is included on the waterway and has access to truck and rail would have a choice set with all three options. However, a shipper located off the waterway would have only truck and rail in the choice set.

Estimation then proceeds with differential choice sets. Our paper differs from this approach by explicitly recognizing that shippers without access to rail, barge, or both, have the option of shipping to an access point. We find that the costs of access have a very important effect on shipment decisions and form the basis for aggregation to points of interest. Specifically, the results are combined with models of access costs (truck rates) over distance, and aggregated to form demand functions which can be directly integrated with simulated equilibrium models which can be used to assess policy decisions related to infrastructure.

The advantage of our approach has become very important in the last 25 years. The railroad industry was deregulated by the Railroad Revitalization and Regulatory Reform Act (4-R Act) and the Staggers Rail Act of 1980 and subsequent legislation. Under regulation, the railroad network was substantial with over 1,80,000 miles of road. Under deregulation, the railroad network has decreased to less than 1,20,000 miles of road (Association of American Railroads). Further under deregulation, the number of Class I railroads has fallen to only seven.[3] Each of these changes implies fewer options available to shippers. As noted in Train and Wilson's (2004) survey of agricultural shippers in the Upper Midwest, about one-half of shippers have direct access to only the truck mode. That is, the shipper cannot ship by rail or barge without first shipping by truck. Despite the fact that modal options are limited at the origin point, shippers do have a number of "routing" options. That is, to get the product to market, they are not limited to a single mode. Rather, they do have the option of shipping to rail or barge, which are, in most cases, lower cost modes, particularly for shipments of longer distances.

In addition to a reduction in the number of rail access points, there is also a considerable interest in the spatial decisions of demanders in evaluating the costs and benefits of major infrastructure improvements. For example, the Army Corps of Engineers (ACE) manage the nation's waterways. They routinely evaluate the costs and benefits of different investment decisions. Their models use aggregations of shipper decisions across both shipments and space to model the demands for waterway traffic. The demands are delineated by commodity and origin–destination "pools." A pool is a body of water between two different reference points. In most applications, a pool is commonly defined as the body of water between two locks on a river, and market demand functions are defined as a commodity, originating pool, and destination pool triple.

In the simulation models, ACE has used two different types of demand structures. In the Tow-Cost and Ohio River Investment Model (ORNIM), pool-to-pool demands are taken as exogenous up to a threshold rate, typically taken as the least cost overland rail rate. At barge rates above this threshold level, pool-to-pool barge demands for the commodity are zero. A second demand structure is used in the ESSENCE planning model. In this model, the quantity varies continuously to this same threshold rate above which demands are zero. In both cases, the quantity shipped emanates from off-river shippers through a barge access point. Over the past five years, the National Research Council and others (NRC, 2001, 2004a, 2004b; Berry, Hewings, & Levin, 2001) have reviewed the models used by ACE. A primary criticism is the treatment of demands in the models. In particular, the various reviews point to the need to develop models that reflect the alternatives of spatially separated shippers. In the present paper, after demand function estimates are presented, we illustrate how the resulting estimates can be used to provide for aggregations across modes reflecting the spatial environment and locations of shippers.[4]

2. THE MODEL

The model is framed as a profit-maximizing choice between two alternatives. That is, shippers have a set of two alternatives. Each alternative (c) has a payoff (π^c), and the shipper chooses the alternative with the higher payoff. The payoff, however, consists of two components. These include a deterministic component ($\bar{\pi}^c$), which is commonly specified in terms of a function of unknown parameters, and a random component (ε^c), which captures attributes that are not observed by the researcher.

To illustrate, we use the demand decisions of shippers in Eastern Washington who ship grain to Portland.[5] Jessup and Casavant (2004, 2005) provide comprehensive summaries of grain shipments and shippers in the region. A brief summary is provided here en route to modeling the decisions of shippers. Eastern Washington is one of the primary wheat producing regions in the United States. Almost all of the wheat travels to export terminals located in or near Portland, and almost all arrive by rail or barge. Eastern Washington and Portland are connected by an interconnected transportation system that consists of a series of rail lines and the Columbia-Snake Waterway. However, not all shippers have direct access to either rail or barge, and typically truck to points with direct access. Throughout access is defined as having the ability to load a particular mode. They may not be located on a river and must truck (or rail) to the river to access the barge mode. Alternatively, they may not receive rail service. The premise of this research is that the access costs affect the mode (rail/barge) of shipper decisions that are central to defining spatially motivated demand models to examine equilibrium and the welfare effects of policy.

In the model, shippers have one of two options modeled: ship to Portland by a sequence of link movements involving barge, i.e., barge alone or truck–barge; or to ship to Portland by a sequence of link movements involving rail, i.e., rail alone or truck–rail. Shippers are distributed over space. Some have rail-loading facilities,[6] some have barge-loading facilities, some have both, and some have neither. Yet, they can still access both rail and barge facilities by using trucks.

In applying the model, two alternatives for each shipper are used (barge or rail). The connection to barge and/or rail facilities is treated as an access cost. As discussed above, a shipper is taken to choose barge if returns from barge exceed returns by rail. Returns for each alternative consist of a deterministic component $\left(\bar{\pi}_i^c\right)$ and a random component $\left(\varepsilon_i^c\right)$. That is,

$$\begin{aligned}\pi_i^c &= \bar{\pi}_i^c + \varepsilon_i^c \\ &= f(rate_i^c,\ access_i^c,\ cars_i) + \varepsilon_i^c \\ &= \beta^c + \beta_r \times rate + \beta_a \times access + \beta_{cars}^c \times cars + \varepsilon_i^c \qquad (1)\end{aligned}$$

In this model, the β's are unknown parameters to be estimated.[7] There is an alternative specific intercept β^c that captures mode-specific differences, i.e., unobserved differences across barge and rail that are systematically different (e.g., speed, reliability, etc.). β_r is the coefficient on rate (technically, this captures the effects on profits from changes in rates). If zero, it means that rates do not affect the payoffs and does not affect decisions. This is a key coefficient in that if it is zero, demands are perfectly inelastic. However, in standard demand modeling, most researchers believe that rates are an important determinant of decision making and should negatively influence the profits and choices of decision makers. β_a is the coefficient on access costs to barge and rail terminals (access costs are measured by truck costs). In some cases, this is zero, i.e., the shipper has direct access to barge and/or rail. In other cases, this is nonzero. That is, to access the option (barge and/or rail), the shipper must truck to the barge and/or rail terminal. β_{cars}^c is the coefficient on rail car loading capacity. Rail car loading capacity (the number of rail cars that can be placed on the shipper's siding) is an important shipper attribute in that shippers with large capacity tend to obtain rate discounts (which is captured in the rate variable) and also incur lower loading costs, which increases profits and, therefore, makes rail more favorable relative to barge.[8]

The empirical foundation for estimation is based on maximizing profit through a discrete choice (i.e., barge or rail). Let $\delta_i = 1$, if shipper i chooses to ship by barge; and zero if the shipper chooses to ship by rail. Since the choice involves both observed and unobserved determinates, the choice is the outcome of a random variable. Through the observation of the choice and an assumption of the distribution of the unobserved component, the econometrician can estimate the unknown parameters. More specifically, the empirical foundation is

$$\begin{aligned} Pr(\delta_i = 1) &= Pr\left(\bar{\pi}_i^{Barge} + \varepsilon_i^{Barge} \geq \bar{\pi}_i^{Rail} + \varepsilon_i^{Rail}\right) \\ &= Pr\big(\beta^{Barge} + \beta_r \times rate^{Barge} + \beta_a \times access^{Barge} \\ &\quad + \beta^c_{cars} \times cars + \varepsilon_i^{Barge} \geq \beta^{Rail} + \beta_r \times rate^{Rail} \\ &\quad + \beta_a \times access^{Rail} + \beta^c_{cars} \times cars + \varepsilon_i^{Rail}\big) \end{aligned} \tag{2}$$

This type of model can be estimated with a wide variety of techniques and assumptions. The approach here is to estimate the model with a logit specification and the method of maximum likelihood. That is,

$$\begin{aligned} Pr(\delta_i = 1) &= Pr\left(\bar{\pi}_i^{Barge} + \varepsilon_i^{Barge} \geq \bar{\pi}_i^{Rail} + \varepsilon_i^{Rail}\right) \\ &= \frac{e^{\bar{\pi}_i^{Barge}}}{e^{\bar{\pi}_i^{Barge}} + e^{\bar{\pi}_i^{Rail}}} \\ &= \frac{1}{1 + e^{\bar{\pi}_i^{Rail} - \bar{\pi}_i^{Barge}}} \end{aligned} \tag{3}$$

Estimation proceeds after substitution of the definition of profits by logit. In the model, the intercept and the coefficient on car capacity are normalized to zero for barge, and the coefficients are interpreted relative to barge. The estimates are presented in Section 4 after presentation of the data sources in Section 3.

3. DATA

All data employed are the result of a survey conducted by the Social and Economic Sciences Research Center at Washington State University. Jessup and Casavant (2005) describe the data, survey techniques, and provide a copy of the survey instrument. The survey was pre-tested and reviewed both by academics and target survey recipients. It was conducted in the fall of 2004. There were 167 firms contacted, representing 414 warehouses.

Of these, 80 firms completed the questionnaire, and provided information for 181 warehouses.[9]

In these data, there are a number of descriptive statistics of immediate relevance. First, the choice data collected consisted of six alternatives. Three of these involve barge as an option, while two involved rail as an option.[10] The other alternative was "other." In about 25 percent of the cases (51 cases), shippers reported that they only had one alternative (the one used) and as such were omitted from the estimation. Another 25 percent (49 cases) involved other locations/modes.[11] After removal of observations with missing values and a small number of responses that substituted within the same mode, there were 55 observations which comprise the data used.

Table 1 provides descriptive statistics. There are 35 shippers that chose rail, and 20 shippers that chose barge. Overall, shippers have an average of about 11 rail cars loading capacity. Those that ship by rail (the column with Rail = 1) tend to have more car capacity than barge shippers (about 16 cars versus 2 cars). The rates per ton are lower (as expected) for barge. For all shippers, the rate per ton by rail is about $11.66, while by barge the rate per ton is about $8.28. These averages are about the same for shippers that choose barge and for those that choose rail. The access cost (truck cost per ton) is larger for barge than for rail, but again there is little difference across rail and barge shippers. One reason for the difference in rail and barge access costs is that the mean distance to barge access points is about

Table 1. Descriptive Statistics.

Variable	Overall		Rail = 1		Barge = 1	
	Mean	Standard Deviation	Mean	Standard Deviation	Mean	Standard Deviation
Barge = 1/Rail = 0	0.36	0.49	0.00	0.00	1.00	0.00
Rail car capacity	10.78	22.76	15.74	27.09	2.10	5.88
Rate/ton-barge	8.28	1.35	8.21	1.33	8.41	1.42
Rate/ton-rail	11.66	2.82	11.51	2.31	11.91	3.61
Access cost/ton-barge	7.32	3.49	7.92	2.91	6.26	4.19
Access cost/ton-rail	2.66	3.69	2.75	4.29	2.51	2.41
Barge distance	252.67	53.75	248.23	37.07	260.45	75.18
Rail distance	345.44	93.11	364.63	60.19	311.85	127.64
Distance to barge	97.67	66.14	105.66	50.43	83.70	86.95
Distance to rail	7.84	8.81	5.94	7.92	11.15	9.48
No. of shippers (N)	55		35		20	

Note: The category labeled Rail = 1 indicates that the chosen alternative involved rail; while the category labeled Barge = 1 indicates that the chosen alternative involved barge.

98 miles (for all shippers), while for rail access points the distance is only about eight miles. Of course, the distance to barge access points tends to be smaller for barge shippers than for rail shippers (about 84 miles versus 106 miles). This reflects the basic point that shippers that use barge tend to be "closer" to the waterway than shippers that use rail. Finally, the barge and rail distances reflect the distance of the barge and rail legs of shipments. Rail distances tend to be longer than for barge, but it is noted that the distance to barge access points is also larger for barge movements.

4. EMPIRICAL APPLICATION AND RESULTS

The logit model of Section 2 was estimated with estimates reported in Table 2.[12] Despite the fact that there are only 55 observations, the model appears to fit the model reasonably well with a χ^2 statistic of 20.26 with four degrees of freedom, and the log-likelihood at convergence suggests a likelihood ratio index of .2658. Further, the coefficients are of the a priori expected sign, and with the exception of the rail dummy, are statistically significant at the 90-percent level.

In this model, the alternative specific dummy is positive, but not statistically significant. A positive value means that relative to barge, profits are higher for rail.[13] The coefficient on rate is negative and statistically significant at the 90-percent level. This suggests that profits decrease as the rate increases. The coefficient on access is also negative and statistically significant at the 90-percent level. This suggests that as the costs of trucking to a barge or rail terminal increase, payoffs decrease, and the likelihood of using barge or rail decreases. That is, as access costs increase for a particular alternative relative to the other, the likelihood of that alternative decreases. Finally, the coefficient on rail car loading capacity is positive and statistically significant at the 90-percent level. This means that profits for shippers that have greater car loading capacities have higher profits from rail relative to barge.

Table 2. Coefficient Estimates.

Variable	Coefficient	Standard Error	*t*-Value
Rail dummy	0.10	0.51	0.2
Rate per ton	−0.64**	0.33	−1.91
Access cost per ton	−0.46**	0.25	−1.82
Car loading capacity	0.09**	0.05	1.93

**indicates statistical significance at the 90-percent level.

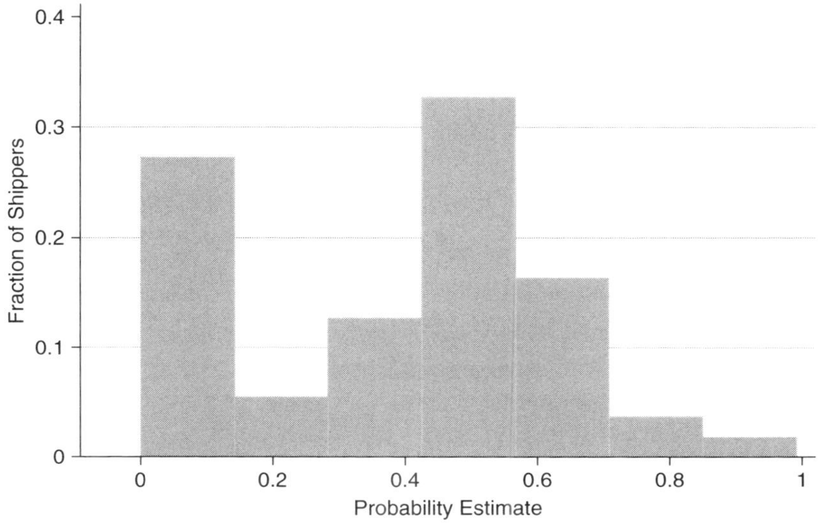

Fig. 1. Probability Estimates Histogram.

A histogram of the probability estimates (the probability of using barge) is given in Fig. 1.

The histogram is quite interesting. There is a cluster of probabilities close to zero, indicating that there are a number of shippers that are essentially "rail-captive." Inspection of the probability estimates suggests that these tend to be shippers with a lot of rail car capacity. There are also a number of estimates that lie close to .5 (over 30 percent of the shippers). Thus, the predominant number of shippers is "on the margin," i.e., probabilities of shipments involving barge are at or near .5. Such shippers are likely "reactive" in their mode choice to changes in barge, rail, or truck rates, and point to shippers that form the source of downward sloping demand functions derived below.

5. ILLUSTRATIONS

There are numerous illustrations and uses of the model. These include the use of the probability function to consider adjustments of shippers to changes in barge and rail rates, the costs of access (i.e., truck costs), distance from the waterway, car loading capacity. The results can also be used to define market areas of rail and barge and, perhaps, most importantly, pool level demands. Each is considered in turn. We note that in all illustrations, we assume that shippers have rail and barge options. However, the survey data collected here and in other surveys, suggest that some shippers do not view themselves as having more than one option in the choice set. Such cases can be easily incorporated in the calculations that follow simply by specifying the mode choice as a zero or a one.

The basis for the choice models is that profits depend on multiple attributes, not just rates. For the illustrations, reference points for the attributes other than barge rate are necessary. For this purpose, the attributes used are based on consideration of sample means and medians. The specific values used are:

Cost of access for rail and barge (truck costs \$5 per ton)
Rail rates (\$11.6 per ton)
Barge rates (\$8.3 per ton)
Car loading capacity (consideration of 0 car and 25 cars)

5.1. Probabilistic Responses of Shippers to Changes in Barge Rates

Given the reference points above, the probabilities of using barge and rail are calculated using a range of barge rates and presented in Fig. 2. Note these two probabilities must sum to one. Further, since rail shippers with lots of car loading capacity likely have a very different probability schedule than shippers without any car capacity, two sets of schedules are presented – one set for shippers with 25 car capacities and one for shippers with no rail car capacity.

As can be seen in the schedules, the probability of using barge at low barge rates is quite high as expected, and the probability of using rail is quite low. As rates rise, however, the probability of using barges falls and rail rises. These results are the foundation for the statement that demand functions slope downward in the context of a choice model. That is, controlling for all else, the likelihood of using barge falls as rates increase. Of course, similar figures can be presented for rail shippers.

There are large differences between shippers with 25 car loading capacities and shippers with no rail capacity. At the mean barge rate of \$8.3 per ton, the difference is about 45 percentage points. That is, at mean values, the probability of using barge is about 90 percent for shippers without rail car capacity, and only about 45 percent for shippers with 25 car capacity. Indeed, equating the probability of using barge and rail for each shipper type identifies the "transition" point wherein the discrete predicted outcome

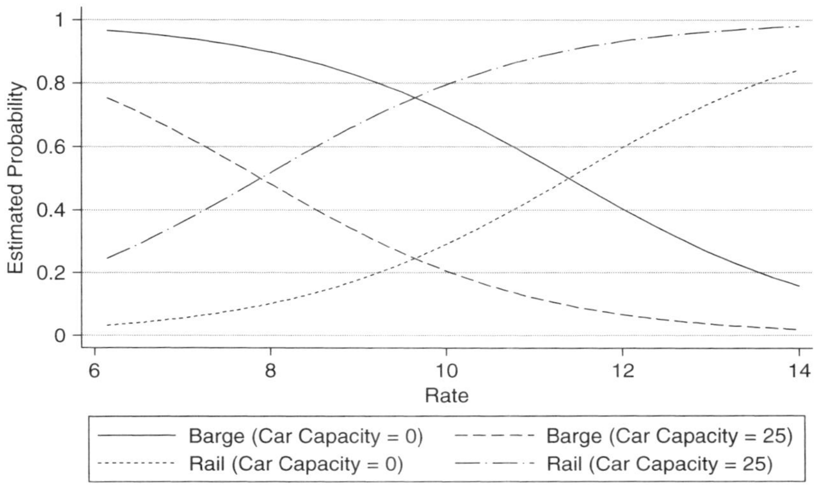

Fig. 2. Probability of Barge Shipments, Rates, and Rail Car Capacity.

changes. For the 25 car capacity shipper, the barge rate necessary for a switch to barge is less than $8.3 per ton. For shippers without rail, it is about $11 – a $3 difference.

5.2. Probabilistic Responses to the Costs of Access

Shippers without access to barge must truck to barge terminals, if they choose barge. An important attribute is, of course, the cost of access. Indeed, as might be expected as the cost of accessing barge increases, the likelihood of using barge falls (and rail increases). This is illustrated with Fig. 3. The probability of using barge is extremely high for shippers with low costs of accessing the river, particularly if they do not have rail access. As the costs increase, the likelihood of using barge falls. This means that shippers with a high cost per ton of shipping to the waterway (e.g., $10 per ton) have a small likelihood of using the waterway, especially for shippers with rail access and significant loading capacity.

5.3. Probabilistic Responses to Access Distance and Costs

As stated above, access costs are measured as truck cost per ton. Of course, truck costs per ton are a function of distance. This allows *spatial*

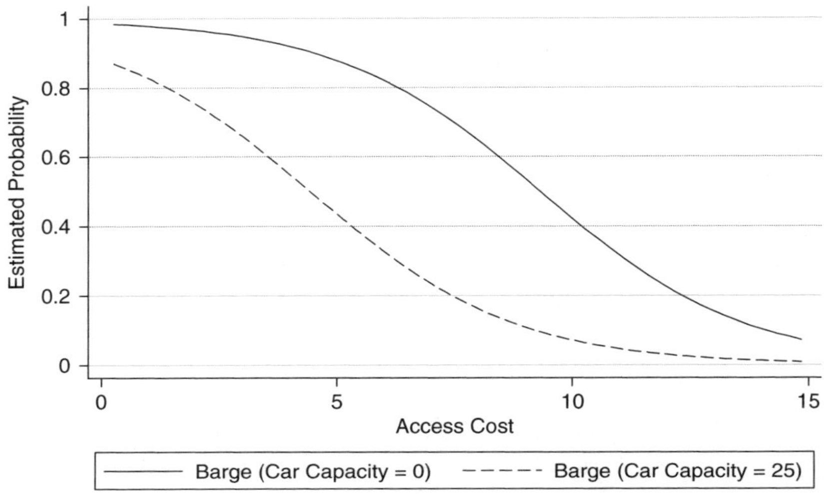

Fig. 3. Estimated Probability of Barge Shipments and Costs of Access.

considerations to be directly integrated into the choice function. In illustrating, truck rates are fit to distance and the result is used in a constructed transportation network. There are two possibilities in construction of the latter. First, we can vary the distance to the waterway, inferring the truck rate *given a constant cost of accessing rail.* Such a procedure means that the distance to the rail access point is fixed as distance to the waterway changes. Second, we can fix the locations of the rail and barge access points and then vary the distance across different shippers. Both procedures were followed and yield similar qualitative results. In the following, we focus on the second approach.

To develop the effects of space on choices, the relationship between truck rates and distance must be determined. This relationship is well known to be a positive relationship (rate per ton as a function of distance), but increasing at a decreasing rate due to the tapering principle. To estimate the relationship, truck rates observed in the sample were regressed on associated distances with a double-log specification.[14] The results are

$$\log(\text{truck rate}) = -0.366 + 0.526 \times \log(\text{distance to access point}) \qquad (4)$$
$$(-2.25) \quad (14.29)$$

where t-values are in parentheses and indicate a strong relationship which is also reflected with an R^2 of about 80 percent.

Given the relationship between access costs (truck rates) and distance, we now fix the distance between rail and barge access points at 200 miles. We then consider the probability of using barge as distance to water increases (and rail falls). This changes the relative access costs of using barge and rail, and sketches out the market area for each. To calculate the probabilities, reference points for barge and rail rates are needed. We fit double log specifications to each and used predicted values for barge and rail of \$9.3 and \$11.1 per ton, respectively. These correspond to barge and rail legs of 350 miles in the shipment. The result is provided in Fig. 4.

The figure indicates that the probability of using barge is quite high close to the river and falls for shippers located "closer" to rail. The two are equivalent for a distance of about 125miles.

6. DEMAND SCHEDULES

A primary feature of this research is to estimate demand schedules for shippers that can be aggregated to the pool level. As discussed earlier, this is a central definition of markets in ACE planning models. In this section, we illustrate choice models such as that presented earlier can be used to define pool level aggregate demands. In this particular case, we assume that

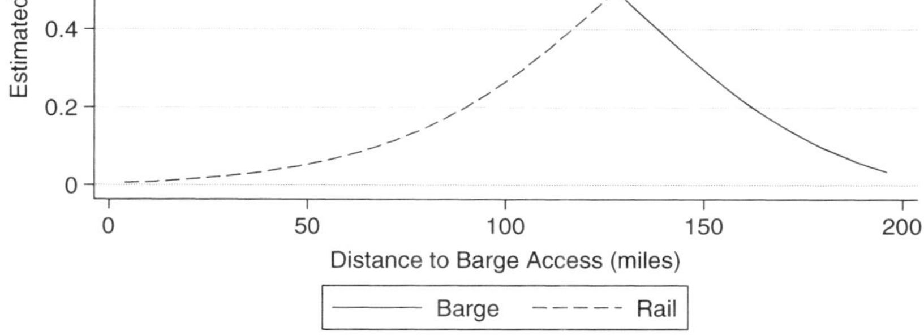

Fig. 4. Market Areas for Rail and Barge and Distance to Waterway.

there are two terminals, a river terminal and a rail terminal, located 100 miles apart on a line. There are 50 shippers and each ships 100 tons for a total quantity of 5,000 tons.[15]

Each of the shippers faces a different set of access costs and, therefore, has different probabilities of using barge (and rail). Therefore, the demand for each mode (not the function but the expected quantity shipped by each shipper)[16] differs by location. In presenting the demand schedules, there are two levels – the individual level and the pool level. Each is presented in turn.

6.1. Individual Demand Schedules of Spatially Separated Shippers

First, at the shipper level, there are three schedules presented below. Each shipper ships a total of 100 tons, shipper one is 10 miles from the river, shipper two is 50 miles from the river, and shipper three is 10 miles from the rail terminal. In Fig. 5, the expected barge quantity for each shipper is plotted against rate – these form the demand equation for spatially differentiated demands.

This figure gives expected shipper level demand functions for barge for shippers located 10, 50, and 90 miles away from the waterway. As expected, at very low barge rates, all quantities go by barge, given the rail rate. As the

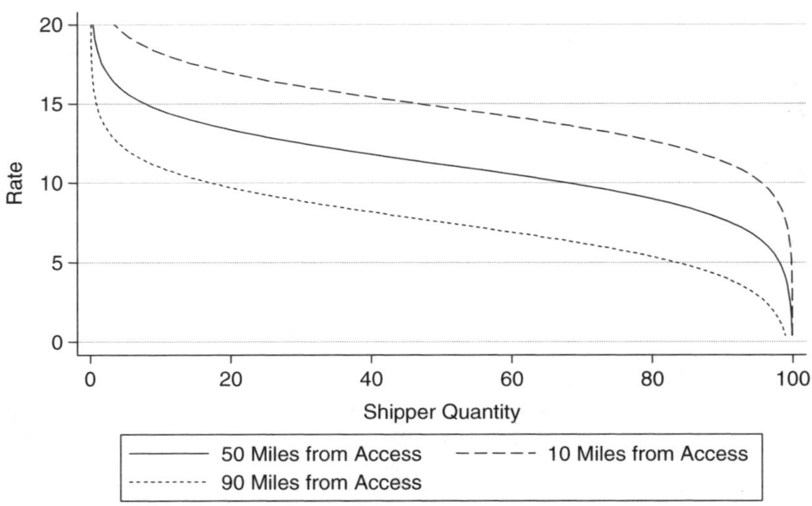

Fig. 5. Shipper Demand Functions and Distance from Barge Access Point.

barge rate increases, shippers located "near" the river continue to select the river, while shippers located further away from the river begin to substitute to rail. At the predicted barge (and rail) rates for a 350-mile movement ($9.1 and $11.3 per ton), shippers located near the river continue to select truck-barge with a high probability, while shippers close to rail are more likely to use truck-rail. According, quantities by barge are lower for such shippers.

6.2. Pool Level Demand Schedules and Spatially Separated Demanders

Central to Army Corps of Engineer Planning models are "pool-to-pool" transportation demands by commodity. A pool is typically regarded as the body of water between two fixed points on the river. Most typically, the two points are two locks. In this illustration, there are two pools. One is the pool in which the terminal location of the total movement, e.g., ocean terminals in Portland, is located. The other pool is the pool above a lock where a barge access point, i.e., a barge loading facility, is located. The "pool" level demand is the aggregation of the individual shipper demands.[17]

To illustrate, we construct a network. In that network (summarized in Fig. 6), there are 50 shippers; each shipping 100 tons. The shippers are

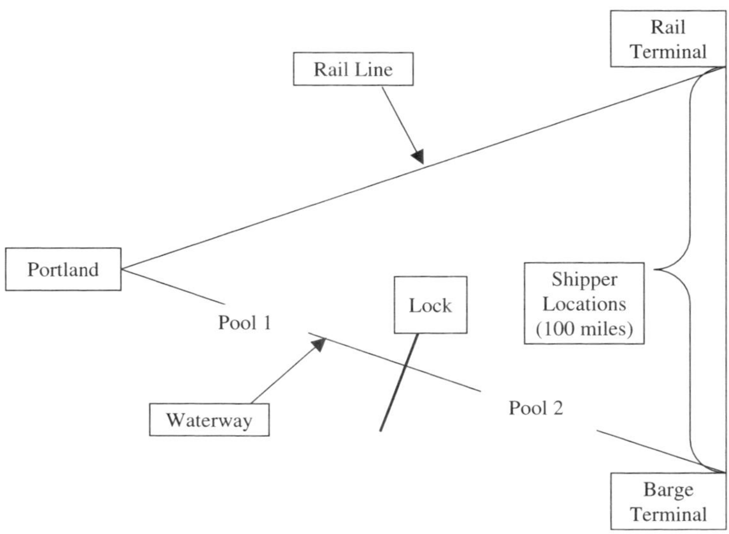

Fig. 6. Network for Illustration.

located two miles apart on a line connecting a barge access and a rail access facility. The access facilities are located 100 miles apart, and each is 350 miles from the terminal location.

Given the network structure, all barge quantities can be aggregated to the barge terminal and, thus, provide the origin–destination–commodity (ODC) triple that defines the demands that are commonly used in ACE modeling. The demand function is built on choice models, and the spatial environment of shippers. The demand function for the given structure and reference values is given in Fig. 7.

There are a total of 5,000 tons that move from the region. At high barge rates, very little moves by water, while, at very low barge rates, most moves by water. At the predicted barge rate of about \$9 per ton, about 3,500 tons move by water (given a rail rate).

An important characteristic of such demand equations is the effect of substitution as rates change. Below, we consider the effects of changes in the rail rate. In this case, we generate, in addition to that of Fig. 7, two additional demand schedules – one with the rail rate reduced by \$2 and one with the rail rate increased by \$2. The result is presented in Fig. 8. This figure indicates that when rail rates increase, the barge demand function shifts to the right, and when rail rates decrease it shifts to the left. The substitution effects appear quite large. Consider, for example, at a barge

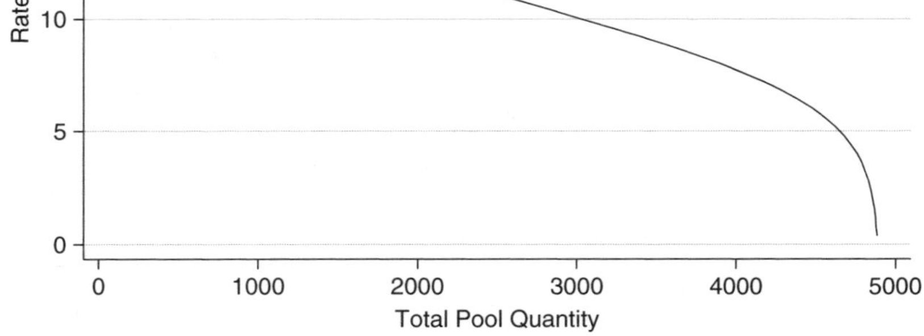

Fig. 7. Pool Level Demand for Spatially Separated Demanders.

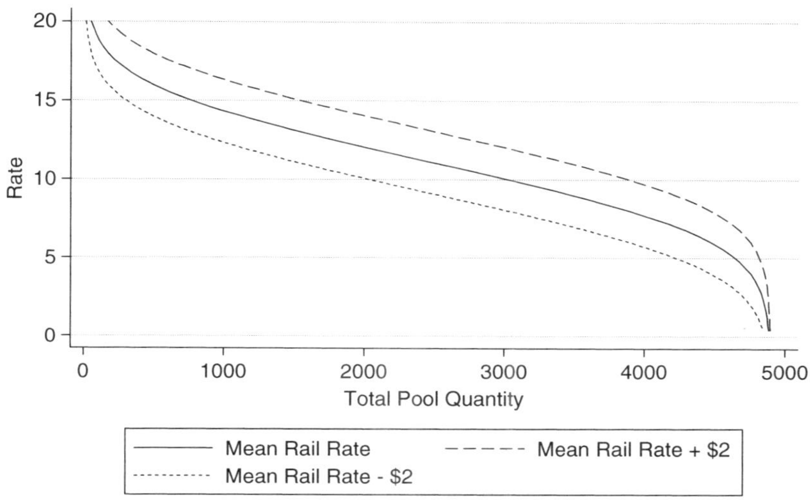

Fig. 8. Pool Level Barge Demands and Changes in Rail Rates.

rate of 10 the quantity moved at the mean rail rate is estimated as 3,031. However, if the rail rate falls \$2 from \$11.3 to \$9.3 per ton, the estimated quantity moved is about 2,036, a 32 percent decline.

7. EQUILIBRIUM AND CONCLUDING COMMENTS

Economic evaluations of markets are often made at fixed locations such as ports, pools, etc. However, the quantities shipped are from spatially distinct locations. The demands then are implicitly or explicitly generated from decisions made by spatially separated demanders. This research makes explicit the role of space in defining spatially aggregated demand functions which are central to establishing market clearing conditions to analyze the effects of policy. The spatially distributed demanders have options in moving goods to markets, and we illustrate in this paper that the choices made are directly connected to spatial considerations. The results illustrate not just choice modeling but also how the results can be used to inform ACE and other equilibrium models. In the specific case at hand, there is but one commodity–origin–destination triple. In this regard, equilibrium in the barge market obtains by adding the supply of barge transportation, equating the demand function above to supply and solving for the equilibrium *given rail rates*. Alternatively, rail supply (or pricing relations if railroads are not competitive) can be added to determine the rail and barge rates and quantities. In both cases, the total quantity moved is exogenous to the equilibrium. In this way, the equilibrium described here is equivalent to a modal split model (total quantity is moved is determined exogenously) such that only the modal split is endogenous.

There are a number of venues in which the apparatus above can be modified to allow for the total quantity moved to become endogenous, and the above framework can easily be adapted to accomplish this goal. In particular, the demand for transportation by mode as modeled above is the mirror image of the decision to supply the port by mode. This supply decision can be complicated by a myriad of factors that essentially capture reservation prices of shippers (supplier of wheat to Portland) to the Port (storage, alternative terminal markets such as local markets for ethanol). In all of these cases, this means that the supply function has a nonzero slope. Another source beyond alternative points to supply (storage, local markets, alternative export markets) is the intensity of production. In the present case, each shipper ships 100 tons. If prices were higher, it is plausible that shippers (for at least some products) could be induced to produce more. In the present case, the total supply to Portland is perfectly inelastic and the total demand for transportation is fixed for the time period of analysis. This allows the barge equilibrium to be separated from its up or downstream markets. In grain markets, the resulting equilibrium rate levels may impact the intensity of production vis-à-vis the planting decision of the next or future time period(s).

If the supply of products to the port has a nonzero slope, total supply, and therefore, transportation demand depends on the price at the Port. This model can be easily adapted to model equilibrium. Essentially, in our illustration, there is a demand for wheat in Portland that depends on a set of factors such as ocean rates to the importer both from Portland and other ports considered, demand factors in the foreign country, etc. This demand is set equal to the supply of the commodity in Portland *which is identically equal to the sum of quantities shipped by each transportation mode to Portland.* This equality defines equilibrium in the Portland export market given equilibrium in the barge market. In this model, total quantities shipped, barge demands, and supply of wheat to Portland by barge, each depends on prices in alternative market, exchange rates, ocean freight rates, demands and supplies in foreign countries. This is the classic Samuelson–Takayama Judge type framework (Samuelson, 1952; Takayama & Judge, 1964). Our contribution has been to aggregate the domestic supply of product by mode *in a full spatial framework*, and illustrate how transportation demand is a mirror image of supply by mode. Once estimated, the model can be adapted for a wide range of settings and shipper locations.

NOTES

1. Oum (1989), Oum, Waters, and Yong (1992), Winston (1983, 1985), and Small and Winston (1999) each provide comprehensive surveys of the transportation demand literature. Boyer (1997) discusses the need to model spatial differences among firms. Apart from discrete choice models, where econometricians may model differences in the choice set of different shippers, we are not aware of any model where access to modes is directly modeled.

2. See, for example, Winston (1981), Inaba and Wallace (1989), and Train and Wilson (2004, 2006, 2007). In the latter, Train and Wilson also combine revealed and stated preference data. Abdelwahab and Sargious (1992) also model shipment data using the Commodity Flow Survey. These data, as they recognize, do not have rate and shipment attributes available, but there is good information on shipments. They use supplemental data to provide the attribute data. In recent work, Sitchinava et al. (2006) use a tobit model with stated preference data to estimate the level of production as a function of rates. In their model, mode choice is exogenous, and the level of production provides for individual demand functions for different shippers.

3. See Wilson (1997), Bitzan (1999, 2003), Bitzan and Keeler (2007), and Ivaldi and McCullough (2001) for more complete discussions.

4. Anderson and Wilson (2004, 2005, 2007) develop theoretical models of spatial equilibrium and the locations of shippers under conditions of network congestion, pricing in spatial model, and the effects of space on the measurement of welfare vis-à-vis models used by ACE. The empirical research in this paper can be directly applied to their models.

5. The same framework can be applied to multiple market outlets. In the case of Eastern Washington, the bulk of shipments are to Portland (Jessup & Casavant, 2004, 2005) and allows the illustration in this paper to be more concise.

6. In addition, the level of rail car loading capacity (the number of rail cars that can be placed on the shipper's siding) is an attribute in the model. Shippers with larger capacities are able to access lower rail rates and may find that loading costs are much lower for a given shipment size.

7. In addition to rates and access costs, times in transit and reliability may also have an influence on demand decisions. These effects may fuel differences in modes which are captured in the alternative specific dummy variable. An alternative specific dummy variable is a standard term in choice modeling. There are two alternatives in this model. Barge is normalized to zero, and there is a rail dummy included in the specification. This captures unobserved differences in attributes across the alternatives.

8. We note that there are two types of variables. The car loading capacity variable is a shipper attribute. It does not vary across the choices. Rates and access costs are

alternative specific. That is, for any given shipper, these variables vary across the choice set. Both the alternative specific dummy and the car loading capacity variables require that they are normalized for identification (i.e., the ability to estimate the parameter). For both purposes, the coefficients on barge are normalized to zero, which means that the coefficients measure the effect on profit of rail relative to barge.

9. After adjusting for ineligible, return to sender, etc., the response rate was 70 percent for grain businesses and 35 percent for nongrain business.

10. In the survey instrument (see Jessup & Casavant, 2005), the six alternatives are: 1. truck to Pasco, WA, and then barge to Portland; 2. truck to a different river terminal then barge to Portland; 3. rail to Portland; 4. truck to rail, and rail to Portland; 5. barge to Portland; and 6. other.

11. Only two of these trucked to Portland, six were of nongrain products, and 21 reported destinations other than Portland. It is not known whether the destinations "other than Portland" were stops along the way to Portland or not. The other 20 did not provide any information.

12. A variety of other models were also examined. Specifically, we imposed a constraint that the coefficients on rate and access were identical. A likelihood ratio test yielded a *chi-square* statistic of 6.88 with one degree of freedom, which suggests that the restriction cannot be imposed at the 5-percent level. In addition, if only total rates matter, then the rail dummy and car loading capacity coefficients are both zero, and the rate and access coefficients equivalent. A likelihood ratio test with these three constraints yielded a *chi-square* statistic of 8.9, which suggests that the three restrictions cannot be imposed at the 5-percent level. Finally, a referee suggested that the choices may be jointly determined with capacity. To evaluate, we regressed capacity on distance from river, but did not find any statistically meaningful results. We also removed capacity from the model estimated and obtained estimates on the rate and access coefficients that were nearly identical to those reported.

13. This coefficient reflects systematic differences across attributes of the mode that are not included in the model (speed, reliability, etc.).

14. We also estimated the model with a linear specification. The results were very similar in terms of predicted values, and when the log predictions were converted to levels, the correlation between the two was in excess of .95. Because of the tapering principle, the rest of this paper is based on predictions from Eq. (4).

15. In related research, Train and Wilson (2004) provide evidence that the 100 tons shipped by each shipper is also a function of the rates confronted by shippers, and this relationship can also be integrated. For this illustration, quantities are taken as exogenous, but note that they can be integrated into the analysis.

16. This is in a statistical sense. For a shipper that has 100 tons, and a 60 percent chance of using barge, we use 60. An alternative would be to predict that they would use barge and allocate 100 tons to barge.

17. In this illustration, there is a single ODC market for barge services. In this frame of reference, the ODC demand is the demand for lock services. In more complicated settings, there might be multiple ODC markets which share the services of an individual lock. In those cases, equilibrium may be obtained by using either the ODC levels or by using aggregations of the ODC markets to form a demand for lock services.

REFERENCES

Abdelwahab, W., & Sargious, M. (1992). Modeling the demand for freight transportation. *Journal of Transport Economics and Policy*, *26*(1), 49–70.

Anderson, S., & Wilson, W. (2004). *Spatial modeling in transportation I: Congestion and mode choice*. Institute of Water Resources, Department of the Army Corps of Engineers. Available at http://www.corpsnets.us

Anderson, S., & Wilson, W. (2005). *Spatial modeling in transportation II: Railroad pricing, alternative markets, and capacity constraints*. Institute of Water Resources, Department of the Army Corps of Engineers. Available at http://www.corpsnets.us

Anderson, S., & Wilson, W. (2007). Spatial modeling in transportation. In: J. Plant (Ed.), *Handbook of transportation policy and administration*. Boca Raton, FL: CRC Press.

Berry, S., Hewings, G., & Levin, C. (2001). *The adequacy of research on Upper Mississippi-Illinois river navigation project*. Washington, DC: Northeast-Midwest Institute.

Bitzan, J. D. (1999). The structure of railroad costs and the benefits/costs of mergers. *Research in Transportation Economics*, *5*, 1–52.

Bitzan, J. D. (2003). Railroad costs and consolidation – The implications of introducing competition to railroad networks. *Journal of Transport Economics and Policy*, *37*(2), 201–225.

Bitzan, J. D., & Keeler, T. E. (2007). Economies of density and regulatory change in the U.S. railroad freight industry. *Journal of Law and Economics*.

Boyer, K. D. (1997). *Principles of transportation economics*. Reading, MA: Addison-Wesley.

Friedlaender, A. F., & Spady, R. H. (1980). A derived demand function for freight transportation. *The Review of Economics and Statistics*, *62*(3), 432–441.

Inaba, F. S., & Wallace, N. E. (1989). Spatial price competition and the demand for freight transportation. *The Review of Economics and Statistics*, *71*(4), 614–625.

Ivaldi, M., & McCullough, G. (2001). Density and integration effects on Class I U.S. freight railroads. *Journal of Regulatory Economics*, *19*(2), 161–182.

Jessup, E., & Casavant, K. L. (2004). Understanding grain movements for demand estimation: The Columbia-Snake river system in Washington State. Available at http://www.corpsnets.us, Accessed on June 15, 2005.

Jessup, E., & Casavant, K. L. (2005). Columbia/Snake river transportation study. NETS Report. Available at http://www.corpnets.us, Accessed on June 15, 2005.

National Research Council. (2001). *Inland navigation system planning: The Upper Mississippi river-Illinois waterway*. Washington, DC: National Academy Press.

National Research Council. (2004a). *Review of the U.S. army corps of engineers restructured Upper Mississippi-Illinois waterway feasibility study*. First Report. Washington, DC: National Academies Press.

National Research Council. (2004b). *Review of the U.S. army corps of engineers restructured Upper Mississippi-Illinois waterway feasibility study*. Second Report. Washington, DC: National Academies Press.

Oum, T. H. (1979). A cross-sectional study of freight transport demand and rail truck competition in Canada. *Bell Journal of Economics*, *10*, 274–287.

Oum, T. H. (1989). Alternative demand models and their elasticity estimates. *Journal of Transport Economics and Policy*, *5*, 163–187.

Oum, T. H., Waters, W.G. II, & Yong, J.-S. (1992). Concepts of price elasticities of transport demand and recent empirical estimates: An interpretative survey. *Journal of Transport Economics and Policy*, *26*(2), 139–169.

Samuelson, P. A. (1952). Spatial price equilibrium and linear programming. *American Economic Review*, *42*, 283–303.

Small, K. A., & Winston, C. (1999). The demand for transportation: Models and applications. In: G.-I. Jose, B. T. William & C. Winston (Eds), *Essays in transportation economics and policy: A handbook in honor of John R. Meyer* (pp. 11–56). Washington, DC: The Brookings Institution.

Takayama, T., & Judge, G. G. (1964). Equilibrium among spatially separated markets: A reformulation. *Econometrica*, *32*, 510–524.

Train, K., & Wilson, W. (2004). *Shippers' responses to changes in transportation rates and times: The Mid-American grain study.* Institute of Water Resources, Department of the Army Corps of Engineers.

Train, K., & Wilson, W. (2006). Spatial demand decisions in the pacific Northwest: Mode choices and market areas. *Transportation Research Record: Journal of the Transportation Research Board.* No. 1963, pp. 9–14.

Train, K., & Wilson, W. (2007, forthcoming). Econometric analysis of stated-preference experiments constructed from revealed-preference choices. *Transportation Research Part B.*

Westbrook, M. D., & Buckley, P. A. (1990). Flexible functional forms and regularity: Assessing the competitive relationship between truck and rail transportation. *The Review of Economics and Statistics*, *72*(4), 623–630.

Wilson, W. W. (1997). Cost savings and productivity gains in the railroad industry. *Journal of Regulatory Economics*, *11*, 21–40.

Wilson, W. W., Wilson, W. W., & Koo, W. W. (1988). Modal competition and pricing in grain transport. *Journal of Transport Economics and Policy*, *22*(3), 319–337.

Winston, C. (1981). A disaggregate model of the demand for intercity freight transportation. *Econometrica*, *49*(4), 981–1006.

Winston, C. (1983). The demand for freight transportation: Models and application. *Transportation Research A, 17A*, 419–427.

Winston, C. (1985). Conceptual developments in the economics of transportation. *Journal of Economic Literature*, *23*, 57–94.

Yu, T.-H. E., & Fuller, S. W. (2005). The measurement of grain barge demand on inland waterways: A study of the Upper Mississippi river. *Journal of the Transportation Research Forum*, *44*(1), 27–40.

RAIL PASSENGER DEMAND FORECASTING: CROSS-SECTIONAL MODELS REVISITED

Mark Wardman, William Lythgoe and Gerard Whelan

ABSTRACT

This chapter revisits cross-sectional models of rail travel demand, a much neglected area in recent years, by covering three developments in the context of inter-urban travel. First, the models are extended to allow a detailed analysis of catchment areas; the ticket-sales data that are used to estimate these models only cover journeys between stations. Second, access to and egress from stations are investigated by refining functions of population and accessibility to stations separately from rail service quality. The best models are achieved with inverted s*-shaped access and egress functions rather than assuming constant elasticity. Third, station choice is modeled using a multinomial logit model that yields fresh insights into rail travel demand.*

1. INTRODUCTION

Econometric demand models have for many years been used to provide important behavioral insights into the passenger railway businesses in many

Railroad Economics
Research in Transportation Economics, Volume 20, 119–152

ISSN: 0739-8859/doi:10.1016/S0739-8859(07)20005-8

countries (e.g., Lave, 1972; Bureau of Transport Economics, 1977; McGeehan, 1984; Owen & Phillips, 1987; Andrikopoulos & Brox, 1990; Koshal, Koshal, Gupta, & Nandola, 1996; Oum, Ooststroom, & Yoon, 1996; Coto-Millán, Banos-Pino, & Inglada, 1997; Rolle, 1997; Kulshreshtha & Nag, 2000; van Vuuren & Rietveld, 2002; Wardman, 2006). There has been particularly extensive application of these methods in Great Britain to a wide range of issues as is testified by the Passenger Demand Forecasting Handbook (PDFH), which is unique amongst railway administrations and has for over 20 years recommended a forecasting framework and set of demand parameters with a firm basis in empirical evidence (ATOC, 2005). Whilst this chapter focuses upon British evidence and specifically inter-urban travel, the methodological advances reported have broader interest and there is considerable potential to apply the methods in a suburban context.

The purpose of the research reported here was to revisit the neglected area of rail cross-sectional modeling with a view to advancing methodology and providing new empirical insights in areas where traditional time-series approaches can contribute little. The chapter essentially covers three developments. The first is based on a recognition of the potential of cross-sectional models, after many years in which time-series-based approaches have dominated, and addressed the issue of catchment areas around stations when the ticket-sales data, which forms the basis of the analysis, covers only the portion of the overall journey that is between stations. The second extends the investigation of access to and egress from stations, refining the functions used to represent population and accessibility to the rail network, and exploring whether it is better to consider the latter in isolation from or alongside the other aspects of rail service quality. The third extends the modeling approach to cover competition between stations and the extent to which new stations or improved services at existing stations generate new rail traffic or merely abstract it from elsewhere. The structure of the chapter is based around these three developments after placing the research into its background context.

2. BACKGROUND

Data on the number of trips and associated revenue between stations can provide a readily available, very large, and extremely valuable source of reliable information on rail travel behavior, and this has proved to be the case in Great Britain. The direct demand modeling approach (Manheim, 1973), so-called because it deals directly with variations in total rail demand rather than its separate components of trip generation, distribution, and mode choice, has allowed the estimation of a large number of influences on rail demand. These include: factors external to the rail industry, such as GDP, car ownership, employment levels, and competition from other modes (Fowkes, Nash, & Whiteing, 1985; Owen & Phillips, 1987; Wardman, 1997a, 2006; NERA, 1999; Steer Davies Gleave, 2003), various aspects of rail service quality, such as journey time, service frequency, interchange and rolling stock (Rail Operational Research, 1989a, 1993; Wardman, 1994, Wardman & Whelan, 2004); and fare (Rail Operational Research, 1989b; NERA, 2003; Wardman & Toner, 2003).

What is common to all the studies cited above is that either they were based purely on time-series data or else, more commonly, they pooled data across routes but rely on time-series variations for their informational content. Time-series data has underpinned much analysis and yields unique insights into lagged adjustments in behavior, time trends, and asymmetries between the effects of improvements and deteriorations in travel attributes. Even though early rail direct demand models in the United States (Quandt & Baumol, 1966) and Great Britain (Tyler & Hassard, 1973; White & Williams, 1976) tended to be cross-sectional in nature, a contributory factor here was the absence of sufficiently long and reliable time-series data, and as soon as such data became available, through advances in information technology, models estimated to purely cross-sectional data became extremely rare.

In part, this was because of concerns regarding identification and the isolation of cause and effect, although the issue of whether, for example, high-service frequency is the cause or consequence of high demand arises for time series as well as cross-sectional models. The specification of station catchment areas when, as with ticket sales data, the precise origin and destination of travelers is not known, was not adequately addressed and this failure also contributed to the demise of cross-sectional models. For example, some rail travelers do not use their most local station but instead 'railhead' at a key regional station to take advantage of its better levels of service quality. Failing to specify the true extent of the catchment areas of major stations, where service quality is good or overstating the catchment areas of stations with poorer service quality where traffic is lost to competing stations will lead to inflated service quality elasticity estimates.

Cross-sectional models, in practice, typically relate the volume (V) of rail demand between stations i and j to factors which generate trips from a station, factors which attract trips to a station, and variables which characterize the attractiveness of the rail service between stations. We here simply represent these as a measure of population around the origin station (P_i)

and the destination station (P_j), and the generalized cost of travel by train between i and j (GC_{ij}), although a wide range of other terms could be entered. In typical constant elasticity form, this is specified as

$$V_{ij} = \mu P_i^{\alpha} P_j^{\beta} GC_{ij}^{\gamma} \tag{1}$$

GC typically contains the fare for travel between i and j and the levels of time, service frequency, and interchange after their conversion into equivalent monetary amounts. It does not include the time and cost of accessing and egressing the rail network.

Casual inspection of rail ticket sales data reveals that it exhibits enormous variations across routes and that it is clearly the generating and attracting variables, and notably the population around origin and destination stations, that drive this difference in the magnitude of trips. We refer to this cross-sectional dimension as the 'size' effect. The specification of the population terms is, therefore critical, with the attractiveness of rail having a lesser influence in varying rail demand around this basic size.

The size effect is not generally an issue in pure time-series models, since it can often be reasonably assumed that the generating and attracting potential of stations do not vary much over time or else can be discerned by time trend terms. However, the size effect must be addressed in models which contain a cross-sectional dimension.

As far as British cross-sectional evidence is concerned, we are aware of six studies. All of them report population elasticities for the origin, with nine estimates in total, whilst three report destination population elasticities. Holt and White (1981) and Jones and White (1994) used the population in each station's local authority area, with adjustments for obvious anomalies, whilst Wardman (1983, 1996) reports models based on crudely specified population terms relating to the district around the station. Tyler and Hassard (1973) weighted population according to distance from the station, although the weights were not directly estimated. Preston (1991) specified the population that was up to 800 m from a local station and between 800 m and 2 km from a station, as well as a model estimated to a different data set which only specified the former population term.

The origin population elasticity estimates range from 0.16 to 0.77, with the remaining estimates in the range 0.34–0.65 and a mean of 0.53. The destination population elasticity estimates average 0.77. Whilst there is a high degree of consistency in the estimated population elasticities, the specification of the catchment areas is far from ideal. The crude specification of the district population is clearly unsatisfactory whilst even if the best single population band around a station is selected no account is taken of the impact that distance from the station has on the propensity to make a rail trip and all stations are forced to have the same size catchment area. Population elasticities so far short of one could be a symptom of the failure to correctly specify station catchments.

It makes sense to pool data over a cross-section of flows and over time periods since then there is more data than a pure time series or cross-section and generally more variation in it, both of which impact beneficially on the precision with which demand parameters are estimated. The research issue is, therefore, not that cross-sectional data is revisited, since it is present alongside time-series data in many studies, but that the size effect is revisited and the insights that this can provide into rail demand are exploited to the fullest extent possible. Hence, we should regard the specification of catchment areas not as a problem but rather as an opportunity to obtain behavioral insights not possible with time-series data.

Just as the time-series dimension is well suited to the analysis of particular issues so the cross-sectional dimension brings its own unique information and a number of opportunities to obtain better understanding of rail travel behavior. These are:

- The ability to predict the total number of trips between stations and to allocate these to actual origins and destinations, rather than to simply increment from current demand levels using elasticities. Forecasting the demand for new stations and services is critically dependent upon such models.
- The estimation of access and egress elasticities denoting how improved accessibility to and from the rail network impacts on rail demand. Increasingly, rail operators are appreciating that they should concern themselves with the whole journey rather than just the on-train portion.
- The analysis of competition between stations, since abstraction from other stations might be important in appraisal. Indeed, the models are well suited to the analysis of other choice contexts which are inherently cross-sectional, such as competition between different routes or operators. The rail market in many countries is becomingly increasingly characterized by competition.
- The opportunity to analyze demand sensitivity to rail service quality and cost in the context of the generalized cost of the overall journey rather than just the rail component.
- The analysis of the impact of a range of socio-economic, demographic, and land use variables whose accurate representation and hence reliable

estimation are often dependent upon the specification of station catchments.
- The analysis of variables that do not vary greatly over time, and hence whose effects cannot be reliably estimated using time-series data, but which do exhibit cross-sectional variation.

3. ENHANCING THE CATCHMENT AREA SPECIFICATION

3.1. Enhanced Cross-Sectional Models: The Data

The data used in model estimation related to the volume of trips in 1994 on 4222 Non London flows over 30 miles. This data set contained 124 origin stations and the same number of destination stations. The measure of fare was the commonly used average revenue per trip. The measure of service quality used was the generalized journey time (GJT) of the railway industry's MOIRA system. GJT contains station-to-station journey time, and after conversion into equivalent journey time units, service headway and the number of interchanges required. A detailed description of the construction of this composite term is provided in Wardman, Shires, Lythgoe, and Tyler (2004).

A range of other information was obtained in order to examine the generating and attracting potential of stations and the effects of different levels of accessibility to the rail network. For each of eight bands around each of our stations, the CACI InSite system was used to provide information on population, average household income, car ownership, employment status, socio-economic group, age, gender, and drive time to the station. These concentric rings around stations effectively formed the origin zones a and destination zones b of Eq. (5), and were based on drive times of 4, 6, 8, 10, 15, 20, 30, and 45 min. All but the income and drive times were derived from the 1991 Census.

3.2. Enhanced Cross-Sectional Models: Empirical Results

Station catchment areas can be addressed through the use of dummy variable terms. If there are p origin stations and q destination stations, and assuming that the only other variable is the generalized cost of rail which enters in constant elasticity form, we can specify the cross-sectional model as

$$V_{ij} = \mu M_i N_j \mathrm{GC}_{ij}^{\delta} \tag{2}$$

The M_i and N_j are dummy parameters relating to the origin and destination stations. This is analogous to the specification of flow-specific dummy variables in fixed effect panel models that pool data across time and routes, although in a pure cross-sectional model we cannot specify dummy variables for each flow since we have only one observation per flow. However, we do have some flexibility, such as allowing a station's generating or attracting coefficients to vary with, for example, the type of flow or journey distance.

Whilst this formulation overcomes mis-specification problems, it misses the opportunity to obtain better insights into the determinants of the size effect. It tells us little of the factors which generate and attract trips, notable amongst these being the size and distribution of population around stations, and it is not readily transferable to forecast demand at stations for which generation and attraction terms have not been specified. Nor does it examine station choice or other aspects of competition within the rail market. However, these are not problems if we are concerned primarily with the elasticities to the other elements of the demand model.

We have argued that the inappropriate specification of the size effect could impact on other parameters estimated in the model. In Wardman (1996), the GC elasticity for a large data set of Non London flows varied from −2.6 in the model based on Eq. (2) to −4.2 when local district populations are used instead. The former is much more in line with industry recommendations (ATOC, 2005) than is the latter.

We can enhance the standard approach of Eq. (1) to explicitly include access and egress terms, and a range of socio-economic, demographic, and land use factors which influence the generating potential of origins and the attracting potential of destinations. Ignoring the socio-economic, demographic, and situational factors and transport variables other than the generalized cost of rail, simply for ease of exposition, the number of trips between zone a around the origin station i and zone b around the destination station j can be specified in constant elasticity form as

$$V_{aijb} = \mu P_a^{\alpha} P_b^{\beta} A_{ai}^{\delta} E_{bj}^{\lambda} \mathrm{GC}_{ij}^{\gamma} \tag{3}$$

A_{ai} and E_{bj} represent access to the origin station i from the origin zone a and egress from the destination station j to the destination zone b. These might be journey times or more ideally generalized costs. The generating potential of zone a is represented simply by its population (P_a) and the attracting potential of zone b by its population (P_b).

This is simply a direct demand model specified for movements between a and b which use the i–j rail service. Note that unlike conventional rail demand models, the terms A_{ai} and E_{bj} enter the equation. However, we cannot observe V_{aijb} since rail ticket sales data records travel only between the stations i and j (V_{ij}) and not between the ultimate origin a and destination b. We proceed by noting that the demand between stations i and j is made up of the rail demand from each of the origins a to each of the destinations b, which use services between stations i and j.

$$V_{ij} = \sum_a \sum_b V_{aijb} \tag{4}$$

Given the V_{aijb} demand function of Eq. (3) and substituting into Eq. (4), the model calibrated to station-to-station flows becomes:

$$V_{ij} = \left(\sum_a P_a^{\alpha} A_{ai}^{\delta} \sum_b P_b^{\beta} E_{bj}^{\lambda} \right) \quad \mathrm{GC}_{ij}^{\gamma} \tag{5}$$

The generating potential of station i is the sum across the a zones of the population effects weighted by the deterrence due to the times and costs involved in station access. Similarly, the attracting potential of station j is a weighted sum of the population in each of the b zones around the station and the times and costs involved in station egress. These relationships are intuitively reasonable. We term this a summation model.

The parameters of Eq. (5) can be directly estimated using non-linear least squares. It represents an advance over models which do not recognize the catchment area issue. Although the precise origins and destinations are unknown, we have expressed a known variable in terms of unknown variables but in turn these unknown variables are related to observable travel variables and other relevant factors.

The model can be readily extended to include other terms. Variables which are specific to origin zones, such as car ownership, income levels, and occupation, enter the first summation term. Similarly, variables which are specific to destination zones, such as employment or shopping opportunities, enter the second summation term. Factors which are common to all combinations of zonal movements, such as the journey time and cost of competing coach and air services, enter outside the brackets alongside GC_{ij}. The model can be extended to cover competition from other stations by entering terms relating to the access to or egress from the 'rival' stations along with the generalized cost for the competing station-to-station movements. However, it would be preferable to explicitly include a station choice element and this is addressed in Section 9.

The aim here is not only to estimate the enhanced model of Eq. (5), but also to demonstrate its superiority over other more typical approaches and hence a range of models have been estimated. These are reported in Table 1. In all cases, we used a generalized cost (GC) measure, because of the high correlation between GJT and fare in this pure cross-sectional data set, and a value of time of 10 pence per min was used in creating it. GC enters each model in the conventional constant elasticity form.

Model I contains dummy variables to represent the generating potential of origin stations and the attracting potential of destination stations as in Eq. (2). Model II is based on a crude specification of the catchment areas of the origin and destination stations, based upon the population of the district in which each station lies, and it takes the form

$$V_{ij} = \mu P_i^{\alpha} P_j^{\beta} \mathrm{GC}_{ij}^{\gamma} \tag{6}$$

These two models serve as reference points for the other models developed since Model I provides a very good representation of generation and attraction effects, but Model II is expected to be poor in this regard.

Model III has the same form as Model II but attempts to improve upon it through the identification of the single population band around the origin stations and destination stations, which provide the best fit to the data. The population bands are constrained to be the same across each origin station and destination station, and the model does not contain any accessibility effects.

Model IV develops Model III by entering a series of population terms according to drive times to the station, although again access and egress effects are not explicitly entered into the model. Preston (1991) developed models to explain local rail trips as a function of, amongst other things, the population up to 800 m and between 800 m and 2 km from a station. Separate parameters were estimated for the populations in the two distance bands. Model IV is such a model which enters separate population terms for the drive time bands. Model IVa enters the population terms in a multiplicative fashion along the same lines as Preston (1991). It takes the form

$$V_{ij} = \mu \prod_{a=1}^{p} P_a^{\alpha_a} \prod_{b=1}^{q} P_b^{\beta_b} \mathrm{GC}_{ij}^{\gamma} \tag{7}$$

There are p zones related to each origin station i and q zones related to each destination station j and for each a separate parameter is estimated.

Table 1. Estimated Models.

Model		Adjusted R^2	GC	Origin Population	Destination Population
I	*O* and *D* dummies (Eq. (2))	0.932	−2.02 (±1.5%)	n.a.	n.a.
II	Crude population (Eq. (6))	0.631	−1.72 (±2.9%)	0.79 (±5.5%)	0.87 (±5.0%)
III	Single band (Eq. (6))				
	$O = 10, D = 15$	0.631	−1.72 (±2.9%)	0.91 (±5.4%)	0.85 (±5.1%)
	$O = 15, D = 10$	0.633	−1.72 (±2.9%)	0.80 (±5.3%)	0.97 (±5.1%)
	$O = 15, D = 15$	0.638	−1.68 (±3.0%)	0.82 (±5.2%)	0.87 (±5.0%)
	$O = 15, D = 20$	0.621	−1.67 (±3.1%)	0.81 (±5.5%)	0.78 (±5.3%)
	$O = 20, D = 15$	0.620	−1.67 (±3.1%)	0.74 (±5.8%)	0.85 (±5.2%)
	Distance band populations				
IVa	Multiplicative (Eq. (7))	0.734	−1.89 (±2.4%)	$\alpha_1 = -0.13$ (±41.1%)	$\beta_1 = -0.16$ (±34.3%)
				$\alpha_2 = -0.52$ (±24.3%)	$\beta_2 = -0.86$ (±14.9%)
				$\alpha_3 = 1.31$ (±18.3%)	$\beta_3 = 1.99$ (±12.0%)
				$\alpha_4 = -0.42$ (±58.5%)	$\beta_4 = -0.67$ (±35.4%)
				$\alpha_5 = 0.39$ (±61.5%)	$\beta_5 = 0.08$ (±197.4%)
				$\alpha_6 = 0.65$ (±36.6%)	$\beta_6 = 1.23$ (±19.4%)
				$\alpha_7 = -0.20$ (±99.5%)	$\beta_7 = -0.63$ (±28.8%)
				$\alpha_8 = -0.49$ (±22.0%)	$\beta_8 = -0.41$ (±25.7%)

IVb	Additive 1 (Eq. (8))	0.661	−1.69 (±2.8%)	$\alpha_1 = 1.05$ (±7.6%) $\alpha_2 = 0.96$ (±9.7%) $\alpha_3 = 1.07$ (±6.5%) $\alpha_4 = 0.91$ (±11.8%) $\alpha_5 = 0.97$ (±6.8%)	$\beta_1 = 1.18$ (±6.6%) $\beta_2 = 0.94$ (±22.2%) $\beta_3 = 1.22$ (±5.7%) $\beta_4 = 0.99$ (±12.9%) $\beta_5 = 1.06$ (±6.4%)
IVc	Additive 2 (Eq. (9))	0.665	−1.70 (±2.9%)	$\delta_1 = 1.0$ $\delta_2 = 0.24$ (±66.6%) $\delta_3 = 1.15$ (±23.5%)) $\delta_4 = 0.18$ (±88.8%) $\delta_5 = 0.50$ (±24.0%) $\delta_6 = -0.15$ (±40.0%) $\alpha = 1.03$ (±7.0%)	$\lambda_1 = 1.0$ $\lambda_2 = -0.07$(±154.3%) $\lambda_3 = 1.46$ (±17.8%) $\lambda_4 = 0.09$ (±111.1%) $\lambda_5 = 0.35$ (±23.1%) $\lambda_6 = -0.10$ (±40.8%) $\beta = 1.17$ (±6.0%)
V	Summation (No. A or E) (Eq. (5))	0.637	−1.69 (±3.0%)	0.81 (±5.9%)	0.87 (±5.5%)
VI	Summation (Incl. A & E) (Eq. (5))				
	$O = 10$, $D = 15$	0.638	−1.73 (±2.8%)	0.87 (±8.9%)	1.16 (±6.7%)
	$O = 15$, $D = 10$	0.637	−1.73 (±2.9%)	0.99 (±7.8%)	0.95 (±8.1%)
	$O = 15$, $D = 15$	0.648	−1.71 (±2.9%)	1.01 (±7.6%)	1.14 (±6.5%)
	$O = 15$, $D = 20$	0.643	−1.71 (±2.9%)	1.01 (±7.6%)	1.20 (±6.2%)
	$O = 20$, $D = 15$	0.642	−1.71 (±2.9%)	1.05 (±7.3%)	1.16 (±6.6%)

Note: 95% confidence levels in parentheses.

Model IVb enters the population terms in an additive manner and takes the form

$$V_{ij} = \left(\mu \sum_{a=1}^{p} P_a^{\alpha_a} \sum_{b=1}^{q} P_b^{\beta_b}\right) \mathrm{GC}_{ij}^{\gamma} \tag{8}$$

Model IVc is a variant on Model IVb in that the powers on the population terms (α and β) are constrained to be the same across the population bands but instead there are scalars (δs and λs) associated with the population in each distance band. The model takes the form

$$V_{ij} = \mu \left(\sum_{a=1}^{p} \delta_a P_a^{\alpha} \sum_{b=1}^{q} \lambda_b P_b^{\beta}\right) \mathrm{GC}_{ij}^{\gamma} \tag{9}$$

The δs and λs effectively discern the distance decay effect. The advantage of this is that since the δs and λs are specific to different distance bands, variations in access and egress modes by distance, which are not otherwise accounted for, and non-linearities in distance decay can be discerned. However, there is no guarantee that the estimated δs and λs will be a monotonically decreasing function of distance whilst they do not possess the elegant properties of Eq. (5) with its direct estimates of the access and egress elasticities.

Model V is a special case of the ‘summation’ model of Eq. (5) because the access and egress terms are removed. It is Model IVb but with the population term constrained to be the same across all distance bands. Model VI is the ‘summation’ model of Eq. (5) and is the only one to contain access time to the station and egress time from the station as explicit variables.

Models I, II, III, and IVa are estimated by ordinary least squares and the remaining are estimated by non-linear least squares.

We had expected the GC elasticity to vary across the different model specifications, since a poor specification of station catchments could lead to an inflated service quality elasticity. However, there is little variation in the GC elasticity across the models, and in each case it is extremely precisely estimated. Whilst it is difficult to assess the GC elasticity with evidence from other studies, since it is rarely estimated in this inter-urban rail demand context, we can examine the plausibility of the implied elasticities to the fare and GJT components of GC. These elasticities depend upon the proportion that each variable forms of overall GC. Given that fare forms 40% of GC, a GC elasticity of −1.8 implies fare and GJT elasticities of −0.72 and −1.08. The recommended PDFH elasticities (ATOC, 2005) are −1.0 for fare and between −0.7 and −1.1 for GJT according to whether the GJT change was driven by interchange variation or not. A central value of −0.9 would seem reasonable. The results obtained here are reasonably similar, and we should bear in mind that the value of time used in creating GC might not be the most appropriate. Nonetheless, the sum of the GJT and fare elasticities should equal the GC elasticity and the sum of the recommended elasticities of -1.9 is very similar to that estimated.

We can see that not only does Model I provide, as expected, the best fit to the data but also the goodness of fit is very high. Other, more flexible and informative modeling approaches, must aspire to this level of fit.

Model II has, as expected, one of the worst fits of the models reported. Nonetheless, the population elasticities are broadly in line with those of previous studies. Indeed, the population elasticities are almost the same as Model III that has the single catchment area that gives the best fit to the data of 15 min drive time around both the origin and the destination stations. Nor is the fit of Model III much better than for Model II's crude specification of catchment areas. The main shortcoming of Model III is that the population beyond 15 min drive time is not allowed to influence rail demand yet all other population has the same propensity to make rail trips.

Models IVa, IVb, and IVc each allow for the population parameters to vary across drive time bands. Separate terms were specified for each distance band for Model IVa. For Model IVb, convergence of the iterative estimation procedure could not be achieved when all eight distance bands were specified and instead only five were entered. Model IVc requires that one weight for the origin and destination population is normalized to one and the other coefficients are interpreted in relation to this.

These three models all achieve better fits to the data than all the others except Model I. Model IVa, which enters population in multiplicative form, performs particularly well, even though the additive representation of Models IVb and IVc seems intuitively more reasonable. However, each model has notable limitations. In Models IVa and IVc the population parameters do not exhibit any clear pattern and indeed there are several instances where they are wrong sign. All the parameters in Model IVb are correct sign, and highly statistically significant, but we would have expected the population effect to diminish with distance from the station. Nor do any of these models contain explicit terms denoting the adverse impact on demand of increasing access times to and from stations.

Model V contains population terms up to 15 min for origin and destination stations since this provided the best fit. In comparison with Model VI, the results seem to confirm the possibility that the absence of access and egress terms is a cause of lower population elasticities.

Model VI contains access and egress time elasticities which improve the fit as would be expected. The best fitting model is for 15 min drive time catchment areas around both origin and destination stations. The population elasticities exhibit noticeable variation according to the catchment area specified but the estimated access and egress elasticities are not particularly sensitive to the different catchments. The key attraction of Model VI is in terms of the additional insights it provides. The estimated access elasticity is −0.61 (±28.3%) whilst the estimated egress elasticity is −0.82 (±18.9%). These are estimated very precisely and seem reasonable in absolute and in relation to each other.

Comparison of the access and egress elasticities with other evidence is not straightforward. Whilst mode choice models contain terms relating to out-of-vehicle time, the implied elasticities are volatile given the form of the elasticity function in logit models. The out-of-vehicle time term also tends to include a wait time component. However, we can compare the access elasticity with that estimated by Wardman and Tyler (2000) to variations in rail trip rates obtained from survey data according to the journey time from the station. The access elasticities estimated for the same sort of Non London inter-urban flows were −0.47 (±17.1%) for leisure travel and −0.53 (±12.5%) for business travel. The elasticities estimated by the two means are encouragingly similar.

It is no surprise that egress time elasticity exceeds the access time elasticity since there will tend to be fewer egress modes available at the destination station and also greater uncertainties as to how to get to the ultimate destination.

Further enhancements were made to Model VI in terms of the inclusion of socio-economic variables whose representation relies on the accurate specification of catchment areas. The following statistically significant effects were obtained:

- Income elasticity 0.52 (±63%)
- Car ownership elasticity −0.79 (±23%)
- % Students 0.30 (±32%)
- % Professional/managerial −0.68 (±21%)
- % Non-manual 1.27 (±22%)
- % Skilled −0.55 (±38%)

Income has an expected positive effect on rail demand whilst increases in car ownership, separate from the income effect that drives it, would lead to fewer rail trips. Both elasticities are plausible. As the number of students in a catchment increases, so the number of rail trips increases. There is also a positive effect from the proportion who are non-manual workers. However, both the skilled and professional/managerial socio-economic categories make fewer rail trips.

We have shown that enhanced cross-sectional models which provide important insights into catchment areas and the effects of access and egress time can be developed using ticket sales data where the precise origin and destination of travelers is not known. The pattern that seems to have emerged is that the GC elasticity is not particularly sensitive to the specification of the catchment area but the population elasticity is. The advances reported here provide a basis for further developments which are discussed below.

4. MORE DETAILED INVESTIGATION OF ACCESS TIME EFFECTS

Two further developments are addressed in this section. One is the specification of the zones around stations and the other is more detailed analysis of the functional relationship between demand and both access and egress time.

4.1. Zoning System

The research reported in Section 5 was based on population zones specified by 'isochrones' (contours of equal drive times) around the origin and destination stations. Mainly in anticipation of the models discussed in Section 9, we replaced these zones with the zoning system based around a station as illustrated in Fig. 1. The zones were also used for the access and egress time models reported in Section 8 since there is an intention to further develop these models to include directional effects.

In general, the zoning systems used in earlier models, such as in Tyler and Hassard (1973) and the models reported in Section 5, take no account of the direction of the rail journey, nor of the direction of the access journey. However, it could be surmised that the sizes and shapes of catchment areas will be affected by both the distance and direction of the destination, and also by the impact of competing stations. It is expected, for instance, that those traveling in the direction of the rail journey will be prepared to accept longer access times than those traveling in the opposite direction.

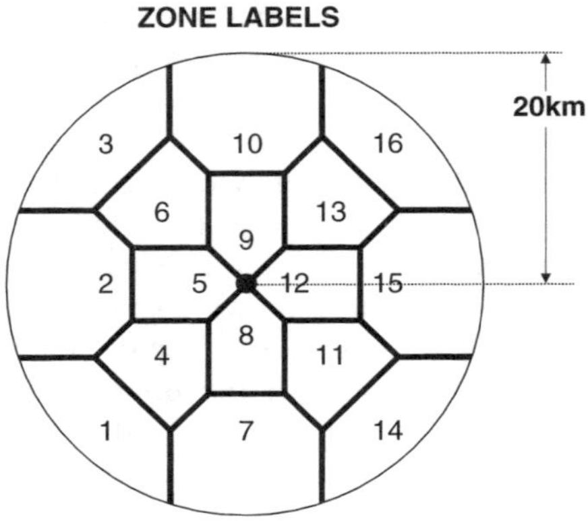

Fig. 1. Station Catchment Area Zoning System.

The choice of a new zoning system was, therefore, dictated by several considerations. The number of zones was chosen to be manageable in the first instance. It is desirable to ensure that within-zone variations in access times and distances to stations (including competing stations) are low relative to between-zone variations; and circular zones would be compact and, therefore, attractive in this respect. The impact of zonal population on the number of trips made from a given station will decrease as the distance from the zone to the station increases, so that larger populations, with larger within-zone variations, are more acceptable in the zones that are further from the station. Allocating population to a zone by finding a nearest 'seed point' is relatively easy, and the resulting zones are polygons (see Fig. 1) which roughly approximate to circles.

For the new zoning system, access times and distances from a zonal center of population, determined using a geographical information system (GIS) representation of the road network, are a reasonable representation of these variables for individual residents of that zone. In contrast, it should be noted that for the earlier models, this property only holds for access to the station on which their zones (the concentric circles) are centered, while access times and distances from different parts of one of these zones to competing stations would vary greatly. Therefore, within-zone variations in access times and distances to competing stations using the grid of zones set out in Fig. 1 are much lower than with the earlier models. This means that models using this new zoning system can now better address the effect of competition from other possible origin stations (or, where applicable, destination stations) than the earlier models, and these are discussed in Section 9. Furthermore, even without considering competing stations, the new zoning system facilitates catchment areas which properly account for the direction of a given rail journey relative to the direction of the access journey.

4.2. Functional Relationship of Access and Egress Time

The research reported in Section 5 not only entered access and egress as separate terms outside of the other time-related variables but also, as is conventional, specified them in constant elasticity form. This functional form does not necessarily provide the best account of the distance decay effect and instead empirical analysis should identify the most appropriate form. A further issue is that it is possible to specify access and egress within an extended GJT expression. The model would take the form

$$V_{aijb} = \mu \mathrm{AEGJT}^{\gamma}_{aijb} F^{\tau}_{ij} P^{u}_{a} P^{v}_{b} \tag{10}$$

where F is the fare and the enhanced GJT term (AEGJT) is composed as

$$\mathrm{AEGJT}_{aijb} = \mathrm{GJT}_{ij} + v_{\mathrm{A}} A_{ai} + v_{\mathrm{E}} E_{bj} \tag{11}$$

Ideally, the weights attached to access time (v_{A}) and egress time (v_{E}) would be freely estimated, and this is possible using the non-linear least squares estimation procedure, but there remains the possibility, if necessary, of using pre-defined values based on available empirical evidence.

By specifying access and egress time within generalized journey time, the implied elasticities to access (e_{A}) and egress time (e_{E}) depend upon the proportion they form of the enhanced GJT.

$$e_{\mathrm{A}} = \gamma \frac{v_{\mathrm{A}} A}{\mathrm{AEGJT}} \tag{12}$$

$$e_{\mathrm{E}} = \gamma \frac{v_{\mathrm{E}} E}{\mathrm{AEGJT}} \tag{13}$$

Thus, shorter distance journeys would tend to have larger access and egress elasticities, whilst the elasticities to the other components of GJT would be lower where access and egress times are higher. Such relationships are intuitively appealing, but they should be the subject of empirical verification rather than being imposed by default.

If we are content to retain separate access and egress time from GJT, we have more flexibility in specifying functions relating to these terms and we can examine them in more detail. The starting point here is the model specified as Eq. (5) in Section 3 which has separate constant elasticities to access and egress time. As a result of concerns raised in Wardman and Whelan (2004) about the appropriate values of time to use in constructing generalized cost, we have here retained fare and GJT as separate terms. The constant elasticity model is therefore

$$V_{ij} = \mu \mathrm{GJT}_{ij}^{\lambda} F_{ij}^{\tau} \sum_a A_a^{\alpha_1} P_a^u \sum_b E_b^{\alpha_2} P_b^v \tag{14}$$

We can instead allow the population elasticity to be defined relative to the access/egress weighted catchment area population rather than the zone-specific population. The model then takes the form

$$V_{ij} = \mu \mathrm{GJT}_{ij}^{\gamma} F_{ij}^{\tau} \left(\sum_a A_a^{\alpha_1} P_a \right)^u \left(\sum_b E_b^{\alpha_2} P_b \right)^v \tag{15}$$

In both these models, the population in zones further away from the station quite sensibly receives less weight than those close to the station. In Eq. (14), the access and egress time elasticities are expressed as α_1 and α_2, and in Eq. (15) they are expressed as $u\alpha_1$ and $v\alpha_2$.

The specification of the population elasticity of demand as in Eq. (15) turns out to be statistically superior. In addition to providing a better fit to the data, a practical advantage of the catchment area population elasticity specification is that stations can be retained that have zones with zero population (for example, as a result of off-coast zones) since the elasticity is estimated relative to the station catchment area and not the individual zone. These models contain substantially more observations. Hence in all the models reported here, which deal with the issue of functional form, only the specification based on what we have termed station catchment area population is reported. Both sets of models for each functional form can be found in Wardman and Whelan (2004).

However, it may be that constant access and egress elasticities are not the most appropriate functions. For example, it is not inconceivable that the rate at which rail trips per head decay with distance is relatively minor within the urban area around the station but then falls off dramatically outside of the built-up area. To examine this particular 'distance decay' effect, four alternative access and egress functional specifications are considered, including the exponential, logit, Gompertz, and quadratic decay functions.

The exponential decay function shows a proportional elasticity to access and egress time and takes the form

$$V_{ij} = \mu \mathrm{GJT}_{ij}^{\gamma} F_{ij}^{\tau} \left(\sum_a \exp(\alpha_1 A_a) P_a \right)^u \left(\sum_b \exp(\alpha_2 E_b) P_b \right)^v \tag{16}$$

The access and egress elasticities are $u\alpha_1 A$ and $v\alpha_2 E,$ and again the population in zones further away from the station receives less weight.

The logit decay function shows a relatively small initial distance decay effect but as access and egress times increase the effect becomes increasingly stronger then the rate of distance decay begins to slow once again. This functional specification shows an inverted s-shaped decay curve. The demand model is specified as

$$V_{ij} = \mu \mathrm{GJT}_{ij}^{\gamma} F_{ij}^{\tau} \left(\sum_a \frac{\exp(\alpha_1 + \beta_1 A_a)}{1 + \exp(\alpha_1 + \beta_1 A_a)} P_a \right)^u \left(\sum_b \frac{\exp(\alpha_2 + \beta_2 E_b)}{1 + \exp(\alpha_2 + \beta_2 E_b)} P_b \right)^v \tag{17}$$

Similar to the logit function, the Gompertz decay function has an inverted s-shape but unlike the logit function it is not symmetrical around its mid-point.

$$V_{ij} = \mu \mathrm{GJT}_{ij}^{\gamma} F_{ij}^{\tau} \left(\sum_a \left(1 - \exp\left(\alpha_1 \exp\left(\beta_1 A_a\right)\right)\right) P_a \right)^u \left(\sum_b \left(1 - \exp\left(\alpha_2 \exp\left(\beta_2 E_b\right)\right)\right) P_b \right)^v \tag{18}$$

Finally, the quadratic distance decay function gives more weight to population in zones close to the station than population in zones further away. This functional specification assigns a zero weight to zonal population beyond an empirically determined threshold.

$$V_{ij} = \mu \mathrm{GJT}_{ij}^{\gamma} F_{ij}^{\tau} \left(\sum_a \left(1 - \alpha_1 A_a^2\right) P_a \right)^u \left(\sum_b \left(1 - \alpha_2 E_b^2\right) P_b \right)^v \tag{19}$$

These different functions have been empirically tested and the results are reported below, where we also illustrate the different shapes of these ‘distance decay’ functions.

4.3. Ticket Sales Data for Accessibility and Station Choice Modeling

The ticket sales data used in the detailed analysis of access to stations, and in the subsequent analysis of station competition, is not the same as that used in the analysis reported in Section 5. Whilst it also relates to non-season ticket sales on inter-urban flows, a much larger data set became available for financial year 1999/2000. However, the 1991 Census was still relied upon for the socio-economic and demographic data.

GJT data was supplied by the railway industry to go alongside the revenue and volume data for each flow. Revenue per trip was again used as a measure of fare. Data on the road network for the whole of Great Britain was downloaded in the form of 1:2,50,000 Ordnance Survey 'Strategi' tiles from EDINA/Digimap, and converted to a MapInfo GIS compatible format. Road distance and time matrices between two sets of locations have been estimated using road network data and road speeds for a series of road types.

For the subsequent station choice aspect of the work, potential competing stations were defined as those within 20 km of at least one origin zone. Candidate competitor stations are ordered by criteria calculated from the product of the total number of journeys originating at the candidate station and the population of a zone, divided by the distance to the center of population for that zone, then summing across all zones for the origin station. The candidate stations are sorted in decreasing order of these criteria, and the top 15 form the competing stations. At an early stage, tests were conducted on whether 5, 10, 15, or 20 competitor stations should be specified, and 15 provided the best fit.[1]

The data contains 44,680 observations for flows over 40 km. This is reduced to 24,076 when we have to remove those origins or destinations which have at least one zone with no population. However, to make the task more manageable, given the additional data relating to competing stations, the estimation of models which allow for competition between stations was restricted to 10,324 observations.

The value of time formula from the PDFH (ATOC, 2002) was used to calculate the money costs of both rail GJTs and road journey times prior to inclusion in GC. This value of time varies with journey distance and, in this study, it was calculated using total journey distance; in other words the sum of the access distance to the origin station and the rail journey distance. For road journeys, the distances are multiplied by a notional but plausible car cost of 7 pence per km and added to the time multiplied by the value of time to give their generalized costs.

4.4. Access and Egress Analysis: Model Estimation Results

Two sets of models are reported for Non London inter-urban flows. The first involves a specification with access and egress time being incorporated as part of GJT and the second involves a specification in which access and egress time are independent of GJT. Given the desire to retain GJT and fare as separate terms, but recognizing the high correlation between the two, we constrained the fare elasticity to be −0.9 in line with then PDFH recommendations (ATOC, 2002).

4.4.1. Access and Egress Time within GJT

Table 2 reports models with access and egress specified within GJT as in Eq. (10) along with the model of Eq. (2), where dummy variables are used to discern the generating potential of the origins and the attracting potential of the destinations. In moving from Eq. (2) to Eq. (10), we lose a considerable amount of data because some stations near coastal areas have zones around them with zero population and undefined access and egress times which cannot be handled by the estimation process.

As expected, Model I achieves a very good fit to the data. Here only the GJT elasticity is being estimated, rather than its equivalent enhanced with access and egress time, and the value of −1.285 is broadly in line with PDFH recommendations. Had we used the more recent recommended fare elasticity of −1.0, the estimated GJT elasticity would have been very similar to PDFH recommendations.

Models II, III, and IV take the form of Eq. (10), the differences being the weights that are attached to access and egress time in GJT. As expected, the

Table 2. Access and Egress Time within GJT.

	Model I (Eq. (2))	Model II (Eq. (10))	Model III (Eq. (10))	Model IV (Eq. (10))
Intercept	18.040 (118.8)	10.393 (63.6)	11.519 (67.4)	23.661 (90.6)
AEGJT	−1.285 (314.1)	−1.433 (90.1)	−1.635 (92.9)	−4.211 (107.1)
Fare	−0.9	−0.9	−0.9	−0.9
Population origin		0.175 (19.1)	0.180 (19.6)	0.487 (39.9)
Population destination		0.434 (45.9)	0.440 (46.2)	0.798 (62.3)
Access (v_A)		1.0 (fixed)	2.0 (fixed)	39.431 (30.8)
Egress (v_E)		1.0 (fixed)	2.0 (fixed)	40.468 (32.1)
R^2	0.946	0.517	0.522	0.588
Observations	44,680	24,076	24,076	24,076

Note: t-ratios in parentheses.

inclusion of access and egress within GJT leads to a higher GJT elasticity, whilst the higher weights that are successively applied to access and egress lead to a higher GJT elasticity as the access and egress times, which turn out to have high elasticities, tend to dominate.

A noticeable finding is that when the weights attached to access and egress time are freely estimated (Model IV), they are far in excess of anything that we would have ascribed to them on the basis of existing behavioral empirical evidence. A widespread convention in transport planning is that the value of out-of-vehicle time is around twice the value of in-vehicle time. Such high weights in Model IV are necessary so that the elasticities to access and egress time implied by the GJT approach are in line with the effect that changes in these variables have on rail demand.

This point is demonstrated in Table 3 where the access elasticities for a weight of unity are implausibly small. This is also the case when a weight of two is used. Nonetheless, the implied access and egress elasticities, when their weights within AEGJT are freely estimated, do seem to be on the high side. It should also be noted that the most reasonable population elasticities are those in Model IV, where the access and egress weights are freely estimated.

The pattern of variation in the access elasticities apparent in Table 3 is driven by the proportion that access time forms of AEGJT, as is clear from Eq. (12). This variation is large but it is enforced given the nature of the function estimated. We subsequently explore whether this implied elasticity variation is empirically justified, but note here that the models reported in Section 8.2, which specify access and egress outside of GJT, provide somewhat better fits to the data.

Table 3. Within GJT Access Elasticities.

Access Time (mins)	GJT (Excluding Access and Egress)									
	100 mins		200 mins		300 mins		400 mins		500 mins	
	$v = 1$	$v = F$	$v = 1$	$v = F$	$v = 1$	$v = F$	$v = 1$	$v = F$	$v = 1$	$v = F$
5	−0.1	−1.7	0.0	−1.4	0.0	−1.2	0.0	−1.0	0.0	−0.9
10	−0.1	−1.8	−0.1	−1.7	0.0	−1.5	0.0	−1.4	0.0	−1.3
15	−0.2	−1.9	−0.1	−1.8	−0.1	−1.7	−0.1	−1.6	0.0	−1.5
20	−0.2	−2.0	−0.1	−1.8	−0.1	−1.8	−0.1	−1.7	−0.1	−1.6
30	−0.3	−2.0	−0.2	−1.9	−0.1	−1.8	−0.1	−1.8	−0.1	−1.7

Note: where $v = 1$ the access/egress weights are constrained to equal 1 and where $v = \mathrm{F}$ they are freely estimated.

4.4.2. Access and Egress Time outside GJT

We now turn to models which have estimated separate terms for access and egress time outside of the GJT term. These take the form of Eqs. (15)–(19) and are reported in Table 4. All of these models are specified with the population elasticity expressed relative to the catchment area.

In general, the more flexible the access-egress function the better model fit. All four model specifications show similar and plausible GJT elasticities, but different properties regarding the access and egress elasticities. The population elasticities do not vary greatly and are generally more plausible than those obtained when access and egress are included within an extended GJT.

All models provide a respectable fit to the data with the Gompertz model giving the best fit. This model, however, has insignificant coefficients which limit the distance decay in early stages and for this reason the logit function is chosen as the preferred model.

Fig. 2 illustrates how the zonal population weight reduces at different access times for each function. The pattern is very similar for egress times. The power and exponential functions show an immediate and relatively steep distance decay compared with the logit, Gompertz, and quadratic models, where the influence of population on rail demand remains relatively constant for zones close to the station then rapidly decays as access times increase. The models imply that at the willingness to use rail is effectively zero for access times in excess of 6 min and egress times in excess of 7 min. Note, however, that access and egress times relate to drive times in uncongested conditions. A six-minute drive time might, therefore, represent a significant distance.

Table 4. Access and Egress Time Outside GJT.

	Model I (Eq. (15)) Power	Model II (Eq. (16)) Exponential	Model III (Eq. (17)) Logit	Model IV (Eq. (18)) Gompertz	Model V (Eq. (19)) Quadratic
Intercept	7.194 (51.0)	5.613 (43.7)	5.765 (43.5)	5.925 (46.7)	4.867 (38.6)
GJT	−1.279 (131.9)	−1.262 (136.7)	−1.250 (139.2)	−1.248 (139.0)	−1.254 (139.0)
Fare	−0.9	−0.9	−0.9	−0.9	−0.9
Population origin	0.549 (61.1)	0.633 (77.7)	0.540 (74.1)	0.532 (79.3)	0.597 (87.3)
Population destination	0.846 (89.7)	0.872 (105.7)	0.755 (103.1)	0.746 (108.9)	0.823 (117.4)
Access (α_1)	−1.738 (70.4)	−0.482 (54.4)	−3.926 (11.2)	−3.480 (10.7)	−0.025 (81.6)
Egress (α_2)	−1.728 (99.9)	−0.442 (69.1)	−3.517 (11.7)	−2.772 (11.5)	−0.022 (75.3)
Access (β_1)			20.916 (10.8)	−79,750,000 (0.6)	
Egress (β_2)			19.646 (11.5)	−3,408,043 (0.7)	
R^2	0.583	0.623	0.644	0.645	0.640
Observations	44,680	44,680	44,680	44,680	44,680

Note: t ratios in parentheses.

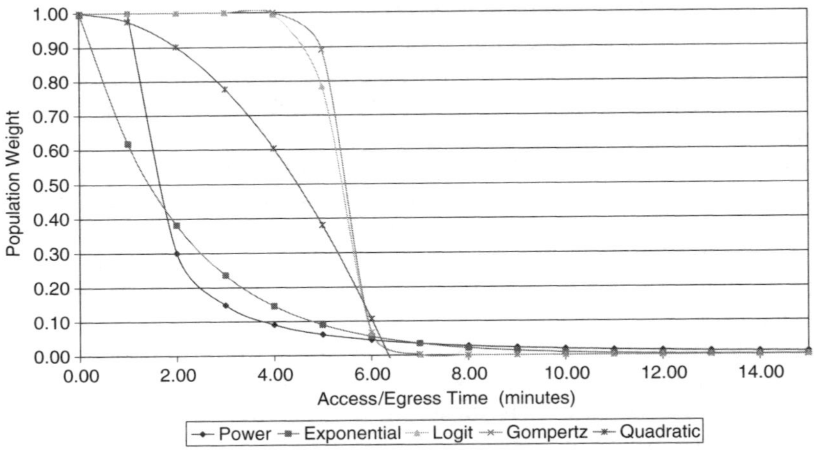

Fig. 2. Access Decay Functions.

The analysis has demonstrated that the 'distance decay' of the propensity to make rail trips is not consistent with a constant elasticity approach. The best explanation of rail travel demand is that trip making is relatively insensitive to changes in access time up to a point and then falls off quite dramatically with few rail trips beyond a threshold. In part, this will be because of the effect of competing stations in a dense network as exists in Great Britain, but it may also be because venturing into congested urban areas to access rail stations has more of an adverse impact on the attractiveness of rail than does access time spent by those already resident in the urban area.

By specifying access and egress outside of GJT, it is possible to improve the behavioral properties of the model by including theoretically justified access and egress decay impacts as well as allowing the population elasticity to be defined relative to the access/egress weighted catchment area population rather than the zone specific population and, therefore, allow more data to be included in model estimation. A possible drawback with this approach is that the impact of access and egress on rail demand is now independent of GJT. In practice, we might expect rail users to accept longer access and egress times for journeys with relatively high GJTs, whilst in general there is intuitively an element of reasonableness about the variation in the GJT and access and egress elasticities that is implied when access and egress are included within an extended GJT. However, this should be subject to empirical verification.

To test this hypothesis a new logit decay function was specified to include different access and egress parameters for journeys in three GJT bands. These were up to 200 min, between 200 and 400 min, and over 400 min. The results from this model were almost identical, indicating that there are no significant differences in access/egress sensitivity across GJT bands, which is in line with the statistical superiority of models which estimate the access and egress effects outside of GJT.

This further development of models estimated to cross-sectional data has provided a number of interesting and significant findings. After accounting for correlation between fare and GJT, the cross-sectional models generate sensible estimates of GJT elasticities of around -1.25 for non-London traffic, whilst the pattern of variation in the access and egress elasticities imposed by adopting the extended GJT approach is not empirically supported. If access and egress were to be specified within an extended GJT, the evidence indicates that the weights attached to them should be freely estimated rather than using conventional behavioral values. Analysis of the functional form of the access/egress decay effect has identified that statistically and theoretically superior models can be achieved by specifying more flexible inverted *s*-shaped decay functions as opposed to typical constant elasticity models.

5. DEALING WITH STATION COMPETITION

We now report modeling that has enhanced the cross-sectional approach to incorporate competition from other stations. This is important since it is necessary to separate out abstraction to or from competing stations from other sources of demand change.

One way of allowing for competition between stations would be to include cross-elasticity terms within the demand model. Thus, for example, the demand in Eq. (3) would depend not only on the generalized cost of rail travel between stations i and j but on the generalized costs of rail between competing origin station k and destination j, the generalized cost between station i and competing destination station l or the generalized cost between k and l. Since there will generally be more than one competing station at both the origin and destination, a large number of cross-elasticity terms would have to be specified. The estimation of such a large set of cross-elasticities would be extremely challenging, and indeed such terms are of little use when dealing with future competition from a station that does not yet exist. An alternative approach to specifying a series of cross-elasticity terms, and one adopted here, is to enhance the cross-sectional direct demand model by the inclusion of a station choice element.

Whilst ticket sales models have analyzed choice contexts, such as route (Rail Operational Research, 1995), operator and ticket type (AEAT, 1999), and station (Rail Operational Research, 1997), much remains unexplored and these models allocate a fixed demand between competing options whereas we are aiming to examine variations in the total market as well as examine competition between rival stations.

The disaggregate equivalent of such choice models, termed discrete choice models, have been employed in the rail market to examine station choice (Wardman & Whelan, 1999), along with a wide range of other choice contexts such as mode (Wardman, 1997b), route (Wardman & Shires, 2001), departure time (Whelan, Preston, Wardman, & Nash, 1997), ticket type (Whelan et al., 2005), and access mode (Wardman & Whelan, 1999). However, this approach requires expensive data collection exercises, whereas very large amounts of ticket sales data are available at modest cost, and it is often reliant upon stated preferences in response to hypothetical scenarios rather than real choices in actual market places. Such models also tend to struggle to link the choice context with the expansion or contraction of the overall market which is vitally important.

We can instead extend our aggregate cross-sectional model to cover the issue of station choice at the origin. Fig. 3 shows the choices for a potential traveler who might choose to travel from origin zone *a* to destination station *j*. He might choose to travel by road or, if traveling by rail, choose one of a number of origin stations (station *i* or one of its competitor stations *k*).

The origin station choice model used here is more fully derived in Lythgoe, Wardman, and Toner (2004). The basic concept is that the annual number of

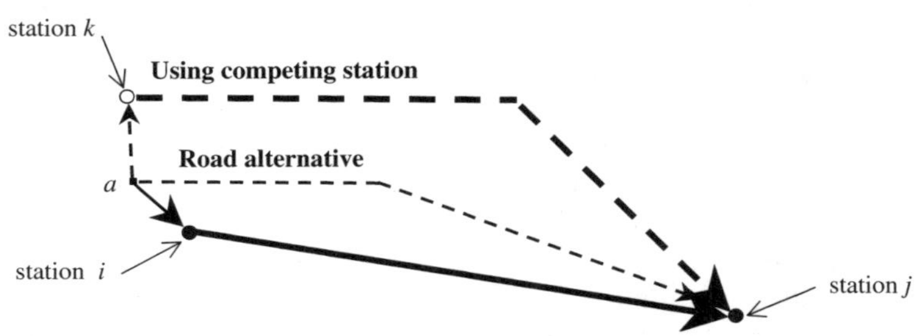

Fig. 3. Journeys from Origin Zone *a* to Destination Station *j*.

journeys from station i to destination station j, with several competing origin stations k, is constructed as a summation model, by adding the numbers of journeys V_{aij} from zone a, via station i, to destination station j. In turn, V_{aij} is the product of three elements: the probability, Pr(i|rail), of using origin station i given that the journey is made by train; the probability, Pr(rail), that the journey will be made by train; and the total number of journeys by either road or rail, V_{aj}, from zone a to destination station j. The two probabilities are based on logit forms.

The annual number of journeys V_{ij} can, therefore, be expressed as follows:

$$V_{ij} = \sum_a V_{aij} = \sum_a \Pr(i|\text{rail}) \Pr(\text{rail}) V_{aj} \tag{20}$$

The total number of journeys by either road or rail, V_{aj}, is given by:

$$V_{aj} = \mu M_{\text{LON}}{}^{O_{\text{LON}}} N_j \left(\sum_{a'} \exp(\alpha_1 \text{GC}_{a'i}) P_{a'} \right)^{u-1} P_a \tag{21}$$

where M_{LON} is a dummy parameter to be applied if London is the origin station; $O_{\text{LON}} = 1$ if London is the origin station (otherwise $O_{\text{LON}} = 0$); N_j is a dummy parameter to be applied for destination station j; and u is the origin population elasticity.

The probability, Pr(rail), that the journey will be made by train is given by the logit form:

$$\Pr(\text{rail}) = \frac{\left(\sum_k \left(\exp(\alpha_1 \text{GC}_{ak}) \text{GC}_{kj}^{\gamma} \right)^{1/\theta} \right)^{\theta}}{\left(\sum_k \left(\exp(\alpha_1 \text{GC}_{ak}) \text{GC}_{kj}^{\gamma} \right)^{1/\theta} \right)^{\theta} + \exp(-\varepsilon L_{aj})} \tag{22}$$

where θ is a parameter, between 0 and 1, that represents the dissimilarity between competing stations; and L_{aj} is the road distance between the origin zone a and the destination station j. Given that Pr(rail) is very small, this can be simplified using the following approximation:

$$\Pr(\text{rail}) \approx \left(\sum_k \left(\exp(\alpha_1 \text{GC}_{ak}) \text{GC}_{kj}^{\gamma} \right)^{1/\theta} \right)^{\theta} \exp(\varepsilon L_{aj}) \tag{23}$$

where the term $\exp(\varepsilon L_{aj})$ picks up the impact of competing road journeys. The probability, Pr(i|rail), of using origin station i given that the journey is made by train is given by a multinomial logit (MNL) model of station choice:

$$\Pr(i|\text{rail}) = \frac{\left(\exp(\alpha_1 \text{GC}_{ai})\text{GC}_{ij}^{\gamma}\right)^{1/\theta}}{\sum_k \left(\exp(\alpha_1 \text{GC}_{ak})\text{GC}_{kj}^{\gamma}\right)^{1/\theta}} \tag{24}$$

Substituting Eqs. (21), (23), and (24) into Eq. (20):

$$V_{ij} = \mu M_{\text{LON}}{}^{O_{\text{LON}}} N_j \left(\sum_{a'} \exp(\alpha_1 \text{GC}_{a'i}) P_{a'}\right)^{u-1} \sum_a \left\{ \left(\exp(\alpha_1 \text{GC}_{ai})\text{GC}_{ij}^{\gamma}\right)^{1/\theta} \left(\sum_k \left(\exp(\alpha_1 \text{GC}_{ak})\text{GC}_{kj}^{\gamma}\right)^{1/\theta}\right)^{\theta-1} \exp\left(\varepsilon L_{aj}\right) P_a \right\} \tag{25}$$

Table 5 reports the parameters estimated for Eq. (25) using non-linear least squares. The estimated rail journey generalized cost elasticity (γ) of -1.82 is in line with results here reported in Table 1, for another data set, and is highly consistent with PDFH recommendations for the elasticities to the fare and GJT components of GC. The access decay parameter (α_1) is negative and the distance decay parameter for road journeys (ε) is positive and these are to be expected. θ is derived from the MNL model of station choice and drives a 'generation ratio' for journeys from station i to station j, defined as the proportion of the increment in newly generated journeys (i.e., not abstracted from competing journeys from k to j) to the increment in

Table 5. Estimated Model Parameters.

Constant (log μ)	18.14 (93.45)
θ	0.505 (78.87)
α_1	−0.00395 (31.01)
γ	−1.82 (75.33)
ε	0.00315 (29.29)
u	0.45 (*)
Adj. R^2	0.61

*Convergence of the iterative estimation procedure could not be achieved when the origin population elasticity was allowed to vary. 0.45 is the constrained value of this elasticity that provided the best fit. t ratios in parentheses.

the total increase in journeys. This incremental generation ratio can range from θ to unity as the total number of journeys increase. The population elasticity (u) is estimated to be 0.45 which is lower than in the summation model of Table 1, but broadly in line with that estimated in Section 4, which dealt with the functional form of the access and egress effects.

M_{LON} and N_j in Eq. (25) are station dummy parameters. The former is applied if London is the origin station, to account for the unique features of London, while the latter is applied for destination station j since these are not being modeled explicitly. These parameters are not listed in Table 5, but are tabulated in Lythgoe et al. (2004). They are broadly correlated with the populations around the destination stations although Edinburgh, York, Brighton, and Norwich, all tourist destinations, attract more journeys than would be expected were population to be the only factor. Another destination attracting more journeys than would be expected for obvious reasons is Gatwick Airport.

We have applied the model to forecast the impact of improved services at Leeds on its competing stations. In this instance, there are 12 stations specified as competing within 40 km of Leeds. Table 6 shows the changes in demand at all 13 stations in response to a 5% decrease in rail GC for journeys from Leeds to London and from Leeds to Edinburgh. Demand at Leeds for journeys to both destinations increases by approximately 15%, while, as would be expected, the demand at all competing stations decreases. By subtracting the journeys lost at the competing stations, the newly generated journeys can be calculated to be approximately 10%. The generation ratio, the ratio of newly generated journeys to the increase in journeys at Leeds, is 0.67 for journeys to both destination stations. Since this is greater than θ (the dissimilarity parameter), and less than one, this is plausible. Although it might be regarded as surprising that switching from other stations is relatively high, given the findings in Section 4 about the sharply declining distance decay effect, it should be noted that this model form allows trips to be attracted from a much broader distance.

We have demonstrated an extension of cross-sectional models to handle competition between stations. Some generally plausible results have been obtained. However, there is one key limitation. θ helps to determine the generation ratio and we might expect it to vary according to the location of the origin station relative to its competitors. The use of a MNL station choice form implies that the proportion that new rail trips form of the total number of rail trips from a station is approximately constant, however far the competing stations are from the origin station. Further work is addressing the limitations of a MNL station choice element. The solution currently

Table 6. Leeds Demand Changes after a 5% Decrease in Rail Generalized Cost.

	Leeds-London	Leeds-Edinburgh
Base demand (Leeds)	511,271	38,581
Changes in demand		
Leeds	77,007	5,744
Bradford	−7,038	−517
Wakefield	−6,455	−367
Huddersfield	−925	−74
York	−378	−57
Dewsbury	−4,691	−390
Shipley	−2,777	−203
Halifax	−747	−62
Keighley	−508	−38
Harrogate	−716	−79
Ilkley	−461	−38
Barnsley	−634	−15
Selby	−306	−30
Newly generated	51,370	3,873
% change		
Leeds	15.06%	14.89%
Newly generated	10.05%	10.04%
Generation ratio	0.67	0.67

being developed is to use a cross-nested logit model. Nonetheless, the forecast generation ratio of 0.67 seems reasonable.

6. CONCLUSIONS

This chapter has revisited cross-sectional models of rail travel demand, a much neglected area in recent years but a form of data that, as we have pointed out, has the potential to provide important and unique insights into rail travel behavior.

Methodological developments have been made to allow station access and egress time elasticities to be estimated when the ticket sales data upon which the models are calibrated relate only to station-to-station movements and without the need for any supplementary data. Further enhancements relate to the functional relationship between rail demand and access and egress time and modeling competition between stations.

In addition to developing more useful cross-sectional models, a number of important findings have emerged in our applications to inter-urban rail travel in Great Britain. For example, the generalized cost elasticity does not seem to depend on the specification of station catchments but the population elasticities do, whilst the use of constant elasticity access and egress functions is inappropriate. Nor should access and egress be included within an extended generalized journey time and the evidence suggests that egress elasticities exceed access elasticities. If access and egress are to be included within an extended generalized journey time, the evidence indicates that the weights attached should be freely estimated rather constrained to standard transport planning values.

An issue that has surrounded cross-sectional models is identification and distinguishing between cause and effect. It should be pointed out that the analysis here is based on many point-to-point flows and that whilst fare and service quality are to some extent under the control of train operators, decisions will be made on the basis of an entire corridor or even on the basis of key flows such that for many point-to-point flows in our data set the fare and GJT can effectively be taken to be exogenous. Moreover, some regulations on fare do remain in Great Britain whilst the regulator has a strong say in the minimum service level offered. In any event, we are here concerned with the effects of access and egress and of population. These are exogenous to the rail industry. Finally, it should be pointed out that the results tend to be sensible. If, for example, we were really estimating movements along a supply curve or various different demand and supply equilibria, it is highly unlikely that the GC and GJT elasticities would be plausible. Nonetheless, more formal allowance for simultaneity bias would be worth pursuing.

Given the plausibility of the emerging results, we can have confidence in using cross-sectional models where time-series models run into data problems. For example, there are often instances where changes in service quality over time on particular routes are so minor that their elasticities cannot be reliably estimated. We might then look at variations across different flows, which tend to be much larger, to estimate their effect.

However, a number of challenges remain. We have seen that the multinomial logit model of station choice has its limitations whilst the appropriate form of access and egress 'distance decays' has been examined somewhat independently of station competition. The issue of the modes used to access and egress stations also requires attention, and the models need to be extended to incorporate the effects of parking availability and other station amenities on which station to use. The money costs as well as the times of access and egress need inclusion in the models. The research reported here is based on a specific form of catchment area zoning. The size and number of zones and also the overall size of the catchment requires further analysis. We might also expect directional effects, whereby people are less likely to use rail if it involves 'doubling-back', whilst urban form might impact on the size of the catchment. The emphasis of the work here has been more on the origin station and further attention needs to be paid to the attractiveness of destination stations and egress from them.

Future rail demand may well depend critically on patterns of land use and the socio-economic and demographic make up of the population. Relatively little is known about many such effects. Since there is a considerable cross-sectional variation in these variables, such models offer considerable opportunities for achieving a better understanding of their effects, although the accurate representation of these variables relies upon the appropriate specification of station catchment areas. Whilst some work was here reported that included socio-economic variables, much more remains to be done. Finally, we have here concentrated on inter-urban trips but significant suburban rail markets exist and the models developed here should be applied in that context.

NOTE

1. Some stations do not have the full 15 competing stations within 40 km.

ACKNOWLEDGMENTS

The research was funded by an Engineering and Physical Sciences Research Council Grant GR/L36826 and PhD studentship, and by the Passenger Demand Forecasting Council of the British Railway industry. The authors are grateful to Jonathan Pugh, then of ATOC, and to Jonathan Tyler, of Passenger Transport Networks, for the provision of data.

REFERENCES

Andrikopoulos, A. A., & Brox, J. A. (1990). Canadian inter-city passenger transportation: A simultaneous equation approach. *International Journal of Transport Economics*, *17*(3), 311–328.

AEAT. (1999). *Evaluating the experience of differential pricing*. Reports SSF013/02 and SSF013/03.

Association of Train Operating Companies (ATOC). (2002). *Passenger demand forecasting handbook* (Version 4). London: ATOC.

Association of Train Operating Companies (ATOC). (2005). *Passenger demand forecasting handbook* (Version 4.1). London: ATOC.

Bureau of Transport Economics (BTE). (1977). *Urban transport: Capital requirements 1977–78 to 1979–80*. Canberra: BTE.

Coto-Millán, P., Baños-Pino, J., & Inglada, V. (1997). Marshallian demand of intercity passenger transportation in Spain 1980–1992: An economic analysis. *Transportation Research, 33E*(2), 79–96.

Fowkes, A. S., Nash, C. A., & Whiteing, A. E. (1985). Understanding trends in inter-city rail traffic in Great Britain. *Transportation Planning and Technology, 10*, 65–80.

Holt, S., & White, P. (1981). *Modelling of interurban passenger demand*. Research Report No. 5, Polytechnic of Central London.

Jones, D. E. S., & White, P. R. (1994). Modelling of cross-country rail services. *Journal of Transport Geography, 2*, 111–121.

Koshal, M., Koshal, R. K., Gupta, A. K., & Nandola, K. N. (1996). Demand for public and private passenger transport in the United States. *International Journal of Transport Economics, 23*(2), 157–172.

Kulshreshtha, M., & Nag, B. (2000). Structure and dynamics of non-suburban passenger travel demand in Indian railways. *Transportation, 27*(2), 221–240.

Lave, L. B. (1972). The demand for inter city passenger transportation. *Journal of Regional Science, 12*(1), 71–84.

Lythgoe, W. F., Wardman, M., & Toner, J. P. (2004). Enhancing rail passenger demand models to examine station choice and access to the rail network. Paper presented at the European Transport Conference.

Manheim, M. L. (1973). *Practical implications of some fundamental properties of travel demand models*. Washington: Highway Research Record 422, Highway Research Board.

McGeehan, H. (1984). Forecasting demand for inter-urban railway travel in the Republic of Ireland. *Journal of Transport Economics and Policy, 18*(3), 275–291.

NERA. (1999). Rail passenger demand analysis. Prepared for the SRA, London.

NERA. (2003). Research on long term fare elasticities. Prepared for the SRA, London.

Oum, T. H., van Ooststroom, H., & Yoon, J. H. (1996). The structure of travel demands in the Netherlands: An application to predict modal shares under the sustainable development goals. *International Journal of Transport Economics, 23*(1), 31–62.

Owen, A. D., & Phillips, G. D. A. (1987). The characteristics of railway passenger demand. *Journal of Transport Economics and Policy, 21*, 231–253.

Preston, J. (1991). Demand forecasting for new local rail stations and services. *Journal of Transport Economics and Policy, 25*(2), 183–202.

Quandt, R., & Baumol, W. J. (1966). The demand for abstract transportation modes: Theory and measurement. *Journal of Regional Science, 6*, 13–26.

Rail Operational Research. (1989a). *Demand changes due to service improvements and sprinter introduction on the North TransPennine*. Report 10323/M7, London.

Rail Operational Research. (1989b). *Estimation of the elasticity of demand to changes in fare*. Report 10329/M2, London.

Rail Operational Research. (1993). *Evaluating the revenue effects of IC225 stock on the East Coast main line*. Report OIH040/M1, London.

Rail Operational Research. (1995). *Differential pricing by route*. Report MPP001/03.

Rail Operational Research. (1997). *Rail heading: Modelling station choice*. Report MPP029/01, London.

Rolle, J. D. (1997). Estimation of Swiss railway demand with computation of elasticities. *Transportation Research, 33E*(2), 117–127.

Steer Davies Gleave. (2003). *The effect of road congestion on rail demand.* Prepared for Passenger Demand Forecasting Council, London.

Tyler, J., & Hassard, R. (1973). Gravity/elasticity models for the planning of the inter urban rail passenger business. In: *Proceedings of the PTRC summer annual meeting*, Warwick.

van Vuuren, D., & Rietveld, P. (2002). The off peak demand for train kilometres and train tickets: A microeconometric analysis. *Journal of Transport Economics and Policy, 36*(1), 49–72.

Wardman, M. (1983). *Interchange and the demand for rail travel.* MA Dissertation, Institute for Transport Studies, University of Leeds.

Wardman, M. (1994). Forecasting the impact of service quality changes on the demand for inter-urban rail travel. *Journal of Transport Economics and Policy, 28*, 287–306.

Wardman, M. (1996). *Cross sectional modelling of inter urban rail demand.* Technical Note 403, Institute for Transport Studies, University of Leeds.

Wardman, M. (1997a). Inter-urban rail demand elasticities and competition in Great Britain: Evidence from direct demand models. *Transportation Research E, 33*, 15–28.

Wardman, M. (1997b). *Disaggregate inter-urban mode choice models: Review of British evidence.* Working Paper 504, Institute for Transport Studies, University of Leeds.

Wardman, M. (2006). Demand for rail travel and the effects of external factors. *Transportation Research E, 42*(3), 129–148.

Wardman, M., & Shires, J. (2001). Comparison of within mode revealed preference and stated preference choice models. Paper presented at AET European transport conference.

Wardman, M., Shires, J., Lythgoe, W. L., & Tyler, J. (2004). Consumer benefits and demand impacts of regular train timetables. *International Journal of Transport Management, 2*(1), 27–37.

Wardman, M., & Toner, J. (2003). Econometric modelling of competition between train ticket types. Paper presented at AET European transport conference.

Wardman, M., & Tyler, J. (2000). Rail network accessibility and the demand for inter-urban rail travel. *Transport Reviews, 20*(1), 3–24.

Wardman, M., & Whelan, G. (1999). *Using Geographical Information Systems to Improve Rail Demand Models.* Final Report to Engineering and Physical Sciences Research Council (EPSRC), Grant GR/L36826.

Wardman, M., & Whelan, G. (2004). Generalised journey time reformulation. ITS University of Leeds. Prepared for Passenger Demand Forecasting Council, London.

Whelan, G., Preston, J., Wardman, M., & Nash, C. (1997). The privatisation of passenger rail services in Britain: An assessment of the impacts of on-the-track competition. Paper presented at PTRC European transport conference.

Whelan, G., Toner, J., Shires, J., Batley, R., Wardman, M., & Nash, C. (2005). Optimal fares regulation for Britain's railways. Paper presented at AET European transport conference.

White, P., & Williams, S. (1976). Modelling cross country rail passenger trips. Paper presented at PTRC summer annual conference. Seminar N, PTRC, London.

RAILROAD PRICING AND REVENUE-TO-COST MARGINS IN THE POST-STAGGERS ERA

Marc Ivaldi and Gerard McCullough

ABSTRACT

The aim of this paper is to look more carefully at the structure of rail rates that has evolved in the 25-year period since the Staggers Rail Act and to assess its impact on the railroad industry. The paper does this by investigating the relationship between car-type-specific marginal costs and car-type-specific rates. These define a set of Lerner indices that are the traditional economic measure of pricing behavior. Taken individually, the Lerner indices are a measure of the market conditions that railroads confront in commodity-specific markets. Taken together in combination with aggregate output measures, the Lerner indices help to determine whether railroad revenues are adequate to cover rail costs. Comparing the ratio of total annual revenues received by each Class I railroad to total (econometrically) estimated costs, we find that this ratio has averaged less than 1.06 in the 23-year period between 1981 and 2004.

Railroad Economics
Research in Transportation Economics, Volume 20, 153–178

ISSN: 0739-8859/doi:10.1016/S0739-8859(07)20006-X

1. BACKGROUND AND INTRODUCTION

The U.S. freight railroads always have practiced price-discrimination among shippers of different commodities. In fact, such discrimination was officially sanctioned under the value-of-service pricing philosophy that the Interstate Commerce Commission (ICC) adopted shortly after its founding in 1887.[1] It continued as official policy for nearly a century and was given renewed authority when the ICC endorsed constrained market pricing as a residual regulatory concept following the passage of the Staggers Rail Act in 1980.[2] It has been reaffirmed by the ICC's successor agency, the Surface Transportation Board (STB), in various rulings since then.[3]

Table 1 reports the real revenue per carload that Class I freight railroads received for carrying various commodities during the post-Staggers era. These are proxies for real rates since they do not reflect distance traveled and that does vary across commodities. Nevertheless, the revenue-per-carload data do provide a broad indication of relative rates and show that while the level of real rates has fallen and the structure has been compressed, the basic pattern of rates has remained constant. Shippers of high-value products such as automobiles continue to pay premium rates for freight service while shippers of lower-valued commodities like grain and coal pay lower rates.

This chapter analyzes the level and structure of rail rates that have prevailed in freight markets since Staggers and assesses their impact on the U.S. railroad industry. It does this by investigating the relationships between car-type-specific rates and car-type-specific marginal costs. These relationships between rates and marginal costs define the set of Lerner indices that are the traditional measure of pricing behavior in particular markets. Taken individually, the Lerner indices are a signal of the varying economic conditions that railroads and shippers confront in different commodity markets.

Table 1. U.S. Class I Railroads Revenue per Carload (1982 Dollars).

	1981	1988	1996	2004
Coal	1,052	1,076	897	830
Grain	1,643	1,210	1,461	1,468
Paper	2,110	2,243	1,980	1,810
Food	2,256	1,776	1,586	1,452
Chemicals	2,554	2,401	2,217	1,796
Motor vehicles	2,557	2,681	1,929	1,466

Taken together and in combination with the level of railroad outputs, the Lerner indices also help to determine whether the revenues that railroad firms receive will be adequate to cover their costs.

The chapter is structured as follows. Section 2 uses a Generalized McFadden (GM) cost function to develop a set of car-type-specific marginal cost estimates based on public data from the Association of American Railroads (AAR) (1981–2004). Section 3 combines these marginal cost estimates with rate estimates drawn from the same public data to create and analyze a set of Lerner indices across railroads, years, and car-type-specific markets. Section 4 uses these estimates to assess whether and to what extent Class I freight railroad revenues covered estimated total costs during the 1981–2004 post-Staggers era. Section 5 states conclusions.

The revenue-to-cost margins presented here cannot be directly compared to the formal revenue adequacy determination made by the STB each year. That determination is based on a comparison of each railroads' accounting rate of return on net investment (ROI) with the STB's estimate of railroad cost of capital. The agency's annual cost of capital estimate is usually about 10 percent and the individual railroads have ROIs which typically range from about 5 to 8 percent. The measure developed in this chapter is the simple ratio of the total annual revenues received by each firm to total (econometrically) estimated costs. It is interesting to note that this ratio has averaged less than 1.06 in the 23-year period between 1981 and 2004. This is not inconsistent with the STB's findings.

2. ESTIMATED RAIL RATES AND MARGINAL COSTS

Griliches (1972) contributed to the early development of modern statistical cost functions to analyze the U.S. railroad technology by pointing out that the "official methods" used by the ICC to evaluate rail costs were inadequate. Subsequent papers by Harmatuck (1979), Brown, Caves, and Christensen (1979), Friedlaender and Spady (1981), Breautigam, Daughety, and Turnquist (1982), Caves, Christensen, Tretheway, and Windle (1985), and others improved the technical sophistication of rail cost functions and applied them to comprehensive data sets. Recent papers by Berndt, Friedlaender, Chiang, and Christopher (1993), Friedlaender, Berndt, Chiang, Showalter, and Christopher (1993), Wilson (1997), Ivaldi and McCullough (2001), and Bitzan (1999) have continued in the same tradition.

Most of the earlier rail cost studies cited here use aggregate ton-miles as the unit of freight output. Ton-mile data are available by railroad and by year on an aggregate basis, but are not available on a commodity-by-commodity basis. This forces the assumption that the outputs of railroad freight firms are homogeneous and that all rail freight services generate similar costs. This is an especially troublesome assumption from our standpoint since freight railroads are multiproduct firms and formal analysis of pricing is impossible unless we can identify the differentiated marginal costs of rail outputs.

Studies by Breautigam et al. (1982) using car-miles rather than ton-miles as outputs are important exceptions in the literature and we adopt their approach. In fact, car-mile outputs are highly correlated with ton-miles and, therefore, serve as a reasonable alternative measure of output. More importantly, data on car-miles by equipment type (open hopper car-miles, closed hopper car-miles, boxcar car-miles, etc.) for each Class I railroad are published annually by the AAR in the *Analysis of Class I Railroads.* These data are significant from an economic standpoint because the different car-types—hopper cars versus boxcars, for example – are involved in freight services that have different cost and demand characteristics. Use of car-mile data for outputs makes it possible to estimate costs in a way that is technologically accurate and that also reflects different market characteristics.

Our use of the car-mile rather than the ton-mile as the measure of railroad operational output does raise the question of whether we have taken into account the differential effect that weight has on railroad costs. In fact, the categories of car-mile by car-type that we use as outputs do represent weight differences in a fairly consistent way. According to data in the *Analysis*, loaded weights of cars in the general freight category range from about 20–25 tons per carload for intermodal and multilevel automobile cars (y_{V}) to 50–70 tons for boxcars, refrigerated cars, and gondolas (y_{E}), and loaded weights of cars in the bulk category are 80–100 tons per carload for tank cars, open hoppers, and covered hoppers (y_{B}). One problem car-type here is the heavy "double-stack" container car. These heavier cars are classified by us as general freight since the *Analysis* does not distinguish them from regular intermodal cars carrying single trailers or containers.

The homogeneous output assumption also creates problems in analyzing the extensive maintenance-related activities of freight railroads. Modern railroad maintenance is highly automated but it still involves lifting track, cleaning ballast, adding additional ballast, and replacing and realigning track. All of this activity is expensive and can disrupt freight service for hours or days. This affects the cost characteristics of both types of activities, but the effects can be analyzed only if we can identify and differentiate between operational outputs and infrastructure outputs.

Our approach to this problem is based on the observation that on mature rail networks most infrastructure-related activity is aimed at maintaining the capacity of the existing network. In 2004, for example, the U.S. railroads installed 13.8 million ties and 4,66,615 tons of new rail, according to the *Analysis*. Some 13.3 million ties (96.4 percent) and 4,43,381 tons of new rail (95.0 percent) were for "replacement" rather than for "addition," according to the AAR. In this respect, maintenance behavior on the rail network is similar to that on mature highway systems, where each additional vehicle-mile imposes a *variable maintenance cost* because it moves forward in time the point at which the infrastructure must be rehabilitated. This suggests that we can view infrastructure-related activity on the rail network as a variable output which imposes costs directly, and which interacts with other (operating) outputs rather than as a fixed capital cost. We use "ties laid-in-replacement" from the AAR's *Analysis* as a measure of output for the infrastructure maintenance entities within each rail firm.

Though we include in our model a measure of infrastructure output, we still account in a variable cost model for a quasi-fixed input whose consumption does not vary as output levels vary. We follow Wilson (1997) in using railroad-owned miles of right of way on which track is located (ROAD) as a measure of quasi-fixed capital. As in the highway case, there is an opportunity cost associated with holding this asset, but it is a cost that is not directly affected by operational levels. In the Wilson paper, the ROAD variable is combined with a measure of track quality as a means of differentiating levels of track investment, while in our paper track-related maintenance activities are treated as outputs. Our assumption here is that the ties-laid-in-replacement variable will capture the different degree of activity that is required to maintain systems with double and triple track segments, while the ROAD variable captures network size and the opportunity cost of holding land.

The general rail cost function (C) is modeled here as

$$C = C^{V}(y_{B}, y_{E}, y_{I}, w_{L}, w_{E}, w_{F}, w_{M}; R, T, \kappa, \theta) + \rho R \qquad (1)$$

where

C^{V} = variable costs,
y_{B} = car-miles of bulk traffic (i.e., open hopper, closed hopper, tank),
y_{E} = car-miles of general traffic (i.e., intermodal, auto-carrier, gondola, box),
y_{I} = replacement ties installed in a given year,
w_{L} = index of labor prices,

w_E = index of equipment prices,
w_F = index of fuel prices,
w_M = index of material prices and other input prices,
R = miles of road operated,
T = counter for years,
κ = degree of network congestion (train-miles per mile of road),
θ = vector of fixed effect parameters.
ρ = opportunity cost of capital.[4]

Our model of railroad production is of a two-stage vertical process. In the first stage, quasi-fixed land assets (miles of roadway) and other inputs (energy, materials, labor, equipment) are converted into infrastructure outputs, which we interpret as actively maintained track miles. In the second stage, these outputs become inputs to an operational production process which also requires energy, materials, labor, and equipment. The actively maintained track miles could be interpreted as outputs, which a separated infrastructure company would sell to operating companies for an access fee.

We have used the specification this way in Ivaldi and McCullough (2001) to analyze the technological feasibility of vertically separating U.S. freight railroads into infrastructure providers and operating companies. We have adopted the same model here because we think that the specification accurately reflects the technology of integrated rail networks. Our assumption is that the *level* of maintenance-of-way activity needed to maintain the capacity of a network will have a direct effect on the cost of freight operations, and vice versa.[5] Traditional rail cost models, which typically use a monetized value of road capital to measure infrastructure, are not able to capture these effects.

The functional form of the cost function used here is the GM cost function derived from McFadden (1978) and introduced by Diewert and Wales (1987). Flexible functional forms were developed by economists to avoid the inherent restriction of the Cobb-Douglas function that all elasticities of factor substitution are equal to 1. The most frequently used functional form in empirical work is the transcendental logarithmic (TL) function. A technical limitation of the TL is that it fails to satisfy the requirement that a cost function be globally concave in input prices. The GM is one of several functions proposed by Diewert and Wales which satisfy this requirement, but do not restrict the elasticities of substitution.

Kumbhakar (1994) proposed an extension of the GM to the multiple-output case and our function further generalizes his form by providing a third-order approximation of the relationship of outputs, factor prices, and quasi-fixed technological factors. This is important to our study because it allows us take into account the complex relationship of multiple rail outputs to each other and to technological characteristics.[6]

More formally, let w be an n-dimensional vector of input prices, t a q-dimensional vector of quasi-fixed technological factors, and y an r-dimensional vector of outputs. Define z as the m-dimensional vector $(m = q + r)$ that includes y and t. The GM cost function is

$$C = \alpha' w + 0.5 \frac{w' \Delta w}{\theta' w} \left(\beta' y\right)^2 + w' \Lambda z + 0.5(\theta' w) z' \Gamma z \tag{2}$$

where a is an unconstrained n-dimensional parameter vector, Δ an $n \times n$ symmetric parameter matrix, Λ an $n \times m$ parameter matrix of nonnegative elements, Γ an $m \times m$ symmetric parameter matrix, and θ is an $n \times 1$ vector of fixed parameters.

For C to provide a second-order approximation to an arbitrary cost function C^*, it must contain $(n+m)(n+m+1)/2$ free parameters. As the cost function in (1) contains $(n+m)(n+m+1)/2+m$ parameters, it is flexible. It is also homogeneous and monotonic in w, and it is concave in w if the estimated matrix Δ is negative semidefinite. If not, concavity can be imposed by setting $\Delta = -BDB'$, where B is a lower triangular matrix with the sum of its diagonal elements equal to 1 and D is a nonnegative diagonal matrix.[7]

To estimate the parameters of C^{V}, the vector of n factor demands is derived by differentiating Eq. (2) with respect to the variable input price vector w. This gives an n-dimensional vector of factor demands that contains all of the cost function parameters. The vector is

$$X = \alpha + \left[\frac{\Delta w}{\theta' w} - 0.5 \frac{(w' \Delta w)\theta}{(\theta' w)^2}\right] \left(\beta' y\right)^2 + \Lambda z + 0.5\theta \left(z' \Gamma z\right) + v \tag{3}$$

Marginal costs are evaluated using the estimated parameters of the cost model. Projected variable costs are

$$\hat{C}^{\mathrm{V}} = w' \left\{ \hat{\alpha} + \left[\frac{\hat{\Delta} w}{\hat{\theta}' w} - 0.5 \frac{(w' \hat{\Delta} w)\theta}{(\hat{\theta}' w)^2}\right] \left(\hat{\beta}' y\right)^2 + \hat{\Lambda} z + 0.5\hat{\theta}(z' \hat{\Gamma} z) \right\} \tag{4}$$

where the term in brackets is the projected factor demand vector. Differentiating Eq. (3) with respect to the relevant output y_{r} gives a vector of n factor-specific resource requirements for that marginal unit of output.

Short-run marginal costs are projected using

$$\hat{C}_{\mathrm{r}}^{\mathrm{MC}} = w'\left\{\left[\frac{2\hat{\Delta}w}{\hat{\theta}'w} - \frac{(w'\hat{\Delta}w)\hat{\theta}}{(\hat{\theta}'w)^2}\right]\left(\hat{\beta}'y\right)\beta_{\mathrm{r}} + \hat{\Lambda}_{\mathrm{r}}'\ y_{\mathrm{r}} + z'\hat{\Gamma}_{\mathrm{r}}y_{\mathrm{r}}\right\} \tag{5}$$

The data used to estimate the cost function are from the *Analysis of Class I Railroads* and *Railroad Cost Indices,* which are both published annually by the AAR. The *Analysis* summarizes official R-1 Annual Reports and other data which railroads file with the STB. The *Cost Indices* are also used for regulatory purposes and are based on periodic surveys of member firms conducted by the AAR. The data used here are an unbalanced panel of 26 Class I freight railroads (currently defined as railroads whose annual revenue is more than $250 million) which operated in the U.S. during the period 1981–2004. These are listed in Table 2. The data set which contains 293 observations is summarized in Table 3.

The measure of rail variable costs includes expenditures for labor, fuel, and materials listed in the *Analysis.*[8] As discussed above, we use bulk car-miles and general freight car-miles for operational outputs, and ties-laid-in-replacement for infrastructure outputs.[9] The technological variables are average length of haul (HAUL), miles of road (ROAD), and a counter for years (TIME).[10]

The actual system estimated includes the four factor demand equations defined by Eq. (3) above, two additional equations for the output variables y_{B} and y_{E} , and a transformation function that specifies the relationship between y_{I} (ties-laid-in-replacement) and the operating outputs y_{B} and y_{E}. The operating outputs are treated as endogenous because the Staggers Rail

Table 2. U.S. Class I Railroads (1981–2004).

Railroad	Symbol	Years	Railroad	Symbol	Years
Santa Fe	ATSF	1981–1995	Milwaukee	MILW	1981–1984
Baltimore & Ohio	BO	1981–1983	Mo.-Kansas-Texas	MKT	1981–1987
Burlington Northern	BN	1981–1995	Missouri Pacific	MP	1981–1985
BN Santa Fe	BNSF	1996–2004	Norfolk & Western	NW	1981–1983
Chesapeake & Ohio	CO	1981–1983	Norfolk Southern	NSC	1986–2004
Chicago Northwestern	CNW	1981–1994	Seaboard Coastline	SCL	1981–1985
Consolidated rail	CRC	1981–1998	Soo Line	SOO	1981–2004
CSX Corp.	CSX	1986–2004	Southern Pacific	SP	1981–1996
Denver Rio Grande	DRGW	1981–1993	Southern Railway	SRS	1981–1985
Grand Trunk West	GTW	1981–2001	Union Pacific	UP	1981–1985
Illinois Central	ICG	1978–1997	UP System	UPSYS	1986–1996
Kansas City Southern	KCS	1978–1997	UPSP	UPSP	1997–2004
Louisville & Nashville	LN	1981–1982	Western Pacific	WP	1981–1984

Table 3. Railroad Cost Data.

Variable	Unit	Mean	Standard Deviation	Minimum	Maximum
Labor spend	$(000)	1,001,453	927,917	88,293	3,918,739
Equip spend	$(000)	755,655	834,971	27,036	4,000,999
Fuel spend	$(000)	197,022	242,015	13,759	1,680,392
Material spend	$(000)	167,344	146,096	11,285	618,222
Bulk output	Car-miles (000)	818,784	984,542	25,209	6,407,584
General output	Car-miles (000)	1,033,887	1,010,107	74,270	5,264,433
Infrastructure output	Ties (000)	1,154	994	27	4,664
Labor price (wL)	Index	243.4	60.4	149.6	376.0
Equipment price (We)	Index	210.6	22.8	160.2	243.4
Fuel price (wF)	Index	202.9	49.6	128.8	355.1
Material price (wM)	Index	167.2	33.2	132.3	244.2
Train-miles/mile	Train-miles	3,223	1,419	786	9,447
Years	Years	13.1	6.65	4	27
Road	Miles	9,601	7,992	550	34,946
Coal consumption	Tons (000)	237,350	149,139	7,444	651,164
Population	Persons (000)	61,500	37,934	4,631	152,092

Act gave firms the right to adjust output levels in response to market conditions. This means that y_{B} and y_{E} could be correlated with the disturbances in (3). The equations have the form

$$\ln y_z = \delta_{0z} + \sum \delta_{nz} \ln w_n + \sum \delta_{qz} \ln t_q + \sum \delta_{fz} \ln g_f + \eta_z \tag{6}$$

The variables used in these equations are the exogenous factor prices (w) and technological variables (t) and two demand shifters (g) – railroad-specific measures of system-wide population and system-wide coal consumption. Railroad system-wide population, a regressor for economic activity, is constructed by summing the total population by state and year from the *Statistical Abstract of the U.S.* that each of the railroads served in each year (available from the AAR). System-wide coal consumption constructed in the same way using data from the Energy Information Agency of the U.S. Department of Energy. The technological variables are used to reflect network size and the input prices are used to further reflect regional economic conditions.

Infrastructure outputs are also considered endogenous and are modeled by a transformation function of the form

$$y_z = \delta_0 + \sum \delta_{z\mathrm{I}}\, y_{z\mathrm{I}} + \sum \delta_{q\mathrm{I}}\, t_{q\mathrm{I}} + \eta_{\mathrm{I}} \tag{7}$$

where the technological variables (t) are miles of road (R) and a counter for time (T). We simplify our analysis here by adopting a linear form for the transformation function though we recognize that this is a much more complicated and dynamic process which involves rationalizing infrastructure and then investing heavily in the rationalized network.[11]

We must also take into account the possibility that there will be fixed effects that influence firms' factor demands. In their 1987 paper, Diewert and Wales suggest that the θ term in the cost function can either be estimated or set by the econometrician based on previous knowledge. To account for fixed effects in each factor demand equation we set the values of θ at the input-specific average value across all years of each firm's input quantities. Since fixed effects are probably the result of network characteristics such as terrain and weather we are implicitly assuming that the fixed network characteristics do not change in a fundamental way as long as the firm is listed as such in the AAR database. This is a rather strong assumption, given the amount of restructuring that has taken place in the industry, but in most cases the θ values are reset to reflect larger merged entities such as BNSF and UP/SP which we treat as new firms.

The system is estimated using the FIML command from SAS 9.1. The regression results reported in appendix Table A1 are consistent with those of earlier rail cost models. The particular specification used here reveals that there are significant cost complementarities between bulk operations (y_B) and general freight (y_E) [parameter *gybye*], and between infrastructure activities (y_I) and general freight [parameter *gyeyi*]. The own-cost effects of bulk and general freight operations [parameters *gybyb* and *gyeye*] are positive, however, suggesting that the U.S. freight railroads have exhausted the economies of density associated with increasing these outputs by themselves.[12]

Cost complements result when there is a shared input, not easily divisible into discrete units, which is an important element in the production of several different outputs. Increased production of one output requires more of the shared input, which then becomes available for production of the second output. General freight operations typically involve more complicated routing and scheduling patterns than bulk traffic, which usually moves in large blocks or unit trains. Our interpretation is that the cost complementarities we observe between general freight and bulk result from the control capabilities that firms develop as traffic volumes increases and they become more adept at coordinating trains, locomotives, and crews. A similar coordination "public good" argument applies to the complementarity we observe between infrastructure activities and freight operations.

The primary focus in this chapter is on the marginal cost of providing rail service. Eq. (5) provides estimates of the variable marginal costs of y_B y_E

Table 4. U.S. Class I Railroads Marginal Effects.

Variable	Estimate	Standard Error	Minimum	Maximum
MC bulk car-miles	$ 0.35	0.19	0.02	0.92
MC general car-miles	$ 0.92	0.51	0.03	2.91
MC infrastructure	$ 380.62	138.17	39.07	759.42
Bulk fee	$ 0.051	0.018	0.005	0.102
General fee	$ 0.009	0.003	0.0009	0.018
Returns-to-density	1.31	0.43	0.49	4.47

and y_I for each of the 293 observations in the data base. Means and standard errors of these projections are presented in Table 4 along with other projected marginal effects. The estimates of operating marginal costs of $0.35 for bulk and $0.92 for general freight are consistent with railroad operating technology. Bulk car-miles typically accrue in unit-train operations that involve less operational complexity and lower marginal costs than general freight operations. The results here suggest that the operational marginal costs of bulk are only slightly more than one-third of the operational marginal costs of general freight. (See the discussion of bulk and general infrastructure fees below.)

The ties-laid-in replacement variable is designed to capture a range of infrastructure expenditures including ballast materials, actual ties, track, and labor. The estimated marginal cost of y_I is $380.62. This is consistent with the fact that between 1981 and 2004, the Class I railroad industry as a whole spent an average of $4.84 million annually on way and structures and installed an average of 14.6 million replacement ties each year (or $351 per tie).[13]

The estimated *operational* marginal costs reported here do not take into account the marginal effects that y_B and y_E have on infrastructure. These effects are reported in Table 4 as a "bulk fee" and a "general fee." The bulk fee is the product of the estimated marginal cost of infrastructure from Eq. (5) and the estimated parameter value for δ_{zI} in Eq. (7). This is the marginal cost that a railroad would incur for moving a bulk carload a mile on its own infrastructure *or* the marginal cost-based access fee that a tenant railroad would pay to move a bulk carload a mile on a host railroad's infrastructure. The general infrastructure fee is calculated in similar fashion using the estimated marginal cost of infrastructure and the estimated parameter value for δ_{zI}. The results suggest that the marginal effect of heavier bulk car-miles is about five times that of general freight car-miles.

The estimated marginal costs of bulk and general freight service are below the average expenditure per car-mile which would be required to cover variable costs. The *average variable cost* for this data – the ratio of estimated variable costs (C^C) to the sum of y_B and y_E with ties-laid-in replacement (y_I) excluded as outputs – would be about $1.20. This is consistent with the mean estimated returns-to-density for this sample which is 1.31 – an indication that the railroads in the sample still exhibit weakly increasing variable costs. This 1.31 figure is also consistent with returns-to-density estimates in earlier rail cost studies which have ranged from about 1.3 to 1.9.[14]

3. PRICING BEHAVIOR

Lerner indices provide a formal assessment of the pricing behavior of firms in diverse markets. The standard representation of the Lerner index assumes that a firm has a degree of market power in all of the markets it serves and that the demands for its outputs are independent. (More sophisticated forms of the index with interdependent demands are available but are not used in our analysis.) The multiproduct objective function of the firm is $\pi = \sum_z p_z(y_z)y_z - C(\sum_z y_z)$. The first-order condition for profit maximization is

$$p_z + \frac{\partial p_z}{\partial y_z} y_z - \frac{\partial C}{\partial y_z} = 0 \tag{8}$$

and the Lerner index is

$$\frac{P_z - \partial C/\partial y_z}{P_z} = \frac{1}{|\varepsilon_{zz}|} \tag{9}$$

where ε_{zz} is the own-price elasticity of demand for a good or service. In our analysis, the indices are calculated in this chapter using the left-hand side of Eq. (9) with estimated short-run marginal costs for each observation derived in Section 2, and estimated rail rates for each firm and each year which are also developed from the *Analysis of Class I Railroads*.

In fact, there is no direct way to estimate commodity-specific rail rates using public data.[15] The STB collects rate data for regulatory purposes in an annual *Waybill Sample* but the detailed records containing rates are confidential. The *Analysis* reports revenues by commodity group (e.g., grain or coal), but it does not report commodity-specific information on ton-miles (e.g., how many ton-miles of grain or coal were moved by each railroad each year). Nevertheless, the car-mile outputs used in this model can be linked to commodities, and this makes it possible to calculate commodity rates indirectly.

Grain revenues and coal revenues, for example, are accrued in closed-hopper, open-hopper, and gondola car-miles. This means that – to a certain extent – the revenue data in the *Analysis* can be combined with firm-specific annual mileage data for these car-type (which is in the *Analysis*) to calculate the average-revenue-per-car-mile associated with bulk car-miles. Similar calculations are performed for intermodal car-miles (intermodal revenue), tank car-miles (chemical revenue), multirack car-miles (motor vehicle revenue), and all other car-miles (all other revenue). The resulting car-mile rate estimates – revenue per car-mile by car-type – are summarized in Table 5.[16]

It is important to recognize here that we cannot present a perfect mapping between car-types and commodity categories. Gondolas, for example, are also used to ship (expensive) coiled steel and inexpensive scrap metal as well as coal, and tank cars are used to ship corn syrup and (now) ethanol as well as chemicals. Nevertheless, we have tried to make the mappings as accurate as possible and we have checked our estimated prices against the price estimates provided by the STB.

The Lerner indices are constructed by combining these rate estimates for the five general car-types with marginal cost estimates for each observation. The estimated marginal cost of y_B is used for the bulk car-type and the estimated marginal cost of y_E is used for the others. The empirical means of the Lerner indices are reported in Table 6.

It is important to recognize in this respect that the Lerner indices reported here are based only on short-run marginal operating costs. As we will develop in more detail in Section 4 below, the markups above these costs must cover variable infrastructure costs and the fixed opportunity costs of holding land.

One must also recognize that the Lerner indices presented here do not provide a detailed structural analysis of the actual pricing behavior of railroads. Our analysis is based on the left-hand side of Eq. (9), but the elasticity measure on the right-hand side reflects market boundaries, complex strategic interactions across railroad firms, and possibly even between car-types such as

Table 5. U.S. Class I Railroads Estimated Rates per Car-Mile (Current Dollars).

	1981	1988	1996	2004
Bulk	0.97	1.14	1.09	0.94
Intermodal	1.68	1.25	1.65	2.31
Chemical	1.82	2.12	3.78	1.75
Auto	2.68	2.07	1.70	2.02
General	1.28	1.77	1.93	2.17

Table 6. U.S. Class I Railroads Estimated Lerner Indices.

	1981	1988	1996	2004
Bulk	.67 (.15)	.69 (.18)	.77 (.29)	.98 (.46)
Intermodal	.73 (.19)	.20 (.58)	.25 (.69)	.44 (.75)
Chemical	.77 (.13)	.62 (.17)	.64 (.35)	.53 (.76)
Auto	.84 (.15)	.56 (.27)	.38 (.55)	.58 (.64)
General	.70 (.20)	.55 (.21)	.51 (.43)	.55 (.54)

intermodal and boxcars. A more detailed analysis would also take into account this fact that prices and quantities are simultaneously determined in a strategic environment. Nevertheless, there are interesting conclusions that we can draw from a comparison of average revenues and estimated marginal costs.

First, the markups in the bulk markets for coal and grain have increased dramatically since 1981, especially in the period between 1996 and 2004. These are traditional, politically sensitive railroad markets where the degree of railroad market power depends heavily on geography. Atkinson and Kerkvliet (1986) found evidence of countervailing pressure on coal rates due to the monopsony power of large coal burning utilities. It would be interesting to explore in more detail whether there is still evidence of countervailing power in these markets, especially in the light of recent rail mergers and electric utility mergers. A second explanation, of course, is that railroads have shown significant productivity gains in these markets, especially as the movement of coal has shifted from shorter eastern hauls to longer hauls from the Powder River Basin. These gains have reduced the marginal costs of bulk movements which in turn increases the Lerner indices.

Second, there has been a significant increase in recent years in the Lerner indices in the intermodal market. Markups on intermodal traffic were lower in the years immediately following Staggers. What may have kept these markups down was not just competition with truckers – this competition also prevails in the chemical and automotive markets – but rail-to-rail competition for intermodal traffic between major cities. Recent years have seen consolidation in some of these markets along with increases in intermodal demand, which would allow railroads to price more strategically. There have also been improvements in rail productivity which would put downward pressure on marginal costs.

Third, the relatively high indices for chemical and automotive traffic are mainly indicative of the high value of these cargoes. Freight demand is a derived demand and the prices shippers are willing to pay are directly related to the value of shipments. While chemical shippers rely heavily on trucks to move finished chemical products, railroads still compete effectively in primary and intermediate markets especially where hazardous chemicals are involved. Automobiles and automotive equipment are also high-valued and railroads have been able to increase their share in these markets by working with automobile manufacturers to develop improved car carriers providing high levels of damage-free service.

Fourth, general freight movements in plain and refrigerated boxcars typically involve what the railroads consider "commonly important commodities": food, paper, lumber, and other manufactured goods, where there is a strong competition between railroads and trucks. Markups on these commodities are significant, nevertheless, and appear to reflect a cost advantage that the railroads have over trucks.

The overall Lerner results show a significant reduction over time in the *level* of markups which the railroads have enjoyed since 1981 (with the notable exception of the bulk markets) and some change in the *structure* of rates. At the beginning of the period, the highest markups were on the highest value commodities, automobiles, and chemicals. This was consistent with value of service pricing. After deregulation, margins on these commodities were reduced while margins on lower-valued bulk commodities increased—this despite a significant decrease in the real rates charged to bulk shippers.

4. REVENUE-TO-COST RATIO

The disaggregated Lerner indices in themselves cannot be given a normative interpretation. The indices reflect quasi-rents, the relationship between the rate the shipper pays and short-run marginal costs that the railroad incurs. Because railroads exhibit weakly increasing variable costs, marginal costs are below the average variable costs that are involved in the movement of particular commodities. Nor do the short-run marginal cost estimates reported here reflect total costs which – as shown in Eq. (1) – include both variable operating and maintenance costs and the opportunity costs of holding land. This means that marginal cost pricing of freight railroad services would eventually force termination of these services or require a subsidy.

To see this more formally, following Friedlaender (1992), let S_Y be the measure of ray economies of density and let Q be the revenue level that the railroad would achieve with marginal cost pricing in all of its output markets. Because this involves proportional increases in the elements of the output vector **y** we have

$$S_Y = \frac{C^{\mathrm{V}}\left(\mathbf{y}_1 \ldots \mathbf{y}_Z\right)}{\sum_z \mathbf{y}_z \,\partial\, C^{\mathrm{V}}/\partial\, y_z} \tag{10}$$

If $S_Y > 1$ (as it is in the current sample) marginal cost pricing will lead to a deficit with respect to variable costs.

The Lerner index results developed above show that railroads have some advantages in truck-competitive markets, and this allows significant mark-ups on intermodal, chemical, automotive, and general freight movements as well as bulk. This raises the prospect of a multiproduct pricing regime in which the set of markups above marginal cost enable the railroads to cover their costs. There is, of course, no guarantee that this will occur but one can use the estimates of marginal costs and rates developed above to assess whether the shipper–carrier configuration, which have emerged since 1981, have enabled firms in the sample to cover costs.

The first step is to compare the actual revenue that railroads in the sample received in each market in a given year with projected revenue that railroads would have received charging marginal cost prices. The sum of these differences is the total margin that the firms would have had available to cover full variable costs plus the opportunity cost of land. The results of this estimate are presented in Table 7 which gives the *average* actual revenues, marginal cost revenues, and margins in each of the five car-type markets for selected years. The table also includes "percent margin" estimates for each car-type and year. This is the percentage of total contribution provided by each type of traffic.

Table 7 confirms the importance of the bulk commodities in contributing to railroad margins but it also shows the extent to which railroads depend on intermodal, chemical, auto, and general freight traffic to cover costs. Bulk and intermodal shares have increased since 1981; chemical's share has remained fairly constant; shares of margin from automotive and general freight have dropped. Nevertheless, general freight traffic is still important. This is seen in Fig. 1 which presents the margin results for the year 2004.

The final revenue calculation is presented in Fig. 2. This shows the ratio of total revenue received by firms in the sample to estimated *total* costs, i.e., the sum of estimated variable costs and land costs. Variable costs for each of the 293 observations in the sample are estimated using Eq. 4. Opportunity costs of road are estimated using *miles of road* for each firm and multiplying this by a fixed value (ρ) of $32,800 per mile per year. This is a value which

Table 7. U.S. Class I Railroads Margin Contribution by Car-Type.

	Bulk	Intermodal	Chemical	Auto	Box	Total
			1981			
Revenue	440,001	131,984	143,536	97,120	497,178	1,358,288
MC Revenue	169,006	34,953	32,270	14,591	152,600	403,421
Margin	270,995	97,030	111,265	81,718	344,578	944,224
% of total margin	28	10	12	9	36	100
			1988			
Revenue	782,059	337,170	298,378	244,832	693,726	2,356,166
MC Revenue	330,576	214,799	98,535	77,105	283,934	1,004,952
Margin	451,482	122,370	199,843	167,726	409,791	1,351,214
% of total margin	33	9	15	12	31	100
			1996			
Revenue	1,205,577	606,215	419,879	258,968	959,128	3,449,770
MC Revenue	415,381	360,054	154,956	140,996	450,070	1,521,958
Margin	790,196	246,160	264,923	117,972	508,558	1,927,811
% of total margin	41	13	14	6	26	100
			2004			
Revenue	1,262,117	693,060	650,724	453,909	1,292,018	4,351,829
MC Revenue	152,425	233,728	187,043	195,740	368,383	1,137,322
Margin	1,109,691	459,331	463,681	258,168	923,634	3,214,507
% of total margin	35	14	14	8	29	100

Lee (1995) has proposed for assessing the opportunity cost of roadway land in the U.S., and takes into account the complexity of urban and rural valuations. The results suggest that the U.S. railroad revenues were less than adequate in the period immediately following the Staggers Rail Act, but the railroads finally achieved a degree of adequacy in 1986. They have remained adequate (by this measure) since then but often by a small margin. The highest degree of positive revenue adequacy (18 percent) was achieved in 1993 and the lowest degree (two percent) in 2003.

We can also use the results developed here to calculate what Lerner index, applied to all traffic, would exactly cover the estimated total costs of railroad operations. The average required Lerner index for all commodities, all years, and all railroads in the sample is 0.55. Table 6 shows that the U.S. freight railroads were almost at or above this index in the bulk, chemical,

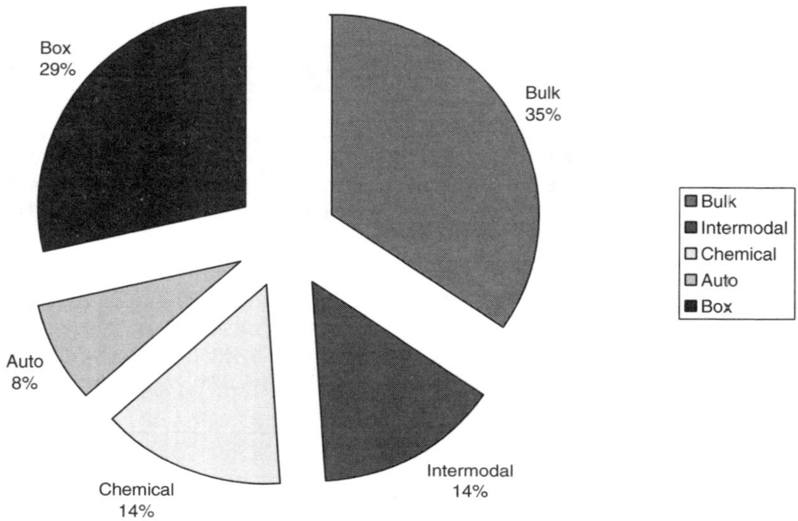

Fig. 1. Margin Contribution by Car-Type 2004.

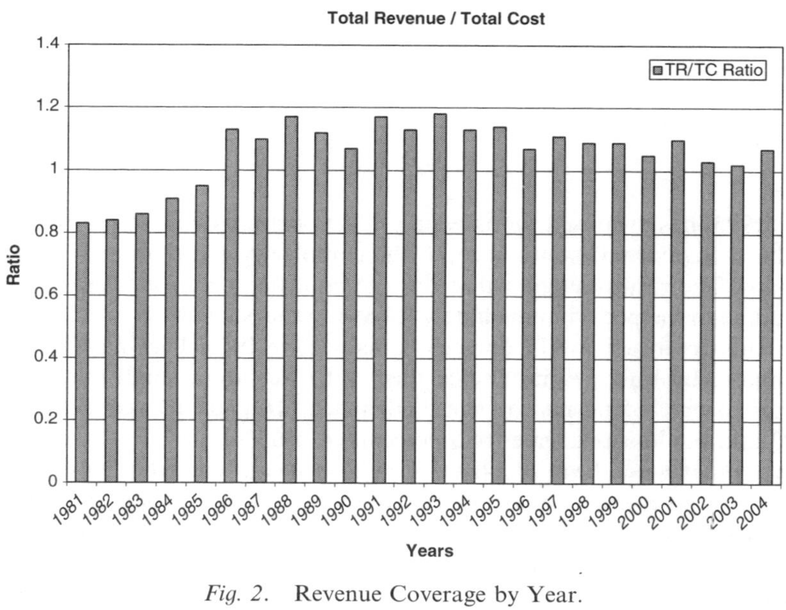

Fig. 2. Revenue Coverage by Year.

automotive, and general freight categories in 2004. It is reasonable to expect that they will be pushing to achieve better margins in the intermodal category in the coming years.

5. CONCLUSIONS

There has been a steady stream of statistical railroad cost studies in the formal economic literature. More recently there has been a series of "natural experiments" in which the regulatory structure of railroads in the U.S. and elsewhere has been dramatically changed. Nevertheless, railroads still present three fundamental questions for policy makers and researchers: (1) Are railroad returns to density such that some degree of natural monopoly is inevitable? (2) Is railroad market power such that some degree of government intervention is essential? (3) Will the complex equilibria involving railroad firms, their customers (freight or passenger), regulatory authorities, and other transportation modes guarantee that railroads will be revenue adequate?

Deregulation of the surface freight markets in 1980 has increased both the commercial freedom of the U.S. freight railroads and the level of truck competition. This has given added significance to questions about pricing behavior and economic viability. This chapter has shown that the U.S. railroad rate structure involves significant differential markups over variable marginal costs, with the Lerner indices currently ranging from 0.44 in intermodal to 0.95 in bulk. It also has shown that the rail freight markets involve an equilibrium in which "captive" (bulk) shippers and "competitive" (higher-value) shippers all contribute to the coverage of total costs. The margin by which total revenue exceeds total cost is not large, however, averaging just 5.6 percent.

This last fact has implications for both policy makers and researchers. The ability of railroads to compete in higher value markets is a function not only of competition policy (antitrust and regulation) but of general transportation policy as well. From an antitrust perspective, it would be useful to understand not just the effect that the Staggers Act and subsequent mergers have had on railroad carriers but also on shippers. That would require a welfare analysis beyond the scope of this paper.[17] From a regulatory perspective, it would also be useful to understand the strategic behaviors that underlie the structure of rail rates that has evolved since Staggers. Carriers, shippers, and regulators have all played roles in this development, especially in the development of contract rates.[18] Finally, there is the broader question of whether the thin margins that railroads have obtained will enable them to play a significant role in 21st century freight markets without a significant revision of transportation investment policies in the U.S., especially policies that affect trucking costs.

The final explanation for railroad revenue-to-cost ratios may lie at the beginning of this paper in Table 1. Between 1981 and 2004, real average revenues from major rail commodities decreased by percentages ranging from 10.6 percent (grain) to 42.6 percent (autos). This downward pressure on rates can be attributed to competition between railroads, to competition with other modes, to the bargaining power of shippers, and to the residual regulatory authority of STB. Whatever the sources, it has been more than adequate to constrain railroad pricing ability and has left the question of whether the industry can "downsize to profitability" is still open.

NOTES

1. See Friedlaender (1969).
2. See Interstate Commerce Commission, Ex Parte 347, *Coal rate guideline-nationwide*.
3. See, for example, Surface Transportation Board, Ex Parte 657, *Major issues in rail rate cases*.
4. We define variable costs as a function that represents cost behavior variable on a given scale of network (R) and for a given degree of technology (fixed by time T). In fact, our econometric estimate of costs does not directly involve the parameter ρ since this variable does not appear in the variable cost function. The variable R does appear in the variable cost function and represents the degree to which network size affects variable costs. The value of R does appear in Section IV of the analysis.
5. In fact, our specification allows us to differentiate between the interaction of infrastructure and bulk service and the interaction of infrastructure activity and general freight service.
6. The GM also allows for the simulation of rail costs in situations where some outputs take on zero values. This is the case in Ivaldi and McCullough (2004) which studies rail subadditivity. Though zero output levels are not directly relevant to the current study, the GM is adopted here because it is more flexible than the translog.
7. This parameterization is from Wiley, Schmidt, and Bramble (1973).
8. The spending categories are labor (Lines 250–251 of the *Analysis* plus an allocated portion of the road maintenance expenditure listed in Line 378), materials (Line 252 plus an allocated portion of road maintenance expenditures in Line 378), fuel (Line 253), and equipment and other (Lines 254–259 less road depreciation in Line 173). The allocation of labor and material expenditures from road maintenance expenditures (which the railroads separate out from operating expenses) are based on the portion of labor or materials to overall freight service expense (Line 262 less Line 173).

9. Bulk car-miles are from Lines 664–666, 673, 680–682, and 689 of the *Analysis*. General freight car miles are from Lines 659–661, 667–670, 675–677. Ties laid in replacement are from Line 350.

10. Miles of road is Line 342 and train-miles are in Line 650.

11. A more thorough analysis of this dynamic relationship is a subject of current research.

12. Economies of density are defined here as efficiencies that result from an increase in traffic $ED = 1/\sum_z(\partial C/\partial y_z)$. These are distinguished from economies of scale which in the rail case involve increases in network size.

13. Spending on infrastructure is in Line 149 of the AAR *Analysis*. Ties laid in replacement are in Line 350.

14. See Ivaldi and McCullough (2001), p. 175, for a summary of earlier findings.

15. See Dennis (2000) for a more detailed discussion of rail rates.

16. Revenues for bulk traffic are from Lines 577–582 of the AAR *Analysis*; bulk car-miles are in Lines 662–666 (loaded) and 678–682 (empty). Revenues for intermodal are in Line 596; intermodal car-miles are in Lines 669 (loaded) and 685 (empty). Revenues for chemical are in Line 588; chemical car-miles are in Lines 673 (loaded) and 689 (empty). Revenues for automotive are in Line 593; car-miles are in Lines 670 (loaded) and 686 (empty). Revenues for general freight include all other revenues and general car-miles include all other car-miles. Intermodal revenues are expanded by a factor of 1.3 based on an estimate by AAR staff that the amount of intermodal revenue *not* included in Line 596 is about 30 percent. Both loaded and empty car-miles are used to estimate average revenues for all categories because the marginal cost estimates are based on empty and loaded mileage.

17. See Ivaldi and McCullough (2005) for a discussion of welfare effects of rail mergers.

18. See Winston, Dennis, and Maheshri (2004) and Ivaldi and McCullough (2005) for a discussion of strategic interactions between carriers and shippers. See Pittman (2005) for a discussion of regulatory experiments outside the U.S.

REFERENCES

Association of American Railroads. (1981–2004). *Analysis of Class I Railroads*. Washington, DC: AAR Economics and Finance Department.

Association of American Railroads. (1981–2004). *Railroad Cost Factors*. Washington, DC: AAR Economics and Finance Department.

Atkinson, S. E., & Kirkvliet, J. R. (1986). Measuring the multilateral allocation of rents: Wyoming low sulphur coal. *The RAND Journal of Economics*, *17*, 416–430.

Berndt, E. R., Friedlaender, A. F., Wang Chiang, J. S.-E., & Christopher, A. V. (1993). Cost effects of mergers and deregulation in the U.S. rail industry. *Journal of Productivity Analysis*, *4*, 127–144.

Bitzan, J. D. (1999). The structure of railroad costs and the benefits/costs of mergers. *Research in Transportation Economics*, *5*, 1–52.

Braeutigam, R. R., Andrew, F. D., & Turnquist, M. A. (1982). The estimation of a hybrid cost function for a railroad firm. *Review of Economics and Statistics*, *64*(3), 394–404.

Brown, R. S., Caves, D. W., & Christiansen, L. R. (1979). Modeling the structure of costs and production for multiple product firms. *Southern Economic Journal*, *46*, 256–273.

Caves, D. W., Christensen, L. R., Tretheway, M. W., & Windle, R. (1985). Network effects and the measurement of returns to scale and density for U.S. railroads. In: A. Daughety (Ed.), *Analytical studies in transport economics*. Cambridge: Cambridge University Press.

Dennis, S. M. (2000). Changes in railroad rates since the Staggers Act. *Transportation Research Part E*, *37*, 55–69.

Diewert, W. E., & Wales, T. J. (1987). Flexible functional forms and global curvature conditions. *Econometrica*, *55*(1), 43–68.

Friedlaender, A. F. (1969). *The dilemma of freight transport regulation*. Washington, DC: The Brookings Institution.

Friedlaender, A. F. (1992). Coal rates and revenue adequacy in a quasi-regulated rail industry. *The RAND Journal of Economics*, *23*, 376–394.

Friedlaender, A. F., Berndt, E. R., Chiang, J. S. W., Showalter, M. H., & Christopher, A. V. (1993). Rail costs and capital adjustments in a quasi-regulated environment. *Journal of Transport Economics and Policy*, *27*, 131–152.

Friedlaender, A. F., & Spady, R. H. (1981). *Freight transport regulation: Equity, efficiency, and competition in the rail and trucking industries*. Cambridge, MA: MIT Press.

Griliches, Z. (1972). Cost allocation in railroad regulation. *Bell Journal of Economics and Management Science*, *3*, 26–41.

Harmatuck, D. J. (1979). Economies of traffic density in the rail freight industry. *Bell Journal of Economics*. (Autumn), 556–564.

Ivaldi, M., & McCullough, G. (2001). Density and integration effects on Class I U.S. freight railroads. *Journal of Regulatory Economics*, *19*(2), 161–182.

Ivaldi, M., & McCullough, G. (2004). *Subadditivity tests for network separation using a generalized McFadden cost function.* Discussion paper #4392. Center for Economic Policy Research (CEPR), London, England.

Ivaldi, M., & McCullough, G. (2005). *Welfare tradeoffs in U.S. rail mergers*. Discussion paper #5000. Center for Economic Policy Research (CEPR), London, England.

Kumbhakar, S. C. (1994). A multiproduct symmetric generalized McFadden cost function. *Journal of Productivity Analysis*, *5*, 349–357.

Lee, D. (1995). *Full cost pricing of highways*. Cambridge, MA: Systems Center Volpe National Transportation.

McFadden, D. L. (1978). Cost, revenue, and profit functions. In: D. L. McFadden & F. Melvin (Eds), *Production economics*. Amsterdam: North-Holland.

Pittman, R. (2005). Structural separation to create competition? The case of freight railways. *Review of Network Economics*, *4*(3), 181–196.

Wiley, D. E., Schmidt, W. H., & Bramble, W. J. (1973). Studies of a class of covariance structure models. *Journal of the American Statistical Association*, *68*(342), 317–323.

Wilson, W. W. (1997). Cost savings and productivity in the railroad industry. *Journal of Regulatory Economics*, *11*, 21–40.

Winston, C., Dennis, S., & Maheshri, V. (2004). *Duopoly in the railroad industry: Bertrand, cournot or collusive.* Working paper.

APPENDIX

Table A1. Nonlinear FIML Parameter Estimates.

Param	Estimate	Standard Error	*t*-Stat.	Pr > |*t*|
al	299.1673	330.6	0.9	0.3663
af	−15.0589	69.2415	−0.22	0.828
ae	1,108.847	481.2	2.3	0.022
am	−228.774	121.7	−1.88	0.0611
dll	−6.41E−06	1.04E−06	−6.14	<.0001
dlf	−1.04E−07	1.18E−07	−0.88	0.3786
dle	3.82E−06	7.90E−07	4.83	<.0001
dff	−4.78E−08	3.91E−08	−1.22	0.222
dfe	2.00E−08	1.41E−07	0.14	0.8877
dee	−4.83E−06	1.04E−06	−4.66	<.0001
dlm	−8.82E−07	2.61E−07	−3.38	0.0008
dfm	8.57E−09	6.54E−08	0.13	0.8958
dem	−2.30E−07	3.28E−07	−0.7	0.4849
dmm	−4.41E−08	2.37E−07	−0.19	0.8527
llyb	0.002202	0.000528	4.17	<.0001
llye	0.002159	0.000503	4.29	<.0001
llyi	1.347148	1.59E−37	8.45E+36	<.0001
lfyb	−0.00022	0.00014	−1.56	0.1211
lfye	0.000588	0.000123	4.79	<.0001
lfyi	0.139251	8.07E−37	1.73E+35	<.0001
leyb	0.00117	0.000791	1.48	0.1405
leye	0.005179	0.000759	6.82	<.0001
leyi	0.367625	8.49E−38	4.33E+36	<.0001
lmyb	0.001302	0.000189	6.89	<.0001
lmye	0.000518	0.000183	2.83	0.0049
lmyi	0.252196	3.88E−37	6.50E+35	<.0001
gybyb	8.95E−14	3.40E−14	2.63	0.0089
gyeye	1.99E−13	4.13E−14	4.83	<.0001
gyiyi	2.88E−08	1.98E−08	1.45	0.1472
gybye	−1.35E−13	3.44E−14	−3.92	0.0001
gybyi	3.86E−11	1.67E−11	2.31	0.0218
gyeyi	−5.27E−11	2.13E−11	−2.47	0.014
llt	−66.5618	34.0896	−1.95	0.0519
lltt	8.91142	2.1402	4.16	<.0001

APPENDIX

Table A1. (*Continued*).

Param	Estimate	Standard Error	*t*-Stat.	Pr > |*t*|
lft	0.921432	6.7186	0.14	0.891
lftt	0.216727	0.4269	0.51	0.6121
let	−94.3454	52.2064	−1.81	0.0719
lett	3.691246	3.2975	1.12	0.264
lmt	11.33997	12.9782	0.87	0.383
lmtt	1.54359	0.824	1.87	0.0621
llr	0.099604	0.0626	1.59	0.1127
llrr	−0.00001	4.63E−06	−2.36	0.0189
lfr	−0.01445	0.016	−0.9	0.3674
lfrr	2.67E−06	1.20E−06	2.22	0.0272
ler	−0.27936	0.0952	−2.93	0.0036
lerr	0.000029	7.22E−06	3.97	<.0001
lmr	0.021039	0.022	0.96	0.34
lmrr	−5.74E−07	1.66E−06	−0.35	0.7302
llh	0.049148	0.162	0.3	0.7619
llhh	0.000074	0.000043	1.71	0.0877
lfh	−0.01132	0.0323	−0.35	0.7266
lfhh	4.08E−06	8.15E−06	0.5	0.6174
leh	−0.40388	0.2438	−1.66	0.0988
lehh	0.000032	0.000067	0.48	0.6296
lmh	0.078755	0.06	1.31	0.1902
lmhh	0.000025	0.000016	1.53	0.1279
lltr	−0.01054	0.00269	−3.91	0.0001
llth	−0.00997	0.00487	−2.05	0.0416
llrh	0.000045	0.000015	2.99	0.0031
lftr	−0.00004	0.000527	−0.08	0.9377
lfth	−0.00035	0.000976	−0.36	0.7216
lfrh	0.000012	2.87E−06	4.21	<.0001
letr	0.001426	0.00414	0.34	0.7306
leth	0.007209	0.00752	0.96	0.3383
lerh	0.000034	0.000023	1.51	0.133
lmtr	−0.00673	0.00102	−6.61	<.0001
lmth	−0.0046	0.00181	−2.55	0.0115

APPENDIX

Table A1. (*Continued*).

Param	Estimate	Standard Error	*t*-Stat.	Pr > |*t*|
lmrh	0.000024	5.54E−06	4.32	<.0001
lltyb	0.000092	0.000033	2.75	0.0064
lltye	0.000041	0.000037	1.1	0.2727
lltyi	0.008317	0.0271	0.31	0.759
llryb	−6.42E−09	2.40E−08	−0.27	0.7892
llrye	6.81E−08	2.62E−08	2.6	0.0099
llryi	−0.00002	0.000017	−1.21	0.2264
llhyb	−2.77E−07	1.80E−07	−1.54	0.1257
llhye	−4.78E−07	1.72E−07	−2.78	0.0058
llhyi	−0.00005	0.000139	−0.36	0.7155
lftyb	−0.00002	6.60E−06	−3.53	0.0005
lftye	0.000021	7.68E−06	2.69	0.0077
lftyi	−0.0069	0.00457	−1.51	0.1325
lfryb	2.42E−08	7.19E−09	3.37	0.0009
lfrye	−2.90E−08	7.41E−09	−3.92	0.0001
lfryi	−9.28E−06	4.06E−06	−2.28	0.0231
lfhyb	1.48E−08	3.56E−08	0.42	0.678
lfhye	−1.05E−07	3.77E−08	−2.8	0.0055
lfhyi	0.000024	0.000031	0.78	0.4373
letyb	−0.00018	0.000051	−3.44	0.0007
letye	0.000265	0.000056	4.69	<.0001
letyi	−0.09051	0.0388	−2.34	0.0203
leryb	1.11E−07	3.54E−08	3.12	0.002
lerye	−2.18E−07	3.41E−08	−6.4	<.0001
leryi	−0.00008	0.000018	−4.18	<.0001
lehyb	−9.14E−09	2.71E−07	−0.03	0.9731
lehye	−1.31E−06	2.63E−07	−4.98	<.0001
lehyi	0.00054	0.000207	2.61	0.0096
lmtyb	0.000048	0.000013	3.71	0.0003
lmtye	0.000048	0.000014	3.47	0.0006
lmtyi	−0.00841	0.00913	−0.92	0.3577
lmryb	−8.78E−09	8.16E−09	−1.08	0.2826
lmrye	2.00E−08	8.36E−09	2.39	0.0175

APPENDIX

Table A1. *(Continued).*

Param	Estimate	Standard Error	t-Stat.	Pr > |t|
lmryi	−9.49E−06	5.08E−06	−1.87	0.0632
lmhyb	−2.65E−07	6.82E−08	−3.88	0.0001
lmhye	−2.90E−07	6.36E−08	−4.55	<.0001
lmhyi	0.000074	0.00005	1.48	0.1397
byi	390.1271	173.3	2.25	0.0252
gama0	197.9471	67.613	2.93	0.0037
gamae	0.000024	0.000076	0.32	0.7515
gamat	−8.53561	4.315	−1.98	0.0489
gamar	0.097288	0.00791	12.29	<.0001
c0yb	3.235948	1.4315	2.26	0.0245
c1yb	1.105272	0.0273	40.47	<.0001
c2yb	0.036199	0.0615	0.59	0.5565
c3yb	0.042728	0.0642	0.67	0.5063
c4yb	1.681985	0.1967	8.55	<.0001
c5yb	−2.03333	0.4163	−4.88	<.0001
c6yb	0.146078	0.0781	1.87	0.0624
c0ye	5.686309	2.0118	2.83	0.005
c1ye	0.932994	0.0375	24.89	<.0001
c2ye	−0.33416	0.0862	−3.87	0.0001
c3ye	0.377676	0.0895	4.22	<.0001
c4ye	1.084537	0.2717	3.99	<.0001
c5ye	−1.03112	0.5844	−1.76	0.0787
c6ye	−0.1831	0.1047	−1.75	0.0814
gamab	0.000134	0.000083	1.61	0.1077

OPTIONS FOR RESTRUCTURING THE STATE-OWNED MONOPOLY RAILWAY☆

Russell Pittman

ABSTRACT

Vertical separation in the freight railways sector may sacrifice significant economies of integration. Economies of density suggest that corresponding benefits may be elusive. We examine competitive alternatives to vertical separation. One option is the creation of competition among restructured vertically integrated railways, an option generally limited to relatively large countries absent willingness to create multinational railway networks. Second is the opening of the infrastructure of the integrated railway to access by train operating companies. Rarely are the benefits of separation of train from track likely to be so great as to outweigh the losses from the vertical separation itself.

1. INTRODUCTION

A broad consensus has emerged that the traditional arrangement of a state-owned monopoly railway is inefficient and unworkable and so should be

☆The views expressed are not those of the U.S. Department of Justice.

Railroad Economics
Research in Transportation Economics, Volume 20, 179–198

ISSN: 0739-8859/doi:10.1016/S0739-8859(07)20007-1

replaced by an institutional arrangement that allows for the introduction of market forces.[1] State-run monopoly railways have been judged *inefficient* because of the poor incentive properties of state ownership and the soft budget constraint generally, and because state-owned railways have been unable to resist political demands for over-manning, above-market wages, and restrictive work rules. They have been judged *unworkable* because of the combination of the resulting high operating costs with the inability of state owners to resist the temptation to continually postpone expenditures on maintenance and new investment, eventually allowing even long-lived plant and equipment to deteriorate.

The introduction of private investment, control, and ownership into the system has been considered a part of the solution to these problems. However, while a private monopolist may have better incentives to operate efficiently than a public monopolist – in both the short and long run – arguably any type of monopolist continues to enjoy the incentive to increase price and restrict output vis-à-vis the levels that a firm facing significant competition would choose. In this chapter, we assume that private sector "participation" in the railway sector has been chosen as a policy decision – though we will address some details, in particular the question of control of the infrastructure itself – and focus on the question of how to restructure the system in such a way as to protect customers from the presence and exercise of monopoly power.

First we must separate freight rail service from passenger rail service for analysis. Most railway systems around the world offer both types of service, but the two service types are generally characterized by very different cost structures and competitive conditions, so that the preferred policy choices for a system that provides mostly freight service (for example, the US and Canada) may differ from that for a system that provides mostly passenger service (for example, most western European countries).

In particular, it is very rare under current conditions in any country that the passenger service operations of a railway can pay even their direct costs, much less pay their fully allocated costs, and much less support competing service providers. The combination of widespread automobile ownership with quick and inexpensive air travel has taken a great deal of personal travel off the rails. Thus in almost every country – Japan is the principle exception – what passenger rail service remains, both commuter and long distance, is subsidized by governments, generally in an effort to reduce traffic congestion, fuel consumption, and air pollution, and sometimes to keep transportation available to the poor as well. (When the latter concern is the principle rationale for subsidies, buses rather than passenger trains are often the more efficient and economical policy choice.)

This means that the question of how to restructure the state-owned monopoly *passenger* railway is generally the question of the most efficient way to provide subsidies, along with, sometimes, the most efficient way to administer and target universal service obligations. There is a widespread presumption among economists that the correct policy choice here is the creation of competition *for* the market through a franchise bidding scheme with a negative price (Chadwick, 1859; Demsetz, 1968), though Williamson (1976) has shown that in the presence of long-lived assets there may be problems in rebidding process that make the process less competitive and/or less efficient than it might otherwise appear, and Affuso and Newbery (2002a, 2002b) confirm the importance of this issue in the context of British Rail privatization. Otherwise, however, passenger rail policy would seem to raise few competitive issues, and we focus mostly on questions involving freight rail policy in this chapter.

For freight services, the answer to the question of how businesses may be protected against abuses by a monopoly railway is for many classes of commodity shippers a straightforward one: make sure that shipment via other modes is an economic alternative. It is important to note, however, that the determination of whether particular classes of shippers have economic alternatives may require a complex and fact-specific investigation. In general, higher valued commodities such as manufactured goods are more likely to be shipped economically by motor carrier than lower valued commodities such as bulk minerals and construction materials, and, in both categories, motor carriers are generally able to compete better for shorter distance hauls than for longer distance (Pittman, 1990; Kwoka & White, 2004). Water transport, though generally slower than rail or motor, is often competitive for the long-distance transport of bulk commodities, but of course only under the right geographic circumstances and hydrologic conditions.

The general policy lessons from the consideration of "intermodal competition" – note that economists use this term in a different sense than do railroaders – is twofold. First, tax and infrastructure policies that improve the ability of motor and water carriers to compete for the custom of freight shippers may directly reduce the level of market power held by rail freight carriers and so be directly welfare enhancing in that respect. Second – as generally accepted in rail merger analysis in the US and Canada – individual shippers and categories of shippers who can economically substitute among different transport modes for shipping their goods are not at risk of exploitation by a rail "monopolist": this is a "monopolist" without market power.

The interesting and difficult questions appear when there are significant magnitudes of commodities to ship that are rail-captive – that have no economic shipping alternatives other than rail. In countries such as the US and the UK with a history privately constructed, vertically integrated railroads competing against each other for freight traffic, shippers have relied upon two different forms of intramodal (i.e., railway versus railway) competition, generally labeled "parallel" (or sometimes "end-to-end") competition and "source" competition. Countries lacking such a history have been more likely to attempt to create rail competition by introducing new train operating companies on the same track infrastructure used by the incumbent train operating company. Let us consider these differing options in more detail.

2. OPTIONS FOR CREATING RAIL VERSUS RAIL COMPETITION

The most obvious and direct form of intramodal rail competition occurs when two independent vertically integrated railways provide service between the same city-pairs.[2] So, for example, companies seeking to ship freight between Chicago and Los Angeles can choose between the Union Pacific/Southern Pacific Railway and the Burlington Northern/Santa Fe Railway, while those seeking to ship freight between Toronto and Vancouver can choose between the Canadian National Railway and the Canadian Pacific Railway. This *parallel competition* is typically abetted by institutions like reciprocal trackage rights and terminal railroads that allow any railway company that reaches a particular city to have access to most shippers in that city.

A second form of intramodal rail competition occurs when a shipper can send its product to an alternative destination using a different railroad, or a customer can receive a product from an alternative source using a different railroad. This *source competition* – sometimes called "geographic" competition – is not so "obvious and direct" as parallel competition, but it has been shown to provide important constraints on the behavior of rail companies that would otherwise enjoy market power.[3] A company seeking to ship commodity X – and in particular *bulk* commodity X – from origin O to destination D may appear to face a rail monopolist, if only one railway connects these two points. However, if the shipper has access to other railways at point O – even if they do not reach D, perhaps going in completely different directions – and if there are potential customers for its commodity located on these other railways, then these options may in many circumstances provide sufficient competition to the O–D "monopolist" that its market power is significantly constrained. Similarly, for the customer at D seeking to receive goods to have protection from this O–D "monopolist," the customer must have access to other railways serving D from different origins – with, of course, corresponding access to substitute products to those available from O.

Source competition is clearly an imperfect substitute for parallel competition, and a close, fact-specific investigation is required to determine whether in particular circumstances the apparent market power of an O–D rail monopolist is in fact tempered significantly by the presence of other railways at both origin and destination. If a producer at point O absolutely requires that its output reach a customer at point D, the fact that another railway serving O could take the output to point E may not be relevant, and similarly for a customer at point D who absolutely requires a particular product available only from point O. Nevertheless, many shippers confirm that if they have a second railway soliciting their business – even if the origin or destination would be a different one from that offered by the first railway – the very presence of the second railway provides them alternatives and hence protection from the ability of the first to charge high tariffs. Furthermore, there is strong econometric evidence confirming the ability of source competition to affect O–D rates; examples include MacDonald (1987, 1989a, 1989b) for grain rates and Winston, Dennis, and Maheshri (2004) for coal rates.[4] Source competition has become a more widespread limitation on rail rates as globalization has increased the size of geographic markets, for example forcing the US railroads to set rates for grain haulage constrained by the ability of the ultimate international customers to receive grain from other countries.

Parallel and source competition are the foundations upon which freight railway deregulation has been constructed in the US and Canada, though Canada especially has relied to some degree upon third-party access as well. (We do not consider here a further source of competition that may be effective on occasion: *product competition*, the ability of a customer to use a substitute product delivered by another railroad.) Source competition, in particular, was relied upon in the restructuring of the railways of Argentina and Mexico (and to a lesser degree Brazil) into vertically integrated railways competing with each other for freight customers at common points.[5]

In contrast to the situation in the Americas, in Europe policy makers have generally chosen a different strategy for the creation of intramodal rail competition: they have sought to create competition "above the rail" between different train companies operating over a common track infrastructure – and so leaving the infrastructure monopoly intact. As with the American model, this strategy comes in two variants, typically labeled "third-party access" and "vertical separation." The parallel to widely used reform strategies in other infrastructure sectors such as electricity, natural gas, and telecommunications should be clear (Newbery, 1999; von Hirschhausen, 2002; Pittman, 2003).

Third party access (TPA) imposes upon an integrated railway the obligation to provide access to its track infrastructure to independent, non-integrated train operating companies (TOCs). Under the railway directives of the European Union, for example, vertically integrated railways are required not only to allow such TOC access but also to create sufficient internal organizational separation to allow regulators to verify that the independent TOCs have access to the infrastructure on the same terms as those available to the affiliated trains of the integrated company. Of course, as with any access mandated by regulators, the integrated company is likely to have the incentive to discriminate in subtle ways, and in practice this has been a serious challenge for regulatory and competition authorities.[6]

A second problem with the TPA model – "problem" from the standpoint of reformers, "advantage" from the standpoint of both integrated railways and those worried about the downside risks of reform – is that it can be imposed and implemented very, very gradually – so gradually, in some cases, as to make it almost imperceptible. The experience with TPA in freight railways in Europe and Russia to this point – though it does vary by country – is that not much competition has been created, at least not very quickly. Russia's railways restructuring plan is in its second phase – a phase in which competition is to be introduced – but so far the principal events in this regard have been the continued delays in getting parliament to enact the law formally creating a regime for granting access permits to third party TOCs, and widespread complaints that the integrated railway discriminates even against shippers who seek to use their own rolling stock on RZhD trains.[7]

The solution often proposed to the problems of TPA is complete *vertical separation*: the splitting of the vertically integrated railway into two independent enterprises, one controlling the infrastructure and the other operating trains, with the assumption that the incentive for discrimination by the infrastructure operator is thereby removed and that new TOCs will now enter. Indeed in the railway sector as in other infrastructure sectors this vertical separation model has come to be considered a sort of "default option" for public utilities restructuring. For example, Laffont (2004) states that

> The general trend is to separate the monopolistic segment from the competitive ones. In other words, vertical separation is taken to be the mainstream restructuring form of industrial structure.

Newbery (2005) agrees:

> The new conventional wisdom is that network utilities should be unbundled, with the potentially competitive network services under separate ownership from the natural monopoly network, so that the network owner has no incentive to favour its own service provider.

In the European railway system, former EU competition director Mario Monti made clear his opinion that while TPA was all very well, effective competition among independent TOCs would take place only once there was complete vertical separation (Monti, 2002).[8]

3. CHOOSING AMONG THE ALTERNATIVES

How might a policy maker or analyst choose among these reform options for creating competition for freight shippers on the state-owned monopoly railway in their country?

Let us begin the discussion with a brief return to passenger-related issues. If the country's railway is mainly a passenger railway, parallel competition is unlikely to be economically viable, and source competition is unlikely to provide much protection to customers. (For a very large proportion of the travelers leaving origin O, most destinations E are not close substitutes for destination D.) Furthermore, as noted earlier, the world experience seems to confirm that it is an exceedingly rare event for a passenger train operation to cover its direct expenses even as a "monopoly," much less for demand to be sufficient to support competing train operators. In the UK, initial plans to create competing passenger train operating companies for the same locations were significantly scaled back.[9]

For a railway that is mostly or solely a passenger operation, then, the choice for creating competition in restructuring would seem to be between auctioning a concession for the integrated railway – that is, for infrastructure and train operations performed by the same franchisee – and auctioning a concession for train operations while making other arrangements (continued state ownership? a separate auction?) for the infrastructure.

From purely a competition standpoint, there would seem to be no advantage to forcing vertical separation in this case beyond possibly expanding the list of potential franchisees, if the integrated package would be so large as to exclude some potential bidders from the process. However, some countries have chosen for other reasons not to relinquish government control of infrastructure, even in the form of a long-term franchise, in which case auctioning off the passenger train operation becomes an attractive outcome. Whether the integrated railway operation or only the train operation is auctioned off, the length of the franchise period is a difficult and important issue, introducing a tradeoff between the ability and incentive to invest in capital equipment and the force of potential and then actual competition for the franchise as a disciplining device (Welsby & Nichols, 1999; Affuso & Newbery, 2002a, 2002b).

In contrast to passenger rail operations, freight rail operations are generally expected to be self-supporting; thus the need for subsidies does not complicate the discussion of options for creating competition. Perhaps the most important issue distinguishing the American-style restructuring models discussed above versus the European-style models is that of vertical integration between the infrastructure operations and the train operations. As I have argued elsewhere (Pittman, 2005a), there are strong a priori reasons to believe that economies of vertical integration are significant in the railways sector; the very locus of vertical separation, between the wagon wheel and the track, is a point where investments, maintenance, and other actions on one side may have a significant impact on costs on the other. The econometric estimates of Ivaldi and McCullough (2004) suggest a cost advantage of 20–40 percent for an integrated railway versus separate infrastructure operators and diversified train operators based on the US data, and Wetzel and Growitsch (2006) derive similar results using the European data.[10]

In addition to these static results, the experience with vertical separation in rail and other sectors has begun to suggest that it is difficult to create appropriate incentives for investment – in both maintenance and new capacity – for a vertically separated, regulated infrastructure company. Several observers argue that incentive problems for maintenance and improvement of the track infrastructure were the single most important reason for the failure of the UK experiment with vertical separation of the railway.[11]

All this would seem to suggest that some burden of proof be placed on those who argue for vertical separation as a policy for creating competition. How would they go about trying to meet this burden?

The first response is that it may be difficult to create intramodal rail competition while maintaining vertical integration. If that is the case, then there may be an explicit tradeoff to consider between the gains from competition and the losses from vertical separation.

Consider the two forms of intramodal competition among integrated railways discussed above. There is little dispute that parallel competition works well to protect shippers from rail market power in those locations where it exists today – principally the US and Canada. (There are strong arguments that it worked even better in the US before the most recent round of large rail mergers; see, e.g., Chapin and Schmidt (1999) and Kwoka and White (2004).) And there seems no reason to doubt that it would be at least theoretically possible to restructure some existing monopoly railways in such a way as to create vertically integrated railways that could compete in parallel fashion – across national borders in the EU, for example, or in Russia (Friebel, Guriev, Pittman, Shevyakhova, & Tomova, 2007), or China (Pittman, 2004a).

The principal argument for caution in the creation of parallel competition among vertically integrated freight railways is the fear that these competing lines would operate with insufficient business to achieve the available economics of density in rail freight hauling. Econometric studies have generally found that existing freight railways are operating at levels where economies of density are not yet exhausted; this is the conclusion of a review of the literature by Savignat and Nash (1999) and of more recent studies of the US Class I railways by Wilson (1997), Ivaldi and McCullough (2001), and Bitzan (2003). The estimates of the magnitude of unexhausted economies of density of course vary across studies, but it is interesting to note that Wilson's estimate of 31 percent at the mean of his sample is squarely in the middle of the range of economies of vertical integration estimated by Ivaldi and McCullough (2001), cited above. Of course, unexhausted economies of density would seem to argue against competing train-operating companies on the same track as well as against competing parallel integrated railway companies.

It is interesting to note, however, that estimates of unexhausted economies of density do *not* appear to be accompanied by suggestions of unexhausted economies of system size, i.e., track mileage. Though "railwaymen" would certainly point to such factors as longer average lengths of haul, fewer interchanges, more alternatives for direct routing, and better utilization of equipment as economies available with increased system size, econometric estimates suggest that these decreasing costs flatten out at fairly moderate scales of operation. Savignat and Nash (1999) report a consensus in the literature that only relatively small railways operate at a level of unexhausted economies of system size, and Wilson (1997) finds that at the mean of his sample, the US Class I railways are operating with slight diseconomies of system size. The results of Bitzan (1999) suggest a flattening of the cost curve for system size at around 5,000 miles, while Chapin and Schmidt (1999) also find a flattening of the cost curve, but at about twice that mileage level.[12]

This finding leads directly to the consideration of the second form of intramodal competition among vertically integrated railways: source competition. Savignat and Nash (1999) conclude from their literature review that

> The general finding of economies of density might suggest that a single operator on each route is best, whilst the lack of economies of scale [i.e., system size] beyond a certain point would suggest that … several integrated railways per country would be possible, at least in the larger countries.

They go on to suggest that such a system "might at least provide some possibilities of yardstick competition between regional operators," but the more important point for our purposes is that such a system might also provide some possibilities for direct competition for the business of shippers and customers located at points served by two or more such vertically integrated railways.

Indeed the experience with competition among vertically integrated "regional" railways in the US, Canada, and Mexico suggests that other competitive forces may be set in motion by this form of restructuring as well. First, it is quite common in these countries now for railway companies to compete with each other to provide incentives for firms to build new plants located on their lines rather than those of a rival. Second, as I noted in Pittman (1990), many rail freight shippers – including but not limited to those using containers – are not located directly on a railroad line, but rely on motor carriers to haul their products to a rail line for shipment. (When not related to containers, this practice is called transshipment.) Once the product has been loaded onto a motor carrier, it may be economical to have it hauled to a more distant rail line if that railway is offering better terms, and this then becomes a second way for these "regional" railways to compete with each other. Finally, at locations where two such railways are not far from each other, it is not unusual for a large shipper to threaten to build – or actually to build – a spur line connecting with an alternative railway, when dissatisfied with the terms offered by the incumbent. Even a threat to build may evoke more attractive terms from the existing railway.

Some, including this author, would argue that the preceding factors should render the creation of vertically integrated railways competing for traffic at common points, a more attractive default option for railways restructuring than vertical separation. However, it must be admitted that this model has its own weaknesses as a restructuring option. First, until the world becomes more ready for multinational integrated railway companies, this is mostly a large and medium-sized country option: the results of Bitzan (1999) and Chapin and Schmidt (1999) cited above suggest that creating multiple, competing vertically integrated railways smaller in size than 5,000–10,000 mile track networks would sacrifice economies of system size. (For reference, the size of the French railway network is about 20,000 miles; the Czech, about 6,000.)

Second, it is clear that source competition offers more effective protection against a railway holding a monopoly over service on a particular origin–destination corridor in some circumstances than in others. As usual with the evaluation of competition in railways, the devil is in the details. Levin (1984) argues that source competition

> Tends to be effective when sources of supply are numerous, when cost conditions of alternative sources of supply are homogeneous, when transport costs from alternative sources are similar, when the delivered products are close substitutes, and when the share of transport costs in the delivered price of the product is high.

(He is focusing on competition from alternative origins to a single destination; corresponding arguments would apply to competition for traffic from a single origin to alternative destinations.) Further and more specifically, my own interviews with shippers have suggested that

> Source competition tends not to be effective in constraining market power for the carriage of commodities that are strongly differentiated by brand name, because maintenance of the goodwill stock of the brand name may require service to particular locations. (Pittman, 1990)

On grounds of network size alone, then, and assuming a requirement that restructured railways remain within the borders of a single country, probably only three countries in the world remain obvious candidates for a restructuring plan that would create multiple vertically integrated railways competing among themselves in parallel fashion and at common points: Russia, China, and India. However, if we note that Mexico's experience with this restructuring plan is generally evaluated as quite successful, that Mexico's network is of only moderately large size (12,000 miles), and that many railway freight operations in transition economies operate with relatively dense traffic loads, another group of candidates suggests itself, including perhaps Poland, Ukraine, Kazakhstan, and Romania.[13]

Finally, given the high and growing importance of international freight railway haulage – on which more below – it seems worth emphasizing at least the possibility of the adoption of railways restructuring plans that would create vertically integrated railways whose networks cross national borders. This would of course render this restructuring option feasible in several regions where at least some within-country integrated railways would be too small to be viable, and of course would face no direct rail competition, except at international borders. The most obvious examples would seem to be Central Europe, Southeastern Europe, Central Asia, and Central and Southern Africa.

However, if national railways are in fact to be restructured and reorganized on a national basis, at least in the foreseeable future, it is clear that some are too small for the creation of what is called in the telecommunications world "facilities-based competition" – i.e., competition among multiple firms that each have their own infrastructure. In that case the only possibility for creating intramodal rail freight competition is by granting infrastructure access to competing operators of trains. This option is all the more relevant for those countries that are in a position to serve as transit countries for long-distance freight rail haulage – most conspicuously, countries through which one of the competing routes for hauling freight from Asia to Europe may pass.

For these small and medium-sized countries, deciding between the TPA model and the vertical separation model would seem to create a set of stark tradeoffs involving at least four factors: economies of vertical integration, economies of density, regulatory capacity, and the relative importance of domestic versus transit traffic.[14] In particular:

1. As argued above, the importance and apparently significant magnitude of *economies of vertical integration* in the rail sector argue against vertical separation. It is true that these economies are something of a weakness for the TPA model as well, since the creation of competition under that model requires the TOCs that have no vertical economies to exploit to compete with the vertically integrated incumbent. Still, the likelihood that vertical separation imposes a discrete 20–40 percent negative shock on efficiency constitutes a serious reason for hesitating to adopt this option – and, one might argue, particularly in developing countries with mining, manufacturing, and agricultural sectors already struggling to compete on world markets.
2. The generally accepted result that most railways are operating in a region of continued *economies of density* suggests that neither TPA nor vertical separation is likely to lead to a vibrantly competitive train operating sector in any but the most densely operated rail systems: more often one can expect that the first mover – that is, the incumbent – will enjoy lower operating costs than smaller entrants and thus maintain a dominant position vis-à-vis rail-captive shippers. This factor also would seem to argue against vertical separation, since it suggests that the gains from competition to counterbalance the losses from vertical separation are likely to be small.

3. However, one relative attraction of the vertical separation model is that it imposes fewer demands on a country's *regulatory capacity*, since detecting and preventing discrimination by a vertically integrated firm against its non-integrated access customers is likely to be a difficult, complex, and never-ending task, in rail as in, say, electricity and telecommunications.
4. Finally, the greater the percentage of non-integrated TOCs that are international freight operators using the infrastructure for transit as opposed to domestic freight operators serving domestic shippers, the more attractive seems the TPA model, since the vertically integrated incumbent will have generally less reason to discriminate against international transit operators than against domestic competitors.

4. ACCESS PRICING

n those cases where non-integrated TOCs are given access to the infrastructure – whether in competition only among themselves or in competition with the vertically integrated incumbent – a policy question that sometimes receives less attention than it merits is how to set the access charges. It is a truth universally acknowledged – especially among competition enforcers – that any access pricing regime for a monopoly infrastructure like the railway track system must be transparent and non-discriminatory. It is also generally assumed – especially in the developing world – that one reason for restructuring the state-owned monopoly railway is to end government subsidization of the system. What is not always recognized is the set of tradeoffs implied by these two goals.

The problem is a straightforward one.[15] Economically efficient pricing requires that prices – in this case, access prices – be set at the level of marginal costs. However, sectors with high levels of fixed costs exhibit large ranges of output where marginal costs are below average cost, meaning that marginal-cost pricing does not cover fixed costs. One solution is for the government to pay the fixed costs, and indeed in many countries, especially in Western Europe, marginal-cost access pricing accompanied by government subsidies to infrastructure maintenance and investment is the planned long-term arrangement.[16] However, government subsidies may create undesirable incentive problems for the operation of the railway – as noted at the opening of this chapter – and one must in addition account for the shadow price on government funds, generally accepted as quite high (sometimes over 100 percent) in developing countries.[17]

A second solution is average-cost pricing, which is essentially some form of the old fully allocated cost pricing common in rate-of-return regulation schemes.[18] This solution avoids the problems created by subsidization but unavoidably causes welfare losses by denying access to the infrastructure to potential users who would be willing to pay their marginal cost of usage but not their fully allocated cost. I estimate in Pittman (2004b) that the welfare cost from this inefficiency in Russia could be on the order of 1 percent of GDP.

The standard, widely accepted solution that avoids either of these two problems is some sort of discriminatory pricing regime – generally, using Pigou's categories, either second-degree (two-part tariffs) or third-degree (Ramsey pricing) price discrimination. Either of these options is specifically designed to cover fixed costs while minimizing the inefficiencies imposed by the resulting departures from pure marginal-cost pricing. Unfortunately, either is – by definition – discriminatory, and the former in particular, while generally easier to implement and manage, ends up charging more intensive users a lower price than less intensive users (if not, no one would move off of the low fixed cost/high variable cost option). Since the most intensive user is usually the incumbent, non-integrated TOCs can be expected to complain of favoritism.[19]

As BTRE (2003), Pittman (2004b), and others emphasize, the significant level of fixed costs in the rail sector makes it impossible to avoid this dilemma – and this is true whether one is setting shipper tariffs for an integrated railway or access charges for TOCs. What BTRE (2003) suggest, however, is the rather surprising idea that the very necessity of discriminatory pricing in order to cover fixed costs may weigh in as an additional argument against the TPA and vertical separation models. Experience has shown, they argue, that while shippers of a particular commodity will complain if they have to bear a greater share of the fixed costs of the rail sector than shippers of other commodities, so long as their competitors are in a similar situation they will not complain much, because they are not harmed competitively. Thus, a vertically integrated freight railway setting tariffs for hundreds or thousands of shippers may use some form of Ramsey pricing, charging a higher mark-up over marginal costs to shippers with inelastic demands (bulk commodities over long distances) than to shippers with elastic demands (non-bulk commodities over shorter distances), and do so in a fairly direct, straightforward manner. This is what has occurred in the US since the Staggers Act created the possibility for flexible tariff setting.

However, BTRE (2003) argues, when an infrastructure operator seeks to set access charges that are in some way discriminatory to a much smaller number of TOCs – even if there is no integrated incumbent being favored – experience suggests that the result may be an endless round of negotiations, complaints to regulators, and jockeying over rents.

The argument, in summary, is that if one seeks to avoid either the inefficiencies and deadweight losses imposed by government financing of infrastructure, or the inefficiencies and deadweight losses imposed by average cost rather than marginal cost pricing, discriminatory shipper tariffs set by a vertically integrated rail freight enterprise may result in lower transactions costs, and may be more politically acceptable, than discriminatory access charges set by an infrastructure operator.

Otherwise one must face the marginal cost versus average cost access pricing dilemma directly. Since there seems no a priori reason to believe that the inefficiencies from average cost access pricing would differ systematically between developed and developing countries, the much higher shadow price on government resources in developing countries would seem to argue for average cost pricing there, ceteris paribus (Beato & Laffont, 2002).[20]

5. CONCLUSION

Common sense and econometric analysis both suggest that the application of the reformers' "default option" of vertical separation in the freight railways sector may impose high costs on the system in their destruction of economies of vertical integration; thus arguments for the adoption of this option would seem to require the demonstration of high levels of corresponding benefits. Unfortunately, certain other aspects of the railways sector, especially the apparently widespread persistence of economies of density, suggest that such high levels of benefits may be difficult to achieve.

In this chapter we focus on methods of protecting shippers from monopoly abuses by a restructured railway that do not require vertical separation. The first and most straightforward policy option is the encouragement of intermodal competition wherever economically feasible. The second is the creation of parallel and/or source competition among restructured vertically integrated railways, an option generally limited to medium sized and large countries unless and until countries are willing to create truly multinational railway networks. The third is the opening up of the infrastructure of the vertically integrated railway to access by non-integrated TOCs, accepting the likelihood that these TOCs will be disadvantaged in competing with the incumbent but counting on their competition to provide at least some relief to shippers.

Only in very rare circumstances, we argue, are the benefits of complete vertical separation of train operations from the infrastructure operator likely to be so great as to outweigh the losses from the process of vertical separation itself.

NOTES

1. See, for example, Kopicki and Thompson (1995) and ECMT (2004, 2005).
2. I have elsewhere (Pittman, 1990) quoted Alfred Marshall (1920, V, XIV, 5) on this form of competition: "One of the most interesting and difficult applications of the theory of monopolies is to the question whether the public interest is best served by the allotment of a distinct basin to each great railway, and excluding competition there. ... It must be admitted that, other things being equal, the "monopoly revenue price" fixed by a railway will be lowered by every increase in the demand for its services. ... But, human nature being what it is, experience has shown that the breaking of a monopoly by the opening out of a competing line accelerates, rather than retards the discovery by the older line that it can afford to carry traffic at lower rates."
3. See, e.g., STB (1998).
4. Clark (1910) was one of the first to emphasize the importance of this factor, which he terms "competition of markets," in constraining tariffs charged by railways over particular O–D paths. Clark (1908) described how this factor operated in Southeastern Australia.
5. See, e.g., Kohon (1995) for Argentina, Pittman (2004a) for Mexico, and Estache, Andrea, and Pittman (2001) for Brazil.
6. I discuss a case involving the Bundeskartellamt in Pittman (2004b). Bayliss (2001) is eloquent regarding the same issue in the electricity sector: "Even now – ten years since privatization – Ofgem, the UK regulator – is struggling to prevent market abuses by private firms. This is in a wealthy country where the regulator has substantial resources. How much more difficult then is the job of the regulator in developing countries where organizations are staffed by poorly paid public sector workers with little exposure to international corporate activities and where the "opposition" consists of highly paid internationally trained corporate executives. What is more, the regulator has little at hand in the way of sanctions, should the firm refuse to adhere to the rules of the regulator."
7. See "RZhD side-track" (Vedomosti, February 27, 2006); Ekaterina Glazunova and Svetlana Khabirova, "Telegrams that Shocked Railway Network" (*RZhD-Partner*, March 1, 2006); and Anastasiya Lebedev, "RZD Criticized for Halting Foreign-Owned Freight Cars" (*Moscow Times*, March 3, 2006).
8. See also Stehmann and Zellhofer (2004).
9. See, for example, Welsby and Nichols (1999), Nash (2001), and Preston (2001).
10. Bitzan (2003) similarly finds cost savings from joint production of infrastructure and freight services (i.e., vertical integration) in the US; however, the earlier results of Ivaldi and McCullough (2001) are more ambiguous.
11. BTRE (2003); Gomez-Ibanez (2003); Mercer Management Consulting (2003). See also Vickerman (2004); Buehler, Schmutzler, and Benz (2004) for a theoretical

discussion; and Newbery (1999) for network investment issues in the restructured electricity sector.

12. I am grateful to John Bitzan and Stephen Schmidt for confirming my interpretations of their published results in personal communications.

13. I propose one such system for Romania in Pittman (2002) and another for China in Pittman (2004b). Five of these seven countries – all except China and India – have taken at least some steps to restructure their railways, and so far all are following some form of either the TPA or vertical separation models. Russia's three-part long-term restructuring plan calls for future consideration of the creation of competing vertically integrated companies in the European portion of the country, but there is no indication that this option is being seriously considered at this point. See, e.g., ECMT (2004) and Pittman (2004b, 2005b).

14. See Pittman (2003) for a discussion of factors such as these in the context of the rail, electricity, and telecommunications sectors.

15. See Pittman (2004b) for a more detailed discussion, with a focus on restructuring options in Russia.

16. See, e.g., BTRE (2003); Peter (2003); ECMT (2005).

17. See, e.g., Beato and Laffont (2002) and Jamasb (2006).

18. See, e.g., Kahn (1970).

19. In addition, in rail as in other sectors, any discriminatory set of access charges may be time-inconsistent. If we assume that users paying access charges below or equal to the average will be satisfied with that arrangement, while users paying above the average will seek relief from the regulator, access charges above the average may turn out to be non-sustainable – in which case charges below the average are non-sustainable as well.

20. We do not consider here three additional and quite relevant issues: (1) the desirability of setting access charges according to social rather than private marginal costs (Bicket, Friedrich, Link, Stewart, & Nash, 2006); (2) the difficulties of measuring marginal costs – private and social – with any accuracy (Nash & Matthews, 2002; Thomas, 2002); and (3) problems of the "second best" arising from possible divergences of access prices from social marginal costs in competing transport modes (Nilsson, 1992).

ACKNOWLEDGMENT

Thoughtful and helpful comments from two referees are gratefully acknowledged.

REFERENCES

Affuso, L., & Newbery, D. (2002a). *Investment, reprocurement, and franchise contract length in the British railway industry*. Unpublished paper. Department of Applied Economics, University of Cambridge.

Affuso, L., & Newbery, D. (2002b). The impact of structural and contractual arrangements on a vertically separated railway. *Economic and Social Review*, *33*, 83–92.

Bayliss, K. (2001). *Privatisation of electricity distribution: Some economics, social and political perspectives*. Working paper. Public Services International Research Unit, School of Computing and Mathematical Sciences, University of Greenwich, April.

Beato, P., & Laffont, J.-J. (2002). Pricing monopoly segments of regulated industries in developing countries. In: P. Beato & J.-J. Laffont (Eds), *Competition policy in regulated industries: Approaches for emerging economies*. Washington: Inter-American Development Bank.

Bicket, P., Friedrich, R., Link, H., Stewart, L., & Nash, C. (2006). Introducing environmental externalities into transport pricing: Measurement and implications. *Transport Reviews, 26*, 389–415.

Bitzan, J. D. (1999). The structure of railroad costs and the benefits/costs of mergers. *Research in Transportation Economics, 5*, 1–52.

Bitzan, J. D. (2003). Railroad costs and competition: The implications of introducing competition to railroad networks. *Journal of Transport Economics and Policy, 37*, 201–225.

Buehler, S., Armin, S., & Benz, M.-A. (2004). Infrastructure quality in deregulated industries: Is there an underinvestment problem? *International Journal of Industrial Organization, 22*, 253–267.

BTRE. (2003). *Rail infrastructure pricing: Principles and practice*. Report 109. Bureau of Transport and Regional Economics, Canberra, Australia.

Chadwick, E. (1859). Results of different principles of legislation and administration in Europe; Of competition for the field, as compared with competition with the field, of service. *Journal of the Royal Statistical Society, Series A, 22*, 381–420.

Chapin, A., & Schmidt, S. (1999). Do mergers improve efficiency? Evidence from deregulated rail freight. *Journal of Transport Economics and Policy, 33*, 147–162.

Clark, J. M. (1910). Standards of reasonableness in local freight discriminations. *Studies in History, Economics and Public Law (Columbia University), 37*, 1.

Clark, V. S. (1908). Australian economic problems. I. The railways. *Quarterly Journal of Economics, 22*, 399–451.

Demsetz, H. (1968). Why regulate utilities? *Journal of Law and Economics, 11*, 55–65.

ECMT. (2004). *Regulatory reform of railways in Russia*. Paris: European Conference of Ministers of Transport.

ECMT. (2005). *Railway reform & charges for the use of infrastructure*. Paris: European Conference of Ministers of Transport.

Estache, A., Goldstein, A., & Pittman, R. (2001). Privatization and regulatory reform in Brazil: The case of freight railways. *Journal of Industry Competition & Trade, 1*, 203–236.

Friebel, G., Guriev, S., Pittman, R., Shevyakhova, E., & Tomová, A. (2007). Railroad restructuring in Russia and central and eastern Europe: One solution for all problems? *Transport Reviews, 27*.

Gomez-Ibanez, J. (2003). *Regulating infrastructure: Monopoly, contracts, and discretion*. Cambridge, MA: Harvard University Press.

Ivaldi, M., & McCullough, G. J. (2001). Density and integration effects on Class I U.S. freight railroads. *Journal of Regulatory Economics, 19*, 161–182.

Ivaldi, M., & McCullough, G. J. (2004). *Subadditivity tests for network separation with an application to U.S. railroads*. CEPR Discussion paper 4392. London.

Jamasb, T. (2006). Between the state and market: Electricity sector reform in developing countries. *Utilities Policy, 14*, 14–30.

Kahn, A. E. (1970). *The economics of regulation*. New York: Wiley.

Kohon, J. C. (1995). Argentina railways case study. In: R. Kopicki & L. Thompson (Eds.), *Best methods of railway restructuring and privatization*. CFS Discussion paper 111. World Bank, Cofinancing and Financial Advisory Services (Privatization Group).

Kopicki, R., & Thompson, L. S. (1995). *Best methods of railway restructuring and privatization*. CFS Discussion paper 111. Washington, DC: World Bank.

Kwoka, J. E., Jr., & White, L. J. (2004). Manifest destiny? The Union Pacific and Southern Pacific railroad merger (1996). In: J. E. Kwoka & L. J. White (Eds), *The antitrust revolution: Economics, competition, and policy* (4th ed., pp. 27–51). New York: Oxford University Press.

Laffont, J.-J. (2004). Management of public utilities in China. *Annals of Economics and Finance (Beijing)*, *5*, 185–210.

Levin, R. C. (1984). *Verified statement in control application of Atchison, Topeka, and Santa Fe railway for southern Pacific transportation company*. Interstate Commerce Commission Finance Docket No. 30400, KCS-14.

MacDonald, J. M. (1987). Competition and rail rates for the shipment of corn, soybeans, and wheat. *RAND Journal of Economics*, *18*, 151–163.

MacDonald, J. M. (1989a). Railroad deregulation, innovation, and competition: Effects of the Staggers Act on grain transportation. *Journal of Law and Economics*, *37*, 63–95.

MacDonald, J. M. (1989b). Concentration and railroad pricing. In: L. W. Weiss (Ed.), *Concentration and price* (pp. 205–212). Cambridge, MA: MIT Press.

Marshall, A. (1920). *Principles of economics* (8th ed.), Philadelphia: Porcupine Press. Reprinted in 1982.

Mercer Management Consulting. (2003). *The GB rail industry: In its own words*. London: Mercer Management Consulting.

Monti, M. (2002). Effective competition in the railway sector: A big challenge. Speech at UNIFE Annual Reception, Brussels, 21 May.

Nash, C. (2001). Competition and growth in railways: Alternative approaches and thoughts on the British experience. Paper presented at the Conference on competition and the development of European railways, Rome, 14–16 February.

Nash, C., & Matthews, B. (2002). *Implementing rail infrastructure charging reform – barriers and possible means of overcoming them*. Paper prepared for seminar of IMPRINT-EUROPE, Brussels, 14–15 May.

Newbery, D. M. (1999). *Privatization, restructuring, and regulation of network utilities*. Cambridge, MA: MIT Press.

Newbery, D. M. (2005). *The relationship between regulation and competition for network utilities*. Paper presented at conference in tribute to Jean-Jacques Laffont, Toulouse, June.

Nilsson, J.-E. (1992). Second-best problems in railway infrastructure pricing and investment. *Journal of Transport Economics and Policy*, *26*, 245–259.

Peter, B. (2003). *Rail infrastructure charging in the European Union*. Unpublished paper. TU Berlin.

Pittman, R. W. (1990). Railroads and competition: The Santa Fe/Southern Pacific merger proposal. *Journal of Industrial Economics*, *39*, 25–46.

Pittman, R. W. (2002). Restructurarea căilor ferate române – pe orizontală, nu pe verticală (in Romanian). *Economica*, *11*, 289–297.

Pittman, R. W. (2003). Vertical restructuring (or not) of the infrastructure sectors of transition economies. *Journal of Industry Competition & Trade*, *3*, 5–26.

Pittman, R. W. (2004a). Chinese railway reform and competition: Lessons from the experience in other countries. *Journal of Transport Economics and Policy*, *38*, 309–332.

Pittman, R. W. (2004b). Russian railways reform and the problem of non-discriminatory access to infrastructure. *Annals of Public and Cooperative Economics*, *75*, 167–192.

Pittman, R. W. (2005a). Structural separation to create competition? The case of freight railways. *Review of Network Economics, 4,* 181–196.

Pittman, R. W. (2005b). *Make, buy, or some of both? The case of Russian railways*. EAG Discussion paper 05-11. Economic Analysis Group, Antitrust Division, U.S. Department of Justice.

Preston, J. (2001). The franchising and re-franchising of passenger rail services in Britain. *Transportation Research Record, 1742*, 1–9.

Savignat, M. G., & Nash, C. (1999). The case for rail reform in Europe: Evidence from studies of production characteristics of the rail industry. *International Journal of Transport Economics*, *26*, 201–217.

STB. (1998). *Market dominance determinations – Product and geographic competition.* Washington, DC: Surface Transportation Board, Decision, STB Ex Parte No. 627, December 10.

Stehmann, O., & Zellhofer, G. (2004). Dominant rail undertakings under European competition policy. *European Law Journal, 10*, 327–353.

Thomas, J. (2002). EU task force on rail infrastructure charging: Summary findings on best practice in marginal cost pricing. Paper prepared for seminar of IMPRINT-EUROPE, Brussels, 23–24 October.

Vickerman, R. (2004). Maintenance incentives under different infrastructure regimes. *Utilities Policy, 12*.

von Hirschhausen, C. (2002). *Modernizing infrastructure in transformation economies: Paving the way to European enlargement*. Northampton, MA: Edward Elgar.

Welsby, J., & Nichols, A. (1999). The privatisation of Britain's railways: An inside view. *Journal of Transport Economics and Policy*, *33*, 55–76.

Wetzel, H., & Growitsch, C. (2006). *Economies of scope in European railways: An efficiency analysis.* Discussion paper No. 5. Institut fur Wirtschaftsforschung Halle, Halle, Germany.

Williamson, O. E. (1976). Franchise bidding for natural monopolies – In general and with respect to CATV. *Bell Journal of Economics*, *7*, 73–104.

Wilson, W. W. (1997). Cost savings and productivity in the railroad industry. *Journal of Regulatory Economics*, *11*, 21–40.

Winston, C., Dennis, S. M., & Maheshri, V. (2004). *Duopoly in the railroad industry: Bertrand, Cournot, or collusive*? Unpublished paper. Brookings Institution and U.S. Department of Transportation, August 2004.

TRESPASSING ON THE RAILROAD

Ian Savage

ABSTRACT

Greater than half of all the fatal injuries on the United States railroads are sustained by trespassers. The paper provides a statistical analysis of the demographics of trespassers, the activities they were engaged in, and the causes of injury. It also analyzes trends over time. The paper finds that the risks of injury and death are particularly acute for males in their 20s and 30s. The annual casualty count has remained relatively stable in recent decades because growing affluence, which tends to reduce risk-taking behavior, has been balanced by increases in railroad activity and the size of the population.

1. INTRODUCTION

In 2005, 471 people died while trespassing on the railroads in the United States. Since 1970, the annual fatality count has fluctuated in a range between 376 and 543. The lack of a sustained improvement is in stark contrast to the considerable reduction in the risks faced by railroad employees and users of highway-rail grade crossings. In 2005, trespassers represented 53% of the 892 fatalities in railroad operations, whereas as recently as the late 1970s the proportion was only 25%.

Railroad Economics
Research in Transportation Economics, Volume 20, 199–224

ISSN: 0739-8859/doi:10.1016/S0739-8859(07)20008-3

A landmark year was 1997 when the number of trespasser fatalities exceeded the number killed in collisions at highway-rail grade crossings for the first time since 1941. In the late 1960s, crossing fatalities exceeded trespasser deaths by a ratio of three to one. Now there are 25% fewer crossing fatalities than trespassing deaths. A public outcry in the late 1960s led to a series of programs to improve crossing safety. These initiatives included making federal funds available to install gates and/or warning lights at a greater proportion of crossings, upgrading the lighting on the front of trains to improve conspicuity, closing little-used crossings, and starting a public education campaign called Operation Lifesaver. Taken together, these initiatives were and are remarkably successful in saving lives, and doing so in a cost-effective way (Mok & Savage, 2005; Savage, 2006). In contrast, solutions to the trespassing problem have been far more elusive. With the public policy spotlight shifting in the past decade from grade crossings to trespassing, there is an increasing need for the professional community to understand the causes of trespassing and what can be done to reduce the annual casualty count.

2. DATA

The analysis in this paper concerns mainline railroads. It does not deal with urban mass transit or streetcars, but it does include commuter railroads. Railroads are required to report deaths (excluding suicides) or injuries of all severities to the Federal Railroad Administration (FRA) on form 6180.55a. They have been required to do so since 1910. However, casualty data can be found for as far back as 1890. The data were published from 1901 to 1965 by the Interstate Commerce Commission (ICC), and since 1966 by the FRA (Federal Railroad Administration, annual from 1901–2005). Throughout this paper "trespassers" will be defined as those people trespassing at locations other than grade crossings. (The term is also used to describe persons at grade crossings who pass through or around closed crossing gates, but the data are reported separately.)

3. DOCUMENTED SUICIDES

Railroads are not supposed to report fatalities that are judged suicides by a coroner to the FRA. We will refer to these as "documented suicides." Coroners and local medical examiners do report suicides to the federal

Centers for Disease Control and Prevention (CDC) for inclusion in the annual *National Vital Statistics Report* (see Hoyert, Heron, Murphy, & Kung, 2006, for the 2003 report). However, deaths are categorized using the World Health Organization's *International Statistical Classification of Diseases and Related Health Problems*, and suicides by railroad trespassers can be classified in a number of different ways. Therefore, it is difficult to accurately establish the annual fatality count. General professional opinion is that the number of documented trespasser suicides on mainline railroads is at least 100 per year, but that number may be higher, and perhaps is considerably higher. This means that the total number of trespasser fatalities is at least 20% higher than the approximately 500 deaths reported to the FRA.

While the number of documented suicides is substantial, the problem is much worse in Europe and Japan than it is in the United States. In Britain, documented suicides on the mainline railways are equal in number to the number of trespassing fatalities not deemed a suicide by a coroner (Rail Safety and Standards Board, 2005). Consistent with this, 2.6% of all documented suicides in Britain are by means of mainline trains, while the proportion in the United States based on an annual fatality count of 100 is 0.3%. The explanation for the different experience across countries is the greater density of rail lines and the higher frequency of trains in Europe and Japan, and the easier access to firearms in the United States (Hoyert et al., 2006, report that firearms are used in 54% of suicides in the United States).

4. HISTORICAL PERSPECTIVE

While the annual fatality count has not changed much in recent decades, the situation is much improved compared with a century ago. A graph of the total number of trespassing casualties (deaths plus injuries) for each year from 1890 to the present is presented in Fig. 1. The graph also distinguishes between deaths and injuries. Caution is required in comparing data over such a long period. In particular, documented suicides were included in the data at one time, and prior to1922 deaths that occurred more than 24 hours after an incident were classed as an injury rather than as a fatality.

Comparing 1905 and 2005, one is struck by the fact that fatalities were almost ten times more numerous (4,650 versus 471) at a time when the country was less than a third as populous (84 million versus 296 million). The fatality risk per head of population in 1905 was thirty-five times larger than it is today. Of course, part of the explanation is that there were 50% more train miles running over a much larger network, and in some cases the

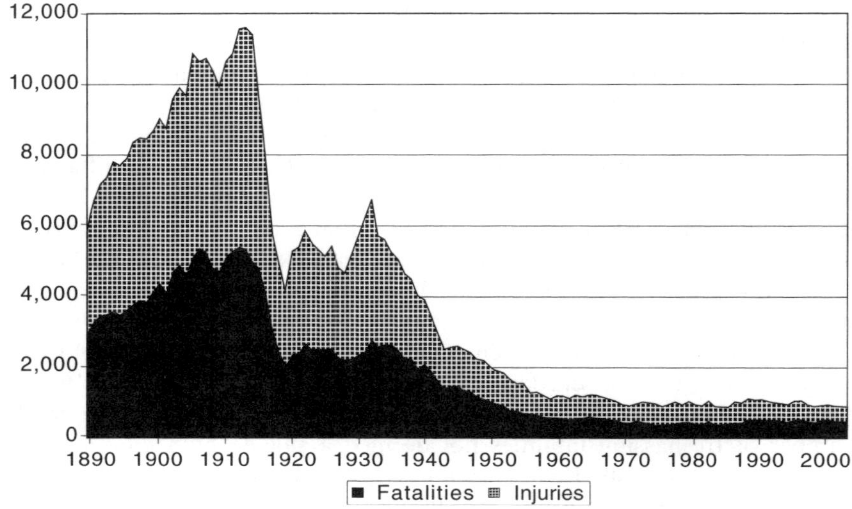

Fig. 1. Annual Trespasser Casualties by Type.

railroad literally ran down the middle of the main street of many towns. In addition, prior to the development of paved roads, the railroad right of way was used as an unofficial pathway (Aldrich, 2006).

Fig. 2 plots the combined number of trespassing fatalities and injuries relative to two measures of exposure: population in millions and line-haul train miles in tens of millions. (The latter measure excludes train miles in yard and switching operations, which have not been reported in a consistent manner over time. It should be noted that the majority of trespassing casualties occur on the main line.) Immediately noticeable from both Figs. 1 and 2 is the very substantial decline in risk between 1915 and 1919, and again between 1939 and 1945. While some of this decline is understandable in that the segment of the population most likely to trespass (men in their 20s and 30s) was away in military service, the improvement persisted even after cessation of hostilities. One might well conclude that the wartime experience changed the risk-taking behavior of this segment of society.

There is also evidence of a spike in trespassing during the Great Depression of the early 1930s. The image in popular culture of people riding freight trains while looking for work during the dust bowl years is not that inaccurate. In the 1930s, a quarter of the trespasser casualties were described as "hoboes or tramps." The proportion fell to about 20% in the 1950s and was less than 10%

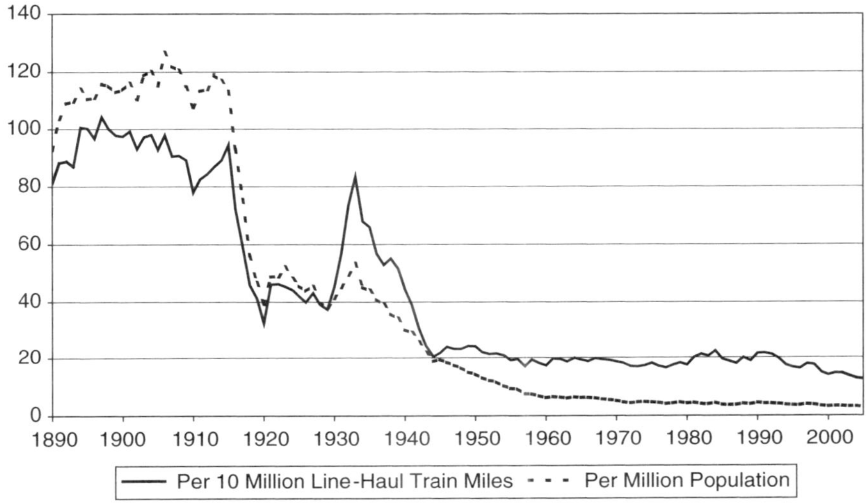

Fig. 2. Trespasser Casualty Rates.

in the early 1970s when the published reports ceased using this description. Similarly, about a quarter of the casualties in the 1930s occurred onboard trains (albeit that this would include injuries sustained aboard passenger trains by people who had not purchased a ticket). This had fallen to about 12% in the 1950s, and today it is relatively rare despite the use of freight trains by illegal immigrants in the Southwest.

Fig. 3 is an enlarged version of Fig. 2 showing the post-Second World War years, with the rates per head of population and per line-haul train mile shown as indices with 1947 set equal to 100. The rate per head of population declined quite steadily until 1960. It then leveled out at about 35% of the rate in 1947. There was then a substantial decrease of about 25% between 1967 and 1975, followed by more than 20 years of stagnation. There is evidence of a reduced risk in the past five years, but it is too early to tell whether this will be a sustained improvement. The rate per line-haul train mile improved between 1947 and 1955, but then fluctuated around a level that was 20% lower than in 1947 until the mid-1990s. Since the mid-1990s, there has been a considerable improvement of about 30% primarily because the number of train miles has increased but the number of trespasser casualties has not.

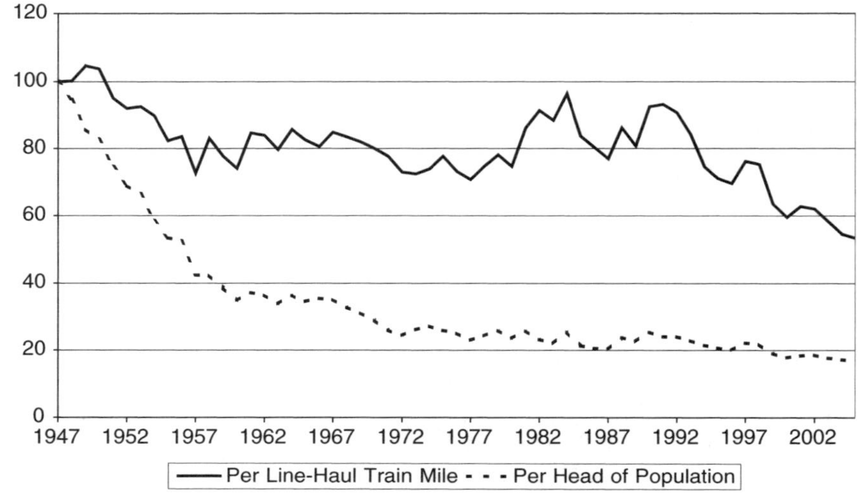

Fig. 3. Index of Trespasser Casualty Rates since 1947 (1947 = 100).

The improvement in casualty rates relative to both train miles and population size in recent years have been counterbalanced by the growth in both population and train miles (up by 25% and 60%, respectively since the early 1980s). This explains why the absolute count of fatalities has remained relatively constant.

5. WHO, WHERE, AND WHAT

A distinction needs to be made between the characteristics of trespassers in general, and the characteristics of the subset of trespassers who sustain fatal and non-fatal injuries. The total number of trespassers is clearly many orders of magnitude larger than the number of casualties. The BNSF Railway Company, the nation's second largest, reports that its police officers removed or arrested 23,200 trespassers in 2003. This compares with a total of 111 trespassers killed or injured in that year on the BNSF. Moreover, we can be certain that the vast majority of acts of trespass go unnoticed by BNSF police given that the railroad's network extends for 33,000 miles.

Information on the general trespassing problem can be obtained when cameras are set up along the right of way. In addition, some railroads have recently started installing cameras on the front of their locomotives with the primary intention of collecting evidence to use in law suits resulting from highway-rail grade crossing collisions. It would be possible to review a sample of the tapes to gain some idea of the locations of trespass, the nature of the persons involved, and the activities they are engaged in.

I am not aware of any published research that has used photographic data to quantify trespass in general. (While, daSilva, Carroll, & Baron, 2006; report on a camera installation on a bridge in Pittsford, New York, the purpose of their research was to test a deterrence system rather than to quantify the frequency and purpose of trespass.) The increasing use of cameras on locomotives may make suitable data available in the future. In contrast, data on incidents in which an injury occurs can be obtained from the FRA database, and from reports filed by attending police officers and, in the case of fatalities, by coroners and medical examiners. Of course, society is most interested in obtaining information to prevent cases in which a fatal or non-fatal injury is sustained.

In Table 1, the 3,628 trespassing deaths and injuries that occurred between 2001 and 2004 are categorized by the event that caused the injury and the activity the trespasser was engaged in at the time. Three-quarters of

Table 1. Proportion of 3,628 Trespassing Casualties by Event and Activity, 2001–2004.

Activity	Event			Total (%)
	Struck by On-track Equipment (%)	Slips, Falls, Electric Shock, Crushed, Striking Object (%)	Other (%)	
Walking or running	29.8	1.7	0.5	31.9
Standing, bending, or stooping	7.5	0	0	7.5
Sitting	7.4	0	0	7.4
Laying, lying down, sleeping	22.9	0	0.9	23.7
Jumping, climbing, crawling, boarding	5.2	3.5	0	8.7
Driving or riding, or operating (bicycle, snowmobile, etc.)	3.5	4.8	0	8.3
Other activities	0.7	0	11.9	12.5
Total	76.8	10.0	13.2	100

Note: Data shown here are rounded, so columns and rows may not add up exactly. *Source:* FRA downloadable database the casualties occur when the trespasser is struck by a train. A further 10% of casualties result from slips, falls, or striking a fixed object while on railroad land or on trains. The remaining 13% of casualties are due to a mixed bag of circumstances that include assault, exposure to the environment, and cases where the event and activity cannot be determined. Of course, those trespassers that are struck by a train are much more likely to sustain fatal injuries. Almost 90% of trespasser fatalities occur when the trespasser is struck by a train, while almost 40% of non-fatal injuries occur in circumstances that do not involve being struck by a train.

Especially notable is that almost a third of all casualties involve a train striking a trespasser who was sitting or lying down. These data are often cited to support the contention that some of the entries in the FRA database represent suicidal people who do not leave notes or other evidence of their intentions. Consequently, coroners are unable to determine conclusively whether or not the fatality was a suicide. In addition, some fatalities are determined by coroners to be suicides subsequent to being reported to the FRA as a trespasser, and there is no formal system in place to reconcile the data at the end of the year. George (2006) matched up 61% of the 1,523 trespassing fatalities in the FRA database that occurred in 2002, 2003, or 2004 with the records held by local coroners and medical examiners. He found that in 164 of the 935 available cases (17.5%), the coroner had used the words "suicide" or "intentional" somewhere in their report. An additional 49 cases (5.2%) contained a written narrative that would suggest suicide as a motive. One might conclude from George's analysis that approximately 20% of the deaths in the FRA database are either "undocumented suicides" or documented suicides that were mistakenly reported. This proportion is far lower than in Europe. Railroad management in Britain investigated the circumstances of all trespasser deaths not deemed a suicide by a coroner, and found a strong suspicion of suicidal intent in 60% of cases (Rail Safety and Standards Board, 2005). Again, the ready access to firearms in the United States seems to reduce the popularity of trains as a method of suicide.

An analysis of casualty age is presented in Table 2. The age distribution of all the casualties occurring between 1999 and 2001 is shown in the middle column. A risk rate is shown in the final column. This is calculated by dividing the average annual casualty count in an age group by population data from the 2000 Census. There is a popular image in the press that children under the age of 10 are at particular risk. In reality, children in this age group represent only 2.2% of casualties and have a casualty rate that is smaller than that for senior citizens. People between the ages of 16 and 45 years old face the greatest risk. This age group represents 45% of the general

Table 2. Distribution of Trespasser Casualties and Casualty Rates by Age.

Age Range (years)	Total Trespasser Casualties 1999–2001 (%)	Annual Rate per Million Population
0–5	0.7	0.27
6–10	1.5	0.67
11–15	5.2	2.33
16–20	10.6	4.74
21–25	14.0	6.77
26–30	11.0	5.00
31–35	9.4	4.08
36–40	11.5	4.54
41–45	9.5	3.90
46–50	6.6	3.05
51–55	3.9	2.15
56–60	1.5	1.03
61–65	1.2	1.01
66–70	1.0	1.00
71–75	0.8	0.81
76–80	0.8	1.00
> = 81	0.9	1.00
Not given	10.0	

Source: Trespassing casualties from downloadable FRA database for 1999–2001. Rate calculated as the average annual count 1999–2001 divided by population data from the 2000 US Census.

population but 75% of the trespasser casualties whose age is known. People in their early twenties are particularly at risk, and face an annual casualty risk of 1 in 1,50,000.

While the FRA reporting form has a field for recording the victim's age, no additional demographic information is collected. There is not even a field for reporting gender. Consequently, additional insights on demographics have come from special studies that rely on police and/or coroners' reports. There has been just a handful of studies. The earliest of these was a National Transportation Safety Board (NTSB, 1978) study that looked at 280 fatalities that occurred between March 1976 and October 1977. A widely cited CDC study (Pelletier, 1997) examined coroners' reports for all of the 138 trespasser deaths in North Carolina for the years 1990–1994. Another CDC study analyzed 132 fatalities and 156 injuries that occurred in Georgia between 1990 and 1996 (Centers for Disease Control and Prevention, 1999). Finally, a recent consulting report to the FRA analyzed 935 deaths that occurred nationwide between 2002 and 2004 (George, 2006). There is also a small literature by medical examiners' (see Davis, Alexander, & Brissie, 1997 and the references therein). The results of the studies are similar.

About 90% of victims are found to be adult males, with the vast majority between the ages of 20 and 49. Consequently, the risk rates shown in the final column of Table 2 considerably understate the risk to males. Eighty percent of the adult victims are unmarried. Pelletier's study found that for those adults whose education was known, only 45% had graduated from high school. Pelletier found that African-Americans were over-represented at 38% of the victims whereas they formed only 22% of the population of North Carolina. George also found that African-Americans were over-represented (16% of victims compared with 12% of the general population), and that Native Americans were even more over-represented at 5% of the victims while they only form 1% of the general population.

Contrary to the popular image of trespassers as "hoboes or tramps," Pelletier found that only 10% of victims were transients, and 80% of deaths occurred within the victim's county of residence. Similarly, George found that only 9% were "homeless" or "transients." The Georgia study found that 60% were injured in the city in which they resided, suggesting that trespassing occurs close to home. The trespasser problem appears to be an urban one with less than a quarter of fatalities occurring outside of city or town limits. The NTSB found that nearly all of the fatalities occurred on multiple-track mainlines (albeit that there is no indication that the NTSB selected a random sample of incidents). In 85% of the cases there was no fence erected to protect the right of way.

Alcohol would appear to be involved in most cases. A disproportionate number of fatalities occur at night on the weekends. Sixty percent of the victims in the NTSB study and 80% in Pelletier's study had been drinking heavily. The Georgia study found that 65% of victims tested positive for alcohol or drugs. George found that 57% of victims tested positive for alcohol and/or drugs, 30% tested negative for both, and the remainder were not tested. The average blood–alcohol content was 0.23 mg/100 mL in the NTSB study, and the median was 0.26 in the North Carolina study and 0.22 in the Georgia study. These are about three times the legal limits for driving, and according to the National Safety Council puts a person in a state of "confusion." Twenty-eight percent of victims in the North Carolina study had previously received medical treatment for alcoholism.

Based on what we know at the moment, and at the risk of generalizing, one might conclude that about two-thirds of the trespasser casualties can be characterized as single adult males in their 20s and 30s under the influence of alcohol. It would appear that the railroad right of way is an attractive place for people to socialize and imbibe, or to sleep off the effects of alcohol or drugs. Almost a third of the trespasser casualties are sitting or lying in the right of way at the time of impact, which clearly indicates considerable negligence on the trespasser's part or suicidal intentions.

That said, the other third represent people on railroad property for the purposes of theft, vandalism, thrill seeking, catching a ride on a freight train, or taking a short cut over or along the right of way. The railroad is generally unfenced, and it bisects many small towns. Pedestrians are tempted to take a short cut rather than walk to the nearest grade crossing or bridge. In urban areas the temptation to take a short cut leads to the destruction of existing fencing. In rural areas, there is evidence that hunters, fishermen, and the operators of snowmobiles and all-terrain vehicles use the railroad right of way. There is also evidence that residents of homes for senior citizens can become disoriented and wander onto neighboring railroad tracks.

6. TIME SERIES ANALYSIS 1947–2003

The stagnation in the number of annual trespasser casualties in the past 35 years has proved to be frustrating and mystifying to both railroads and the government. Some insights into the reasons for this stagnation can be found by conducting a time-series analysis on the period since the end of the Second World War. Two different regression techniques will be used to analyze annual data from 1947 to 2003. Both techniques produce similar results.

The first type of regression is a log-linear regression on the rate of trespasser casualties per head of population. The AR(1) (Prais & Winston, 1954) estimator is used to reduce the problems commonly found in time-series analysis caused by serial correlation. It does so by transforming both the dependent and explanatory variables in the regression by subtracting a proportion, ρ, of the variable's value in the previous period. Hence variables take the form

$$X_t - \rho X_{t-1}$$

The Prais–Winsten method also ensures that the regression does not "lose" one observation in making this transformation.

The second is a negative binomial regression with the count of casualties as the dependent variable, population as the exposure variable, and the other explanatory variables expressed in logarithms. The negative binomial regression is a more generalized version of the Poisson regression. It assumes that the mean, $E(Y)$, and variance, $\mathrm{Var}(Y)$, of the count of casualties for a group of years with identical values of the explanatory variables have the following relationship:

$$\mathrm{Var}(Y) = E(Y) + aE(Y)^2$$

While the estimation algorithms of the two equations are very different, the functional form is very similar. The negative binomial equation can be usefully visualized as having the form

$$\text{count of casualties} = \text{population} \times e^{\left(\alpha + \sum \beta_i \ln(X_i)\right)} + \varepsilon$$

while the log-linear function is

$$\ln(\text{count of casualties}/\text{population}) = \alpha + \sum \beta_i \ln(X_i) + \varepsilon$$

or

$$\text{count of casualties}/\text{population} = e^{\left(\alpha + \sum \beta_i \ln(X_i)\right)} + \varepsilon$$

Consequently, the magnitudes of the estimated coefficients of the explanatory variables in the two equations can be directly compared. In effect, the log-linear regression and the negative binomial regression are two different estimation techniques for the same basic functional form for the variables. Moreover, as all but one of the explanatory variables is expressed in logarithms, the coefficients can be interpreted as elasticities. In both regressions, the dependent variable measures trespassing casualties, which is the combination of both fatal and non-fatal injuries. The use of this broader measure of victims is designed to overcome the problem of random year-to-year variation that is found in fatality data.

The regression results are shown in Table 3. The negative binomial regression has an alpha value significantly larger than zero, thereby rejecting the Poisson model. As the estimated value of α is positive, the data are referred to as overdispersed. This model has a pseudo R^2 of 0.25. The pseudo R^2 is a measure, using the estimated log-likelihoods, of the explanatory power of the full regression compared with a regression with a constant as the sole explanatory variable. In the log-linear model, a Durbin–Watson test finds that a Prais–Winsten AR(1) estimator, with a value of ρ 0.55, removes serial correlation. The adjusted R^2 of the equation is very high.

The overall goodness of fit of the equations can be seen in Fig. 4, which shows the actual casualty rates per million population (shown as the dots) versus the predictions of the negative binomial (represented by the solid line)

Table 3. Time Series Regression Results.

Dependent Variable	Negative Binomial		Prais-Winsten AR(1)	
	Coefficient	*t*	Coefficient	*T*
	Count of Trespassing Casualties		Trespassing Casualties per Head of Population	
Constant	−15.6171	3.78	−13.7662	2.29
United States Population	Exposure		Part of Dependent variable	
Log of Railroad Road Miles	1.0070	4.08	0.9364	2.51
Log Of Average Daily Number Of Trains	0.9180	8.55	0.8547	6.33
Log of Proportion of Population between Ages 15 and 44	1.1888	4.24	1.2904	3.01
Log of Real Gross Domestic Product per Capita	−0.9633	8.08	−1.0408	6.12
Proportion of Locomotives with Ditch Lights	−0.1360	2.02	−0.0780	0.85
Alpha	0.0041	4.35		
Observations	57		57	
Constant-only Log Likelihood	−442.26			
Log Likelihood	−331.37			
rho			0.5555	
Original Durbin–Watson statistic			0.9318	
Transformed Durbin–Watson statistic			2.0157	
Pseudo R^2/Adjusted R^2	0.2508		0.9852	

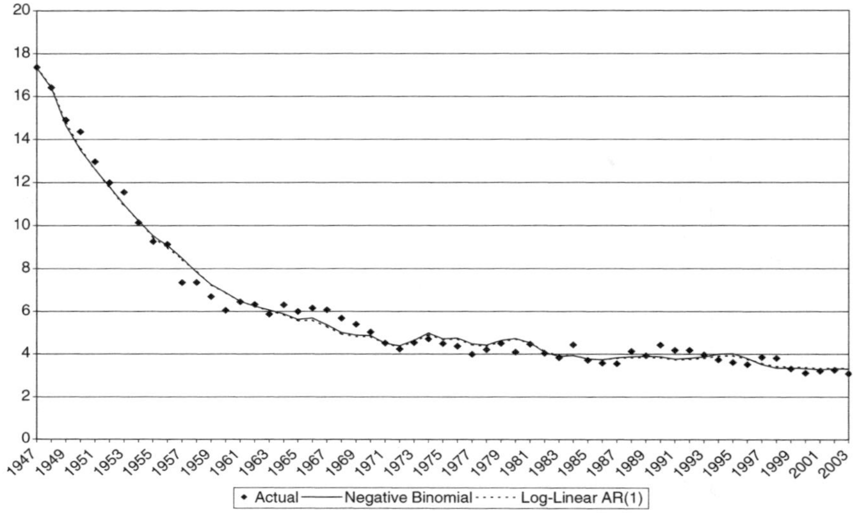

Fig. 4. Actual versus Predicted Trespasser Casualty Rates per Million Population.

and log-linear AR(1) (dashed line) regressions. The two predicted regression lines are very similar, and track the actual data quite well, with the exception of the period between 1960 and 1967, when the actual rate reached a temporary plateau.

In interpreting the results, one should not forget that the size of the population is treated by both regressions as having a direct 1:1 effect on the number of casualties. The population has more than doubled from 143 million in 1947 to 291 million in 2003. Consequently, had nothing else changed, we would expect to have twice as many casualties in 2003 as there were in 1947. That said, there are some concerns with this variable. Fifty years ago, settlement patterns were heavily influenced by the rail network, and many, if not most, people had some interaction with railroads on a daily basis. Widespread automobile ownership has changed settlement patterns in such a way that new development has occurred in places remote from the railroad.

The first explanatory variable is the national railroad route length, known in the industry as "road miles." This was obtained from the ICC's annual statistical publication and later from the Association of American Railroad's *Railroad Facts* (Interstate Commerce Commission, annual from 1888–1994; Association of American Railroads, annual from 1924–2005). The national network shrunk by 35% between 1947 and 2003, with most of the reduction occurring in the decade between 1974 and 1984. The 1976 *Railroad Revitalization and Regulatory Reform Act* and the 1980 *Staggers Act* gave railroads more freedom to abandon unremunerative lines. A reduction in the network should reduce casualties, as fewer people live in close proximity to the tracks. The estimated coefficient is very close to unity in both regressions. Indeed one cannot reject a null hypothesis that it is unity. Casualties change proportionately, all other things being equal, with the size of the network.

In an ideal world, one might want to use an exposure measure that incorporates population increases, changes in settlement patterns, and line abandonment. Perhaps the most appropriate exposure measure would be the number of people who live, work, or go to school within, say, a mile of the tracks. Nowadays such data are available in geographic information systems, based on Census Bureau data and a digitized representation of the rail network. Such information is used to model the population exposed to movements of hazardous materials (see for example, Han, Chin, Hwang, & Peterson, 2006). However a time series of such data is not available, especially when one wishes to track changes back to the 1940s.

Of course, the lines that were abandoned were those with the least amount of rail traffic. The effect of closing little-used lines, along with general trends in rail traffic are captured by a second explanatory variable measuring the average daily line-haul trains per mile of network. The number of national train miles was obtained from the ICC's annual statistical publication and later from the FRA's annual safety publication. The variable representing the average daily trains is calculated as

$$\text{Daily Trains} = \frac{\text{Annual Line - Haul Train Miles}}{\text{Road Miles} \times \text{Days in Year}}$$

The average daily number of trains fell from 13 a day in 1947 to 8 in 1960. It then fluctuated around this number until 1991. Rail traffic density then started to increase, and by 2003 the number of daily trains had almost returned to its 1947 level. The estimated coefficient is in the range of 0.85–0.9, implying that casualties change slightly less than proportionately with rail activity. This is to be expected given that a quarter of all casualties result from slips and falls rather than from being struck by a moving train.

The third variable measures the proportion of the population that is between the ages of 15 and 44 (U.S. Census Bureau, 2002). Table 2 indicates that persons in this age range have a disproportionate involvement in trespassing incidents. As the post-World War II "baby boom" generation has aged, the proportion of 15–44 year olds has followed a wave pattern.

It decreased from 0.46 in 1947 to a low of 0.39 in 1961, increased to a high of 0.48 in 1986/7, and has subsequently fallen to 0.43 in 2003. This variable is found to have a very strong effect on the number and rate of casualties.

The fourth variable measures the real per capita gross domestic product (GDP). GDP data from the Bureau of Economic Analysis were converted to 2003 dollars using the Consumer Price Index, and expressed as a per capita rate. Real GDP per capita has increased from $14,000 in 1947 to $38,000 in 2003. Standard economic theory suggests that citizens demand more lifesaving activities as a country becomes richer. This manifests itself in increased health care expenditures, a demand for more product safety features, and perhaps a reduction in undertaking risky activities such as trespassing on the railroad. Consistent with this theory, the National Safety Council (annual) reports that the rate of non-work-related unintentional deaths in the United States fell from about 55 per 100,000 people in 1947 to 33 per 100,000 in 2003. In addition, increased wealth reduces the prevalence of transients who hop trains while traveling to find work. The regressions find that the increase in wealth has the expected negative effect on casualties and casualty rates, with an elasticity close to unity.

The final variable measures a technological change that was found by Mok and Savage (2005) to be particularly effective in improving safety at grade crossings. A 1995 federal rule required increased lighting of trains. The traditional single headlight had to be augmented by two additional lights lower down on the front of the locomotive. These are known as ditch or crossing lights, and provide added illumination of the sides of the track and, what is more important, the triangular pattern provides trespassers with a greater perception of an approaching train's speed and how far it is away. Assuming that locomotives were fitted with these additional lights at a constant rate between the announcement of the rule in September 1995 and the deadline for fitting them in December 1997, the average proportion of locomotives so fitted would be 0.33 in 1996, 0.78 in 1997, and unity from 1998 onwards. Unlike the other variables, this is not expressed in logarithms. Also, unlike the other variables, the regressions suggest a weaker statistical relationship with the number of casualties. The negative binomial regression suggests that installing ditch lights reduced casualties by 13%. This relationship is marginally significant at the 95% confidence interval. The relationship is statistically insignificant in the log-linear equation, which estimates that ditch lights reduced casualties by 7.5%.

There were two other variables that were tested but were found to be less satisfactory and were dropped from the analysis. The first was the implementation of Operation Lifesaver. The public outcry concerning grade crossing safety in the late 1960s led to the formation, starting in Idaho in 1972, of state-based non-profit organizations to promote education and awareness of railroad-related hazards. The program spread state by state across the nation between 1972 and 1986. A variable was constructed indicating the proportion of the population in a given year who resided in a state in which Operation Lifesaver had been established. Unfortunately from an analytical perspective, the growth in Operation Lifesaver coincided with the peak period for railroad abandonment. A high correlation between these variables made it impossible to include both in the regressions. Subsequent discussions with officers of Operation Lifesaver revealed that the organization primarily focused on the risks at grade crossings in its early years, and only since 1997 have activities also been directed toward trespassing and suicide prevention.

With an eye to examining possible trends in the portion of reported casualties who are undocumented suicides, data were obtained on the national rate of suicide (National Center for Health Statistics, annual). The rate has fluctuated over the years between 97 and 131 per million population. The rate was particularly low between 1951 and 1961, and in the period since 1999. It was particularly high between 1975 and 1978, and again between 1984 and 1988. If a large proportion of reported trespasser casualties are really undocumented suicides then one would expect a strong positive correlation between the national suicide rate and the trespassing casualty rate. In fact, the correlation is a counterintuitive −0.36. This would lend additional support to the notion that undocumented suicides are a smaller proportion of the reported trespasser fatalities in the United States compared with the situation overseas.

7. DECOMPOSITION OF TIME-SERIES TRENDS

From 1947 to 2003, the number of annual trespassing casualties fell by 1,594 from 2,490 to 896. The regressions can be used to estimate the contribution of the various causes to the decline. Using the negative binomial regression results, the change in the predicted number of casualties from year t to year $t+1$, can be decomposed into its constituent parts. The theory of the decomposition methodology can be explained by considering a simple function where $Z = A \times B$. The change in Z from one period to the next can be defined as

$$\begin{aligned} Z_{t+1} - Z_t &= A_{t+1} \times B_{t+1} - A_t \times B_t \\ &= A_t \times (B_{t+1} - B_t) + B_t \times (A_{t+1} - A_t) + (A_{t+1} - A_t) \times (B_{t+1} - B_t) \end{aligned}$$

The analysis in this paper has many more variables, and the decomposition will take the following form

$$\begin{aligned}\text{Casualties}_{t+1} - \text{Casualties}_t = {} & \left[\text{Population}_{t+1} - \text{Population}_t\right] e^a e^{b_1 \ln(\text{RoadMiles}_t)} \\ & e^{b_2 \ln(\text{Trains}_t)} e^{b_3 \ln(\text{Age15-44}_t)} e^{b_4 \ln(\text{Wealth}_t)} e^{b_5 \text{Ditch Lights}_t} \\ & + \text{Population}_t e^a \left[e^{b_1 \ln(\text{RoadMiles}_t)} - e^{b_1 \ln(\text{RoadMiles}_{t-1})}\right] e^{b_2 \ln(\text{Trains}_t)} \\ & e^{b_3 \ln(\text{Age15-44}_t)} e^{b_4 \ln(\text{Wealth}_t)} e^{b_5 \text{Ditch Lights}_t} + \cdots + \varepsilon_t - \varepsilon_{t-1}\end{aligned}$$

The equation will also include (in place of the ellipses) similar terms to the first two that involve changes from year t to $t+1$ for the variables trains, age 15–44, wealth and ditch lights. In addition, there will be cross-product terms involving every possible combination of the value of variables in period t and changes in variables. There will be 63 terms in total. Of course, most of the cross-product terms will be quite small as they involve the product of two (or more) relatively small changes in the constituent variables. In addition some of the cross-product terms will be positive and some negative, and will tend to cancel each other out.

The decomposition was carried out for each of the annual changes, starting with the predicted change from 1947 to 1948 and concluding with the predicted change from 2002 to 2003. The annual changes are then added together to produce a predicted decomposition over the entire 57-year period. This is shown in the final column of Table 4. The first-order effects are shown explicitly, while the cross-product terms are summed together. Over the entire period, the regression predicts that increases in population should have increased casualties by 904 a year. However, this was counteracted by abandonment of parts of the network (reducing casualties by 498), reductions in the number of average daily trains (369), changes in the age distribution of the population (232), installation of ditch lights (136), and increases in wealth which promote less risk-taking behavior (1,133). The cross-product terms produce a further reduction of 62 casualties a year. The sum of the error terms, which is to say the changes not explained by the regression, total a net decrease of 68 casualties. As inspection of Fig. 4 would suggest, the explanation for the latter is that the actual number of casualties in 2003 was somewhat below the predicted value, whereas in 1947 the actual and predicted numbers are much closer.

While the decomposition of the changes over the entire period is interesting, breaking down the decomposition into four sub-periods provides even more insight. The sub-periods chosen are 1947–1960 (that is to say, the sum of the predicted changes from 1947 to 1948 through 1959 to

Table 4. Decomposition of Change in Annual Totals.

	Sub-Periods				Overall 1947–2003
	1947–1960	1960–1974	1974–1988	1988–2003	
Actual annual totals					
Start of period	2,490	1,088	1,004	1,010	**2,490**
End of period	1,088	1,004	1,010	896	**896**
Change	−1,402	−84	+6	−114	**−1,594**
Changes explained by regression					
Increased population	415	184	135	170	**904**
Decreased road miles	−68	−84	−218	−128	**−498**
Changes in average daily trains	−806	−1	65	374	**−369**
Changes in proportion of population between 15 and 44	−338	110	109	−114	**−232**
Increased per capita real gross domestic product	−436	−373	−181	−142	**−1,133**
Locomotives with ditch lights	0	0	0	−136	**−136**
Sum of cross product terms	−15	−9	−27	−11	**−62**
Changes not explained by regression	−154	89	123	−127	**−68**

Note: Totals may not add due to rounding.

1960), 1960–1974, 1974–1988, and 1988–2003. The break points were chosen because of observed changes in the trend of one, or more, of the explanatory variables. The decompositions are shown in the middle columns of Table 4. In interpreting the table, there are a number of notable features. Increases in population and wealth have affected casualties in all four time periods. However, the numerical size of both the population and wealth effects are much larger in the earlier time periods because trespassing risks (as explained by the other variables) were much higher 50 years ago. The reduction in the railroad network size had its primary effect in the 1974–1988 period. The aging of the baby boom generation is reflected in the high proportion of people between the ages of 15 and 44 in the period from 1960 to 1988. The reduction in the average number of daily trains in the 1950s had a particularly large negative effect. The reverse is true when train traffic density started to increase rapidly after 1988.

The decomposition suggests that the perception that there has not been any discernable change in trespassing in the past few decades is incorrect. There have been some strong trends, but they have tended to counteract each other. Increases in train traffic coupled with an increase in population have been almost exactly balanced by factors that tend to reduce trespassing, such as line abandonment, increasing wealth, the installation of ditch lights, and an aging population.

8. THE WAY FORWARD

Trespassing on the railroad is a problem that does not seem to be going away. The lack of success is disheartening to all involved in attempting to improve the situation. In charting out future public policy initiatives, it may be useful to think of trespassers as falling into four broad categories: people who are loitering near the tracks, suicides, those looking for transportation, and everyone else. Such a classification is useful, as the applicability of potential countermeasures will vary depending on the nature of the trespasser.

By far the largest group of trespassers casualties, probably representing about half of all casualties, are males in their 20s and 30s, who are socializing or loitering on or near the tracks. From what we know from the CDC studies, many of these trespassers are under the influence of alcohol, have a history of alcohol abuse, are unmarried, and have a low level of educational attainment. It would be probably fair to say that these persons probably engage in risky behaviors of many types in addition to trespassing on the railroad. Consequently, the most productive public policy responses would probably fall into the realm of public health, rather than being specific to the railroad.

That said, there is presumably some reason why this segment of society decides to congregate along the right of way. In the absence of any relevant studies, let me suggest that the most likely explanation is that one can engage in things on the railroad that one could not do in a public park or a parking lot. Persons drinking in a public park would be in full view of the street, and it would likely result in citizen complaints and an intervention by the city police or county sheriff. In contrast, the railroad right of way is what sociologists would call a quasi public-private place. It is technically private property, yet access is easy and the probability of enforcement by railroad police is very low. Moreover, vegetation shields activities on the right of way from public view, and the local police have no jurisdiction and little interest in removing trespassers (albeit that the latter may be changing since the terrorist attacks of September 2001). For this type of trespasser, deterrence in the form of fencing the right of way may actually prove to be counter-productive as it may further shield the tracks from public view, and this type of trespasser values privacy. Clear cutting the vegetation, and where appropriate installing some lighting, might be far more productive.

Because all evidence suggests that these trespassers exist on the fringe of society, mainstream activities such as public service announcements and the current program of Operation Lifesaver presentations may be an ineffective way of communicating the dangers. It may be productive for Operation Lifesaver to redirect some of its activities away from presentations to schools and civic groups toward activities in soup kitchens and taverns that are located close to the tracks.

The second group is suicides. While the number of coroner-determined suicides is not known for sure, the number is thought to be at least 100 a year. It may be much higher than this number. In addition, George (2006) reports that about 23% of the FRA database of trespasser casualties, which in theory should exclude suicides, are most likely also suicides, which would represent another 100 suicides a year. Taken together, perhaps a third of the persons who died on the tracks away from grade crossings are actual or probable suicides. There is a small literature on suicides on railroads, primarily dealing with urban transit systems, and mainline railways in Europe (see Mishara, 1999 and the references cited therein). The FRA in cooperation with Transport Canada has recently commissioned a research study that will investigate and provide detailed background information on 60 cases of suicide over the course of the next few years. This study will provide demographic information, the medical background, and information on why the railroad was chosen as a method of suicide.

Possible countermeasures include posting the phone number of suicide helplines at intervals along the right-of-way and at stations, and instructing staff to be aware of antecedent behavior. Suicidal people often reconnoiter the site of the proposed suicide in advance. Because many suicidal persons have lapsed from a program of psychiatric treatment and a drug regimen, an intervention can get them back into their programs and deter a suicide attempt. Evidence from Britain suggests that fencing of the right of way has relocated suicide attempts to station platforms and other places of public access such as highway-rail grade crossings.

Perhaps the first step in addressing the suicide problem is to obtain a clear picture of its magnitude. By not requiring the reporting of suicides, the FRA is sweeping the problem out of public sight. It should be required that all deaths on the railroad are reported to the FRA, and procedures put in place to cross check the reports to the verdicts of coroners and medical examiners. It is clear from George (2006) that even the current reporting requirements are not being followed consistently with some coroner-confirmed suicides entering the FRA trespasser database. In the proposed regime, suicides would be shown as a separate line item in the FRA safety data. I suspect that the outcome of such a change in reporting requirements will be so shocking as to spur public policy. The government and railroad management might wish to go even further and classify other trespasser deaths as "suspected suicides" based on evidence from police reports and coroners' enquiries. The objective of such an analysis would not be to allow the railroad to evade legal or moral responsibility for a trespasser's death, but to inform public policy because the countermeasures that should be adopted to prevent suicides are different from those that are appropriate to prevent other types of trespass.

The third group is transients using the railroad for purposes of illicit transportation. While the era of the hobo from popular imagery has long since passed into history, there is a problem of illegal immigrants in the Southwestern states hopping freight trains, and using the right of way as a pathway. Clearly, the magnitude of this railroad problem is related to the prevalence of illegal immigration, which is a topic of national debate.

The final group is a mixed bag of thieves, vandals, thrill seekers, and those taking a short cut across or along the tracks. While members of this group probably represent the vast majority of incidents of trespass, they are a minority of those killed and injured. Alcohol-fueled loiterers, suicidal people, and people hopping freight trains are much more likely to sustain an injury while on railroad property than people taking a short cut. Savage (1998, see Chapter 9) discusses the legal duty of care that railroads have in preventing this final type of trespass. In general, courts in the United States have held that the mere existence of a railroad track is sufficient to warn adults of the dangers of trespass, and that neither a fence nor warning signs are necessary.

However, for children under the age of twelve a higher standard of care is required, especially because the law has long recognized that children may be attracted to playing on the railroad. This is formally known as the "attractive nuisance doctrine" and more commonly referred to as the "turntable doctrine" as an early case involved a child injured while he was trespassing on a railroad turntable. The actual conduct expected of the railroad is somewhat unclear. In areas where there are very young children a fence may be required, whereas for older children Operation Lifesaver presentations in neighboring schools warning of the dangers may be sufficient.

A more contentious issue is how the railroad should act when it is aware that trespass takes place repeatedly at certain locations. Some courts have taken the view that railroads have a duty to "anticipate future trespass" at locations where trespass occurs regularly, and to react to a "well-worn path" crossing the railroad. In situations where a landowner is aware of repeated trespass but has taken no action to prevent access, courts may regard the trespasser as a "licensee." In general, landowners are held to a higher standard of care in warning licensees of the dangers than they would be for trespassers. In general, the posting of signs by the railroad is regarded as a sufficient action. Railroads do take further actions such as conducting patrols and working with local authorities and police departments. Where there appears to be a well-used informal foot crossing then the railroad might be expected to provide a regular crossing, a footbridge, or erect fencing to make people use nearby formal crossings.

In North America, as in continental Europe and many other parts of the world, the railroad is generally unfenced. The NTSB (1978) study indicates that 85% of trespasser fatalities occurred at unfenced locations. At various times Congress has raised the issue of imposing regulations to require railroads to erect fences along sections of their right of way that pass through populated areas. Savage (1998) made some calculations on the economics of fencing approximately 10,000 miles of right of way that pass through areas with population densities of greater than 800 persons per square mile. He estimated that installing and maintaining urban fencing would cost about $300 million a year, and would reduce trespassing fatalities by a maximum of 100 persons a year. At this level of fatalities averted, fencing would be marginally justified in a cost-benefit analysis given commonly used values of a statistical life saved. However, Savage points out that this calculation is based on the most optimistic assumptions about the effectiveness of fencing. Fencing is routinely destroyed, and may not be effective against persons who value privacy while loitering on the right of way, or potential suicides who relocate to accessing the tracks at grade crossings and stations. From a public policy point of view, Savage argues that society would be much better off if the money was spent on installing flashing lights and gates at the large number of highway-rail grade crossings that currently do not have them. At these locations, the payoff in terms of lives saved is larger and much more predictable.

9. CONCLUSIONS

The good news is that the nation's increasing affluence has reduced the propensity for people to expose themselves to the risks of trespassing on the railroad. The bad news is that increases in train traffic and the size of the population conspire to ensure that the annual toll of injuries and fatalities has remained reasonably constant for the past three decades.

There is a strong epidemiological aspect to the trespassing problem, with the risks concentrated on males in their 20s and 30s. Consequently, the amount of trespassing will be directly related to the demographic trends affecting the size of the population in the target group. While the baby boom generation has aged, lowering the proportion of the population in this high-risk group, the total size of the population is increasing, meaning that the absolute number of 15–44 year olds is still rising. Absent any innovative countermeasures, there is little prospect that the annual casualty count will be reduced anytime soon.

A hurdle to designing effective countermeasures is that we are only now developing an understanding of the demographics of trespassers and their motivation for being on the tracks. The 1990s studies by the CDC (Pelletier, 1997; CDC, 1999), and the recent work by George (2006), which was envisioned by the FRA as a pilot study, point in the right direction. There is a great need for a nationwide comprehensive study that combines FRA data with information that can be gained from coroners and local police reports, supplemented by interviews with those suffering non-fatal injuries, and relatives and friends of the deceased.

Insights from more detailed studies are essential, as the effectiveness of possible countermeasures will vary depending on the nature of the trespassing.

It is clear that innovative thinking is necessary if society wishes to see a reduction in the annual casualty toll, but without a good understanding of the problem we risk wasting resources or, even worse, doing things that may be counterproductive.

REFERENCES

Aldrich, M. (2006). *Death rode the rails: American railroad accidents and safety 1828–1965*. Baltimore: Johns Hopkins University Press.

Association of American Railroads. (annual from 1924–2005). *Railroad facts*. Washington, DC: Association of American Railroads.

Centers for Disease Control and Prevention. (1999). Injuries among railroad trespassers in Georgia, 1990–1996, *Mortality and Morbidity Weekly Report*, *48*(25), 537–541.

daSilva, M., Carroll, A., & Baron, W. (2006). *Railroad infrastructure trespass detection research*. Report to the Federal Railroad Administration. Cambridge, MA: Volpe National Transportation Systems Center, U.S. Department of Transportation.

Davis, G. G., Alexander, C. B., & Brissie, R. M. (1997). A 15-year review of railway-related deaths in Jefferson County, Alabama. *American Journal of Forensic Medicine and Pathology*, *18*(4), 363–368.

Federal Railroad Administration. (annual from 1901–2005). *Accident/incident bulletin*. Washington, DC: FRA, U.S. Department of Transportation. (Prior to 1966, it was published by the Interstate Commerce Commission under the title *Accident Bulletin*. In 1997, it was renamed *Railroad Safety Statistics*)

George, B. F. (2006). *Rail-trespasser fatalities: Developing demographic profiles*. Preliminary report to the Federal Railroad Administration. Edgewater, MD: Cadle Creek Consulting.

Han, L. D., Chin, S., Hwang, H., & Peterson, B. E. (2006). A tool for railroad hazmat routing under shipment bans in major cities. In: *Proceedings of the Transportation Research Board 85th annual meeting*.

Hoyert, D.L., Heron, M.P., Murphy, S.L., & Kung, H. (2006). Deaths: Final data for 2003. *National vital statistics reports*, *54*(13). Hyattsville, MD: National Center for Health Statistics.

Interstate Commerce Commission. (annual from 1888–1994). *Annual report on the statistics of railways in the United States*. Washington, DC: Interstate Commerce Commission. (From 1954 renamed *Transport statistics in the United States*.)

Mishara, B. L. (1999). Suicide in the Montreal subway system: Characteristics of the victims, antecedents, and implications for prevention. *Canadian Journal of Psychiatry*, *44*(7), 690–696.

Mok, S. C., & Savage, I. (2005). Why has safety improved at rail-highway grade crossings? *Risk Analysis*, *25*(4), 867–881.

National Center for Health Statistics. (annual). *Vital statistics of the United States*. Hyattsville, MD: National Center for Health Statistics. (Previously published by the Census Bureau.)

National Safety Council. (annual). *Injury facts*. Itasca, IL: National Safety Council. (Prior to 1999 this was known as *Accident facts*).

National Transportation Safety Board. (1978). *Safety recommendation R-78-42*. Washington DC: National Transportation Safety Board.

Pelletier, A. (1997). Deaths among railroad trespassers: The role of alcohol in fatal injuries. *Journal of the American Medical Association*, *277*(13), 1064–1066.

Prais, S. J., & Winsten, C. B. (1954). *Trend estimators and serial correlation*. Discussion paper 383. Cowles Commission, Chicago.

Rail Safety and Standards Board. (2005). *Annual safety performance report 2004*. London: Rail Safety and Standards Board.

Savage, I. (1998). *The economics of railroad safety*. Boston, MA: Kluwer Academic Publishers.

Savage, I. (2006). Does public education improve rail-highway crossing safety? *Accident Analysis and Prevention*, *38*(2), 310–316.

U.S. Bureau of the Census. (2002). Census 2000 special reports, Series CNSR-4; Demographic trends in the 20th century. Washington DC: U.S. Census Bureau.

ENERGY USE AND POLLUTANT EMISSIONS IMPACTS OF SHORTLINE RAILROAD ABANDONMENT

Michael W. Babcock and James L. Bunch

ABSTRACT

Railroad abandonment has potential negative effects especially in rural areas that rely on railroads for outbound and inbound shipments. The objectives of the study are (1) to develop a model that can measure wheat transport modal ton-mile shifts, (2) measure modal energy use changes, and (3) measure the modal emissions changes resulting from hypothetical shortline railroad abandonment. Total ton-miles are about the same in the simulated shortline abandonment and no shortline abandonment cases, with the abandonment scenario generating 2% fewer ton-miles. Total energy consumption is nearly identical in the two scenarios; 2.1% higher in the shortline abandonment case. Grand total emissions are 1.4% lower in the scenario that does not include shortlines in the logistics system.

1. INTRODUCTION

According to Wilson (2002), in 2001 railroads accounted for nearly 42% of the total U.S. ton-miles of freight and nearly 26% of the total U.S. tons

Railroad Economics
Research in Transportation Economics, Volume 20, 225–257

ISSN: 0739-8859/doi:10.1016/S0739-8859(07)20009-5

originated (Wilson, 2002, pp. 42, 44). In 2004, railroads moved 8.1 million containers and 2.9 million trailers (Association of American Railroads, 2005, p. 26).

Despite the important role of railroads in the U.S. transportation system, railroad mileage has been declining. Table 1 displays Class I railroad mileage of the top 10 states in railroad mileage in 1975 and 2004.[1] As a group, railroad mileage plunged 31.7% in these states. The largest decline occurred in Iowa (47.7%) and the smallest in California (20.5%). Table 2 contains miles of road operated by Class I and non-Class I (i.e., Classes II and III) railroads during the 1987–2004 period.[2] The data indicate that Class I miles operated fell from 147,568 (1987) to 97,496 (2004), a 33% decline. In the same period, non-Class I miles of road operated rose from 33,645 (1987) to 42,750 (2004), a 27.1% gain. However in the 1997–2000 period, non-Class I miles peaked at slightly less than 50,000 miles. Then, between 2000 and 2004, non-Class I miles fell 14.4%. Total mileage operated in the 1987–2000 period by all three classes of railroads declined from 181,213 (1987) to 170,512 (2000), a decrease of 5.9%. In the 2000–2004 era, total miles operated decreased an additional 17.8%. Thus, the net change in the national railroad network is nearly a 23% decrease. The data in Tables 1 and 2 clearly indicate that the rail system has declined as a result of abandonment.

Table 1. Top 10 States in Class I Railroad Mileage[a] 1975 and 2004.

State	1975 Mileage	2004 Mileage	Percent Change
			1975–2004
Texas	13,255	10,246	−22.7
Illinois	10,555	7,338	−30.5
California	7,291	5,796	−20.5
Ohio	7,506	5,179	−31.0
Pennsylvania	7,837	5,060	−35.4
Kansas	7,514	4,936	−34.3
Minnesota	7,294	4,589	−37.1
Indiana	6,357	4,192	−34.1
Missouri	6,010	4,122	−31.4
Iowa	7,547	3,946	−47.7
Total	81,166	55,404	−31.7

Source: 1975, Association of American Railroads (1978), *Yearbook of Railroad Facts*, 1978 edition, p. 47; 2004, Association of American Railroads, *Railroad Facts*, 2005 edition, p. 46.
[a]Georgia was in the top 10 states in 2004 but not in 1975. Georgia's rail mileage fell from 5,414 (1975) to 4,779 (2004), a decline of 11.7%.

Table 2. Miles of Road Operated Class I and Non-Class I Railroads 1987–2004.

Year	Class I Railroads	Non-Class I Railroads	Total
1987	147,568	33,645	181,213
1988	140,767	34,037	174,814
1989	137,504	39,770	177,274
1990	133,189	42,712	175,909
1991	129,839	43,969	173,808
1992	126,237	43,427	169,664
1993	123,738	45,226	168,964
1994	123,335	45,441	168,776
1995	125,072	45,361	170,433
1996	126,682	47,214	173,896
1997	121,670	49,615	171,285
1998	119,813	49,985	169,798
1999	120,986	49,672	170,658
2000	120,597	49,915	170,512
2001	97,631	45,002	142,633
2002	99,943	41,448	141,391
2003	98,944	41,995	140,939
2004	97,496	42,750	140,246
Percent change 1987–2004	−33.9	27.1	−22.6

Source: Association of American Railroads, *Railroad Facts* (various issues).

Railroad abandonments have occurred for a wide variety of reasons. The Staggers Rail Act of 1980 made railroad mergers and abandonments easier to accomplish by establishing strict time limits for making regulatory decisions. Significant government investment in the interstate highway system and the adoption of just-in-time (JIT) inventory practices have increased the demand for motor carrier service and have had a negative impact on railroad demand.

Railroad abandonment has potential negative effects, especially in rural areas that rely on railroads for outbound shipments of goods and inbound shipments of raw materials and other inputs. Among the potential negative impacts on rural areas are the following:

- higher transport costs for railroad shippers;
- reduction of market options for shippers;
- lost economic development opportunities;
- loss of local tax base to fund basic government services;
- increased road damage costs.

Changes have occurred in the Great Plains region of the U.S. that have contributed to increased trucking of grain. Class I railroads have encouraged the construction of unit train (100 or more railcars) loading facilities (shuttle train locations) on their mainlines. Due to the scale economies of unit trains, Class I railroads offer lower rates to shuttle train shippers. This enables shuttle train shippers to pay a relatively high price for wheat. Thus, wheat producers will truck their grain a much greater distance to obtain a higher wheat price at the shuttle train location. Farmers will bypass the local grain elevator and the shortline railroad serving it, and truck their wheat to the shuttle train facility.

Agriculture has consolidated into fewer, larger farms. With the increased scale of operations, farmer ownership of semitractor trailer trucks has increased (Babcock & Bunch, 2002b, pp. 34–35). With these trucks, farmers can bypass the local grain elevator and the shortline railroad serving it, and deliver grain directly to more distant markets.

However, the shift of grain transport from railroads to trucking is not limited to the Great Plains region. According to U.S. Department of Agriculture (2004, p. 10), for all U.S. grain, the market share of motor carriers has risen from 38.2 (1987) to 49.7% (2000), while the rail share has fallen from 42.7 (1987) to 32.2% (2000). For all the U.S. wheat tonnage, the motor carrier market share increased from 18.1 to 31.3% in the 1987–2000 period, while the railroad share declined from 67 to 50.6% (U.S. Department of Agriculture, 2004, p. 16). The motor carrier market share for the U.S. corn rose from 43.4 (1987) to 53.4% (2000). In the same period, the railroad share decreased from 37.7 to 30.1% (U.S. Department of Agriculture, 2004, p. 13).

Grain is the principal commodity market of most shortlines serving rural regions. Prater and Babcock (1998) found that the most important determinant of shortline railroad profitability is carloads per mile of track. Thus, increased trucking of grain at the expense of shortline railroads threatens the economic viability of these railroads, possibility resulting in their abandonment.

The objective of this paper is to develop a methodology to measure the impact on energy use and emissions resulting from potential abandonment of shortline railroads. Although Kansas wheat transport is used to empirically implement the methodology, the models can be used by other researchers to measure similar impacts for any modal substitution situation. The specific objectives of the paper are:

1. Develop a model that can measure wheat transport modal ton-mile shifts resulting from hypothetical shortline railroad abandonment.

2. Measure modal energy use changes attributable to hypothetical shortline abandonment using energy use coefficients for railroads and motor carriers.
3. Measure the modal emissions changes related to potential shortline abandonment using mobile source emissions factors.

To achieve the second and third objectives, it is necessary to measure the wheat market ton-mile changes resulting from abandonment of Kansas shortlines. This is achieved by computing the minimum transportation and handling costs for moving Kansas wheat from farms, through grain elevators, and then through unit train loading locations to the export terminals at Houston, Texas. Using Arc View Geographic Information software and a truck routing algorithm from Babcock and Bunch (2002), wheat is routed through the logistics system to achieve minimum total transportation and handling costs. This analysis is performed with and without study area shortlines in the wheat logistics system. Thus, rail and truck ton-miles before and after shortline abandonment are one of the outputs of the model. Energy use by mode is computed by multiplying ton-miles by energy use coefficients (Btus per ton-mile). Energy use by mode is converted into emissions by mode through the use of truck and locomotive emission factors (pounds of pollutants per 1,000 gallons of diesel fuel). The approach is similar to that found in Lee and Casavant (2002) and Ball and Casavant (2003).

2. LITERATURE REVIEW

There are a number of possible impacts of railroad abandonments on highway users and taxpayers. These impacts can be classified into five categories which are as follows:

(a) increased highway wear with resultant costs to highway users and taxpayers;
(b) increased highway congestion and reduced safety, with resultant costs on highway users;
(c) reduced local area employment and income;
(d) higher transport costs to local plants;
(e) impacts on energy costs and emissions.

A number of recent studies have examined the road damage costs resulting from abandonment-related incremental truck traffic as well as changes in grain logistics systems. Casavant and Lenzi (1990) outlined a methodology for determining the pavement costs of potential abandonments and applied the approach to potential abandonments in the state of Washington. They found that the amount of road damage due to abandonments is heavily dependent on the volume of abandonment-related truck traffic relative to the type of roads used. Rigid, well-structured pavements with high structural design standards were hardly affected by increased truck traffic. However, county roads built to lesser design standards were greatly impacted from increased truck use.

Tolliver (1989) applied the Highway Pavement Monitoring System (HPMS) model to calculate pavement damage costs due to subterminal development in the state of North Dakota. One of the study scenarios predicted pavement damage costs resulting from a grain subterminal in the study region to be $58 million for 452 miles of highway. The author concluded that the collector and minor arterial roads would be the most severely affected by subterminal development due to the mismatch between pavement structural characteristics and truck weights and volume.

Following Casavant and Lenzi (1990) and Tolliver (1989), Eusebio and Rindom (1991) developed a procedure for estimating road damage impacts related to potential abandonments, and applied the procedure to a group of counties in south central Kansas. They found that in the six-county area, abandonment resulted in 740,000 bushels of wheat being diverted from rail to truck shipment for movements from country elevators to large grain terminals. Total abandonment-related road damage cost was $194,000 per year.

Tolliver, Andres, and Lindamood (1994) used an analysis similar to Eusebio and Rindom (1991) to simulate the loss of all rail service in the state of Washington and measure the resulting road damage costs. He found that the loss of all mainline rail service in Washington would result in incremental annual pavement resurfacing cost of $65 million and annual pavement reconstruction cost would be $219.6 million. If all branchlines were abandoned, the annual resurfacing costs ranged from $17.4 to $28.5 million, and the annual reconstruction cost would be $63.3 to $104 million.

Russell, Babcock, and Mauler (1996) estimated potential road damage costs resulting from hypothetical abandonment of 800 miles of railroad branchline in south central and western Kansas. The authors employed a network model developed by Chow, Babcock, and Sorenson (1985) to simulate wheat movements in the region both before and after hypothetical abandonment. The authors employed Highway Performance Monitoring System (HPMS) pavement functions and American Association of State

Highway Transportation Officials (AASHTO) traffic equivalency functions to measure road damage costs. They found that total annual abandonment-related road damage costs would be slightly more than $1 million.

Lenzi, Jessup, and Casavant (1996) estimated state and county road damage costs in the state of Washington resulting from a potential draw-down of the lower Snake River. They assumed two drawdown scenarios: One of these only involving two months and the other four months. In both scenarios the authors assumed that grain formerly moved by barge from eastern Washington would be shipped by truck to the nearest elevator with rail service. The authors found that road damage was actually 63% *less* for both scenarios, primarily because the average length of haul for trucks declined from 45 miles for truck-barge movements to 15 miles for truck–rail shipments.

Rindom, Rosacker, and Wulfkuhle (1997) measured road damage costs related to subterminal (unit train) locations at Dodge City and Colby, Kansas. The research included two study areas that included all Kansas farms within a 50-mile radius of Dodge City and Colby. The authors employed the Chow et al. (1985) model to simulate grain flows in the two study areas for a base case that assumed no subterminals in the logistics system and several scenarios for which subterminals were included in the system. The authors found that for the Dodge City study area the maximum incremental road damage cost relative to the base case was $3.3 million per year, while the corresponding figure for the Colby study area was $7.6 million. These results were due to substantial increases in truck average length of haul in the subterminal scenarios.

Babcock and Bunch (2002) measured the road damage costs related to the hypothetical abandonment of four shortline railroads serving western and central Kansas. Using a 12-step process to measure road damage costs, they found that the four shortlines annually save the State of Kansas $49.5 million in pavement damage costs.

Bitzan and Tolliver (2003) investigate potential railroad abandonment in North Dakota resulting from a rail industry switch from 263,000-pound covered hopper cars to 286,000-pound cars. The authors estimate highway impacts for four scenarios representing a range of possibilities for lines that could be abandoned (895–1,202 miles) as a result of the shift to larger hopper cars. They found that if all the abandonment-related truck traffic moved on rural minor arterial roads, the incremental annual road damage cost would range from $2.5 to $4.3 million.

Babcock, Bunch, Sanderson, and Witt (2003a) measured the change in Kansas state highway damage costs resulting from assumed abandonment of shortline railroads. Using the methodology in Tolliver and HDR Engineering (2000), the authors measured the road damage cost that would occur if 1,761 miles of four shortline railroads were abandoned. They found that the total annual road damage costs would be $57.8 million.

Fewer studies have measured the highway safety impacts of abandonment. Tolliver and HDR Engineering (2000) described a method by which the safety costs of rail abandonment-related truck traffic can be measured. The four-step procedure starts by converting existing annual rail freight into equivalent truck trips. Next, the incremental abandonment-related truck traffic is associated with a statistically probable quantity of accidents, injuries, and fatalities. Then the increased annual quantity of accidents are multiplied by their respective cost estimates. Finally, the costs are aggregated into a dollar figure that represents the safety impact of rail abandonment.

Witt (2004) estimated incremental highway accident costs and benefits associated with shortline abandonment in Kansas. He measured the safety costs of shortline abandonment by multiplying the incremental truck miles by the accidents per mile traveled. This result was multiplied by the cost per accident. The safety benefit of abandonment was obtained by multiplying highway-rail crossings eliminated by accidents per highway-rail crossing. This figure was multiplied by the cost per highway-rail crossing accident. He found that abandonment of four Kansas shortlines would result in a safety cost of $1.3 million and a safety benefit of $2.7 million.

There have been a few studies that have quantified the impact of railroad abandonment on local area income and employment. Public Interest Economic Center (1974) employed a general equilibrium model to estimate the income and employment effects of the reorganization of several bankrupt eastern U.S. railroads that became CONRAIL. The study concludes that for most counties, abandonment of rail service according to the CONRAIL system plan would have small impacts relative to the size of the affected economies. However, in some counties real income would be reduced by as much as 3.3%.

Eusebio, Rindom, and Abderrezak (1992) used the Public Interest Economic Center (1974) model to measure the economic impacts of abandonment on Kansas county income and employment. The study concluded that most counties have reductions in employment of 4% or less, and payroll declines of about 2% or less. However, some Kansas counties had employment declines of greater than 4%.

Sanderson and Babcock (2005) used econometric panel data techniques to measure the impact of rail abandonments on Kansas county income and employment. Estimates were measured for rural, urban, and metropolitan counties. The authors concluded that abandonments produce an initial period of income and employment growth that may be temporary for some counties, and that any adverse impacts appear with a time lag of a few years.

Comparatively, few studies have specifically addressed the issue of the impact of abandonment on transport costs to local delivery points. Chow et al. (1985) found that the simulated abandonment of the Rock Island railroad in northwest Kansas would increase total wheat logistics costs in that region by only 1.4%. However, increases in trucking and storage costs were additional burdens for farmers who delivered wheat to elevators on the former Rock Island line.

Babcock, Bunch, Sanderson, and Witt (2003b) measured changes in transportation and handling costs resulting from simulated abandonment of all the shortline railroads in the western two-thirds of Kansas. The authors found that total transportation costs were about the same with or without shortline railroads in the wheat logistics system. However, total wheat handling costs rose nearly 30% once shortlines were removed from the transportation network.

Lee and Casavant (2002) and Ball and Casavant (2003) used a transportation cost minimizing model in combination with modal energy intensities and emission factors to identify potential effects on energy consumption and emissions output, attributed to wheat and barley transportation in eastern Washington, if breaching of the lower Snake River dams occurs. However, to our knowledge, this is the only study that has investigated changes in energy use and emissions resulting from freight railroad abandonment.

3. THE STUDY AREA

The study area corresponds to the western two-thirds of Kansas encompassing the three central and three western Kansas crop reporting districts (Fig. 1). During the 2000–2004 period, the study area accounted for 88.2% of total Kansas wheat production, 81.1% of the state's sorghum production, 75.7% of Kansas corn production, and 39.8% of the soybean output (Kansas Agricultural Statistics Service, 2002b, 2004, 2005, Kansas Farm Facts). The study area produced 78.5% of Kansas production of the four crops combined.

Four shortline railroads serve the study area – Kansas and Oklahoma Railroad, Kyle Railroad, Cimarron Valley Railroad, and Nebraska, Kansas, and Colorado Railnet. The Kansas and Oklahoma began operations in 2001 and serves the central part of the study area from Wichita, Kansas, and west

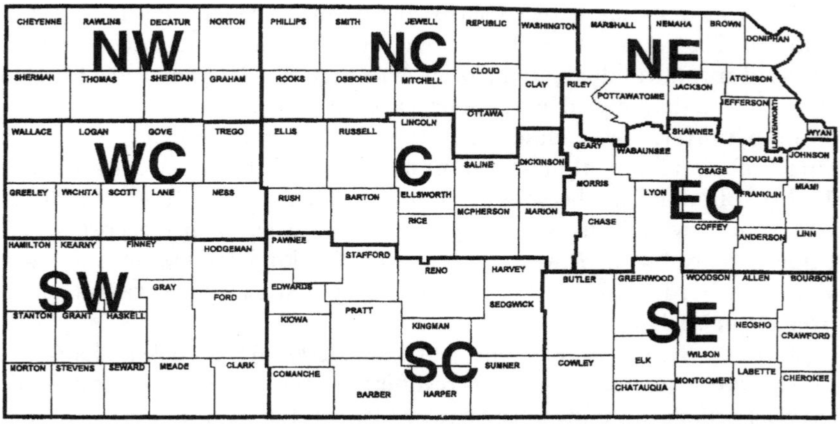

Fig. 1. Kansas Crop Reporting Districts.

to the Colorado border. It also serves south central Kansas and has a line in north central Kansas as well. The Kansas and Oklahoma Railroad has 877 route miles in Kansas and 82 employees.

The Kyle Railroad serves the northern part of the study area with a 479-mile system. The Kyle began operations in 1982 and has 77 full-time employees. The Cimarron Valley Railroad (CV) has 254 route miles with 182 miles in southwest Kansas. The CV was purchased from the Santa Fe Railroad and began operations in 1996. The CV has 15 full-time employees in Kansas. The Nebraska, Kansas, and Colorado Railnet (NKC) serve five Kansas counties in the northwest part of the study area. The railroad has 122 miles in Kansas and 17 miles of trackage rights on the Kyle Railroad. The NKC began operations in 1996 and has 30 full-time employees.

The study area is also served by two Class I railroads, the Burlington Northern Santa Fe (BNSF) and the Union Pacific System (UP). The BNSF has 1,072 miles of mainline track in Kansas and 188 branchline miles. The UP has 1,378 mainline miles and 127 branchline miles.

4. DESCRIPTION OF THE KANSAS WHEAT LOGISTICS SYSTEM

Fig. 2 portrays a simplified version of the Kansas wheat logistics system. Wheat is shipped from farms in five axle, 80,000-pound semitractor trailer

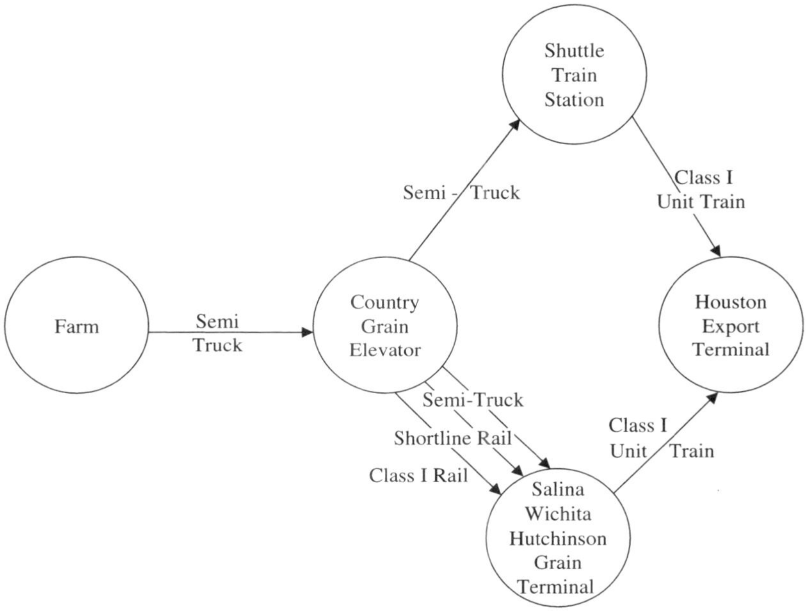

Fig. 2. Wheat Logistics System.

trucks (hereafter referred to as semi-truck) to country grain elevators, which are usually no more than 10–15 miles from the farm origin. Wheat is shipped from country elevators to either shuttle train stations (100-railcar shipping facilities at former country elevator locations) or the terminal elevators at Salina, Wichita, and Hutchinson, Kansas. Wheat moves exclusively by semi-truck to shuttle train stations, but movements to Salina, Wichita, and Hutchinson can be semi-truck, shortline railroad, and Class I railroad. Wheat is then shipped by Class I unit train from the shuttle train facilities and the grain terminal elevators in Salina, Wichita, and Hutchinson to Houston, Texas for export.

As noted above, this is a simplified version of the wheat logistics system. In some cases, farmers deliver wheat by semi-truck directly to shuttle train stations or Salina, Wichita, and Hutchinson grain terminals. This occurs if the farm origins are relatively close to one of these facilities. Also Kansas wheat is shipped to many domestic flour milling locations as well as the Texas Gulf region for export.

5. THE WHEAT LOGISTICS SYSTEM MODEL

The movement of Kansas wheat is modeled as a transshipment network model with individual farms serving as supply nodes, grain elevators and unit train loading facilities serving as transshipment nodes, and the final demand node being the export terminals at Houston, Texas. The county and state road networks, shortline railroads, and Class I railroads constitute the arcs which connect these nodes.

Given the magnitude and complexity of the wheat logistics system, the movement of wheat through the various possible network paths is most clearly analyzed in four distinct steps. Step I involves the collection of wheat from production origins, or farms, into an intermediate storage facility (grain elevator) which can ship wheat to the export node. Since it is not economically feasible for firms to ship wheat by truck from Kansas to Houston, Step I consists of moving wheat from the farm to an elevator that has rail access capable of reaching the final demand node. Step II involves the handling of wheat at intermediate storage facilities. Step III analyzes the shipment of wheat from unit train shipping facilities to the network model export node. Step IV includes Steps I to III except shortline railroads are assumed to be abandoned and are deleted from the transportation network.

Although profit maximization is assumed to be the main goal of all agents (farmers, elevators, transport firms) in the wheat logistics system, costs serve as the most consistent influence on agents' behavior because all agents face a world price at the export terminal. Profits ultimately decide individual behavior; however, cost minimization is the consistent strategy for maximizing profits, regardless of the type of market involved. Farmers seek to minimize both the financial and time costs of getting wheat from the field to the grain elevator or unit train facility; grain elevators and unit train shipping facilities operate so as to minimize the cost of handling wheat and shipping it to various market destinations. Thus, the goal of the model is to determine the least cost transport route for wheat from production origin to final destination utilizing the available transportation network. Kansas wheat is shipped to both domestic and international export markets. The Port of Houston is assumed to approximate the cost of shipping wheat to the many destinations to which it is normally shipped in a given year.[3] Thus, it is assumed that all agents minimize the costs involved in shipping wheat to market. This relationship is summarized in mathematical form by the following objective function:

$$\text{Minimize TSC} = \sum_{i}(H_i + T_i + R_i)X_i \quad (1)$$

Subject to the following constraints:

H_i, T_i, $R_i \geq 0$
Total wheat demanded = Total wheat supplied
Actual wheat stored at elevator $i \leq$ Maximum storage capacity of elevator i
Actual transport by truck $i \leq$ Maximum transport capacity of truck i
Actual transport by railcar $i \leq$ Maximum transport capacity of railcar i
Flow of wheat into elevator i = Flow of wheat out of elevator i

where TSC is the total wheat logistics system transportation and handling costs, H_i is the sum of all handling costs of unit of wheat i, T_i is the sum of all trucking costs of unit of wheat i, R_i is the sum of all rail costs of unit of wheat i, and X_i is the total amount of wheat shipped from farms to the Port of Houston.

5.1. Assumptions of the Network Model

Several assumptions were necessary in order to implement the network model. With respect to Step I, although other methods are available, the optimal methodology for determining wheat movements is individual routing choice analysis. By this method, the initial movement of wheat is determined independently by each farmer. A farmer may choose to truck wheat to a country grain elevator, a shuttle train station, or a terminal grain elevator. This choice is based on the wheat price offered by each available destination market and the costs of transporting wheat to that destination. Based on the spatial distribution of farms and potential destinations, the principal determinant in this choice of destination is usually the transportation cost. That is, the difference in wheat prices between destinations tends to be negligible due to low-cost information and high levels of competition, while each farm is usually much closer to one destination than any other potential destination. Thus, producers are assumed to always choose the least-distant, least transport cost destination.

Three key assumptions were made governing system behavior for the Step II handling aspect of wheat transport. First, vehicle and storage capacities are available in equilibrium quantities such that a capacity constraint never influences wheat movements. The second key assumption for Step II is that a country grain elevator does not ship wheat to another country grain elevator. Instead, country grain elevators ship to unit train facilities because of the large volumes of wheat that must be handled, stored, and shipped to Houston. And finally, input costs and technologies across the study area are assumed to be uniform, thereby making it possible to characterize economic entities by type. Thus, all country elevators have the same characteristics, as do all grain trucks, Class I railroads, and shortline railroads.

Two additional assumptions were made for Steps III and IV of Kansas wheat movement. A key assumption is that wheat must use rail transport to reach Houston. The high motor carrier variable (with distance) costs of shipping wheat makes trucking wheat to Houston economically infeasible. The large economies of scale associated with unit train transport make rail the least cost mode of transport for every wheat long distance movement. Thus, if rail service is available from a grain elevator, it will be utilized, and wheat shipments will never change modes of transport once loaded on a rail car.

5.2. Structural Elements of the Model

Before analyzing the movement of wheat, some structural elements had to be quantified and geo-spatially referenced. First, the farms where wheat is produced were determined. Second, the transshipment nodes (i.e., country grain elevators, shuttle train facilities, and Salina, Wichita, and Hutchinson, Kansas grain terminals) and the terminal node (Houston) were defined. Next, the road and rail systems available for transporting the wheat had to be specified. And finally, system behaviors as defined by the cost functions of activities were approximated using the four-step approach.

In traditional agricultural network models, an area of the magnitude used in this study would probably be divided into 10 mile × 10 mile squares, with each square representing a "simulated farm" origin. While the simulated farm assumption was the best available approximation in the past, tremendous advances in computer technology have enabled a much more detailed approximation of reality. Using GIS software and satellite imagery data on land usage in each county, a specific land use map was generated for the entire study area. Distinct parcels of urban area, woodland, water, and cropland were defined for the entire study area, and all cropland was identified for its possible contribution to wheat production. The entire study area was subdivided into 640 acre plots which contained various parcels of cropland and other land uses that were further analyzed to estimate simulated wheat farms in the model.

After the actual amount of cropland in a section (640 acres) was identified, the amount of wheat that it would be estimated to produce for the simulation had to be determined. The wheat production of origin points for study area wheat is determined by dividing the average wheat produced in a particular county by the total cropland in that county and multiplying this result by the exact amount of cropland in each section in that county. That is

$$\text{SectionWheat}_i = \text{SectionCropLand}_{i,t} \times \left[\text{Wheat}_{j,\text{avg}}/\text{CountyCropLand}_{j,t}\right] \quad (2)$$

where SectionWheat_i is the amount of wheat originating in section i, $\text{SectionCropLand}_{i,t}$ is the land used to produce crops in section i in year t, $\text{Wheat}_{j,\text{avg}}$ is the average wheat produced in county j over a four-year period, $\text{CountyCropLand}_{j,t}$ is the total land in county j used to produce crops in year t.

By applying the resulting estimated wheat production for a particular section to the centroid, or center point of the simulated farm, the result was a geo-referenced set of origin points which served to spatially distribute the average county wheat production according to the actual distribution of study area cropland. This approach, therefore, allowed the model to account for geographical variances in both land usage patterns and historic wheat yields, thereby offering a vastly more accurate estimate of origin point locations and wheat production than postulating homogenous 10 mile × 10 mile simulated farms.

Having established the origin nodes for the model, transshipment and terminal nodes were identified. The numbers of country grain elevators, shuttle train stations, Salina, Wichita, and Hutchinson, Kansas grain terminals, and terminal nodes (Houston) were small enough that actual data concerning these entities could be used. Street addresses for facilities licensed to handle and store grain in the State of Kansas were used to identify and geo-reference the transshipment nodes in the model. The Salina, Wichita, and Hutchinson grain terminals and shuttle train facilities were those identified in Babcock et al. (2003b). The geographic center of the Port of Houston served as the terminal node for the model.

Having defined all of the nodes in the system, the next step in formulating a model of the wheat logistics system was to define the arcs that serve to connect the different origin, transshipment, and terminal nodes of the network. The actual Kansas road system maintained by state and county governments was utilized to define road network arcs. Likewise, systems of railroads operating in Kansas were used to specify railroad network arcs.

See the appendix for a detailed mathematical presentation of the network model.

5.3. Data

The model in this study requires much more data than traditional agricultural network models. Identifying wheat origin points requires two sets of data. Data describing the *location* and *amount* of all cropland in the study area are required. These are is available through the State of Kansas Data Access and Support Center (DASC), an initiative of the state's GIS policy board. The data of interest to this study is collected by DASC for each county, so the data for the 66 counties in the study area were obtained from DASC and used to form a single land use map of the entire study area, providing the spatial location of all origin points. The amount of wheat produced at each origin point is the subject of the second set of data. The amount of wheat produced per Kansas county in 2000–2003 is found in Kansas Agricultural Statistics Service (2002b, 2004). The wheat production for each county was averaged over this four-year period and the county average production is distributed across all wheat origins in the county.

The system of county and state roads in the study area was provided in digitized form by the Kansas Department of Transportation (KDOT). The locations and storage capacities of country grain elevators and terminal grain elevators were obtained from Kansas Grain and Feed Association (2003). Shuttle train facility locations were from Babcock et al. (2003b). Rail systems for Class I (UP and BNSF) and shortline railroads were obtained through Kansas rail maps provided by KDOT and the Kansas Corporation Commission.

The key data for generating wheat movements are the various transport costs involved in the wheat logistics system. Truck costs incurred by farmers when transporting wheat from origin points to the nearest destination (Step I) are from the Kansas Agricultural Statistics Service (2001b). In the study area, the costs vary from a low of .89 cents to a high of 1.17 cents per bushel per mile. Thus, truck movements from origin points are assumed to cost 1.0 cent per bushel per mile.[4]

Truck shipments of wheat by grain elevators typically involve for-hire trucking companies. To estimate the for-hire truck costs (per 100 lbs) for various distances, the study by Berwick (2002) was used. For-hire truck costs for wheat are based on the assumptions of a 100-mile loaded trip by a five-axle semi-tractor trailer operating at a gross vehicle weight (GVW) of 80,000 lbs and hauling 943 bushels of wheat, with a 100-mile empty return trip.[5] The cost per mile is $1.13.

Elevator charges for loading and unloading wheat by truck and rail are required under Kansas statute to be publicly posted. Based on the reported averages of 345 country grain elevators, truck unload and loadout costs were found to average nine cents per bushel. The rail loadout cost at country elevators, based on 238 reports, was also found to average nine cents per bushel. Rail and truck unloading and loadout costs at 16 shuttle train facilities and Salina, Wichita, and Hutchinson terminal elevators were all found to average seven cents per bushel.

The rail costs of shipping wheat per 100 lbs were obtained through the Uniform Rail Costing System (URCS) Phase III Movement Costing Program, which is maintained by the Surface Transportation Board. These costs range from a low of $656 to $990 per car, depending on the distance of the wheat shipment from the unit train shipping locations to Houston.

6. TRANSPORTATION ENERGY CONSUMPTION

Energy intensity for freight transportation is measured in British thermal units (Btu) per ton-mile, the number of Btus required to move one ton-mile. A single Btu is the amount of energy required to raise the temperature of 1 lbs of water by 1°F at or near 39.2°F.

Class I railroad energy intensity coefficients (Btus per ton-mile) for 2001 and 2002 were obtained from Davis and Diegel (2004, pp. 2–18). Data to calculate the coefficient for 2003 was obtained from Association of American Railroads (2004, pp. 27, 61).[6]

According to Babcock and Bunch (2002, pp. 16–17), farmers and commercial grain trucking companies use large trucks (semi-tractor trailer) to deliver grain to elevators. Thus, energy intensity coefficients were calculated for combination trucks, defined by Davis and Diegel (2004) as a power unit (truck tractor) and one or more trailing units (a semi-trailer). Energy intensity coefficients for 2001–2003 were calculated for combination trucks as follows:

$$\text{Btus per Vehicle Mile} = \left(\frac{\text{Combination Truck Gallons of Fuel Consumed}}{\text{Combination Truck Vehicle Miles}}\right) \times 138{,}700 \quad (3)$$

where 138,700 is the heat content used to convert a gallon of diesel fuel to Btus.

$$\text{Btus per Ton Mile} = \frac{\text{Btus per Vehicle Mile}}{\text{Tons of Grain per Vehicle}} \tag{4}$$

Since the data to calculate Class I railroad energy intensity is based on net tons (revenue ton-miles), the energy intensity for combination trucks is based on net tons per vehicle (tons of grain per vehicle) to ensure comparability. As noted above, the trucks used to haul wheat in Kansas are five-axle semi-tractor trailers that haul 943 bushels of wheat. Since a bushel of wheat weighs 60 lbs, the net tons per vehicle is 28.3 (56,580/2000).

The data to calculate Eq. (3) for 2001 and 2002 was obtained from Davis and Diegel (2004, pp. 5–3), while the data for 2003 was from U.S. Department of Transportation (2005, Table 4–14).

The calculated energy intensities (Btus per ton-mile) for Class I railroads and combination trucks for the 2001–2003 period are as follows:

Year	Class I Railroads	Combination Trucks
2001	346	915
2002	345	935
2003	344	953
Average 2001–2003	345	934

The energy intensities in this analysis are the average intensities over the 2001–2003 period, or 345 and 934 Btus per net ton-mile for Class I railroads and combination trucks, respectively. Thus, the energy intensity of combination trucks is nearly 171% higher than Class I railroads. There is no published data source for energy intensity of shortline railroads, so shortlines are assumed to have the same energy intensity as Class I railroads. This is a strong assumption since shortlines operate older, less energy efficient locomotives. However, since there is no information, there is no realistic alternative to making this assumption.

The energy intensities are used in conjunction with truck and rail ton-miles derived from the wheat logistics system model to determine energy consumption with and without shortlines in the grain logistics system.

7. EMISSION FACTORS

7.1. Mobile Source Emissions

Mobile sources such as trucks and locomotives emit a number of air toxics associated with adverse effects on human health including heart problems, asthma, eye and lung irritation, and cancer. The principal air pollutants are the following:

1. Hydrocarbons (HC) – are chemical compounds that contain hydrogen and carbon, which are in diesel fuel. Hydrocarbon pollution results when partially burned fuel is emitted from the engine as exhaust, and also when fuel evaporates directly into the atmosphere.
2. Carbon monoxide (CO) – is a colorless, odorless, poisonous gas that forms when carbon in diesel fuel is not burned completely.
3. Nitrogen oxide (NO_X) – is formed when the oxygen and nitrogen in the air react with each other during fuel combustion. Nitrogen oxides can travel long distances, causing a variety of environmental problems including smog and ozone.
4. Particulate matter – comes from diesel exhaust and refers to tiny particles or liquid droplets suspended in the air that can contain a variety of chemical compounds. Larger particles (PM-10) are visible as smoke or dust and settle out relatively rapidly. The smallest particles (PM-2.5) are not visible to the naked eye but are major contributors to haze. Virtually all particulate matter from mobile sources is PM-2.5.
5. Sulfur dioxide – is found in diesel exhaust and contributes to the formation of particulate matter and other air toxics.

7.2. Rail and Truck Emission Factors

Emission factors (pounds per 1,000 gallons of diesel fuel) for Class I railroads, shortline railroads, and Class 8 trucks are displayed in Table 3.[7] The emission factors for Class I railroads and Class 8 trucks are national averages for the 2001–2003 period. The emission factors for Kansas shortline railroads were based on a survey of these railroads conducted in July 2005 and USEPA publications.

The emission factors for line-haul Class I railroads were calculated using the following procedure:

1. Convert tons of each pollutant to thousands of pounds per year.
2. Divide (1) by annual fuel use (thousands of gallons) of Class I railroads.

3. Multiply (2) by 1,000 to obtain annual pounds of pollutant per 1,000 gallons of diesel fuel.

Annual tons of each pollutant was obtained from USEPA (2005), and Class I railroad annual fuel use was from Association of American Railroads (2004, p. 61).

The emission factors for Class 8 trucks were calculated using a similar procedure.

1. Convert tons of each pollutant to millions of pounds per year.
2. Divide (1) by millions of Class 8 truck vehicle miles and multiply the result by 5.25.[8]
3. Multiply (2) by 1,000 to obtain annual pounds of pollutant per 1,000 gallons of diesel fuel.

Annual tons of each pollutant and vehicle miles of Class 8 trucks were obtained from USEPA (2005). Average miles per gallon were from USDOT (2005, Table 4–14).

Emission factors for Kansas shortline railroads were estimated by combining a survey of Kansas freight-carrying shortlines with data in USEPA (1992). Four of the five carriers surveyed provided information on a combined total of 73 line-haul locomotives used to haul grain. The shortlines provided five pieces of information for each locomotive including:

- locomotive manufacturer;
- year of manufacture;
- locomotive model;
- locomotive engine type;
- locomotive horsepower.

USEPA (1992, Appendix 6–6) has HC, CO, NO_X, and PM emission factors (pounds per gallon) for all the engine types of locomotives used by the Kansas shortlines. USEPA (1992, Appendix 6–7) outlines a five-step procedure for calculating average emission factors for the sample of 73 line-haul locomotives. Locomotives built after 1972 were required to meet lower emission rate standards. About one-third of the shortlines' locomotives were built or rebuilt after 1972. USEPA (1997, p. 3) provides estimated emission factors for HC, CO, NO_X, and PM for locomotives manufactured between 1973 and 2001. These emission factors were used to calculate weighted average emission factors for Kansas shortline locomotives. The USEPA

Table 3. Emission Factors for Railroads and Class 8 Trucks[a] 2001–2003 National Averages.

Emission Type	Class I Railroads	Shortline Railroads	Class 8 Trucks[b]
Hydrocarbons (HC)	13.41	20.02	12.06
Carbon monoxide (CO)	35.80	66.45	67.02
Nitrogen oxide (NO_X)	321.62	474.75	219.88
Particulate matter (PM-10)	8.95	12.20	6.71
Particulate matter (PM-2.5)	8.68	11.83[c]	5.84
Sulfur dioxide (SO_2)	22.33	22.33[d]	4.97

Sources: Class I railroads, U.S. Environmental Protection Agency, Office of Transportation and Air Quality, ASD at http://www.epa/otaq/m6.htm. Association of American Railroads, *Railroad Facts 2004*, Washington DC, 2004; Shortline railroads, survey of Kansas shortline railroads; Class 8 trucks, U.S. Environmental Protection Agency, Office of Transportation and Air Quality, ASD at http://www.epa/otaq/m6.htm, U.S. Department of Transportation, Bureau of Transportation Statistics, *National Transportation Statistics 2005* (Table 4–14) at http://www.transtats.bts.gov/.

[a]Pounds per 1,000 gallons of diesel fuel.

[b]Class 8 trucks are the largest diesel semi-tractor trailer trucks and have gross vehicle weight of 33,001 lbs or more.

[c]Estimation based on Class I rail data.

[d]Assumed to be the same as Class I railroads since the data to calculate the emission factor was unavailable.

publications provided no SO_2 emission factors for shortlines, so the Class I railroad estimate was used.

The data in Table 3 indicate that, with the exception of carbon monoxide, the emission factors for Class 8 trucks are less than that of Class I railroads and substantially lower than shortline railroads per 1,000 gallons of fuel.

Energy use by mode is converted into emissions by mode through the use of truck and locomotive emission factors. Emissions by mode are calculated with and without shortline railroads in the wheat logistics system to measure the pollution impact of shortline abandonment.

8. EMPIRICAL RESULTS

8.1. Energy Use

Table 4 contains the ton-miles by mode for the Kansas export wheat logistics system with and without shortline railroads in the system. The ton-mile values were obtained by solving the network model discussed above,

Table 4. Ton-Miles by Mode (Millions of Ton-Miles).

Mode	With Shortlines	Without Shortlines	Percent Change
Truck	216.8	445.4	105.4
Shortline railroad	414.8	0	−100
Class I railroad	8,693.4	8,693.4	0
Total	9,325.0	9,138.8	−2.0

assuming the two scenarios of no shortline abandonment and complete abandonment. Truck ton-miles increase from 216.8 million in the logistics system that includes shortline railroads to 445.4 million without them, a 105.4% increase. Shortline railroad ton-miles are 414.8 million in the wheat logistics system that includes them, and zero in the simulated shortline abandonment scenario. The combined truck-shortline ton-miles declines from 631.6 million in the no abandonment case to 445.4 million in the abandonment scenario. After hypothetical abandonment, truck shipments to shuttle train stations on Class I rail lines will increase. According to Babcock and Bunch (2002, p. 16), 97% of the shuttle train grain receipts originate within 70 miles of the facility. In contrast, most of the shortline destinations are the grain terminals in Salina, Wichita, and Hutchinson. The shortline shipping distance to these destinations from origins in western Kansas are 180–240 miles. The shift from relatively long haul shortlines to relatively short haul trucks accounts for the lower truck-shortline combined ton-miles in the abandonment case.

Class I railroad ton-miles are unaffected by shortline abandonment and are 8,693.4 million in both scenarios. Since Class I railroads are the dominant mode in the export wheat logistics system and Class I ton-miles are unaffected by simulated shortline abandonment, total ton-miles are about the same in the simulated abandonment and no abandonment cases, with the abandonment scenario generating 2% fewer ton-miles.

Table 5 displays energy consumption by mode for the export wheat logistics system for the shortline abandonment and no abandonment cases. The values in Table 5 were computed by multiplying modal energy intensities (Btus per ton-mile), which were 345 for railroads and 934 for trucks, by the corresponding modal ton-miles in Table 4. Since energy consumption is directly proportional to ton-miles, the modal percentage changes for energy consumption are identical to the percentage changes in ton-miles, i.e., 105.4% for trucks, −100% for shortline railroads, and no change for Class I railroads. The combined truck and shortline railroad Btus increase from 345,597 million in the no abandonment case to 416,004 million in the

Table 5. Btu per Ton-Mile and Btus Consumed by Mode (Millions of Btus).

Mode	Btu per Ton-Mile	Btus Consumed with Shortlines	Btus Consumed without Shortlines	Percent Change
Truck	934	202,491	416,004	105.4
Shortline railroad	345	143,106	0	−100
Class I railroad	345	2,999,223	2,999,223	0
Total Btus consumed		3,344,820	3,415,227	2.1

shortline abandonment scenario, a 20.4% increase. The change is significant since the lower truck-shortline combined ton-miles in the abandonment case is more than offset by the higher energy intensity of trucks. However, due to the dominance of Class I railroads in the export wheat logistics system, combined with the same Class I energy consumption in both scenarios, the difference in total energy consumption in the two cases is small, 2.1% higher in the abandonment case. The abandonment case results in 70,407 million additional Btus. Since there are 138,700 Btus per gallon, the abandonment case generates consumption of an additional 507,621 gallons of diesel fuel.

Although the average energy intensity of the Kansas shortline locomotive fleet is unknown, it is possible to test the sensitivity of the results to the assumption that shortlines have the same energy intensity as Class I railroads. The energy efficiency differential of Class I and Kansas shortline locomotive fleets is unknown. Therefore, three scenarios are assumed, involving the assumption that average Kansas shortline locomotives are 10, 20, and 30% less efficient than the Class I railroad locomotive fleet.

The Class I Btu per ton-mile figure of 345 (Table 5) is increased by the assumed percentages resulting in shortline energy coefficients of 379.5, 414, and 448.5, respectively. The millions of Btus consumed with shortlines in the system (Table 5) are recalculated using these revised energy intensities. The results are 3,359,131, 3,373,441, and 3,387,752 million Btus for the three scenarios, respectively. As indicated by the data in Table 5, total Btus consumed without shortlines in the logistics system are 3,415,227 million. Thus, comparing this figure to the Btus consumed with the three scenarios results in the system without shortlines consuming 1.6, 1.2,, and 0.8% more Btus than the system that includes shortlines. Assuming Kansas shortlines have the same energy intensity as Class I railroads resulted in the system including shortlines having 2.1% fewer Btus consumed than the system without shortlines. Thus, the energy consumption results are not sensitive to the assumption that Kansas shortline locomotives have the same average energy intensity as Class I railroads. This is primarily because Class I railroads dominate the energy consumption of the two logistics systems and their energy consumption is unaffected by shortline abandonment.

8.2. Pollutant Emissions

Pounds of emissions by type of pollutant and mode were calculated using the following procedure:

1. Since the heat content of a gallon of diesel fuel is 138,700 Btus, divide millions of Btus from Table 5 by 0.138700. For example, Class 8 truck emissions of hydrocarbons for the with shortline scenario is 202,491/ 0.138700 = 1,459,921 gallons of energy use.
2. Divide (1) by 1,000 to obtain thousands of gallons of energy usage or 1,459,921/(1,000) = 1,459.9.
3. Multiply (2) by the appropriate emission factor. Thus, pounds of Class 8 truck emissions for hydrocarbons is 1,459.9 (12.06) = 17,606 lbs.

Table 6 contains total emissions by type of emission for the wheat logistics system with and without shortline railroads. Since system ton-miles and energy consumption are dominated by Class I railroads, the total emissions data in Table 6 also reflect this fact. Although the percentage changes in Class 8 truck and shortline ton-miles and energy consumption are large (Tables 4 and 5), between the no abandonment and abandonment scenarios, Class I railroads account for the great majority of ton-miles and energy

Table 6. Total Emissions of Truck and Railroad Transportation of Wheat, with and without Shortline Railroads (lbs).

(1) Emission Type	(2) With Shortlines	(3) Without Shortlines	(4) [(3)/(2)−1] × 100 (%)
HC	328,237	326,147	−0.6
CO	940,538	975,147	3.7
NO_X	7,765,489	7,614,139	−1.9
PM-10	215,917	213,658	−1.0
PM-2.5	208,427	205,211	−1.5
SO_2	513,155	497,767	−3.0
Total	9,763,336	9,626,858	−1.4

Note: Total does not include PM-2.5 since it is included in PM-10.

consumption, and neither variable is affected by shortline abandonment. Thus, the percentage changes in total emissions are relatively small for all emission types. Total emissions of carbon monoxide increase 3.7% as a result of shortline abandonment, while emissions of all other types decrease by 0.6–3.0% in the without shortlines case. This is expected since the estimated emission factors were relatively lower for Class 8 trucks with the exception of carbon monoxide, and energy use was about the same for both logistics systems. Grand total emissions are 1.4% lower in the scenario that does not include shortlines in the export wheat logistics system.

If it is assumed that the Kansas shortline locomotive fleet is 30% less efficient than Class I railroad locomotives, total emissions for the logistics system including shortlines are 9,947,739 lbs. Thus, the system that excludes shortlines would have 3.2% fewer total emissions (9,626,858 lbs) rather than 1.4% (Table 6). Thus, the assumption of 30% less energy efficiency for Kansas shortline locomotives results in virtually no difference (1.8%) in grand total emissions.

Table 7 displays emissions data by emission type and mode for the with and without shortlines scenarios. As indicated in Table 3, Class 8 trucks have substantially lower emission factors than Kansas shortline railroad locomotives, except for carbon monoxide. Class 8 truck emissions increase from 453,509 lbs in the with shortline case to 931,706 lbs in the without shortline scenario, an increase of 105.4%. Likewise, shortline railroad emissions fall from 614,675 lbs to zero. Grand total emissions decrease because combined truck and shortline railroad emissions decline from 1,068,184 (453,509 + 614,675) in the with shortlines case to 931,706 lbs in the without

Table 7. Emissions by Emission Type and Mode, with and without Shortline Railroads (lbs).

Emission Type	Class 8 Truck		Shortline Railroad		Class I Railroad	
	With Shortlines	Without Shortlines	With Shortlines	Without Shortlines	With Shortlines	Without Shortlines
HC	17,606	36,172	20,656	0	289,975	289,975
CO	97,844	201,014	68,561	0	774,133	774,133
NO_X	321,007	659,488	489,831	0	6,954,651	6,954,651
PM-10	9,796	20,125	12,588	0	193,533	193,533
PM-2.5	8,526	17,516	12,206	0	187,695	187,695
SO_2	7,256	14,907	23,039	0	482,860	482,860
Total	453,509	931,706	614,675	0	8,695,152	8,695,152

Note: Total does not include PM-2.5 since it is included in PM-10.

shortlines scenario, a decrease of 12.8%. This result is the net impact of three factors. Although trucks have higher energy intensity than shortlines, this factor is more than offset by lower truck emission factors and fewer combined truck-shortline ton-miles in the abandonment case. However, as noted above, this relatively large percentage change is offset by the dominance of Class I railroads whose total emissions are 8,695,152 lbs in both scenarios.

9. OTHER EXTERNAL EFFECTS OF SHORTLINE RAILROAD ABANDONMENT

As discussed in the Literature Review, several studies have measured various external impacts of shortline abandonment, other than the effects on energy consumption and emissions. These include highway safety costs, reduced local area income and employment, higher transport costs to local delivery points, and road damage costs. At this time the literature indicates that road damage cost is the most significant impact, involving tens of millions of dollars annually when measured for an entire state.

No research has been published regarding measurement of other negative impacts of shortline abandonment on rural areas. For example, following abandonment, rural shippers lose market options. Markets that are more efficiently served by rail (i.e., large volume shipments over long distances) are less available to the rural shipper after abandonment. Also, abandonment would result in a loss of economic development opportunities for rural communities. Firms that require railroads for inbound and/or outbound transport (i.e., shippers of food, lumber, paper, chemicals, and steel products) would not consider locating in a community that has no rail service. The lack of studies of these impacts may be attributable to the difficulty of measuring the value of lost opportunities.

There is a need for regional and national studies to measure the external effects of abandonment on passenger vehicle owners. The significant increase in heavy truck movement associated with shortline abandonment will increase the frequency and magnitude of rutting and cracking of the pavement. As a result, the vibration of a vehicle's frame and parts increases. This leads to additional maintenance costs for the life of the vehicle. Poor pavement quality also reduces the useful life of the vehicle. Also as the severity of rutting and cracking of the pavement increases, the vertical and lateral motion of the vehicle increases. This increases wind and rolling resistance, requiring more fuel to travel a given distance at a particular speed.

10. CONCLUSION

This paper developed a methodology to measure the impact on energy use and emissions from potential abandonment of shortline railroads. Although the Kansas wheat transport market was used to empirically implement the methodology, the models can be used to measure similar impacts for any modal substitution situation. For example, Class I railroad versus TL motor carrier, shortline railroad versus TL motor carrier, and Class I railroad versus truck-barge.

To the authors, some of the results of the study were expected while others were surprising. The conventional wisdom is that railroads are more energy efficient than motor carriers. This expectation was confirmed by the result that during the 2001–2003 period, Class 8 combination trucks consumed 2.7 times as much energy (Btus) per net ton-mile as Class I railroads. However, the conventional wisdom of railroads producing fewer emissions than trucks was not confirmed by the study. Emission factors (pounds per 1,000 gallons of diesel fuel), with the exception of carbon monoxide, were lower for Class 8 combination trucks than either Class I or shortline railroads.

The results indicate that the ton-mile, energy use, and emission impacts of modal substitutions depend on the geographical context of the transport market and the unique mix and characteristics of modes operating in that market. For example in this study, the shortline abandonment scenario generated 2% fewer ton-miles. However, this effect was offset by the greater energy efficiency of railroads with the result being 2.1% more energy consumption in the abandonment case compared to the no abandonment scenario. Also, while combination trucks have substantially lower emission factors (with the exception of carbon monoxide) than shortlines, grand total emissions were only 1.4% lower in the shortline abandonment scenario. This result was attributable to the dominance of Class I railroads in the wheat logistics system whose emissions are not affected by shortline abandonment.

Since this study was based on the situation in a single state and one commodity group, no implications can be drawn regarding shortline abandonment, energy, or emissions policy. A first step toward policy prescriptions would require many more studies in different geographic areas with different traffic mixes and intensity of intermodal and intramodal competition. However, even this body of knowledge would be only one factor among many in the formulation of national shortline, energy, and emissions policies.

NOTES

1. Three classes of freight railroads are designated by the Surface Transportation Board based on the railroads' operating revenue. For 2004, the annual revenue threshold for Class I railroads is $289.4 million or more, for Class II $23.1–$289.3 million, and for Class III less than $23.1 million. These thresholds are adjusted annually for inflation.

2. The AAR identifies two groups of non-Class I railroads based on their revenue and mileage characteristics. Regional railroads are defined as line-haul railroads operating at least 350 miles of road and/or earn annual revenue between $40 million and the Class I revenue threshold. Local railroads are line-haul railroads earning less than $40 million per year and/or operate less than 350 miles of road. The local group also includes switching and terminal railroads. Thus, the regional and local groups include all railroads, except Class I, i.e., Classes II and III.

3. Texas Gulf ports, of which Houston is the largest, is the most important single destination of Kansas wheat, accounting for about 50% of the shipments [Kansas Agricultural Statistics Service (2001a, pp. 13, 15), and Kansas Agricultural Statistics Service (2002a, pp. 13, 15)].

4. The rates in Kansas Agricultural Statistics Service (2001b) are rates actually charged by custom harvesters of wheat to haul grain from the farmers' field to the nearest elevator up to a maximum of 12 miles in which case additional charges may apply. The rates may include costs for preparation of the shipment from the field to the elevator. These rates are reported to the Kansas Department of Agriculture each year.

5. Empty backhauls are assumed since the objective is to minimize costs for the one-way movement of wheat through the logistics system to Houston.

6. Class I railroad fuel use in 2003 was 3,849.229 gallons and revenue ton-miles was 1,551,438, where both variables are measured in millions. Btus per gallon of diesel fuel are 138,700. Thus, Class I railroad Btus per ton-mile in 2003 are calculated as follows:

$$\left(\frac{3,849.229}{1,551,438}\right)\bullet 138,700 = 344.$$

7. Class 8 trucks are the largest diesel semi-tractor trailer trucks with gross vehicle weight of 33,001 lbs or more.

8. Combination truck average miles per gallon in the 2000–2003 period was 5.25.

REFERENCES

Association of American Railroads. (1978). *Yearbook of railroad facts, 1978 edition*. Washington, DC.

Association of American Railroads. (2004). *Railroad facts, 2004 edition*. Washington, DC.

Association of American Railroads. (2005). *Railroad facts, 2005 edition*. Washington, DC.

Babcock, M. W., & Bunch, J. L. (2002). *Impact of Kansas grain transportation on Kansas Highway damage costs*. Topeka, KS: Kansas Department of Transportation.

Babcock, M. W., Bunch, J. L., Sanderson, J., & Witt, J. (2003a). Impact of short line railroad abandonment on highway damage costs: A Kansas case study. *Transportation Quarterly*, *57*(4), 105–121 (*Journal of the Transportation Research Forum*).

Babcock, M. W., Bunch, J. L., Sanderson, J., & Witt, J. (2003b). Impact of short line railroad abandonment on wheat transportation and handling costs: A Kansas case study. *Transportation Quarterly*, *57*(4), 87–104 (*Journal of the Transportation Research Forum*).

Ball, T., & Casavant, K. L. (2003). Alternative evaluations of a river drawdown: Reassessing the environmental paradox. *Transportation Quarterly*, *57*(4), 123–133 (*Journal of the Transportation Research Forum*).

Bellman, R. (1958). On a routing problem. *Applied Mathematics*, *XVI*(1), 87–90.

Berwick, M. (2002). *Motor carrier estimates for Kansas grain*. Fargo, ND: unpublished.

Bitzan, J. D., & Tolliver, D. D. (2003). The impacts of an industry switch to large rail grain hopper cars on local infrastructure. *Transportation Quarterly*, *57*(2), 135–154 (*Journal of the Transportation Research Forum*).

Casavant, K. L., & Lenzi, J. C. (1990). Preparing for rail line abandonment: Prediction of financial and locational impacts on roads. *Journal of the Transportation Research Forum*, *30*, 264–274.

Chow, M. H., Babcock, M. W., & Sorenson, L. O. (1985). The changing logistics structure for grain marketing: A case study of export wheat in Northwest Kansas. *Transportation Journal*, *24*(3), 39–46.

Davis, S. C., & Diegel, S. W. (2004). *Transportation energy data book* (24th ed.). Oak Ridge, TN: Center for Transportation Analysis, Oak Ridge National Laboratory.

Dijkstra, E. W. (1959). A note on two problems in connection with graphs. *Numerische Mathematik*, *1*, 269–271.

Eusebio, V. E., & Rindom, S. J. (1991). Methodology for estimation of road damage cost resulting from potential rail branchline abandonment: The case of South Central Kansas. *Transportation Research Record*, No. 1305.

Eusebio, V. E., Rindom, S. J., & Abderrezak, A. (1992). *Economic impacts of rail line abandonment on rural communities in Kansas*. Topeka, KS: Kansas Department of Transportation.

Kansas Agricultural Statistics Service. (2001a). *Kansas grain transportation*. Topeka, KS: Kansas State Board of Agriculture.

Kansas Agricultural Statistics Service. (2001b). *2000 Kansas custom rates*. Topeka, KS: Kansas Department of Agriculture.

Kansas Agricultural Statistics Service. (2002a). *Kansas grain transportation*. Topeka, KS: Kansas State Board of Agriculture.

Kansas Agricultural Statistics Service. (2002b). *Kansas farm facts*. Topeka, KS: Kansas State Board of Agriculture.

Kansas Agricultural Statistics Service. (2004). *Kansas farm facts*. Topeka, KS: Kansas State Board of Agriculture.

Kansas Agricultural Statistics Service. (2005). *Kansas farm facts*. Topeka, KS: Kansas State Board of Agriculture.

Kansas Grain and Feed Association. (2003). *2003 Kansas official directory*. Topeka, KS: Kansas Grain and Feed Association.

Lee, N. S., & Casavant, K. L. (2002). Transportation energy, emissions, and endangered species: An environmental paradox. *Transportation Quarterly*, *56*(2), 77–88 (*Journal of the Transportation Research Forum*).

Lenzi, J. C., Jessup, E. L., & Casavant, K. L. (1996). *Prospective estimates for road impacts in eastern Washington from a drawdown of the lower Snake River*. Pullman, WA: Washington State Department of Transportation.

Neudecker, K. (1999). *Shortest network paths (SNP)*. http://arcscripts.esri.com

Prater, M., & Babcock, M. W. (1998). Determinants of profitability of grain dependent short line railroads. *Transportation Research, Part E, Logistics and Transportation Review*, *34*(3), 187–200.

Public Interest Economics Center. (1974). *Community impact of abandonment of railroad service*. Washington, DC: U.S. Railway Association.

Rindom, S. J., Rosacker, J. J., & Wulfkuhle, M. (1997). *The transportation impact of grain subterminals in Kansas*. Topeka, KS: Kansas Department of Transportation.

Russell, E. R., Babcock, M. W., & Mauler, C. (1996). Study of the impact of rail abandonment on local roads and streets. In: *Conference Proceedings, Sixth international conference on low volume roads*, (Vol. I, pp. 110–119).

Sanderson, J., & Babcock, M. W. (2005). County-level impacts of rail line abandonments: A Kansas case study. *Journal of the Transportation Research Forum*, *44*(3), 93–112.

Tolliver, D. D. (1989). *The impacts of grain subterminals on rural highways* (Vol. II). Fargo, ND: Upper Great Plains Transportation Institute, North Dakota State University.

Tolliver, D. D., Andres, K., & Lindamood, B. (1994). *Washington rail impact analysis: Executive summary*. Olympia, Washington: Washington Department of Transportation.

Tolliver, D. D., & HDR Engineering Inc. (2000). *Benefits of rail freight transportation in Washington: A multimodal analysis*. Olympia, Washington: Washington Department of Transportation.

U.S. Department of Agriculture. (2004). *Transportation of U.S. grains: A modal share analysis, 1978–2000*. Washington, DC: Agricultural Marketing Service.

U.S. Department of Transportation, Research and Innovative Technologies Administration, Bureau of Transportation Statistics. (2005). *National Transportation Statistics 2005*. Table 4–14. Washington, DC: Bureau of Transportation Statistics. http://www.transtats.bts.gov

U.S. Environmental Protection Agency. (1992). *Procedures for emission inventory preparation (Vol. IV: Mobile Sources)*. Ann Arbor, MI: Office of Mobile Sources.

U.S. Environmental Protection Agency. (1997). *Technical highlights, emission factors for locomotives*. Washington, DC: Office of Mobile Sources.

U.S. Environmental Protection Agency. (2005). Clean air interstate rule, emissions inventory technical support document. Washington, DC: Office of Transportation and Air Quality. http://www.epa.gov/air/interstateairquality/pdfs/finaltech01.pdf

Wilson, R. A. (2002). *Transportation in America* (19th ed.). Washington, DC: Eno. Transportation Foundation Inc.

Witt, J. (2004). Highway safety effects from rail line closure in Kansas. *Journal of the Transportation Research Forum*, *43*(1), 5–17.

APPENDIX: MATHEMATICAL STRUCTURE OF THE NETWORK MODEL

The model minimizes the total Kansas wheat logistics system costs subject to several constraints. The objective function is as follows:

1. Minimize

$$TSC = \sum_{i=1}^{a} \sum_{j=1}^{b+c+d} F_{ij} f_{ijt} + \sum_{i=1}^{b} \sum_{j=1}^{c+d} C_{ijt} c_{ijt} + \sum_{i=1}^{b} \sum_{j=1}^{d+e} C_{ijr} c_{ijr} + \sum_{i=1}^{c} \sum_{j=1}^{e} S_{ijr} s_{ijr} + \sum_{i=1}^{d} \sum_{j=1}^{e} T_{ijr} t_{ijr}$$

The constraints are as follows:

2. The flow of wheat into an elevator equals the flow out of that elevator.

$$Q_i = \sum_{j=1}^{b+c+d} F_{ij} \quad \text{for } i = 1, \ldots, a \tag{2a}$$

$$QE_i = \sum_{j=1}^{c+d} C_{ijt} + \sum_{j=1}^{d+e} C_{ijr} \quad \text{for } i = 1, \ldots, b \tag{2b}$$

$$QS_i = \sum_{j=1}^{e} S_{ijr} \quad \text{for } i = 1, \ldots, c \tag{2c}$$

$$QT_i = \sum_{j=1}^{e} T_{ijr} \quad \text{for } i = 1, \ldots, d \tag{2d}$$

3. The total amount of wheat supplied equals the total amount of wheat demanded.

$$\sum_{i=1}^{a} Q_i = \sum_{i=1}^{e} OG_i \tag{3a}$$

4. All coefficients and variables are ≥ 0.
5. Actual wheat stored at elevator i must be $\leq$ the maximum storage capacity of elevator i.

$$QE_i \leq \text{total storage capacity}, \quad \text{for } i = 1, \ldots, b \tag{5a}$$

$$QS_i \leq \text{total storage capacity}, \quad \text{for } i = 1, \ldots, c \tag{5b}$$

$$QT_i \leq \text{total storage capacity}, \quad \text{for } i = 1, \ldots, d \tag{5c}$$

$$QG_i \leq \text{total storage capacity}, \quad \text{for } i = 1, \ldots, e \tag{5d}$$

The model has no vehicle or storage capacity constraints since it is assumed that vehicle and storage capacities are available in equilibrium quantities such that a capacity constraint never influences wheat movements.

The model is solved using dynamic programming techniques initially developed by Bellman (1958). Eq. (1) incrementally evaluates each component (arc) of the alternative routes and selects the least expensive arc for the next stage of the trip. The sum of all the least cost arcs is the minimum transportation costs. Solving for the least cost network using this technique requires an algorithmic evaluation of nodes in the network to identify the route combination of nodes and arcs that constitute the least cost route among all the possible routes. In this study, the software utilized to identify the least cost routes was the ESRI Arc GIS platform and a Visual Basic Script titled *Shortest Network Paths* (SNP) developed by Neudecker (1999). The SNP script employed the most commonly used shortest path algorithm known as the Labeling Method, which was initially developed in an algorithm by E.W. Dijkstra (1959).

Handling costs were determined exogenously. Wheat delivered from farms in trucks to an intermediate storage facility was assessed as a truck unloading cost. If the storage facility has rail service, the wheat was assessed a railroad loadout charge. For elevators without rail service, an additional unload and loadout cost was incurred when transporting the wheat to a storage facility with rail service. Thus, to measure total wheat logistics system handling costs, the number of bushels of wheat estimated to be stored at each elevator by the network model was multiplied by the corresponding per bushel unload and loadout cost for that type of elevator, i.e., country elevator or unit train shipping elevator, using Microsoft Excel.

The variable definitions are as follows:

TSC – Total transportation and handling costs
F_{ij} – Quantity of wheat shipped from production origin i to its next destination j
C_{ijt} – Quantity of wheat shipped by truck from country elevator i to its next destination j

C_{ijr} – Quantity of wheat shipped by railroad from country elevator i to its next destination j
S_{ijr} – Quantity of wheat shipped by railroad from shuttle train station i to its next destination j
T_{ijr} – Quantity of wheat shipped by railroad from Salina, Hutchinson, and Wichita, Kansas grain terminal i to its next destination j
f_{ijt} – Unit shipping cost from production origin i to its next destination j by truck
c_{ijt} – Unit shipping cost from country elevator i to its next destination j by truck
c_{ijr} – Unit shipping cost from country elevator i to its next destination j by railroad
s_{ijr} – Unit shipping cost from shuttle train station i to its next destination j by railroad
t_{ijr} – Unit shipping cost from Salina, Hutchinson, and Wichita, Kansas grain terminal i to its next destination j by railroad
a – Number of production origins
b – Number of country elevators
c – Number of shuttle train stations
d – Number of Salina, Hutchinson, and Wichita, Kansas grain terminals
e – Number of Houston, Texas port grain terminals
Q_i – Total quantity of wheat produced at production origin i
QE_i – Quantity of wheat received at country elevator i
QS_i – Quantity of wheat received at shuttle train station i
QT_i – Quantity of wheat received at Salina, Hutchinson, and Wichita, Kansas grain terminal i
OG_i – Quantity of wheat received at Houston, Texas port grain terminal i

EARNINGS DIFFERENTIALS OF RAILROAD MANAGERS AND LABOR

James Peoples and Wayne K. Talley

ABSTRACT

This chapter investigates the separate earnings pattern of managers, union, and non-union employees in the U.S. rail industry during regulatory and deregulatory regimes. Such an empirical investigation is significant, in part, because economic theory does not provide an obvious prediction on post-deregulation earnings patterns in the rail industry. Findings reveal uneven earnings declines for the three groups of rail employees, as the earnings of railroad non-union labor experienced a greater decline in the deregulation period than those for union labor. The decline in earnings for railroad managers was generally smaller than that for union and non-union labor.

1. INTRODUCTION

The U.S. Federal regulation of the railroad industry began with passage of the Interstate Commerce Act in 1887, establishing the Interstate Commerce Commission (ICC) as the regulatory authority over industry rates, entry,

Railroad Economics
Research in Transportation Economics, Volume 20, 259–281

ISSN: 0739-8859/doi:10.1016/S0739-8859(07)20010-1

services, and finances. The Act protected railroads from intramodal, but not from intermodal competition. By 1900, the railroad was the dominant mode for intercity freight movements. After World War I, the speed advantage of trucks began a long-term shift of less-than-carload traffic and time sensitive traffic in general from rail to truck, continuing over the following decades, accompanied by declining rail market shares and subnormal rates of return on investment (Talley, 1983). In 1944, the U.S. railroads were responsible for 68.6% of the total U.S. freight ton-mile volume. Their share declined to 56.2, 44.1, 39.8, and 36.7% in 1950, 1960, 1970, and 1975, respectively (Association of American Railroads (AAR), 1994). In 1947, railroads' rate of return on net investment, the ratio of net railway operating income to average net investment in transportation property, was 3.44%, falling to 2.13, 1.73, and 1.20% in 1960, 1970, and 1975, respectively (AAR, 2002).

By the 1970s, the poor financial status of railroads prompted Congress to deregulate the industry by passing the Railroad Revitalization and Regulatory Reform (the 4-R) Act of 1976 and the Staggers Rail Act of 1980, substituting competitive market forces (i.e., providing greater freedom for railroads to compete with the trucking industry) for regulatory decree. The 4-R Act introduced limited rate-making freedom to the industry and made it easier for railroads to receive authority to abandon unprofitable lines. The Staggers Act allowed contract rates on a very wide scale; established rate floors and ceilings that allowed railroads considerable rate flexibility; permitted the ICC, now the Surface Transportation Board (STB), to exempt commodities from rate regulation when intermodal competition was strong enough to ensure that competitive prices would be realized; and expedited the ICC timetable on merger applications.[1]

Subsequent to deregulation, rates of return have risen significantly. In 1980, railroads' rate of return on net investment was 4.22%, rising to 4.58, 8.11, 7.04, and 6.48% in 1985, 1990, 1995, and 2000, respectively (AAR, 2002). McFarland (1987, 1989) has investigated whether this improvement resulted in excess profits for the industry. Based on an analysis of 1980–1984 data in his 1987 paper and an analysis of 1985–1986 data in his 1989 paper, McFarland found no such evidence. The ICC also tests annually for excessive railroad profits utilizing the revenue adequacy test: A railroad is judged to be revenue-adequate if its rate of return on investment exceeds the market cost of capital; if so, it becomes subject to stricter rate regulation than a revenue-inadequate railroad. For the 1982–1987 period, the ICC never found a railroad to be revenue-adequate; subsequently, however, several railroads have been so classified.

The rising rates of return on net investment are attributable in part to cost savings from mergers and acquisitions, from more efficient labor usage, and from reductions in track-mileage. Prior to the Staggers Act, rail mergers were typically parallel mergers, i.e., involving the consolidation of rail systems having a substantial amount of parallel trackage. In the Staggers environment, proposed mergers have typically been end-to-end consolidations. From 1980 to 1988, there were 18 mergers involving Class I railroads. In 1993, the 13 Class I railroads (excluding Amtrak) accounted for 73% of rail mileage operated, 89% of employees and 91% of freight revenue for all the U.S. railroads. In 1995, Burlington Northern acquired the Atchison, Topeka, and Santa Fe; in 1996 Union Pacific acquired the Southern Pacific, a merger creating the largest U.S. railroad. On July 23, 1998 the STB approved purchase (for over $10 billion in cash) of Conrail by Norfolk Southern and CSX railroads that acquired legal control of Conrail on August 22, 1998. In 1999, Canadian National acquired Illinois Central. In 1999, a merger was proposed between Canadian National and the Burlington Northern and Santa Fe, but was abandoned in July 2000 because of the STB's 15-month rail-merger moratorium in December, 1999. For a discussion of railroad deregulation and mergers, see Davis and Wilson (1999). In January 2005, Kansas City Southern (KCS) purchased 51% of the Mexican railroad Transportacion Ferroviaria Mexicana (TFM) and plans to fold it into its U.S. rail holdings under a new entity called Nafta Rail.[2]

The productivity of rail labor has increased. The revenue ton-miles per employee for Class I railroads has increased from 1.6 in 1975 to 2.1, 2.9, 7.0, and 8.7 in 1980, 1985, 1995, and 2000, respectively (AAR, 2002). In 1970, the U.S. railroad industry had 319,092 miles of track, declining to 310,941, 270,623, 242,320, 200,074, 180,419, and 168,535 miles in 1975, 1980, 1985, 1990, 1995, and 2000, respectively (AAR, 2002). In the post-Staggers period (from 1980 to 1990), the miles of track declined 26%, substantially less as a percentage than the decline in demand for rail labor. Hence, the ratio of track-mileage to labor increased in the period. Friedlaender, Berndt, and McCullough (1992) suggest that the disparity in rates of decline between labor demand and trackage has been reinforced by factors slowing the rate of capital adjustment: (1) failure to minimize costs, (2) the lumpiness of capital, and (3) substantial institutional barriers to capital adjustment.

The rising rates of return on net investment are also attributable to improvements in service and managerial effectiveness. The Staggers Act permitted railroads to enter into separate service contracts with shippers. In the first five years of the Staggers period, 41,021 contracts were filed with the

ICC, resulting in railroads becoming more time-sensitive. For example, automakers are using rail service to deliver parts to the factory door in as little as two hours before the part is needed on the assembly line. Freight loss and damage costs for Class I railroads as a percentage of freight revenue declined from 1.83% in 1975 to 1.08, 0.44, 0.33, and 0.31% in 1980, 1985, 1995, and 2000, respectively (AAR, 2002). Friedlaender et al. (1992) hypothesize that the railroad industry has steadily evolved under deregulation from a regime in which railroad managers balanced their own interests against the interest of shareholders to a regime in which rail managers are more directly subject to shareholder influence.

Railroads have shared the benefits of deregulation with shippers, in the form of lower real rates and improved service, and with shareholders, in the form of higher returns. Wilson (1994) concludes that real rail rates have fallen since passage of the Staggers Act. Initially, deregulation increased rates for some commodities, decreased rates on others, and had no effect on still others, but by 1988 deregulation had lowered real rates significantly for almost all commodities.[3] In 1980, the U.S. railroads provided 37.5% of all the U.S. domestic ton-miles of freight service. This percentage rose to 41.0% by 2000 (AAR, 2002); making the U.S. system the only major railroad system in the world to increase its share of the domestic freight transportation market over that period (Thompson, 1998).

Prior to deregulation the heavily unionized rail industry operated in a high labor-cost environment, reflecting use of an excessive amount of labor, costly work and pay rules, and high wage rates. Under regulation, increases in labor costs were typically passed on to customers through higher rail rates. Adhering to this strategy, however, has become increasingly difficult in the post-deregulation period, as railroads face competition from a deregulated trucking industry as well as from one another.[4]

While shareholders and shippers have benefited from railroad deregulation, the impact on labor has been negative. The bargaining power of rail workers has declined in the post-deregulation period. The settled 1985 industry-wide union contract resulted in a shift in the balance of power from rail labor to management. Before 1985, pay increases were granted at least annually and supplemented by regular cost-of-living adjustments (COLA) payments. In the 1985–88 agreement, pay increases were smaller and certain types of pay were frozen or modified; the COLA provision was less liberal; a two-tier pay system was introduced; and the mileage in the mileage day rule (miles traveled for determining a day's pay) was increased from 100 to 108 miles. Between December 1987 and July 1991 no changes were made in base pay; the 1991–1995 agreement called for moderate nominal increases in base pay, but no COLA until January 1995, and a considerable larger increase in the mileage day rule, from 108 to 130 miles.

The number of railroad jobs has also declined significantly in an effort by the industry to reduce labor costs. In 1975, the industry had 548,000 (488,000 Class I) employees; by 1985 and 1995 the number had fallen, respectively, to 372,000 (302,000 Class I) and 265,000 (188,000 Class I) employees; and by 2000 the number had declined to 246,000 (168,000 Class I) employees (Association of American Railroads (AAR), 1994, 2002). By 2003, the number of Class I railroad employees had dropped to 155,000, but increased to 165,000 employees in 2005, reversing decades of job losses brought about by industry restructuring and increased use of technology. In 1980, railroads typically operated four-man crew trains (one locomotive engineer, one conductor, and two brakemen).[5] Since then, the brakemen have gradually disappeared under union agreement through attrition and buy-outs.[6]

The erosion of labor protection programs and a politically conservative environment less supportive of union objectives have facilitated the elimination of jobs. In the pre-Staggers era, federal labor protection programs covered rail mergers, but the Staggers Act was passed without rail employee guarantees.[7] Although there were major rail strikes preceding 1985 and 1991, the Presidential Emergency Board recommendations of 1985 and 1991 accepted the railroads' arguments for eliminating firemen and unnecessary train service employees.[8] The adoption of industry labor-saving technologies has also facilitated this decline: Electronic-based communications and information systems have made it possible to automate almost every phase of traffic control, signaling, car management, train dispatching and make-up, and train movement (resulting in the elimination of cabooses) as well as such administrative functions as waybill transmission and the handling of freight and loss-and-damage claims. Also, truck competition has contributed to the decline in rail's share of the total U.S. freight ton-mile volume and the accompanying loss in rail jobs.

The elimination of jobs, however, has also become more palatable through the railroad industry's willingness to provide generous labor buy-out programs; its use of attrition rather than layoffs to eliminate jobs; and the potential for retaining a high wage structure for remaining union workers through improved productivity. Generous separation packages have, however, limited short-run rail labor cost savings and is one of the reasons why labor cost savings have lagged behind the rate of employee decline. Between 1980 and 1990, the industry's labor force fell by 44%, but labor costs dropped only 23% (see Tully, 1991). Railroad revenue ton-miles per employee increased 650% in the 1946–1984 period and 162% in the 1985–1999 period (Schwarz-Miller & Talley, 2002). The increase in railroad labor productivity is attributed to public policy changes, changes in competitive conditions, and labor-saving technological advances, e.g., advances in locomotive technology, track technology, car technology, and electronics, communications, and information technology.[9] The erosion of labor protection programs and labor-saving technology have provided railroad managers with greater flexibility in the allocation of rail labor for improving railroads' intramodal competitiveness.

This study contributes to our understanding of economic deregulation's influence on railroad employee earnings by investigating the regulatory earnings patterns of railroad managers and labor. Specifically, have union rail workers been able to withstand downward pressure on labor costs better than non-union rail workers following deregulation? Do the wages of managers have a similar pattern to that of non-managerial employee wages following deregulation? Individual railroad employee data taken from the Bureau of the Census' Current Population Survey (CPS) are used in the investigation. These data allow for the examination of the regulation-deregulation earnings differentials of railroad managers and labor. Such an examination allows for the testing of whether railroad manager earnings follow the deregulation pattern of eroding labor earnings (see Hirsch, 1988; Rose, 1987), and increasing managerial earnings found in other transportation sectors (see Burks, Guy, & Maxwell, 2004) or whether the railroad unions' control over the supply of labor in the railroad industry provides railroad union workers with the ability to avoid a widening managerial-union wage gap.

2. DEREGULATION AND RAILROAD LABOR EARNINGS

Economic theory provides no clear a priori predictions on the effect of deregulation on railroad non-managerial labor earnings. On the one hand, the elimination of unprofitable routes and competitive cost-cutting steps may reduce the demand for labor and depress earnings; on the other hand, improvements in productivity and profitability may improve the earnings for workers left in the industry. Economic rent theory reinforces the argument for declining labor earnings in deregulated environments. Regulation may create economic rents for regulated firms by restricting entry and price competition which, in turn, provides an opportunity for increased wages, in particular for highly unionized industries. Under deregulation, economic rents and labor earnings are expected to decline as a result of increased competition. However, such declines may differ by union status as the collective voice of union members may help them avoid relatively large wage reductions. The potential for limiting losses, though, is dependent, in part, on rail unions' ability to maintain control over the supply of workers following deregulation.

The challenge in providing a single post-deregulation wage differential prediction is reflected in the mixed results findings from past research. For instance, in his estimation of earnings equations using 1973–1988 CPS files, Hendricks (1994) found that the earnings of railroad operators increased in the post-Staggers period. MacDonald and Cavalluzzo (1996), relying upon CPS files as well as collective bargaining agreements, also found that the wages of railroad operators increased following passage of the Staggers Act of 1980, but reached a peak in 1985 and then declined substantially thereafter. Estimates of railroad union earnings equations by Talley and Schwarz-Miller (1998) using 1973–1993 CPS files suggest that the weekly earnings of union operatives remained stable in the 4-R period. Union wages then rose initially in the post-Staggers period, but peaked in 1988. The earnings peak in 1988 is consistent with the fact that there were no increases in nominal contract pay for the 1988–1991 period and moderate increases thereafter. Talley and Schwarz-Miller further found that engineer earnings declined overall in the Staggers deregulation period, but the decline in conductors' pay was not statistically significant, likely the result of reduced crew allowances paid in compensation for the elimination of brakemen. Talley (2001) in using 1973–1995 CPS files also found a significant decline in the earnings of brakemen/switchmen in the Staggers post-deregulation period. These results, in particular for engineers and brakemen/switchmen, are consistent with the Staggers Act spawning a more competitive railroad industry environment that provided the basis for railroads to press more effectively for work- and pay-rule changes and moderation in wage increases.

While findings using CPS data suggest declining real wages following the mid-1980s, it is possible that lucrative buyouts at that time contributed to the total compensation for rail workers actually increasing following deregulation. Indeed, utilizing 1978–1994 Class I Railroad firm-level data, Davis and Wilson (2003) found that the total compensation of railroad employees increased by over 40% for the period. Mergers contributed 5–15%, deregulation contributed 20% and changes in firm operating and network characteristics contributed 4–5% to the 40% overall increase in total compensation. Even though these results on total compensation differ from wage findings, they are not contradictory, since buyout packages could more than offset wage losses during the post-deregulation period.[10]

Theories on labor earnings are just as unclear on the expected effect of deregulation on the earnings of rail mangers. On the one hand, economic rent theory predicts that the earnings of managers, like those of labor, will decline in a deregulation period. Rail managers were highly likely to share rent given the industry's internal labor market practice of selecting managers from the pool of rail engineers and other professional rail occupations (Grimm, Kling, & Smith, 1987). Managerial earnings would be closely tied to union wages under the pre-deregulation internal labor market structure, since workers promoted to managerial positions would command a premium over their previous earnings received as a non-management employee. However, post-deregulation wage levels for managers would be difficult to sustain in a more market oriented business environment that emphasizes cost-cutting. In contrast to the hypothesis derived from economic rent theory, performance theory predicts that the earnings of managers will rise or at least not decline at the rate of non-managerial wages (Joskow, Rose, & Shepard, 1993). Regulation based on a cost mark-up removes performance as an objective of mangers of regulated firms and hence removes performance indicators such as productivity as incentives for managerial compensation. Given the incentive to improve firm performance following deregulation, owners are more likely to compensate managers for enhancing productivity.

The impact of railroad deregulation on the earnings of railroad managers was first examined in a study by Belzer (1998), using CPS files for the years 1973–1991. He found no significant decline in manager earnings with respect to the 4-R Act, but a significant decrease for the Staggers post-deregulation period through 1991. The post-Staggers act earnings decline for managers resemble his wage results for railroad engineers and brakemen. This managerial wage pattern is consistent with the notion that rail managers as well as other rail employees were the beneficiaries of pre-deregulation rent sharing, and these high wages were difficult to justify economically even during a post-deregulation period of significant productivity gains. The parallel earnings pattern of rail managers and non-managers is unique to surface transportation freight services, as past research into the trucking industry indicates earnings gains for managers but earnings losses for drivers in the post-deregulation period (Burks et al., 2004).

Table 1. Mean Union Density.

Occupation	Regulation[a]	Deregulation[b]
Engineer	.926	.935
Conductor	.885	.873
Brakeman/Switchman	.923	.936
Mechanic	.882	.864

[a]Years 1973–1980.
[b]Years 1981–2001.

However, past rail findings on relative wages using CPS data uncover interesting results, such work does not distinguish wage patterns for union and non-union workers when making a comparative analysis with managerial earnings.[11] Making that distinction is important in part because rail unions' members following deregulation continue to comprise a large share of the industry's work force. As reported in Table 1 mean union densities for the rail occupations were quite high during regulation and remained so under deregulation. For the regulation period, the percentages of rail engineers and brakemen/switchmen belonging to unions were on average 92.6 and 92.3%, increasing slightly to 93.5 and 93.6% during deregulation. The mean union densities for the regulation period for conductors and mechanics were slightly lower, i.e., 88.5 and 88.2%, respectively, falling slightly to 87.3 and 86.4% in the post-deregulation period.[12]

3. DATA AND LABOR EARNINGS MODEL

The U.S. Current Population Survey (CPS) data for individual railroad managers and labor for the years 1973–2001 are used in this investigation. This data source also provides information on railroad workers' occupation, union status, and other personal characteristics. Railroad labor occupations utilized in the study include the locomotive engineer, conductor, brakeman/switchman, and mechanic. Railroad managers are those that manage, coordinate, and supervise: train operation systems; the construction and maintenance of railroad structures, facilities and systems; and rail terminal activities such as storage and distribution of rail cars. While this data source provides the benefit of examining wage trends separately for union, non-union, and managerial employees, there are shortcomings that are associated with its use. For instance, CPS reports information on labor earnings and identifies whether workers receive employer-supported

Table 2. Union Mean Real Earnings and Hours Worked.

Occupation	Regulation[a]			Deregulation[b]		
	N	Weekly Earnings	Weekly Hours	*N*	Weekly Earnings	Weekly Hours
Engineer	225	$643.30	47.3	1,101	$577.04	49.1
Conductor	131	605.23	49.3	1,014	557.19	48.9
Brakeman/Switchman	227	550.61	46.0	755	486.51	45.4
Mechanic	157	466.75	39.7	465	410.70	41.0

[a]Years 1973–1980.
[b]Years 1981–2001.

pensions and health care plans; however, these data do not report the value of such non-wage compensation. In addition, information that is provided on non-wage compensation is only reported for a very small sample of rail employees and hence precludes its use for labor compensation analysis. Ideally, one would prefer to analyze employees' total compensation packages of earnings and benefits.[13] Nonetheless, labor earnings provide a good indicator of rail compensation without buyouts. Another shortcoming of the CPS survey is that information is typically not collected on respondents' employers. Consequently, the investigation may suffer from omitted variable bias associated with the inability to control for firm characteristics varying across employees.[14]

Mean real weekly earnings and hours worked for union railroad occupations for regulation and deregulation periods taken from the CPS are presented in Table 2.[15] This study selects as deregulation years, the years following passage of the Staggers Act. The initial railroad deregulation act, the 4-R Act of 1976, "was largely emasculated by the ICC, which was inclined to oppose deregulation or move only slowly toward deregulation" (Grimm & Windle, 1998, p. 18). Further, no significant changes have been found in the real weekly wages of union railroad operators following passage of the 4-R Act and prior to passage of the Staggers Act (see Talley & Schwarz-Miller, 1998; Belzer, 1998). Since the Staggers Act was passed by Congress in October 1980, 1981 is used as the first year of the railroad deregulation period. Hence, the railroad regulation and deregulation years used in the investigation are 1973–1980 and 1981–2001, respectively. The 1981 date chosen for distinguishing regulatory regimes coincides with the expiration of the railroad labor contract period prior to the Staggers Act.

The findings in Table 2 reveal that the union mean real weekly earnings of all occupations declined during the post-deregulation period. The

Table 3. Non-Union Mean Real Earnings and Hours Worked.

Occupation	Regulation[a]			Deregulation[b]		
	N	Weekly Earnings	Weekly Hours	*N*	Weekly Earnings	Weekly Hours
Manager	184	$688.58	46.2	382	$648.06	47.1
Engineer	18	510.37	42.4	76	412.08	44.3
Conductor	17	437.11	42.4	147	515.95	45.9
Brakeman/Switchman	28	489.63	42.8	52	352.12	43.3
Mechanic	21	447.84	46.0	73	337.66	41.9

[a]Years 1973–1980.
[b]Years 1981–2001.

percentage decreases in the mean weekly earnings for engineers, conductors, brakemen/switchmen, and mechanics are 10, 8, 12, and 12%, respectively. Information on hours worked suggests that these wage declines were not the result of reductions in weekly hours worked. For instance, the mean weekly hours worked by union conductors and brakemen/switchmen are similar for both time periods. The mean hours worked actually increased for union engineers and mechanics during the post-deregulation period.

Comparable mean statistics for non-union labor and managers appear in Table 3. The mean real weekly earnings of all non-union occupations except conductors were lower during the post-deregulation period. The mean weekly earnings of managers fell 6%, the smallest decline among non-union and union occupations. Conductors' non-union earnings rose 18%. The decreases in non-union mean earnings were greater than the declines in union mean earnings for comparable occupations—mean weekly earnings of non-union engineers, brakemen/switchmen, and mechanics dropped 19, 28, and 25%, respectively, during the post-deregulation period. Mean weekly hours worked for non-union brakemen/switchmen were similar for both time periods, but increased for managers, engineers, and conductors and decreased for mechanics during the post-deregulation period.

In sum, mean results on earnings and hours reveal two key patterns. (1) Changes in managers' earnings more closely resemble earnings changes for union than for non-union workers. (2) Still, mean union earnings fell more than managerial earnings even though the industry work force remained highly organized following deregulation. Caution is suggested, however, before deriving conclusions from these results. Worker characteristics varying over regulatory regimes and over occupations introduce bias when examining earnings trends. For example, the increasing weekly hours worked for managers might contribute to their relative lower wage declines compared to union workers. Hence, multivariate estimation techniques are needed to address such bias.

The multivariate earnings equation used to examine the impact of railroad deregulation on the weekly earnings differentials of railroad union and non-union labor and managers (i.e., to examine regulatory earnings differentials) is depicted by

$$\text{LWKEARN}_{ij} = \alpha_1 \text{DEREG}_{ij} + \alpha_2 \text{LHOURS}_{ij} + \sum \alpha_k X_{ijk} + \varepsilon_{ij} \qquad (1)$$

where LWKEARN_{ij} is the natural log of weekly earnings in 1983 dollars of the *i*th railroad employee in the *j*th year; DEREG is the deregulation binary variable equal to 1 for the deregulation years 1981–2001 and 0 for the regulation years 1973–1980; and LHOURS is the natural log of the weekly hours worked by the *i*th worker in the *j*th year. X is a vector of control variables which includes a constant term as well as the variables: worker's age (AGE), worker's age squared (AGESQ), and the U.S. annual unemployment rate (UNRATE). The inclusion of the annual employment rate is needed to address potential estimation bias caused by time variant distortions. The more common time fixed-effects approach introduces perfect collinearity with the deregulation dummies. The vector X also includes binary variables equal to 1, if the worker is a female (FEMALE), married (MARRIED), full-time employee (FULLTIME), black (BLACK), white (WHITE), not a high school graduate (NODIPLOMA), a high school graduate at most (DIPLOMA), residing in a consolidated metropolitan statistical area (CMSA), or residing in the Northeast (NEAST), South (SOUTH), or North Central (NCENT), as opposed to residing in the West region of the country. The coefficient α_1 measures the log weekly earnings differential for a given railroad occupation in the Staggers deregulation period relative to the regulation period. The estimated coefficients on the deregulation binary variable are used to investigate whether non-union and union rail workers experience appreciable declines in their earnings following deregulation. An explanation of the expected signs on the estimated coefficients is provided in Table 4.

A shortcoming associated with interpreting the findings from estimating Eq. (1) is the inability to compute the statistical significance of the differences in the deregulation earnings effects across rail occupations. Hence, the occupational earnings analysis relies on comparing the magnitude of earnings changes. The benefit of estimating Eq. (1), though, is that it allows the earnings returns to worker characteristics to vary by occupation, whereas an earnings equation that allows the statistical significance testing of

Table 4. Hypotheses on the Predicted Earnings Effect of Determinants in Equation (1).

Variable	Hypothesis
LHOURS	An increase in weekly hours worked is expected to be associated with higher weekly earnings
AGE	An increase in individual workers' age is expected to be associated with higher weekly earnings
AGESQ	An increase in the square of individual workers' age is expected to be associated with declining weekly earnings, which depicts earnings increasing at a decreasing rate over time
UNRATE	Periods of high national unemployment is expected to be associated with lower weekly earnings due to a weak labor market
FEMALE	The potential for labor market discrimination can lead to lower earnings for women compared to men
MARRIED	Married workers are expected to receive higher weekly earnings than single workers in part because they are likely to gain from long employment tenure at the same place of business
FULLTIME	Full-time workers are expected to receive higher weekly earnings than part-time workers because they are able to gain from working long hours
BLACK	The potential for labor market discrimination can lead to lower earnings for blacks compared to the control group of non-black minorities. For the sample population used in this study Asian Americans comprise the largest share of non-black minorities
WHITE	The potential for labor market discrimination can lead to higher earnings for whites compared to the control group of non-black minorities
NODIPLOMA	The lack of a high school diploma is expected to be associated with weekly earnings below that of the control group of college educated workers
DIPLOMA	The lack of a college education is expected to be associated with weekly earnings below that of the control group of college educated workers
CMSA	Workers residing in metropolitan areas are expected to receive higher earnings than workers in rural non-metropolitan areas due to the higher cost of living in metropolitan areas
NEAST	Workers residing in northern states are expected to receive earnings that resemble earnings of workers in the control group of western states due to the high cost of living in both regions
SOUTH	Workers residing in southern states are expected to receive lower earnings than workers in the control group of western states due to the higher cost of living in the west
NCENT	Workers residing in north central states are expected to receive lower earnings than workers in the control group of western states due to the higher cost of living in the west

deregulation earnings effects across rail occupations may restrict the earnings returns to worker characteristics to be the same across occupations.[16] Using such a model is highly likely to provide confounding results given that unions negotiate contracts that suppress returns to education and instead emphasize returns to experience. In contrast, educational attainment is a key wage determinant for managers.

4. ESTIMATION RESULTS

Estimates of earnings equation (1) for railroad union labor and non-union labor and managers for the time period 1973–2001 are presented in Tables A1 and A2 of the appendix.[17] Since earnings differentials are the primary concern of this study, the DEREG coefficient estimates found in Tables A1 and A2 of the appendix are presented in Table 5. The DEREG coefficient estimates for all union railroad occupations are negative and statistically significant. The coefficients indicate that the weekly earnings of union railroad engineers, conductors, brakemen/switchmen, and mechanics have declined 31.0, 22.4, 22.2, and 24.0%, respectively, during the deregulation period. Apparently, controlling for differences in worker characteristics addressed biases associated with examining mean earnings patterns as these estimated post-deregulation earnings declines are markedly larger than the mean earnings results.

The DEREG coefficient estimates for all non-union railroad occupations (managers and non-union labor) are also negative and depict earnings declines that are larger than declines reported for mean earnings. The coefficients are statistically significant except for the coefficient for conductors. The estimated coefficient for managers indicates that their weekly earnings have declined 13.9% during the deregulation period. The DEREG

Table 5. Estimated Weekly Earnings Differential Coefficients: Deregulation versus Regulation[a].

Occupation	Union	Non-union
Manager	–	–.1494 (–3.16)
Engineer	–.3715 (–6.70)	–.8575 (–3.20)
Conductor	–.2540 (–3.74)	–.0130 (–0.07)
Brakeman/Switchman	–.2504 (–5.17)	–.6412 (–3.33)
Mechanic	–.2745 (–4.69)	–.5766 (–4.03)

[a] *t*-Statistics are in parentheses; years 1973–2001.

coefficient estimates of the non-union railroad labor – engineers, brakemen/switchmen, and mechanics – indicate that their weekly earnings have declined 57.6, 47.3, and 43.8%, respectively, during the deregulation period. There was no appreciable change in the earnings of non-union conductors.

The DEREG coefficient estimation results are consistent with the view that deregulation promoted a more cost-conscious business environment that placed downward pressure on earnings gains for both union and non-union labor as well as for managers. With the exception of the conductor category, the earnings of non-union labor experienced a greater decline during the deregulation period than the earnings of union labor. The decline in the earnings of managers during the deregulation period was smaller than that for labor (both union and non-union), except for non-union conductors. Managers' and union workers' abilities to avoid the significant post-deregulation earnings differential loss experienced by non-union labor supports the view that managers and union workers were better able than non-union workers to negotiate relatively small wage losses during the deregulation period. Union workers would benefit from their negotiation strength associated with a highly unionized work force. Managers would benefit from a post-deregulation business environment that encourages performance pay.

5. CONCLUSION

While shareholders and shippers have benefited from railroad deregulation, the impact on railroad union and non-union labor and managers has been negative. Has the negative impact on labor been greater than that on managers? Has the negative impact on non-union labor been greater than that on union labor? Has the negative impact been greater for certain non-managerial railroad occupations than for others? This chapter has addressed these questions with respect to the earnings of railroad union and non-union labor, and managers by estimating the regulation-deregulation earnings differentials of railroad managers and labor (i.e., regulatory earnings differentials). The findings indicate that the earnings of railroad union labor experienced a smaller decline in the deregulation period than the earnings of non-union labor (except for conductors). The percentage decline in the earnings of railroad managers during the deregulation period is smaller than that for both railroad union and non-union labor, except for non-union conductors.

The earnings losses experienced by railroad occupations during the deregulation period comports well with the notion that railroad employees are less likely to benefit from rent-sharing that apparently prevailed prior to deregulation. Downward pressure on labor cost resulting from greater emphasis on cost-savings seems to have created a business environment that made it difficult to maintain pre-deregulation earnings levels. The relatively smaller earnings loss of managers during the post-deregulation period of high railroad productivity growth is consistent with past research that indicates that rail managers can benefit from greater reliance on pay-for-performance following deregulation. Union members' ability to avoid the large wage losses of their non-union counterparts is the predicted outcome for members belonging to unions that represent an overwhelming majority of the post-deregulation labor force in the railroad industry.

NOTES

1. For further discussion, see Braeutigam (1993). Since neither the 4-R Act nor the Staggers Act completely deregulated the rail industry, some authors prefer to use the phrase "regulatory reform" rather than the term "deregulation." We choose the latter for this paper.

2. From an analysis of annual data of major Class I railroads for the 1974–1986 period, Berndt, Friedlaender, Wang Chiang, and Vellturo (1993) conclude that both mergers and deregulation contributed significantly to railroad cost savings, but that the impact of the latter has been much larger than that of the former, with the cost-reducing effects of mergers being more short-lived. Wilson (1997), utilizing data of Class I railroads for the 1978–1989 period, concludes that the initial effects of deregulation on railroad productivity were large, but have fallen through time; alternatively, the initial effects of deregulation on cost savings were modest, but were substantial by 1989, with costs being 40% lower than they would have been under regulation. Bankruptcies, consolidations, and mergers of Class I railroads have contributed to a rising concentration in the industry: In 1974, 56 railroads had Class I status in comparison to only 21 in 1986 and 13 in 1993 (excluding Amtrak). The latter accounted for 73% of the mileage operated, 89% of the employees, and 91% of the freight revenue for the industry.

3. Other deregulation studies focusing on rail rates of specific commodities include studies by MacDonald (1989) and Burton (1993). For a discussion of the impact of deregulation on aggregate rail rates, see Boyer (1987), Barnekov and Kliet (1990), and McFarland (1989).

4. There are a number of rail labor unions. In January 2005, seven rail labor unions formed the Rail Labor Bargaining Coalition to coordinate contract negotiations with the National Carriers' Conference Committee, which represents 32 U.S. railroads, including five Class I railroads. These seven unions include the: (1) Brotherhood of Locomotive Engineers and Trainmen, (2) Brotherhood of

Maintenance of Way Employees Division, (3) Brotherhood of Railroad Signalmen, (4) American Train Dispatchers of America, (5) National Conference of Firemen and Oilers, (6) Sheet Metal Workers International Association, and (7) International Brotherhood of Boilermakers.

5. In some cases crews were even larger, including an extra brakeman and/or a fireman.

6. Bilateral agreements between railroads and unions allow for two-man crew trains (where the remaining brakeman has been eliminated). The reduction in crew size reflects the elimination of residual work-rule redundancies (carried over from the earlier steam to diesel conversion), the substitution of end-of-train devices for cabooses, and track switching automation, making the brakeman's primary job of manually switching track unnecessary. Crew size collective bargaining agreements have been an impediment to substituting available technologies (e.g., computerized electric sensors) for employees. Keaton (1991) found that crew size reductions are likely to be used to reduce rail operating cost rather than to improve service.

7. In situations in which jobs are being eliminated as a result of mergers, sales, and abandonments, it is the conditions surrounding the reduction, rather than the reductions themselves, that are negotiated. Implementary agreements are required between the individual unions and railroads involved and were negotiated under protective conditions specified by the former ICC, e.g., with respect to minimum pay guarantees or separation payments. ICC rules provided for third-party arbitration of disputes. Both unions and the carriers prefer prior settlement to the uncertainty of arbitration outcomes.

8. Emergency procedures under the Railway Labor Act allow the U.S. President to appoint a Presidential Emergency Board (PEB) to investigate a dispute and report back with recommendations. The decisions of the PEB appointed in 1991 were particularly significant: In the 1991 negotiations, the industry sought 20% wage reductions to compensate for large crew sizes. After an impasse was reached, the PEB recommended to Congress that, in the absence of agreement, parties negotiating crew size were to go to arbitration using an earlier settlement as a basis. This settlement involved a forced buy-out that labor did not want. The PEB recommendations, thus, gave railroads the leverage to make subsequent crew-reduction agreements possible. Congressional willingness to impose the PEB's recommendations, which would not necessarily have been forthcoming in the past, was also vital. For further discussion of government intervention in rail disputes, see Rehmus (1990).

9. For a discussion of these technologies, see Schwarz-Miller and Talley (2002).

10. The differing outcomes for wage and total compensation may also be due to the fact that the firm-level data utilized by Davis and Wilson (2003) only include compensation information for Class I railroads, whereas the CPS data include the earnings of Class I, II, and III railroad employees. Including Class II and III railroad employees is important, since the number of these railroads have increased under deregulation. In 1979, there were 238 short-line and regional railroads; by 1996 there were more than 500 such railroads, employing 13,000 workers and operating almost 27,000 miles of rail track (Wilner, 1997). This increase is traced to two events: (1) the Staggers Act advocated that Class I railroads dispose of uneconomic track through line sales rather than abandonment and (2) the ICC approved line sales without the

imposition of income protection, i.e., the ICC encouraged entrepreneurs to purchase the lines by creating a loophole in the railroad regulation that otherwise required the granting of up to six years of income protection to rail employees adversely affected by line sales. For a discussion of short-line and regional railroads, see Allen, Sussman, and Miller (2002).

11. Hendricks (1994) and MacDonald and Cavalluzzo (1996) examine wage patterns of union and non-union rail workers using an aggregate measure of worker occupation. This measure does not identify managers and specific rail occupations such as engineers, conductors, and brakemen.

12. The small sample size of non-union rail workers may suggest caution when examining union density trends. Nonetheless, the small sample is consistent with the findings of a lack of non-union employment share growth.

13. Fringe benefits are a key component of labor compensation packages for rail workers given the significance placed on the value of pension payments in post-deregulation labor negotiations.

14. CPS files do report information on firm characteristics such as firm size; however, prior to 1983 this information is only reported every five years.

15. The Consumer Price Index (CPI) was used to deflate weekly earnings.

16. An example of such an equation that could be used to examine weekly earnings differentials of railroad managers versus union and non-union labor for the regulation and deregulation periods, i.e., to examine occupational earnings differentials, is

$$\text{LWKEARN}_{ij} = \beta_1 \text{MANAGER}_{ij} + \beta_2 \text{LHOURS}_{ij} + \sum \beta_k X_{ijk} + \varepsilon_{ij} \tag{2}$$

where MANAGER is a binary variable equal to 1 if a railroad manager and 0 if a labor occupation (engineer, conductor, brakeman/switchman or mechanic), and the remaining explanatory variables are the same as those in Eq. (1). The coefficient β_1 measures the log weekly earnings differential between a railroad manager and a given labor occupation for the regulation and deregulation periods. The estimated coefficients on the manager binary variable would be used to investigate the extent to which earnings differentials existed between railroad managers and labor during the regulation and deregulation periods. For an investigation of the earnings differentials between railroad labor and port dockworkers, see Talley (2004).

17. The estimated coefficients on the control variables in Tables A1 and A2 reveal important results. For instance, the returns-to-education variables for union workers are only significant for conductor and positive. In contrast, a lack of a high school diploma is associated with statistically significantly lower wages for all non-union workers except non-union conductors. Findings in these tables also reveal that changes in tightness of the national labor market is associated with changes in labor earnings for non-managerial workers, as the estimated coefficient on the national unemployment rate is negative and statistically significant except for non-union conductors. Managerial earnings, however, are not associated with the national unemployment rate. Such evidence on returns-to-worker characteristics varying by occupation provides support for use of this study's earnings specification (i.e., Eq. (1).

ACKNOWLEDGMENTS

The authors appreciate the comments and suggestions of the participants at the "Conference on Railroad Industry Structure, Competition and Investment" at Northwestern University in 2004, and the Transportation Session of the Annual Meeting of the Eastern Economics Association in 2006.

REFERENCES

Allen, W. B., Sussman, M., & Miller, D. (2002). Regional and short-line railroads in the United States. *Transportation Quarterly*, *56*(4), 77–113.

Association of American Railroads (AAR). (1994, 2002). *Railroad facts*. Washington, DC: Association of American Railroads.

Barnekov, C. C., & Kleit, A. N. (1990). The efficiency effects of railroad deregulation in the United States. *International Journal of Transport Economics*, *17*(1), 21–36.

Belzer, M. (1998). Commentary on railroad deregulation and union labor earnings. In: J. Peoples (Ed.), *Regulatory reform and labor markets* (pp. 155–182). Boston, MA: Kluwer Academic Publishers.

Berndt, E. R., Friedlaender, A. F., Wang Chiang, J. S.-E., & Vellturo, C. A. (1993). Cost effects of mergers and deregulation in the U.S. rail industry. *Journal of Productivity Analysis*, *4*(1/2), 127–144.

Boyer, K. D. (1987). The costs of price regulation: Lessons from railroad deregulation. *Rand Journal of Economics*, *18*(3), 408–416.

Braeutigam, R. R. (1993). Consequences of regulatory reform in the American railroad industry. *Southern Economic Journal*, *59*(3), 468–480.

Burks, S., Guy, F., & Maxwell, B. (2004). Shifting gears in the corner office: Deregulation and the earnings of trucking executives. In: J. Peoples & W. K. Talley (Eds), *Transportation labor issues and regulatory reform* (pp. 137–164). Amsterdam, The Netherlands: Elsevier-JAI.

Burton, M. L. (1993). Railroad deregulation, carrier behavior, and shipper response: A disaggregated analysis. *Journal of Regulatory Economics*, *5*(4), 417–434.

Davis, D. E., & Wilson, W. W. (1999). Deregulation, mergers and employment in the railroad industry. *Journal of Regulatory Economics*, *15*(1), 5–22.

Davis, D. E., & Wilson, W. W. (2003). Wages in rail markets: Deregulation, mergers and changing networks characteristics. *Southern Economic Journal*, *69*(4), 865–885.

Friedlaender, A. F., Berndt, E. R., & McCullough, G. (1992). Governance structure, managerial characteristics, and firm performance in the deregulated rail industry. In: *Brookings papers in economic activity: Microeconomics 1992* (pp. 95–169). Washington, DC: Brookings Institution.

Grimm, C., Kling, J., & Smith, K. (1987). The impact of U.S. rail regulatory reform on railroad management and organizational structure. *Transportation Research*, *21*(A), 87–94.

Grimm, C., & Windle, R. J. (1998). Regulation and deregulation in surface freight, airlines and telecommunications. In: J. Peoples (Ed.), *Regulatory reform and labor markets* (pp. 15–49). Boston, MA: Kluwer Academic Publishers.

Hendricks, W. (1994). Deregulation and labor earnings. *Journal of Labor Research, 15*, 207–234.

Hirsch, B. T. (1988). Trucking regulation, unionization, and labor earnings: 1973–1985. *Journal of Human Resources, 23*, 296–319.

Joskow, P., Rose, N., & Shepard, A. (1993). Regulatory constraints on CEO compensation. In: *Brookings papers in economic activity: Microeconomics 1993* (1–58). Washington, DC: Brookings Institution.

Keaton, M. H. (1991). Train crew size, crew cost, and service levels for single carload freight traffic in the U.S. rail industry. *Logistics and Transportation Review, 27*(4), 333–349.

MacDonald, J. M. (1989). Railroad deregulation, innovation, and competition: Effects of the Staggers Act on grain transportation. *Journal of Law and Economics, 32*(1), 63–96.

MacDonald, J. M., & Cavalluzzo, L. C. (1996). Railroad deregulation: Pricing reforms, shipper responses and the effects on labor. *Industrial and Labor Relations Review, 50*(1), 80–91.

McFarland, H. (1987). Did railroad deregulation lead to monopoly pricing? An application of *q*. *Journal of Business, 60*(3), 385–400.

McFarland, H. (1989). The effects of United States railroad deregulation on shippers, labor, and capital. *Journal of Regulatory Economics, 1*, 259–270.

Rehmus, C. M. (1990). Emergency strikes revisited. *Industrial and Labor Relations Review, 43*(2), 175–190.

Rose, N. L. (1987). Labor rent sharing and regulation: Evidence from the trucking industry. *Journal of Political Economy, 95*, 1,146–1,178.

Schwarz-Miller, A. V., & Talley, W. K. (2002). Technology and labor relations: Railroads and ports. In: J. Bennett & D. Taras (Eds), *Technological change and employment conditions in traditionally heavily unionized industries. A symposium issue of the Journal of Labor Research, 23*(4), 513–533.

Talley, W. K. (1983). *Introduction to transportation*. Cincinnati, OH: South-Western Publishing Co.

Talley, W. K. (2001). Wage differentials of transportation industries: Deregulation versus regulation. *Economic Inquiry, 39*(3), 406–429.

Talley, W. K. (2004). Wage differentials of intermodal transportation carriers and ports: Deregulation versus regulation. In: W. K. Talley (Ed.), *The industrial organization of shipping and ports. A special issue of the journal The Review of Network Economics, 3*(2), 207–227.

Talley, W. K., & Schwarz-Miller, A. V. (1998). Railroad deregulation and union labor earnings. In: J. Peoples (Ed.), *Regulatory reform and labor markets* (pp. 125–153). Boston, MA: Kluwer Academic Publishers.

Thompson, L. S. (1998). U.S. rails: A world apart. *Journal of Commerce*, July, 7A.

Tully, S. (1991). Comeback ahead for railroads. *Fortune, 123*(June), 107–113.

Wilner, F. N. (1997). Gale warnings for short-line rails. *Journal of Commerce*, August, 9A.

Wilson, W. W. (1994). Market-specific effects of rail deregulation. *Journal of Industrial Economics, 42*(1), 1–22.

Wilson, W. W. (1997). Cost savings and productivity in the railroad industry. *Journal of Regulatory Economics, 11*(1), 21–40.

APPENDIX

Table A1. Union Weekly Earnings Equation Results: Deregulation versus Regulation[a].

Variable	Engineer	Conductor	Brakeman/ Switchman	Mechanic
DEREG	−.3715	−.2540	−.2504	−.2745
	(−6.70)	(−3.74)	(−5.17)	(-4.69)
FEMALE	−.2562	−.0041	−.2001	.0268
	(−2.09)	(−0.03)	(−1.15)	(0.15)
MARRIED	−.0646	.0073	.0806	−.0397
	(−1.31)	(0.15)	(1.53)	(−0.69)
UNRATE	−.2737	−.2251	−.3384	−.2742
	(−20.33)	(−16.18)	(−23.54)	(−17.0)
FULLTIME	.0494	−.0291	.2995	.6167
	(0.44)	(−0.25)	(3.44)	(2.05)
LHOURS	.5467	.6906	.5022	−.0013
	(7.03)	(8.87)	(5.66)	(−0.01)
AGE	.0376	.0639	.0404	.0359
	(2.69)	(4.31)	(2.83)	(2.19)
AGESQ	−.0004	−.0007	−.0005	−.0005
	(−2.56)	(−4.25)	(−2.93)	(−2.40)
NODIPLOMA	−.0750	.1251	−.0082	.0536
	(−0.98)	(1.79)	(−0.12)	(0.75)
DIPLOMA	.0467	.0806	.0083	−.0319
	(1.24)	(2.02)	(0.20)	(−0.61)
BLACK	−.3767	−.0638	−.1952	−.2819
	(−1.55)	(−0.24)	(−0.46)	(−0.91)
WHITE	−.1926	.0257	−.1300	−.0932
	(−0.84)	(0.10)	(−0.31)	(−0.31)
NEAST	−.2163	−.2563	−.2346	.0014
	(−3.45)	(−4.27)	(−3.08)	(0.02)
NCENT	−.0635	−.1166	−.1025	.0274
	(−1.37)	(−2.42)	(−2.04)	(0.48)
SOUTH	−.0545	−.2062	−.0949	.0095
	(−1.10)	(−3.81)	(−1.81)	(0.16)
CMSA	−.0312	.0235	−.0659	−.0887
	(−0.81)	(0.60)	(−1.60)	(−1.89)

Table A1. (*Continued*).

Variable	Engineer	Conductor	Brakeman/ Switchman	Mechanic
Constant	5.7040	3.8275	5.7185	6.8230
	(11.68)	(7.71)	(9.49)	(8.15)
R^2	.351	.311	.432	.387
$\bar{R}^2$	.343	.300	.427	.369
No. of observations	1,184	1,013	978	578

[a]Years 1973–2001; *t*-statistics are in parentheses.

Table A2. Non-union Weekly Earnings Equation Results: Deregulation versus Regulation[a].

Variable	Manager	Engineer	Conductor	Brakeman/ Switchman	Mechanic
DEREG	−.1494	−.8575	−.0130	−.6412	−.5766
	(−3.16)	(−3.20)	(−0.07)	(−3.33)	(−4.03)
FEMALE	−0.1440	−.6557	−.3710	—	—
	(−2.27)	(−1.71)	(−1.83)	—	—
MARRIED	.1200	−.1619	−.0919	.0377	.0057
	(2.42)	(−0.98)	(−0.76)	(0.21)	(0.04)
UNRATE	.0184	−.2282	.0320	−.2689	−.2525
	(1.25)	(−4.67)	(0.86)	(−4.17)	(−5.84)
FULLTIME	.3563	−1.3356	−1.0926	−.3100	—
	(1.66)	(−2.42)	(−2.25)	(−1.07)	—
LHOURS	.7679	2.1977	1.1107	1.1741	.5501
	(8.38)	(5.35)	(5.87)	(3.13)	(2.47)
AGE	.0354	.0018	.0747	.0830	.0188
	(2.49)	(0.04)	(2.25)	(1.55)	(0.47)
AGESQ	−.0003	.0002	−.0008	−.0011	−.0001
	(−2.01)	(0.41)	(−2.10)	(−1.63)	(−0.24)
NODIPLOMA	−.2273	−.5753	−.4200	−.4985	−.4961
	(−2.89)	(−2.41)	(−1.31)	(−1.96)	(−2.66)
DIPLOMA	−.1091	.0673	.0041	−.0312	−.0283
	(−2.96)	(0.50)	(0.05)	(−0.19)	(−0.22)

Table A2. *(Continued).*

Variable	Manager	Engineer	Conductor	Brakeman/ Switchman	Mechanic
BLACK	.0548	−.2823	−.2981	.1835	0.0514
	(0.38)	(−0.51)	(−0.77)	(0.33)	(0.25)
WHITE	.1887	−.7668	−.1348	.0975	—
	(1.64)	(−1.43)	(−0.38)	(0.19)	
NEAST	.0196	−.0914	−.2647	−.0778	−.1067
	(0.34)	(−0.38)	(−1.73)	(−0.28)	(−0.50)
NCENT	.0328	−.2135	−.1771	−.0442	−.1688
	(0.66)	(−1.16)	(−1.44)	(−0.20)	(−1.06)
SOUTH	.0856	−.3771	−0.2196	−.5689	−.0469
	(1.66)	(−2.02)	(−1.77)	(−2.76)	(−0.31)
CMSA	.0956	.0016	.0357	−.1050	−.0611
	(2.33)	(0.01)	(0.40)	(−0.60)	(−0.55)
Constant	1.8952	1.6954	1.5896	2.5423	5.3382
	(4.04)	(0.95)	(1.86)	(1.46)	(4.67)
R^2	.313	.608	.463	.594	.474
$\bar{R}^2$	.289	.496	.394	.467	.383
No. of observations	471	73	142	64	89

[a]Years 1973–2001; *t*-statistics are in parentheses.